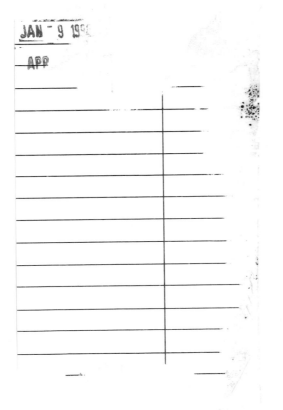

Intervention Research in
Learning Disabilities

Thomas E. Scruggs   Bernice Y.L. Wong
Editors

Intervention Research in Learning Disabilities

With 23 Illustrations

Springer-Verlag New York Berlin Heidelberg
London Paris Tokyo Hong Kong

Thomas E. Scruggs
Special Education
Purdue University
West Lafayette, Indiana 47907
USA

Bernice Y.L. Wong
Faculty of Education
Simon Fraser University
Burnaby, British Columbia V5A 1S6
Canada

Library of Congress Cataloging-in-Publication Data

Intervention research in learning disabilities/Thomas E. Scruggs,
    Bernice Y.L. Wong, editors.
        p.   cm.
    Based on a symposium on intervention research held at Purdue University.
    Includes bibliographical references.
    ISBN 0-387-97280-3
        1. Learning disabilities—Congresses.   2. Learning disabled youth—Education—
    Congresses. I. Scruggs, Thomas E., 1948– .
  II. Wong, Bernice Y.L. - 60 - 805 - 520
  LC4704.I59   1990
   371.9—dc20   90-33001

Printed on acid-free paper

Typeset by Asco Trade Typesetting, Ltd., Hong Kong.
Printed and bound by Edward Brothers, Inc., Ann Arbor, Michigan.
Printed in the United States of America.

9 8 7 6 5 4 3 2 1

ISBN 0-387-97280-3 Springer-Verlag New York Berlin Heidelberg
ISBN 3-540-97280-3 Springer-Verlag Berlin Heidelberg New York

Preface

This book is based on the Symposium on Intervention Research, sponsored by the Division for Learning Disabilities (DLD) of the Council for Exceptional Children, and held on the campus of Purdue University. The Division's purpose in sponsoring this symposium was to bring together a number of the most prominent researchers in learning disabilities to share ideas and discuss critical issues in intervention research. Over an eight-hour period, many of the authors of this volume discussed a wide variety of issues, from theoretical to practical, and gained from one another important insights on the present and future conduct of such research. The Symposium concluded with an additional two days of open panel discussions and individual presentations of the primary research interests of the participants. We believe that those presentations represent the state of the art in effective intervention research with learning disabled individuals. The individual contributions in this volume reflect admirably the wealth of novel ideas and information presented at that Symposium.

Prior to the Purdue Symposium, DLD had sponsored a previous symposium, held in Salt Lake City, which included such topics as models and theories, assessment, eligibility, and public policy. These proceedings were published by College Hill as *Research in Learning Disabilities: Issues and Future Directions*, edited by Sharon Vaughn and Candace Bos. Although this and other scholarly volumes have recently appeared in the area of learning disabilities, the Executive Board of DLD felt (rightly, we think) that it was time to sponsor a work solely devoted to intervention research in learning disabilities. We hope readers will enjoy, as we have, the wealth of practical, relevant, and scholarly ideas contained in these pages.

This volume is organized into four parts: Issues, Academic Interventions, Social and Behavioral Interventions, and Post-Secondary Interventions. After each of the first three sections, a section of commentary has been included, by each of the editors, and by Barbara Keogh, of the University of California–Los Angeles, who generously offered to comment on the third part. The fourth part, on post-secondary intervention, is represented by a single chapter, and we therefore did not include a written commentary.

v

We would like to thank the authors for agreeing to spend three days at Purdue for what resulted in a very exciting and productive meeting, and sharing with us, in their chapter contributions, their most recent research findings. We would also like to thank the Executive Board of the Division for Learning Disabilities for its sponsorship and wholehearted support for this project. We would like to thank the staff at Springer-Verlag for their professional support and encouragement; and Rick Brigham, Jeff Bakken, and Susie Anders, for their editorial assistance. Finally, we would like to dedicate this volume to all children, adolescents, and adults with learning disabilities, in the hope that this book may represent another positive step toward the amelioration of this perplexing condition.

Thomas E. Scruggs
Bernice Y.L. Wong

Contents

Preface   v
Contributors   ix

Part I   Issues in Intervention Research

Chapter 1   Variances and Verities in Learning Disability
              Interventions   3
              Kenneth A. Kavale
Chapter 2   Instruction Derived from the Strategy Deficit
              Model: Overview of Principles and Procedures   34
              H.L. Swanson
Commentary   Foundations of Intervention Research   66
              Thomas E. Scruggs

Part II   Academic Interventions

Chapter 3   Strategy Instruction Is Often Insufficient:
              Addressing the Interdependency of Executive and
              Attributional Processes   81
              *Andrea K. Groteluschen, John G. Borkowski, and
              Catherine Hale*
Chapter 4   Enhancing Academic Performance with
              Mnemonic Instruction   102
              *Margo A. Mastropieri and
              Barbara J. Mushinski Fulk*
Chapter 5   Content Enhancement: A Model for Promoting
              the Acquisition of Content by Individuals with
              Learning Disabilities   122
              B. Keith Lenz, Janis Bulgren, and Pamela Hudson
Chapter 6   Interactive Teaching and Learning:
              Instructional Practices for Teaching Content and
              Strategic Knowledge   116
              Candace S. Bos and Patricia L. Anders

Chapter 7   Unraveling the Mysteries of Writing Through
               Strategy Instruction   186
               Carol Sue Englert
Commentary   Signposts to Future Directions in Learning
               Disabilities Intervention Research   224
               Bernice Y.L. Wong

               Part III   Social and Behavioral Interventions

Chapter 8   Self-Recording of Attending to Task: Treatment
               Components and Generalization of Effects   235
               John Wills Lloyd and Timothy J. Landrum
Chapter 9   Social Skills Training with Learning Disabled
               Children and Adolescents: The State of the Art   263
               Tanis Bryan and John Lee
Chapter 10   Why Social Skills Training Doesn't Work:
               An Alternative Model   279
               Sharon Vaughn, Ruth McIntosh, and Anne Hogan
Chapter 11   The Use of Schema in Research on the Problem
               Solving of Learning Disabled Adolescents   304
               Joanna P. Williams
Commentary   The Effectiveness of Social and Behavioral
               Interventions   322
               Barbara K. Keogh

               Part IV   Postsecondary Interventions

Chapter 12   Intervention Effectiveness at the Postsecondary
               Level for the Learning Disabled   329
               Susan A. Vogel and Pamela B. Adelman

Index   345

Contributors

Pamela B. Adelman, Barat College, Director of Learning Opportunities Program, Department of Education, Lake Forest, Illinois, 60045, USA

Patricia L. Anders, Division of Language, Reading, and Culture, University of Arizona, Tucson, Arizona 85721, USA

John J. Borkowski, Department of Psychology, University of Notre Dame, Notre Dame, Indiana 46556, USA

Candace S. Bos, Division of Special Education and Rehabilitation, University of Arizona, Tucson, Arizona 85721, USA

Tanis Bryan, Department of Special Education, University of Illinois, Chicago, Illinois 60680, USA

Janis Bulgren, Institute for Research on Learning Disabilities, The University of Kansas, Lawrence, Kansas 66045-2342, USA

Carol Sue Englert, Department of Counseling. Educational Psychology and Special Education, Michigan State University, East Lansing, Michigan 48824-1034, USA

Barbara J.M. Fulk, Department of Educational Studies, SCC-E, Purdue University, West Lafayette, Indiana 47907, USA

Andrea K. Groteluschen, Institute of Child Development, University of Minnesota, Minneapolis, Minnesota 55455, USA

Catherine Hale, University of Puget Sound, Psychology Department, 1500 N. Warner, Tacoma, Washington 98416, USA

Anne Hogan, Department of Education, University of Miami, Coral Gables, Florida 33124, USA

Pamela Hudson, Department of Special Education. Utah State University, Logan, Utah 84322, USA

Kenneth A. Kavale, Division of Special Education, Lindquist Center, University of Iowa, Iowa City, Iowa 52242, USA

Barbara K. Keogh, Graduate School of Education, University of California, Los Angeles, California 90024, USA

Timothy Landrum, Curry School of Education, University of Virginia, Charlottesville, Virginia 22903-2495, USA

John Lee, Department of Special Education, University of Illinois, Chicago, Illinois 60680, USA

B. Keith Lenz, Institute for Research on Learning Disabilities, The University of Kansas, Lawrence, Kansas 66045-2342, USA

John Wills Lloyd, Curry School of Education, University of Virginia, Charlottesville, Virginia 22903-2495, USA

Margo A. Mastropieri, Department of Educational Studies, SCC-E, Purdue University, West Lafayette, Indiana 47907, USA

Ruth McIntosh, Department of Education, University of Miami, Coral Gables, Florida 33124, USA

Thomas E. Scruggs, Department of Educational Studies, SCC-E, Purdue University, West Lafayette, Indiana 47907, USA

H. Lee Swanson, Department of Educational Psychology, University of British Columbia, Vancouver, British Columbia V6T125, Canada

Sharon Vaughn, Department of Education, University of Miami, Coral Gables, Florida 33124, USA

Susan A. Vogel, Department of Special Education, Eastern Michigan University, Ypsilanti, Michigan 48197, USA

Joanna P. Williams, Teachers College, Columbia University, New York, New York 10027, USA

Bernice Y.L. Wong, Faculty of Education, Simon Fraser University, Burnaby, British Columbia V5A 1S6, Canada

Part I Issues in Intervention Research

1
Variances and Verities in Learning Disability Interventions

KENNETH A. KAVALE

In one sense, intervention is probably the raison d'être for the field of learning disabilities (LD). The LD field is part of special education, the segment of the educational domain concerned with students experiencing difficulties in the regular system. To deal with these students, special education in general and LD in particular have developed a wide array of particular methods and materials. The promotion of this assortment of special procedures and techniques has led to a fundamental question: Are they effective? Although the question of effectiveness has increasingly been answered through empirical evidence, decisions about efficacy have not reached closure. The empirical data have not been unequivocal and have become entwined in political and ideological rhetoric associated with different "schools of thought" about LD. This state of affairs, it has been suggested (Kauffman, 1981), can lead to cynicism and despair because change in the form of false hopes and easy solutions has been more characteristic than real progress.

The Status of Intervention Research in Learning Disabilities

Although assessing treatment effectiveness is important, surveys of the research literature find that intervention is not a primary topic (Bursuck & Epstein, 1987; Forness & Kavale, 1987). Studies dealing with characteristics of LD outnumber intervention articles by a factor of more than two to one. There is no easy answer to explain this situation but it can be understood within the context of LD as an independent domain with its own philosophy and methodology. As such, the LD field faces a basic tension between its human science side, a helping profession aimed at improving the performance of LD students, and its natural science side, the scientific study of LD students. The strong advocacy stance found in the LD field (Biklen & Zollers, 1986) has led to an emphasis on the human science side with a majority of resources being directed at educating LD students.

The desire to help LD students, however, has minimized the fact that the most effective help (i.e., instruction) should be based on scientific grounds (Gage, 1978). Without a scientific basis, LD intervention becomes a variable enterprise. A respectable scientific base does exist in LD (Summers, 1986) but, unfortunately, has never been communicated effectively and has become confounded with the "conventional wisdom" whose overriding concern is helping (i.e., enhancing LD students' performance). The tension between a humanistic spirit and a scientific reality has caused LD to become a target for those who question its value as a system separate from regular education (Reynolds, Wang, & Walberg, 1987; Stainback & Stainback, 1984). Although the LD field has defended its position (Kauffman, Gerber, & Semmel, 1988), there remains a question of whether LD programs can be justified on a cost-benefit basis. Implied here is a basic policy question that needs to be addressed through an evaluation of the efficacy of the special practices that have come to be associated with LD practice.

Judging the Effectiveness of Learning Disability Interventions

How is the effectiveness of LD intervention judged? Within the scientific context of LD, efficacy is best assessed through an analysis of the existing research. The findings of LD research have not, however, provided a strong basis for appraising the efficacy of its practices. The reason is simple: LD research represents a varied enterprise employing a variety of different paradigms, methods, and procedures.

For example, both experimental and nonexperimental research can be found (Kerlinger, 1986). Nonexperimental research is usually associated with initial efforts to clinically test the efficacy of a new treatment. Although systematic, nonexperimental research possesses the basic flaw of not having the observer in direct control of independent variables making any conditional statement (i.e., if X, then Y) impossible. The lack of control in a nonexperimental study makes it difficult to determine whether the outcome was influenced by the treatment because of the possibility that a whole host of intervening variables may have influenced the outcome (Campbell & Stanley, 1963).

The effectiveness of LD intervention is best addressed through experimental research wherein it is possible to establish a cause and effect relationship. For example, when the question "Does perceptual-motor training improve academic performance?" is posed, it implies that when perceptual-motor training is provided to LD students, their academic difficulties will be reduced *because* of the perceptual-motor training. Three conditions are necessary, however, to establish cause and effect including (1) a statistical relationship established through inferential tests, (2) a temporal sequence wherein the cause occurs before the effect, and (3) all other causes possible for the effect are ruled out (Kaplan, 1964). The unequivocal establishment of these three conditions is difficult and accounts for much of the difficulty encountered in interpreting LD research.

The effectiveness of LD intervention has been investigated by a multitude of experimental research but even the nature of this research is subject to debate. For example, a symposium (see Wong in *Journal of Learning Disabilities*, 1988a, b) explored the question of the relevance and relationship between basic and applied research in LD. Implicit in the basic versus applied research debate is the disagreement alluded to earlier about the tension between LD as a helping profession and LD as the scientific study of LD students. Swanson (1988), in the central paper, argued for an emphasis on basic research and metatheoretical development. Although Swanson's stand was supported in half the responses, the other half did not and suggested that a bias toward applied research is a necessary stance for a field whose emphasis is appropriate education and service for LD students. Kavale (1988) attempted to narrow the basic versus applied split with some tempering of the "versus" idea. Basic and applied research are not incompatible and applied research can be properly viewed as theoretically driven research aimed at practical matters. When viewed this way, applied research can lead to an enhanced relationship between theory and practice because of the potential for a full and complete specification of the LD phenomenon.

The Status of Learning Disabilities

The controversies surrounding LD research led Andreski (1972) to argue that what passes as the scientific study of behavior (e.g., LD) is little more than a form of sorcery. Instead of natural and predictable laws to explain phenomena, sorcery includes a primitive cause and effect termed sympathetic magic where events are assumed to exert influence on other events even though separated by space, time, and distance (Frazer, 1963). Unfortunately, some LD conceptions evidence such magical thinking. For example, the assertion that patterning exercises to enhance neurological organization (see Delacato, 1966) improves language and reading ability represents a form of sympathetic magic because the magic (i.e., patterning) does not influence the phenomenon.

The scientific method in LD has been based upon an approach termed "empiricism" defined as an emphasis upon data collection and analysis (see Phillips, 1983). The primary difficulty with empiricism is that the data collected are not joined theoretically and thus remain as isolated elements with no rational connection. Any individual study is not part of a logical research program building knowledge cumulatively but rather is part of the search for the "perfect" study that will be the all-time true and unassailable fact about the effectiveness of an LD technique (Lindblom & Cohen, 1979). But no single study approaches that perfectness and is thus subjected to criticism about its shortcomings and inconsistencies. The outcome is a variety of schools of thought that function on an ethnocentric bases wherein our ideas are sensible but theirs are not. The consequences are found in a separatism that distinguishes LD and creates an unhealthy competition characterized by complexity, confusion, and chaos.

A symposium focusing on intervention is important because of its emphasis on research. Research needs to be emphasized because much of what is termed intervention research in LD is more properly viewed as evaluation. Research and evaluation are different, and without a proper distinction their outcomes can become confounded. In its formal sense, evaluation is the process of establishing value judgments based on evidence (Worthen & Sanders, 1973). Evaluation has its origins, not in theoretical development, but in securing information for judging the merits of a program. As such, evaluation is parochical rather than universal in scope and is typically more comprehensive in the number and variety of aspects of the technique or program to be studied (Cronbach, 1982). The emphasis on value judgments make criteria like effectiveness and efficiency primary rather than criteria like knowing and understanding (Raizen & Rossi, 1981). Evaluation is thus important but provides only a partial answer about intervention efficacy. Understanding is also important for intervention in the sense of "how" and "why" they either work or do not work and thus can only be achieved through experimental paradigms. Intervention research, while calling itself research, has not provided the understanding but has really focused on-determining the worth of an intervention.

Even within the context of evaluation, intervention "research" in LD has been contentious. Little agreement has emerged about the value of an intervention much less insight in how or why it works. For example, the *Illinois Test of Psycholinguistic Abilities* (ITPA) (Kirk, McCarthy, & Kirk, 1968) has served as the clinical model for a variety of remedial and developmental language programs. These programs assumed that the components of language can be trained but this assumption precipitated much debate. During the 1970s, primary research was synthesized to answer the question about the efficacy of psycholinguistic training. Hammill and Larsen (1974) summarized the findings from 39 studies and concluded that "the idea that psycholinguistic constructs, as measured by ITPA, can be trained by existing techniques remains nonvalidated" (p. 11). Minskoff (1975) offered a critique of Hammill and Larsen's (1974) review and a positive interpretation that was immediately followed by a critical response by Newcomer, Larsen, and Hammill (1975). Three years later the debate continued when Lund, Foster, and McCall-Perez (1978) offered a reevaluation of the 39 studies reviewed earlier and reached conclusions markedly at variance with the statement that psycholinguistic training is nonvalidated.

The debate continued when Hammill and Larsen (1978) reaffirmed their original position and concluded that "the cumulative results of the pertinent research have failed to demonstrate that psycholinguistic training has value at least with the ITPA as the criterion for successful training" (p. 413).

Decisions about efficacy are thus complex and have not been based on data accumulated in a manner that makes it "usable knowledge" (Lindblom & Cohen, 1979). Traditionally, research has been combined through either narrative methods providing a verbal report synthesizing individual studies or numerical methods providing a "box score" tally based on statistical significance and nonsignificance (Jackson, 1980). In the case of psycholinguistic training, it is not important that there was disagreement but rather that the debates were not based on a review methodology that was explicit, unambiguous, and well defined.

Quantitative Methods of Research Synthesis

The theoretical and pragmatic difficulties of traditional methods led to the development of quantitative methods (Glass, 1976, 1977), in what has come to be known as meta-analysis (the analysis of analyses). The methods of meta-analysis have been described and debated (see Glass, McGaw, & Smith, 1981) and, while not universally accepted, are now an established means of summarizing statistically a research domain. Technical advances (see Hedges & Olkin, 1985) in meta-analysis have served to increase the objectivity, verifiability, and replicability of the quantitative review process (Kavale, 1983).

Meta-analysis is based upon a metric "effect size" that transforms individual study data into standard deviation units (z-scores). The effect size is defined by $ES = \bar{X}_e - \bar{X}_c/SD_c$ where $\bar{X}_e$ = average score for experimental group on an outcome measure, $\bar{X}_c$ = average score for control group on an outcome measure, and SD_c = standard deviation of the control group. Individual ES calculations may then be combined and recombined into different aggregations representing average treatment effects ($\overline{ES}$).

Meta-Analysis and Learning Disabilities

Kavale (1984) described the potential advantages of meta-analysis in terms of understanding and explanation. Meta-analysis, as an empirical and systematic form of applied epistemology, imparts a clarity, explicitness, and openness necessary to make research findings believable. The ES statistics can be translated into notions of overlapping distributions and comparable percentiles for interpretation. An ES of +1.00, for example, indicates an average superiority of one standard deviation for the treatment group. This

TABLE 1.1. Meta-analyses of LD interventions.

Intervention	No. of studies	Mean age	Mean ES	Percent negative ES	%ile rank or equivalent
1. Psycholinguistic Training	34	7.5	.39		
reception			.21		
association			.44	5%	65%ile with training
expression			.63		
2. Perceptual-Motor Training	180	8.0	.08		
perceptual			.17		
achievement			.01	48%	53%ile with training
cognitive			.03		
3. Modality Preferences	39	8.6			
testing			.51	35%	70% differentiation
teaching			.14		56%ile with modality instruction
4. Special Class Placement	50	11.0	−.12		
EMR			−.14	58%	45%ile with special
EH			.29		61%ile with special
5. Stimulant Drugs	135	8.8	.58		
behavior			.80		
intelligence			.39	15%	72%ile with drugs
achievement			.38		
6. Diet Treatment	23	8.3	.12		
hyperkinesis			.29		
attention			.02	27%	55%ile with diet
learning			−.05		

translates into a 34 percentile increase and suggests that the average treated subject was better off than 84% of the untreated (control) group, while only 16% of the control group were left better off than the average subject receiving treatment.

Kavale and Forness (1985) presented the findings of meta-analyses investigating techniques and practices that practically define LD intervention (see also Kavale & Forness, 1987, for modality). These data are shown in Table 1.1.

Psycholinguistic Training

Even a cursory examination of Table 1.1 reveals a mixed picture. An obvious conclusion is that LD interventions are both effective and not effective, somewhat like Dickens' suggestion in *A Tale of Two Cities* that "it is the best of times, it is the worst of times." Take the example of psycholinguistic training. Examination of the table reveals that, while training of Receptive Processes does not seem warranted, four abilities—the associative and expressive processes—improve functioning from 15 to 23 percentile ranks. The average subject receiving psycholinguistic training would be better off than approximately 65% to 73% of untrained subjects on associative and expressive processes.

Findings for ITPA total score and subtest scores provided validation for the benefits of some psycholinguistic training. Clearly, the findings regarding the receptiveness to intervention of the Expressive constructs, particularly Verbal Expression, and the Representational Level subtests are encouraging since they embody the "language" aspects of the ITPA and, ultimately, productive language behavior. For a basic area like language, the average elementary school pupil gains about one standard deviation ($\overline{ES}$ = +1.00) over the school year and exceeds about 84% of the pupils' scores made on a language achievement measure at the beginning of the school year. The approximately 60% success rate for training Verbal Expression is thus substantial. In fact, roughly 50 hours of psycholinguistic training produced benefits on the Verbal Expression subtest ($\overline{ES}$ = .63) exceeding what would be expected from one-half year of schooling in language achievement ($\overline{ES}$ = .50).

These findings, however, only fueled the lingering debate over the efficacy of psycholinguistic training. Larsen, Parker, and Hammill (1982) as well as Sternberg and Taylor (1982) questioned the findings on a cost-benefit basis since the gains represented only about 15 to 20 items across ITPA subtests. A distinction was made between statistical significance and practical significance with Sternberg and Taylor (1982) pursuing the question "Does the increase of only two or three items per subtest within this instrument really make a *clinically significant* difference?" (p. 255).

The answer is affirmative and the example of Verbal Expression demonstrates why. In concrete terms, the obtained $\overline{ES}$ for Verbal Expression (.63) translates into improvement by perhaps an additional half-dozen correct responses on a test like the ITPA. If these six items are considered proxies for hundreds of skills, abilities, and bits of information, then an improvement on these seemingly few items is significant. Consider an analogous situation: A child with IQ 130 answers perhaps nine more Information questions or nine more Vocabulary items on the WISC-R than a child with IQ 100. Does this suggest that the difference between IQ 100 and IQ 130 is nine bits of knowledge? Certainly the abilities involved transcend nine pieces of information or words. Likewise, improvement on a test of Verbal Expression represents more than the expected increase of six items since it comprises a complex amalgam of language abilities. Thus, psycholinguistic training programs are likely to provide salutary effects and advantages that probably surpass the abilities themselves.

The example offered by psycholinguistic training revealed that questions about efficacy are not easily answered. The answer was not a simple positive or negative response but rather a differential response resulting in the conclusion that psycholinguistic training is effective and is not effective.

Similar meta-analytic investigations were completed for other popular LD interventions (see Table 1.1).

Perceptual-motor Training

Among the more popular intervention approaches in special education is perceptual-motor training. Its popularity is based partially on historical considerations (since the day of Itard and Seguin) as well as a variety of clinical reports attesting to its efficacy (e.g., Ayres, 1972; Barsch, 1967; Chaney & Kephart, 1968; Cratty, 1969; Frostig & Horne, 1964). Reviews of the reported research, however, (e.g., Balow, 1971; Goodman & Hammill, 1973; Hammill, Goodman, & Weiderholt, 1974) reached conclusions that did not favor perceptual-motor interventions but urged caution because of faulty reporting and unsound methodological procedures.

Table 1.1 shows that the overall $\overline{ES}$ was .082 which in relative terms, indicates that a child who is no better off than average (i.e., at the 50th percentile), rises to the 53rd percentile as a result of perceptual-motor interventions. At the end of treatment, the average trained subject was better off than 53% of control subjects, a gain only slightly better than no treatment at all. Additionally, of 637 ESs, 48% were negative, suggesting that the probability of obtaining a positive response to training is only slightly better than chance (i.e., 50%).

Examination of Table 1.1 reveals perceptual-motor training to have essentially no effect on achievement and cognitive outcomes and only a modest effect on the areas to which the training was directed (i.e., perceptual-motor processes). The data were combined and recombined but, regardless of how global or discrete the aggregation, perceptual-motor training presented an unbroken vista of disappointment. There were essentially zero effects and nothing indicative of any selected benefits.

Perceptual-motor training programs have been developed by individuals whose names read like the roster from the Special Education Hall of Fame. The $\overline{ES}$s for the various training methods (e.g., Kephart, Barsch, Frostig, Getman) did not exceed .15. The findings do not paint a positive picture and their efficacy must be questioned. The studies investigating individual programs included studies performed by both program advocates themselves and independent investigators. A single example will reveal the fragility of such empirical findings. The Delacato program, for example (e.g., Delacato, 1966), based upon the concept of neurological patterning, was assessed by both Delacato disciples and more critical investigators (e.g., Cohen, Birch, & Taft, 1970; Glass & Robbins, 1967). The Delacato sources produced an $\overline{ES}$ of .723 while the non-Delacato sources revealed an $\overline{ES}$ of $-.242$. The range here is significant and a cursory examination of selected sources could lead to very different interpretations.

In summary, the available research evidence, when synthesized quantitatively, appears to offer the negative evidence necessary for questioning the value of perceptual-motor training. Yet, the deep historical roots and strong clinical tradition will make difficult the removal of perceptual-motor training from its position as an LD treatment technique.

Modality Testing and Teaching

The practice of assessing abilities and devising subsequent instruction in accord with assessed modality patterns possesses a long history and an intuitive appeal (e.g., Dunn, 1979). The benefits are thus widely believed (e.g., Dunn & Dunn, 1978) even though the weight of the evidence suggests a negative evaluation (e.g., Cronbach & Snow, 1977; Tarver & Dawson, 1978). Yet, like perceptual-motor training, the deep historical roots and strong clinical support has prevented the modality model from being dislodged from the repertoire of LD (Carbo, 1983).

The findings summarized in Table 1.1 do not offer support for the modality model. On the assessment side, the ES measurements indicated the level of group differentiation between subjects chosen because of assessed modal preferences and these demonstrating no such preferences.

The original testing $\overline{ES}$ was .931 but needed to be modified because of the low reliability of tests used to assess modality (Ysseldyke & Salvia, 1980). The original ES measurements were thus corrected for the influence of measurement error in order to provide a "true" level of group differentiation (see Hunter, Schmidt, & Jackson, 1982).

After correction, the $\overline{ES}$ declined from .931 to .512. This means that, on average, 70% of subjects demonstrating a modality preference could be differentiated clearly on the basis of their test scores while 30% could not be distinguished unequivocally. With the original $\overline{ES}$ (.931) the one standard deviation (SD) difference typically used to establish modality groups was approached but, when corrected for measurement error, found that only 7 out of 10 subjects actually demonstrated a modality preference score different enough to warrant placement in a particular modality preference group. Thus, although modality assessments were presumed to differentiate subjects on the basis of modality preferences, there was, in actuality, considerable overlap between preference and nonpreference groups.

Besides assessing modality preferences, the effect of matching instruction to preferred modalities was evaluated. The $\overline{ES}$ of .144 for modality teaching translates into a 6 percentile rank improvement. This indicates that 56% of experimental subjects were better off after modality instruction but this is only slightly above chance level (i.e., 50%) and indicates conversely that 44% of experimental subjects did not reveal any gain. Furthermore, 35% of ES measurements were negative indicating that over one-third of subjects receiving instruction matched to their preferred learning modality actually scored less well than control subjects receiving no special instruction. These findings were similar across modalities (i.e., auditory, visual, kinesthetic), across standardized achievement measures, and across reading skills.

In providing an answer to the question, "Why teach through modality strengths?," Barbe and Milone (1981) suggested that research supports the contention that modality-based instruction works. The present findings contradict that assumption since research evidence, when integrated statistically, did not render empirical support for the effectiveness of the modality model. With respect to modality assessment, it was shown that groups seemingly differentiated on the basis of modality preferences actually revealed considerable overlap and it was doubtful whether any of the presumed preferences could really be deemed preferences. On the teaching side, little (or no) gain in achievement was found when instructional methods were matched to preferred learning modality. Although the modality model has been long accepted as true, the present findings disclosed that the modality mode is not effective and efforts would be better directed at improving more substantive aspects of the teaching-learning process.

The Problem of Process Training

The question of process training presents a vexing situation for LD practice. For psycholinguistic training, there existed selected benefits especially with regard to basic language skill areas that makes it not an all-or-none proposition and also suggests caution lest "the baby gets thrown out with the bath water." The case for perceptual-motor training and modality training was quite different. Here there were no selected benefits and they can be rightly judged in an all-or-none manner. Yet, they reveal a stubborn resistance because of the seductive statements found in clinical reports. When conjoined with their intuitive appeal and historical foundation, they remain as established LD practices.

The attacks on process training (Mann & Phillips, 1967; Mann, 1971b) have been vigorous but apparently not convincing to a segment of the LD community. Why? Because processes are presumed to possess a reality that then assumes they must be considered in remediation. For a process like language, which is reasonably well understood and readily observed, this assumption is probably true and accounts for the selected benefits of psycholinguistic training. These assumptions, however, were not supported for perceptual-motor training and modality-based instruction where perception, learning style, and the like are not well understood and certainly not obvious. The empirical evaluation of these methods were decidedly negative but yet were not persuasive enough to shake fundamental belief. This belief sets in motion an attitude of questioning about research findings typically centered around the notion, "What if . . . ?" The tension between belief and reality provides a continuing sense of justification for process training. When historical considerations are also included, process training becomes an entrenched element in LD intervention. Debate about the efficacy of process training becomes centered on philosophical issues that are not so easily discussed. Regardless of the weight of the research evidence against it, process training with its established clinical, historical, and philosophical base has proven remarkably resistant to criticism (Mann, 1979).

The "Efficacy" Question

Besides questions of process training, other questions about LD interventions have also spurned debate. One such question surrounds placement of LD students and the best setting for their education. The question is a long-standing one (e.g., Shattuck, 1946) but the burgeoning literature became difficult to interpret (e.g., Guskin & Spicker, 1968; Kirk, 1964; Meyers, MacMillan, & Yoshida, 1980). With the research evidence seemingly inconclusive, legislation and litigation brought about the main-streaming movement (Kavale, 1979) that demanded placement in the "least restrictive environment" which, for a majority of LD students, meant placement in the regular class instead of the previously favored special segregated class. Nevertheless, a nagging question remained: "Was the mainstreaming movement justified?" The most vocal advocates of main-streaming (e.g., Christopolos & Renz, 1969; Dunn, 1968) built their arguments on a philosophical rather than empirical foundation which was more steadfast than warranted by the empirical evidence: The research literature has been criticized for a number of methodological flaws that confounded interpretation (Guskin & Spicker 1968; MacMillan, 1971).

The "efficacy" studies yielded an overall $\overline{ES}$ of $-.12$. (The ES statistic was arranged so that a positive ES favored the special class while a negative ES favored the regular or mainstreamed class). Approximately 58% of the ESs were negative: In more than half the cases, special classes were less effective than regular classes. Since the average comparison regular class subject would be at the 50th percentile, the effects of approximately two years of special class placement was to reduce the relative standing of the average special class subject by 5 percentile ranks. Efficacy studies generally measured two outcomes: achievement and social-personality variables which revealed $\overline{ES}$s of $-.15$ and $-.11$ respectively. Thus, special class placement was inferior to regular class placement regardless of outcome measures. The critics were apparently correct: Special education placement produced no tangible benefits. When the ES measurements were classified and averaged in a number of different ways the primary finding was not challenged: The special class was an inferior placement option.

Tindal (1985) questioned the efficacy literature with respect to the populations included in the studies. It was suggested that aggregations of ill-defined groups does not permit assessment of treatment effects in groups with similar problems. Although definitions of specific categories and heterogeneity within those categories are certainly problematic, it does not preclude aggregating studies by category of exceptionality.

The analysis by category brought to light a significant and surprising findings. The *ES* measurements were classified into three categories: EMR (IQ 50–75), Slow Learner (IQ 75–90), and LD or BD/ED. Special class placement was most disadvantageous for handicapped students whose primary problem was lowered IQ levels (i.e., EMR with an $\overline{ES}$ of −.14 and the slow learner with an $\overline{ES}$ of −.34) as evidenced by a decline of 6 and 13 percentile ranks respectively. The average LD and BD/ED student in special classes improved by 11 percentile ranks and was thus better off than 61% of those placed in a regular class ($\overline{ES} = +.29$).

Although a significant finding, the disturbing question remains as to why some pupils placed in special classes were slightly worse off (in terms of achievement and social/personality adjustment) than they would have been had they been left in regular classrooms. The significant variable appears to be intelligence: If the child was placed in a special class because of a low IQ, it may lower teacher expectations, resulting in less effort on the teachers' part and less learning on the student's (e.g., Rosenthal & Jacobson, 1968; Rosenthal & Rubin, 1978).

On the other hand, the normal intelligence of LD and BD/ED pupils (at least, by definition) apparently did not dampen teacher expectation. Special class teachers apparently took an optimistic view and focused effort on improving academic functioning. Perhaps this effort represents the "real" LD intervention, not a system seeking the status quo but a system focusing upon individual learning needs and abilities in order to design the most effective program of *academic* remediation necessary to overcome *academic* deficits.

In general, these findings suggested that basic questions about the best placement for LD students is complex and not easily answered. It appeared that the differences were related to indeterminate and imperceptible variables not easily assessed or controlled. Tindal (1985) suggested that the efficacy question must be evaluated with new methods that incorporate changes in experimental design, outcome assessments, and data analysis procedures, especially if the indeterminate and imperceptible variables are to be included in placement decisions. MacMillan (1971) suggested that the real issue is not whether special classes or regular classes are better but rather where the best interests of the students might be. The answer to the efficacy question is obviously not an all-or-none response and unconditional judgments must be avoided until both new programs and new methods of evaluation are developed.

Stimulant Medication

Because the LD field has roots in medicine, medically based interventions have become an integral part of LD practice. Yet, questions about the efficacy of these medical interventions have also been a source of contention in the LD field. For example, the treatment of LD students with hyperactivity or attention deficit disorder with stimulant medication is controversial and emotionally loaded. The medical community considers medication to be an efficacious treatment (e.g., American Academy of Pediatrics, 1970, 1975). This conclusion has been challenged: First in the form of critical reviews suggesting no positive interpretation could be drawn from extant research (e.g., Sprague & Werry, 1971; Sroufe, 1975), and second, in the form of ideological, political, and moral attacks upon stimulant drug treatment (e.g, Schrag & Divoky, 1975).

Across 135 studies (see Table 1.1), an overall $\overline{ES}$ of .578 was obtained which indicates that the average drug-treated student moves from the 50th to the 72nd percentile as a result of drug intervention. This 22 percentile rank gain suggested that an average drug-treated student would be expected to be better off than 72% of untreated controls.

The diverse assortment of outcomes measured in drug research makes it difficult to fully interpret a single index of drug efficacy. Three major outcome classes were identified: behavioral, cognitive, and physiological, and this analysis revealed substantial positive effects on behavioral ($\overline{ES} = .80$) and cognitive outcomes ($\overline{ES} = .39$). (Physiological outcomes are beyond the province of this chapter and will not be discussed.)

When aggregated into behavioral outcome classes, impressive gains were noted (with the exception of anxiety). Substantial benefits were found on ratings of behavioral functioning ($\overline{ES} = .89$), lowered activity levels ($\overline{ES} = .85$), and improved attending skills ($\overline{ES} = .78$). Although not of the same magnitude as behavioral improvements, cognitive functioning also exhibited consequential improvement. With respect to cognitive tasks ($\overline{ES} = .39$), the present findings were generally in accord with findings from laboratory studies (see Cantwell & Carlson, 1978; Gittelman & Kanner, 1986; for reviews) regarding the salutary effects of stimulants on tasks that tap various aspects of attention and memory. Unlike past reviews (e.g., Aman, 1980; Barkley & Cunningham, 1978), the meta-analytic findings also showed stimulant medication to have a positive effect on academic performance ($\overline{ES} = .38$). Students on stimulant medication could, in fact, be expected to gain the equivalent of a 15 percentile rank increase in achievement when compared to nontreated controls. To put these gains in perspective, other meta-analyses of interventions deemed to be just as controversial as psychopharmacological treatment (e.g., perceptual-motor training or modality instruction) have only resulted in gains of 5 or 6 percentile ranks.

There appears to be, however, a resistance to acknowledging the positive effects of medication on academic achievement (e.g., Gadow, 1983; O'Leary, 1980). The improved academic performance is usually attributed to improved attention and reduced impulsivity. When the effects of attention were held constant (through partial correlation), however, the positive effect for achievement was reduced by only 20%, suggesting that factors other than simply attention were operating to enhance academic performance.

Pelham (1986) has also questioned the validity of the negative results of stimulant effects on achievement and then suggested that the presumed positive effects of behavioral interventions have resulted in an antimedication bias with different evidential standards being applied to medication studies. Thus, caution is necessary in the interpretation that stimulant medication has no beneficial effect on academic achievement. For example, the $\overline{ES}$s for reading ($\overline{ES}$ = .32) and spelling ($\overline{ES}$ = .37) approximated a level of improvement equal to a half-year's worth of schooling. The effects of drug treatment exhibited a similar gain in achievement in only 10 weeks.

Stimulant drug treatment appears to be an effective intervention for the treatment of hyperactivity and contradict earlier narrative reviews suggesting limited efficacy (e.g., Adelman & Compas, 1977). No empirical analysis, regardless of how positive, can hope to resolve the complex ideological questions associated with drug treatment and the debate is likely to continue.

Diet Modification

Besides stimulant medication, another medically based practice popular in the LD field was offered by Dr. Benjamin Feingold who suggested that the ingestion of artificial (synthetic) food additives (colors and flavors) results in hyperactivity (Feingold, 1976). The suggested treatment was based upon the Feingold Kaiser-Permanente (K-P) diet designed to eliminate all foods containing artificial food additives from the diet (Feingold & Feingold, 1979). It was reported that between 40% to 70% of hyperactive children demonstrated marked improvement (Feingold, 1976). The diet received a favorable and enthusiastic response from the general public but the question remained: Is there any justification for the major dietary changes required by the Feingold K-P diet in terms of reduced hyperactivity?

The literature examining the efficacy of the Feingold diet was not large but sufficient for drawing conclusions. Across 125 ES measurements, an $\overline{ES}$ of .118 was obtained which, in relative terms, indicates that a student no better off than average (i.e., at the 50th percentile) would rise to the 55th percentile as a result of the Feingold K-P diet. When compared to the 22 percentile ranks gain for stimulant drug treatment, the 5 percentile ranks improvement for diet intervention is less than one-fourth as large. Although the average ages and IQ were similar for drug-treated and diet-treated subjects, the average duration of treatment differed: 39 weeks in a diet study and 10 weeks in a drug study. In relation to $\overline{ES}$ (.118 vs. .587), these comparisons suggest that when compared to Feingold K-P diet treatment, drug treatment is approximately five times as effective in about one-fourth the time. Thus, the Feingold K-P diet is cast in an unfavorable light since it produces a substantially lower treatment effect than stimulant medication.

The *ES* data were next aggregated into descriptive outcome categories. The effects of the Feingold K-P diet ranged from a loss of 2 percentile ranks (learning ability) to a gain of 11 percentile ranks (Conners Scale—Teachers, and hyperkinesis ratings). Thus, the only obvious effect of diet treatment is upon overt behavior but such global ratings of improvement possess two major problems, however: objectivity in defining improvement, and psychometric deficiencies (reliability and validity). These problems influence the "reactivity" or subjectivity of outcome measures. Reactive measures are those under the control of observers who have an acknowledged interest in achieving predetermined outcomes (e.g., "improvement"). The correlation of *ES* and ratings of reactivity was significant ($r = .181$) suggesting that larger treatment effects were associated with more reactive measures. Additionally, aggregations of reactive versus nonreactive measures found $\overline{ES}$s of .179 and .001 respectively, suggesting that in those instances where instruments paralleled the valued outcomes of observers, there was a tendency to view more improvement as revealed in larger treatment effects.

The findings offered little support for the Feingold hypothesis. The modest and limited gains found suggest a more temperate view of the efficacy of the Feingold K-P diet than that asserted by the diet's proponents. The slight improvement shown by some students should not interfere with the critical examinations of the Feingold K-P diet since it may postpone more appropriate medical, psychological, or educational intervention (Sheridan & Meister, 1982; Wender, 1977).

Variance in Learning Disability Interventions

The findings from the reported meta-analyses paint a mixed picture of the efficacy of LD interventions: They were shown to be both effective and not effective. Such mixed findings necessarily lead to equivocal judgments and suggests caution in their use. The picture is further confounded by displaying the meta-analytic data in a different way to provide an "efficacy summary" (see Table 1.2).

Two observations about the efficacy summary are important (and also somewhat disconcerting). If an $\overline{ES}$ of 1.00 is used as a yardstick representing the average achievement of the average student in any content area at the end of one year's worth of schooling, then these LD interventions are not impressive. Most of the $\overline{ES}$s were below .50 and represent less advantage than one-half year's worth of schooling. For special practices, these numbers are not an eloquent testimony to the efficacy of the interventions that have come to be associated with LD. This is especially true considering that something as simple (setting aside financial considerations) as

TABLE 1.2. Efficacy summary for meta-analyses in learning disabilities.

Intervention	Number of studies	Average effect size	Standard deviation
Psycholinguistic training	34	.39	.54
Perceptual-motor training	180	.08	.27
Modality instruction	39	.14	.28
Special class placement	50	−.12	.65
Stimulant drugs	135	.58	.61
Diet intervention	23	.12	.42
Early intervention	74	.40	.62
Behavior modification	41	.93	1.16
Reducing class size	77	.31	.70

All of the above are from Kavale and Forness (1985, 1987) with the following added:

Casto, G., & Mastropieri, M.A. (1986). The efficacy of early intervention programs: A meta-analysis. *Exceptional Children*, 52(5), 417–424. (Early Intervention)

Glass, G.V., & Smith, M.L. (1979). Meta-analysis of research in class size and achievement. *Educational Evaluation and Policy Analysis*, 1, 2–16. (Reducing Class Size)

Skiba, R., & Casey, A. (1985). Interventions for behaviorally disordered students: A quantitative review and methodological critique. *Behavioral Disorders*, 10, 239–252. (Behavior Modification)

reducing class size can improve achievement by about one-third standard deviation ($\overline{ES}$ = .31).

There is another facet to the table that should be viewed with some consternation but probably also some optimism. The second column displays the standard deviation (SD) associated with each *ES*. The two statistics may be used to represent a form of expectation (see Kaplan, 1964) about an intervention ($\overline{ES} \pm$ SD). The SD column, however, reveals a disconcerting fact: The SDs revealed magnitudes two to three times greater than the $\overline{ES}$. In each case, the treatment exhibited greater variability than it did average effectiveness. This means that from one setting to the next the effect of any intervention can vary from negative to zero to positive over a wide range. Thus, LD interventions are more variable in their effects than they are beneficial. From an evaluation point of view (i.e., determining the worth of a thing), LD interventions would not receive a positive evaluation. This is because the variability makes the effects of these treatments difficult to determine prior to their application. Therefore, the response to the question of whether or not they work must be equivocal.

In an effort to harness at least some of the variability, meta-analysis techniques attempt to determine if some features of studies (e.g., age, sex, IQ, SES, severity and the like) might correlate substantially with *ES*. If some correlations were significant, then it would be possible to predict, for example, that psycholinguistic training or stimulant medication will be effective here but not there and so on. But across hundreds of calculated correlations only a handful were significant which suggested that the relationships were not of a magnitude permitting useful predictions. Thus, LD interventions may produce benefits but they do so in a manner that is essentially unpredictable.

How is that variability harnessed? Evaluation appears not to be a powerful enough methodology for this purpose. Yet, LD intervention "research" has been structured as evaluation, albeit sometimes very sophisticated, but nevertheless allowing only for judgments about value. To understand why and how an intervention works requires a more powerful methodology such as that found in applied research because intervention is best studied not in the laboratory but rather in real settings with a strong theoretical rationale (Kavale, 1988). The present level of understanding emanating from an evaluation perspective suggested rightly that LD intervention is not perfect knowledge (Brodbeck, 1962) in the sense of being characterized by a complete and closed set of input-output relationships (e.g., do A in circumstance X and Y, and do B in circumstance Z).

Intervention activities in LD thus must be viewed as imperfect knowledge, which makes it largely indeterminate. What this implies is that LD intervention cannot and should not operate on the basis of simple prescriptive action—that is, a single course of action over a wide range of circumstances. The problem is compounded by the fact that any generalizations in the behavioral sciences tend to change over time (Gergen, 1973). The change is brought about because the generalizations rest on values concerning what is desirable and important, and these values are changeable (Eisner, 1979). Intervention in LD thus needs to be treated as an enterprise that is unpredictable, unlawful, and value-laden.

Conceptual Difficulties in Learning Disability Intervention

How then can LD interventions be made more predictable and more lawful? This question is not easily answered because of the complexity surrounding interactions during intervention. Compounding the complexity are a number of conceptual problems that tend to confound the picture of intervention effectiveness. By pointing out these conceptual problems, it is possible to explain partially why intervention research does not often produce the expected results.

The first problem, alluded to earlier, relates to what is believed about intervention effectiveness. The clinical tradition and historical roots of many LD interventions strongly influence perceptions about efficacy. Research evidence is dismissed as inconclusive and, consequently, closure is never achieved and the basic belief is not shaken. A prime example is the modality concept where Arter and Jenkins (1977) found that 99% of teachers surveyed thought that a student's modality strengths and weaknesses should be considered and that a student learned more when instruction was modified to match modality patterns. Although the Kavale and Forness (1987) quantitative synthesis offered a negative evaluation of the modality model, it is important to note that many previous reviews (e.g., Arter & Jenkins, 1979; Derevensky, 1978; Kampwirth & Bates, 1980; Ysseldyke, 1973) reached similar conclusions. Yet, the consistent and persistent nature of negative evaluations, because of the strong intuitive appeal associated with the modality model, are discounted in favor of unsubstantiated claims capitalizing on that intuitive appeal.

The strength of such belief is seen in Swanson's (1984) finding of a significant discrepancy between what teachers say and what they do. Teachers are most comfortable with what they already know, what they have been exposed to, and what the conventional wisdom says. Regardless of how exciting teachers may find new theoretically based strategies, there is a resistance to implementing them in favor of existing practices they find comfortable (like those described earlier in the meta-analytic findings). Thus, a strong theoretical rationale does not appear to guide teaching practice.

A second problem surrounds the nonproductive ways issues have come to be perceived. An example here is the concept of diagnostic-prescriptive teaching. In its classic sense (see Peter, 1965), nothing is more fundamental to LD intervention than the idea that a student is assessed to determine strengths and weaknesses, and then instruction is designed to capitalize on strengths and remediate weaknesses. This basic idea, however, has become polarized into diametrically opposed positions (i.e., Process [ability] Models versus Skill [behavioral] Models) that reflect basic philosophical differences (Ysseldyke & Salvia, 1974). Neither model is satisfactory by itself (Smead, 1977) but debate has deflected attention away from actual instructional practice. Lloyd (1984) emphasized this point in an analysis of individualized instruction. Three models of individualization were analyzed (remedial, compensatory, and preferential) but little support was found for any of them. It was concluded that the assumption that some kinds of instruction are better for some students while other kinds are better for other students may not be valid and instruction instead should be based on "skills students need to be taught."

A final problem is found in instances wherein there has been a confounding of the concept of intervention. Intervention efforts are often approached from the perspective of "cure," which implies that the goal is to "fix" the LD student. This may be an unconscious attachment to the medical model and the assumption that efforts must be focused on removing the source of difficulty because symptoms are simply manifestations of that difficulty which cannot be dealt with directly (Kauffman & Hallahan, 1974). Even though there is often no insight into etiology, intervention proceeds as if the goal were removal of the cause. A consequence of the cure mentality is found in the demand for special interventions that are unique and different (like those reviewed earlier). These special interventions are, however, equivocal in their efficacy. Cure then seems inappropriate and should be replaced by concepts like remediation and compensation (Kavale & Forness, 1985). Although not as glamorous, these concepts would refocus efforts on environmental and instructional variables in addition to student variables.

With the application of special (i.e., unique and different) interventions and the goal of curing the LD students, the outcomes have not been impressive as evidenced by the quite modest $\overline{ES}$ associated with these interventions (see Table 1.1). To be deemed effective, special practices should, at least, enhance learning at a level comparable to regular schooling ($\overline{ES} = 1.00$ after one year). There are, however, special practices that do approximate and exceed the effects of regular schooling. Direct instruction that includes academically focused, teacher-directed learning with sequenced, structured materials and high levels of student involvement produced an $\overline{ES}$ of .84 (White, 1988). More specifically, mnemonic techniques involving elaborative strategies (e.g., keywords, pegwords) to teach, for example, history and science facts to LD students produced an $\overline{ES}$ of 1.62 (Mastropieri & Scruggs, 1989). This means that LD students receiving mnemonic instruction are better off than 98% of students not receiving such instruction, and would gain over one and one-half years of credit on an achievement measure compared, for example, to about one month for modality teaching ($\overline{ES} = .14$). Thus, techniques based on direct and effective instructional practices are anywhere from 5 to 10 times more effective than the "special" practices attempting to cure LD students by influencing unobservable constructs (e.g., perception).

Another example is found in "efficacy research" and the question of where LD students should be educated. Debate has raged so long about what is the best placement for LD students and so many models in varying degrees of restrictiveness have been devised that setting per se has come to be viewed as the treatment itself (Epps & Tindal, 1988). But educational setting is not the salient variable that determines the success of instruction. Setting as the independent variable has provided little insight into what constitutes effective instruction (Burstein & Guiton, 1984). It is thus probably the case that features of instruction systematically affect outcomes but are not unique to setting. Setting is thus a macrovariable and the real question becomes one of examining what happens in that setting (Maher & Bennett, 1984).

Verities in Learning Disability Interventions

Returning now to the original question: How can LD interventions be made more predictable and lawful? It appears that a first step is a reconceptualization of LD intervention, specifically the understanding that LD interventions cannot simply be applied. They do not work automatically but instead are mediated through a whole host of intervening variables that influence the teaching-learning process (e.g., Dunkin & Biddle, 1974; Joyce & Weil, 1972; Peterson & Walberg, 1979). The conclusion is that success is highly variable and what works in one place does not necessarily work someplace else. The context within which intervention is delivered is just as important as the intervention itself. As Simon (1969) suggested in *The Sciences of the Artificial*, man as a behaving system is simple and the real complexity is found in the environment. The artificial is used to denote systems that have a given form because they have adapted to their environment. The goal of an artificial science is to outline the shape of the environment and its influences. Within education, this has come to be termed "contextual appraisal," which emphasizes an ecological view of schools and schooling (Field & Hill, 1988). The question thus becomes: What is the role of mediating variables in producing LD intervention effects? What factors either accentuate or attenuate the effectiveness of any intervention?

The past 10 years have brought to the fore factors that influence school performance and has come to be referred to as the "effective school" research (e.g., Mackenzie, 1983; Purkey & Smith, 1983; Squires, 1983). These practices associated with improvement in student achievement include (1) clearly defined curriculum, (2) focused instruction, (3) consistent behavior management, (4) close monitoring of performance, and (5) strong instructional leadership. These, of course, do not exhaust the possibilities surrounding school effects, teacher effects, curriculum alignment, program coupling, and educational change. For example, Walberg (1984) has synthesized a wealth of information and demonstrated how attention to nine factors can improve the productivity of schools. Similarly, Haertel, Walberg, and Weinstein (1983) analyzed eight models of educational performance and related effective schooling practices to these models to enhance educational productivity.

The implications of the effective schooling research for LD intervention have been discussed (e.g., Bickel & Bickel, 1986; Samuels, 1986) and suggest clearly the necessity of reconceptualizing how instructional services should be conceived and delivered. It has been shown, however, that discrepancies exist between the elements of effective schooling and the observation of actual instructional practice in LD (Morsink, Soar, Soar, & Thomas, 1986). Specifically, Englert (1983) demonstrated that there was only a small amount of time spent on activities that could be considered direct instruction with active learner involvement and teacher attention. Thus, the effective schooling research needs to be better integrated into LD practice. In this way, a broader context can be investigated, that is, the manner through which any specific intervention is mediated within a particular setting. This increases the variability but potentially also will allow us to explain more of the variance (Light, 1979).

The enhanced specification of the LD teaching-learning process indicates the need for applied research because it must be studied in real settings. Particularly for LD, the entire instructional situation needs to be partitioned into components to be studied. Intervention research in LD must then expand upon the predominant "process-product" paradigm where there is a search for processes (teacher behaviors and characteristics) that predict or cause products (educational outcomes like achievement) (see Gage, 1963). But the process-product paradigm has been criticized as too narrow since it omits concern with the events that intervene between teacher behaviors and learning outcomes (Doyle, 1977). The findings have been disappointing and has resulted in conclusions marked by low correlations and methodological disputes. The process-product paradigm has also been criticized because of its inherent assumptions about causation (i.e., teachers cause student achievement), its outcomes in formal rules of pedagogy that may not have a normative bases, and its emphasis on teacher behavior that ignores the content of teaching (Garrison & Macmillan, 1984).

Two other paradigms have been suggested to expand the process-product paradigm (see Doyle, 1977). One is the "mediating-process" paradigm which takes into account the student responses and psychological processes that govern learning. The other is the "classroom-ecology" paradigm which focuses on the relationships between environmental demands and the responses that occur in natural settings. Ethnographic description is a primary method here and provides a richness that cannot be achieved solely from experimental research (Goetz & LeCompte, 1984). Thus, quantitative and qualitative methodologies are necessary for a complete description of the LD teaching-learning process (Rist, 1977). In this way, the contexts of both discovery and justification are incorporated. Qualitative research can discover new hypotheses while quantitative research is most useful for justifying (i.e., testing and validating) the hypotheses (Reichenbach, 1951).

Theoretical and Philosophical Perspectives on Learning Disability Interventions

The next question surrounds the best means to partition the intervention situation into components. Essentially, how are variables best selected? It should not be a random process and theory should play a critical role because it can aid in providing a rational foundation (Kavale, 1987). But here differences about the philosophical basis of LD practice come to the fore. Heshusius (1982) suggested that the foundation provided by a predominantly mechanistic (i.e., behavioral) approach serves only to reduce teaching and learning to the subordinate level of rules and instrumentality.

The required measurement and quantification of instruction and student learning tend not to operate at those levels that are meaningful or worthwhile for the LD student. Heshusius (1982) warned that such mechanistic assumptions are too narrow or simplistic, and, although recognizing that no one model holds ultimate truth or reality, contended that LD practitioners have been trying to do the impossible—"to force the innately unpredictable into the predictable, the unmeasurable into the measurable, and wholeness into fragmentation" (p. 12). Furthermore, a mechanistic approach demands that teachers become behavioral engineers or technicians, a transformation that only serves to promote the reduction of complex reality into quantifiable triviality. Optimal LD intervention requires an understanding of "complexity in its own right and the relationship of the whole to its parts, rather than trying to understand complexity by fragmenting it and reducing it to small, statistically measurable units over which one thinks one has control" (Heshusius, 1986, p. 463). This view did not go unchallenged (Ulman & Rosenberg, 1986) and mechanistic approaches have been credited with being the primary agent for the efficient evaluation and modification of LD interventions (Nelson & Polsgrove, 1984). This debate has not been restricted to LD but extends to all educational research as witnessed by debate about positivism and its influence (see Phillips, 1983, and response by Eisner, 1983). The debate led to an examination of the nature of educational research particularly with respect to its philosophical underpinnings (e.g., Garrison, 1986; Macmillan & Garrison, 1984; Tuthill & Ashton, 1983).

The debate continued with Poplins' (1988b) recent criticism of the reductionistic tendencies of all LD models be they medical, process, behavioral, or cognitive, and further suggested that holistic principles should underlie LD instruction (Poplin, 1988a). Similarly, Iano (1986) suggested that the natural science-technical model failed to capture the complexity of the teaching-learning process and has created an artificial distinction between researchers and practitioners. Researchers tend to reduce classroom behavior to controlled or defensible variables that fail to recognize classroom reality while teachers view these as minor contributors and hence have little confidence in the generalizability of research findings. Iano's (1986) view was followed by commentary (Carnine, 1987; Forness & Kavale, 1987; Lloyd, 1987) either criticizing, expanding, or clarifying specific points which Iano (1987) responded to.

These debates have focused upon the increased attention directed model-based practice in LD intervention. Presently, the validity and worth of any particular model is practically impossible to determine. It may be the case that the LD field will need to accept the fact that multiple models can be equally productive for studying its efficacy (Labouvie, 1975). Although different models would lead to different interpretations of observed intervention effects, all would be retained for utilization in classroom situations. Nonetheless, this relativism, or belief that judgments concerning the adequacy of conflicting models cannot be made, has been challenged (Phillips, 1983). For example, Soltis (1984), while encouraging tolerance for all educational perspectives within an "associated community," emphasized that open-mindedness must not be mistakenly viewed as being synonymous with empty mindedness; LD professionals must exercise judgment when evaluating their interventions. Donmoyer (1985) asserted that relativism has contributed to LD being a "solipsistic morass" where any intervention could by deemed just as effective as any other intervention even when conflicting findings exist. Thus, the theoretical foundation of LD should not be ignored in the search for effective interventions. Theory, in whatever form it takes, provides an all-important "map" for forays aimed at understanding both the phenomenon itself (i.e., LD) and the mean to best treat the phenomenon (i.e., intervention).

Besides debates about the form of LD theory, intervention research itself has demonstrated positive signs. Wong (1988c) provided an instructional model for intervention research in LD. Although the need for a theoretical rationale appears to be becoming better understood, little attention has been paid to the instructional phase of intervention research. Consequently, the instructional phase has tended to be narrow and imbalanced with an emphasis on strategic knowledge. The proposed model included three foci that provide a more comprehensive view of instruction and, ultimately, will permit better judgments about efficacy as well as enhanced understanding about what happened during the intervention.

Mastropicri and Scruggs (1988) have demonstrated the benefits of programmatic research in studying content area learning. The initial research focused on the identification of specific deficits which, in this case, surrounded memory. Next, a specific technique (i.e., mnemonic instruction) was evaluated in a controlled laboratory setting. This technique was next adapted to existing curricular materials. Finally, the mnemonically adaptive materials were evaluated by both students and teachers in different classrooms over time. Positive outcomes were obtained but equally important was the excellent demonstration of how applied research should be conducted. Additionally, these efforts demonstrated the importance of intervention research in understanding not only whether a method is effective but also the "how," "why," and "when" it is effective. This comprehensive view permitted a means-end view that is embedded in what are termed research programs (Lakatos, 1970) or traditions (Laudan, 1977).

Conclusion

In conclusion, one caution is necessary. Although significant strides are being made in intervention research (Algozzine & Maheady, 1986), it is necessary to guard against overspecification in intervention research. More can be learned about intervention but it is also important not to learn too much. Gage (1978), in *The Scientific Basis of the Art of Teaching*, argued that practical enterprises in the real world have both scientific and artistic components and analogies were drawn with medicine and engineering whose scientific basis is unquestioned but artistic elements also abound. Gage (1978) suggested that "To practice medicine and engineering requires a knowledge of much science: concepts, or variables, and interrelations in the form of strong or weak laws, generalizations, or trends. But using science to achieve practical ends requires artistry—the artistry that enters into knowing when to follow the implications of the laws, generalizations, and trends, and especially, when *not* to, and how to combine two or more laws or trends in solving a problem" (p. 18). This has also been termed the *is/ought* dichotomy (Phillips, 1980): Research findings take an *is* form (i.e., *X* is *Y*) while practical implications take an *ought* form (i.e., *A* ought to do *B*). The *ought* form thus requires some translation of research findings. This translation has been aided significantly by recent LD methods texts (see Bos & Vaughn, 1988, and Mastropieri & Scruggs, 1987) but, nevertheless, application will still require judgment which should not be limited by overspecifying the teaching-learning process (Rudner, 1966). Like doctors and engineers, LD practitioners will need to go beyond the scientific basis of their work. An LD student is quite likely to present problems where the generalizations, principles, and suppositions will need to be applied with intelligence and judgment. Therefore, individual LD teacher creativity must not be stifled because quality education for LD students will always be based on the artful application of science.

References

Adelman, H.S., & Compas, B.E. (1977). Stimulant drugs and learning problems. *Journal of Special Education*, *11*, 377–416.

Algozzine, B., & Maheady, L. (1986). When all else fails, teach! *Exceptional Children*, *52*, 487–590.

Aman, M.G. (1980). Psychotropic drugs and learning problems: A selective review. *Journal of Learning Disabilities*, *13*, 89–97.

American Academy of Pediatrics Committee on Drugs. (1970). An examination of the pharmacologic approach to learning impediments. *Pediatrics*, *46*, 142–144.

American Academy of Pediatrics Council on Child Health. (1975). Medication for hyperkinetic children. *Pediatrics*, *25*, 560–562.

Andreski, S. (1972). *Social sciences as sorcery*. London: Andre Deutsch.

Arter, J.A., & Jenkins, J.R. (1977). Examining the benefits and prevalence of modality considerations in special education. *Journal of Special Education*, *11*, 281–298.

Arter, J.A., & Jenkins, J.R. (1979). Differential diagnosis-prescriptive teaching: A critical appraisal. *Review of Educational Research*. *49*, 517–555.

Ayres, A.J. (1972). *Sensory integration and learning disorders*. Los Angeles: Western Psychological Services.

Balow, B. (1971). Perceptual-motor activities in the treatment of severe reading disability. *Reading Teacher*, *25*, 513–525.

Barbe, W.B., & Milone, M.N. (1981). What we know about modality strengths. *Educational Leadership*, *38*, 378–380.

Barkley, R.A., & Cunningham, C.E. (1978). Do stimulant drugs improve the academic performance of hyperactive children? *Clinical Pediatrics*, *17*, 85–92.

Barsch, R.H. (1967). *Achieving perceptual-motor efficiency: Vol. 1*. Seattle: Special Child Publications.

Bickel, W.E., & Bickel, D.D. (1986). Effective schools, classrooms, and instruction: Implications for special education. *Exceptional Children*, 52(6), 489–500.

Biklen, D., & Zollers, N. (1986). The focus of advocacy in the LD field. *Journal of Learning Disabilities*, *19*, 579–586.

Bos, C.S., & Vaughn, S. (1988). *Strategies for teaching students with learning and behavior problems*. Boston: Allyn & Bacon.

Brodbeck, M. (1962). Explanation, prediction, and "imperfect" knowledge. In H. Feigl and G. Maxwell (Eds.), *Minnesota studies in the philosophy of science. Vol. III*. Minneapolis: University of Minnesota Press.

Burstein, L., & Guiton, G.W. (1984). Methodological perspectives on documenting program impact. In B.K. Keogh (Ed.), *Advances in special education: Vol. IV: Documenting program impact* (pp. 21–42). Greenwich, CT: JAI Press.

Bursuck, W.D., & Epstein, M.H. (1987). Current research topics in learning disabilities. *Learning Disability Quarterly*, *10*, 2–7.

Campbell, D.T., & Stanley, J.C. (1963). *Experimental and quasi-experimental designs for research*. Chicago: Rand McNally.

Cantwell, D.P., & Carlson, G.A. (1978). Stimulants. In J.S. Werry (Ed.), *Pediatric psychopharmacology: The use of behavior modifying drugs in children* (pp. 171–207). New York: Brunner/Mazel.

Carbo, M. (1983). Research in reading and learning style: Implications for exceptional children. *Exceptional Children*, *49*(6), 486–494.

Carnine, D. (1987). A response to "False standards, a distorting and disintegrating effect on education, turning away from useful purposes, being inevitably unfulfilled, and remaining unrealistic and irrelevant." *Remedial and Special Education*, *8*(1), 42–43.

Chaney, C.M., & Kephart, N.C. (1968). *Motoric aids to perceptual training*. Columbus, OH: Charles E. Merrill.

Christopolos, F., & Renz, P. (1969). A critical examination of special education programs. *Journal of Special Education*, *3*, 371–379.

Cohen, H.J., Birch, H.G., & Taft, L.T. (1970). Some considerations for evaluating the Doman-Delacato "patterning" method. *Pediatrics*, *45*, 302–314.

Cratty, B. (1969). *Perceptual-motor behavior and educational processes*. Springfield, IL: Charles C Thomas.

Cronbach, L.J. (1982). *Designing evaluations of educational and social programs*. San Francisco: Jossey-Bass.

Cronbach, L.J., & Snow, R.E. (1977). *Aptitudes and instructional methods: A handbook for research on interactions*. New York: Irvington.

Delacato, C.H. (1966). *Neurological organization and reading*. Springfield, IL: Charles C Thomas.

Derevensky, J.L. (1978). Modal preferences and strengths: Implications for reading research. *Journal of Reading Behavior*, *10*, 7–23.

Donmoyer, R. (1985). The rescue from relativism: Two failed attempts and an alternative strategy. *Educational Researcher, 14*, 13–20.

Doyle, W. (1977). Paradigms for research on teacher effectiveness. In L.S. Shulman (Ed.), *Review of Research in Education, 5*, 163–197.

Dunkin, M.J., & Biddle, B.J. (1974). *The study of teaching.* New York: Holt, Rinehart & Winston.

Dunn, L.M. (1968). Special education for the mildly retarded—Is much of it justifiable? *Exceptional Children, 35*, 5–22.

Dunn, R.S. (1979). Learning—A matter of style. *Exceptional Leadership, 36*, 430–432.

Dunn, R.S., & Dunn, K.J. (1978). *Teaching students through their individual learning style.* Reston, VA: Reston Publishing Co.

Eisner, E. (1979). *The educational imagination.* New York: Macmillan.

Eisner, E.W. (1983). Anastasia might still be alive, but the monarchy is dead. *Educational Researcher, 12*, 13–24.

Epps, S., & Tindal, G. (1988). The effectiveness of differential programming in serving mildly handicapped students: Placement options and instructional programming. In M. Wang, M. Reynolds, & H. Walberg (Eds.), *Handbook of special education: Research and practice* (Vol. 1, pp. 213–250). Oxford: Pergamon Press.

Feingold, B.F. (1976). Hyperkinesis and learning disabilities linked to the ingestion of artificial food colors and flavors. *Journal of Learning Disabilities, 9*, 551–559.

Feingold, B.F., & Feingold, H.S. (1979). *The Feingold cookbook for hyperactive children.* New York: Random House.

Field, S.L., & Hill, D.S. (1988). Contextual appraisal: A framework for meaningful evaluation of special education programs. *Remedial and Special Education, 9*, 22–30.

Forness, S.R., & Kavale, K.A. (1987). De-psychologizing special education. In R.B. Rutherford, C.M. Nelson, & S.R. Forness (Eds.), *Severe behavior disorders of children and youth* (pp. 2–14). Boston: College-Hill/Little, Brown.

Forness, S.R., & Kavale, K.A. (1987). Holistic inquiry and the scientific challenge in special education: A reply to Iano. *Remedial and Special Edncation, 8*(1), 47–51.

Frazer, J.G. (1963). *The golden bough.* New York: Macmillan.

Frostig, M., & Horne, D. (1964). *The Frostig program for the development of visual perception.* Chicago: Follett Educational Corp.

Gadow, K.D. (1983). Effects of stimulant drugs on academic performance in hyperactive and learning disabled children. *Journal of Learning Disabilities, 16*, 290–299.

Gage, N.L. (1963). Paradigms for research on teaching. In N.L. Gage (Ed.), *Handbook of research on teaching.* Chicago: Rand McNally.

Gage, N.L. (1978). *The scientific basis of the art of teaching.* New York: Teachers College Press, Columbia University.

Garrison, J.W. (1986). Some principles of postpositivistic philosophy of science. *Educational Researcher, 15*, 12–18.

Garrison, J.W., & Macmillan, C.J.B. (1984). A philosophical critique of process-product research on teaching. *Educational Theory, 34*, 255–274.

Gergen, K.J. (1973). Social psychology as history. *Journal of Personality and Social Psychology, 26*, 309–320.

Gittelman, R., & Kanner, A. (1986). Psychopharmacology. In H. Quay & J. Werry (Eds.), *Psychopathological disorders of childhood* (3rd ed.). New York: John Wiley.

Glass, G.V. (1976). Primary, secondary, and meta-analysis of research. *Educational Researcher, 5*, 3–8.

Glass, G.V. (1977). Integrating findings: The meta-analysis of research. In L.S. Shulman (Ed.), *Review of Research in Education, 5*, 351–379.

Glass, G.V., McGaw, B., & Smith, M.L. (1981). *Meta-analysis in social research.* Beverly Hills, CA: Sage.

Glass, G.V., & Robbins, M.P. (1967). A critique of experiments on the role of neurological organization in reading performance. *Reading Research Quarterly, 3*, 5–51.

Goetz, J.P., & LeCompte, M.D. (1984). *Ethnography and qualitative design in educational research.* Orlando, FL: Academic Press.

Goodman, L., & Hammill, D. (1973). The effectiveness of the Kephart-Getman activities in developing perceptual-motor and cognitive skills. *Focus on Exceptional Children, 4*, 1–9.

Guskin, S.L., & Spicker, H.H. (1968). Educational research in mental retardation. In N.R. Ellis (Ed.), *International review of research in mental retardation* (Vol. 3). New York: Academic Press.

Haertel, G.D., Walberg, H.J., & Weinstein, T. (1983). Psychological models of educational performance: A theoretical synthesis of constructs. *Review of Educational Research, 53*, 75–92.

Hammill, D.D., Goodman, L., & Weiderholt, J.L. (1974). Visual-motor processes: Can we train them? *Reading Teacher, 27*, 469–478.

Hammill, D.D., & Larsen, S.C. (1974). The effectiveness of psycholinguistic training. *Exceptional Children, 41*, 5–14.

Hammill, D.D., & Larsen, S.C. (1978). The effectiveness of psycholinguistic training: A reaffirmation of position. *Exceptional Children, 44*, 402–414.

Hedges, L.V., & Olkin, I. (1985). *Statistical methods for meta-analysis.* New York: Academic Press.

Heshusius, L. (1982). At the heart of the advocacy dilemma: A mechanistic word view. *Exceptional Children, 49*, 6–13.

Heshusius, L. (1986). Paradigm shifts and special education: A response to Ulman and Rosenberg. *Exceptional Children, 52*, 461–465.

Hunter, J.E., Schmidt, F.L., & Jackson, G.B. (1982). *Meta-analysis: Cumulating research findings across studies.* Beverly Hills, CA: SAGE.

Iano, R.P. (1986). The study and development of teaching: With implications for the advancement of special education. *Remedial and Special Education, 7*(5), 50–61.

Iano, R.P. (1987). Rebuttal: Neither the absolute certainty of prescriptive law nor a surrender to mysticism. *Remedial and Special Education, 8*(1), 52–61.

Joyce, B., & Weil, M. (1972). *Models of teaching.* Englewood Cliffs, NJ: Prentice-Hall.

Kampwirth, T.J., & Bates, M. (1980). Modality preference and teaching method: A review of research. *Academic Therapy, 15*, 597–605.

Kaplan, A. (1964). *The conduct of inquiry.* San Francisco, CA. Chandler.

Kauffman, J.M. (1981). Historical trends and contemporary issues in special education in the United States. In J.M. Kauffman & D.P. Hallahan (Eds.), *Handbook of special education* (pp. 3–23). Englewood Cliffs, NJ: Prentice-Hall.

Kauffman, J.M., Gerber, M.M., & Semmel, M.I. (1988). Arguable assumptions underlying the regular education initiative. *Journal of Learning Disabilities, 21,* 6–11.

Kauffman, J.M., & Hallahan, D.P. (1974). The medical model and the science of special education. *Exceptional Children, 40,* 97–102.

Kavale, K.A. (1979). Mainstreaming: The genesis of an idea. *The Exceptional Child, 26,* 3–21.

Kavale, K.A. (1983). Fragile findings, complex conclusions, and meta-analysis in special education. *Exceptional Education Quarterly, 4*(3), 97–106.

Kavale, K.A. (1984). Potential advantages of the meta-analysis technique for research in special education. *Journal of Special Education, 18,* 61–72.

Kavale, K.A. (1987). Theoretical quandaries in learning disabilities. In S. Vaughn & C. Bos (Eds.), *Research in learning disabilities: Issues and fnture directions* (pp. 111–131). Boston: Little, Brown/College-Hill.

Kavale, K.A. (1988). Epistemological relativity in learning disabilities. *Journal of Learning Disabilities, 21,* 215–218.

Kavale, K.A., & Forness, S.R. (1985). *The science of learning disabilities.* San Diego: College-Hill Press.

Kavale, K.A., & Forness, S.R. (1987). Substance over style: Assessing the efficacy of modality testing and teaching. *Exceptional Children, 54,* 228–234.

Kerlinger, F.N. (1986). *Foundations of behavioral research* (3rd ed.). New York: Holt, Rinehart & Winston.

Kirk, S.A. (1964). Research in education. In H.A. Stevens & R. Heber (Eds.), *Mental retardation: A review of research.* Chicago: University of Chicago Press.

Kirk, S.A., McCarthy, J.J., & Kirk, W.D. (1968). *The Illinois Test of Psycholinguistic Abilities* (rev. ed.). Urbana: University of Illinois Press.

Labouvie, E.W. (1975). The dialectical nature of measurement activities in the behavioral sciences. *Human Development, 18,* 205–222.

Lakatos, I. (1970). Falsification and the methodology of scientific research programmes. In I. Lakatos & A. Musgrave (Eds.), *Criticism and the growth of knowledge* (pp. 91–196). Cambridge, England: Cambridge University Press.

Larsen, S.C., Parker, R.M., & Hammill, D.D. (1982). Effectiveness of psycholinguistic training: A response to Kavale. *Exceptional Children, 49*(1), 60–66.

Laudan, L. (1977). *Progress and its problems.* Berkeley, CA: University of California Press.

Light, R.J. (1979). Capitalizing on variation: How conflicting research findings can be helpful for policy. *Educational Researcher, 8,* 7–11.

Lindblom, C.E., & Cohen, D.K. (1979). *Usable knowledge: Social science and social problem solving.* New Haven: Yale University Press.

Lloyd, J.W. (1984). How shall we individualize instruction—Or should we? *Remedial and Special Education, 5*(1), 7–15.

Lloyd, J.W. (1987). The art and science of research on teaching. *Remedial and Special Education, 8*(1), 44–46.

Lund, K.A., Foster, G.E., & McCall-Perez, G.C. (1978). The effectiveness of psycholinguistic training: A reevaluation. *Exceptional Children, 44,* 310–319.

Mackenzie, D.E. (1983). Research for school improvement: An appraisal of some recent trends. *Educational Researcher, 12*(4), 5–17.

Macmillan, C.J.B., & Garrison, J.W. (1984). Using the "new philosophy of science" in criticizing current research traditions in education. *Educational Researcher, 13*, 15–21.

MacMillan, D.L. (1971). Special education for the mildly retarded: Servant or savant? *Focus on Exceptional Children, 2*, 1–11.

Maher, C.A., & Bennett, R.E. (1984). *Planning and evaluating special education services*. Englewood Cliffs, NJ: Prentice-Hall.

Mann, L. (1971a). Perceptual training revisited: The training of nothing at all. *Rehabilitation Literature, 32*, 322–327, 335.

Mann, L. (1971b). Psychometric phrenology and the new faculty psychology: The case against ability assessment and training. *Journal of Special Education, 5*, 3–14.

Mann, L. (1979). *On the trail of process*. New York: Grune & Stratton.

Mann, L., & Phillips, W.A. (1967). Fractional practices in special education: A critique. *Exceptional Children, 33*(4), 311–317.

Mastropieri, M.A., & Scruggs, T.E. (1987). *Effective instruction for special education*. Boston: Little, Brown/College-Hill.

Mastropieri, M.A., & Scruggs, T.E. (1988). Increasing content area learning of learning disabled students: Research implementation. *Learning Disabilities Research, 4*, 17–25.

Mastropieri, M.A., & Scruggs, T.E. (1989). Constructing more meaningful relationships: Mnemonic instruction for special populations. *Educational Psychology Review, 1*, 83–111.

Meyers, C.E., MacMillan, D.L., & Yoshida, R.K. (1980). Regular class education of EMR students, from efficacy to mainstreaming: A review of issues and research. In J. Gottlieb (Ed.), *Educating mentally retarded persons in the mainstream*. Baltimore: University Park Press.

Minskoff, R. (1975). Research on psycholinguistic training: Critique and guidelines. *Exceptional Children, 422*, 136–144.

Morsink, C.V., Soar, R.S., Soar, R.M., & Thomas, R. (1986). Research on teaching: Opening the door to special education classrooms. *Exceptional Children, 533*(1), 32–40.

Nelson, C.M., & Polsgrove, L. (1984). Behavior analysis in special education: White rabbit or white elephant. *Remedial and Special Education, 5*, 6–15 .

Newcomer, P., Larsen, S., & Hammill, D. (1975). A response. *Exceptional Children, 42*, 144–148.

O'Leary, K.D. (1980). Pills or skills for hyperactive children. *Journal of Applied Behavior Analysis, 13*, 191–204.

Pelham, W.E. (1986). The effects of psychostimulant drugs on learning and academic achievement in children with attention-deficit disorders and learning disabilities. In J. Torgesen & B. Wong (Eds.), *Psychological and educational perspectives on learning disabilities* (pp. 160–168). New York: Academic Press.

Peter, L.J. (1965). *Prescriptive teaching*. New York: McGraw-Hill.

Peterson, P.L.,& Walberg, H.J. (Eds.). (1979). *Research on teaching: Concepts, findings and implications*. Berkeley, CA: McCutchan.

Phillips, D. (1983). After the wake: Post positivistic educational thought. *Educational Researcher, 12*, 4–12.

Phillips, D.C. (1980). What do the researcher and the practitioner have to offer each other? *Educational Researcher, 9*, 17–20, 24.

Poplin, M.S. (1988a). Holistic/constructivist principles of the teaching/learning process: Implications for the field of learning disabilities. *Journal of Learning Disabilities*, *21*, 389–400.

Poplin, M.S. (1988b). The reductionistic fallacy in learning disabilities: Replicating the past by reducing the present. *Journal or Learning Disabilities*, *21*, 401–416.

Purkey, S.C., & Smith, M.S. (1983). Effective schools: A review. *Elementary School Journal*, *83*, 427–452.

Raizen, S., & Rossi, P.H. (1981). *Program evaluation in education: When? How? To what ends?* Washington, DC: National Academy Press.

Reichenbach, H. (1951). *The rise of scientific philosophy*. Berkeley: University of California Press.

Reynolds, M.C., Wang, M.C., & Walberg, H.J. (1987). The necessary restructuring of special and regular education. *Exceptional Children*, *53*, 391–398.

Rist, C.R. (1977). On the relations among research paradigms. From disdain to detente. *Anthropology and Education Quarterly*, *8*, 42–49.

Rosenthal, R., & Jacobson, L. (1965). *Pygmalion in the classroom*. New York: Holt, Rineholt & Winston.

Rosenthal, R., & Rubin, D.D. (1978). Interpersonal expectancy effects: The first 345 studies. *The Behavioral and Brain Sciences*, *3*, 377–415.

Rudner, R.S. (1966). *Philosophy of social science*. Englewood Cliffs, NJ: Prentice-Hall.

Samuels, S.J. (1986). Why children fail to learn and what to do about it. *Exceptional Children*, *53*(1), 7–16.

Schrag, P., & Divoky, D. (1975). *The myth of the hyperactive child*. New York: Pantheon.

Shattuck, M. (1946). Segregation versus non-segregation of exceptional children. *Journal of Exceptional Children*, *12*, 235–240.

Sheridan, J.J., & Meister, K.A. (1982). *Food additives and hyperactivity*. New York: American Council on Science and Health.

Simon, H.A. (1969). *The sciences of the artificial*. Cambridge, MA: MIT Press.

Smead, V.S. (1977). Ability training and task analysis in diagnostic-prescriptive teaching. *Journal of Special Education*, *11*, 113–125.

Soltis, J. (1984). On the nature of educational research. *Educational Researcher*, *13*, 5–10.

Sprague, R.L., & Werry, J.S. (1971). Methodology of psychopharmacological studies with the retarded. In M.R. Ellis (Ed.), *International review of research in mental retardation: Vol. 5*. New York: Academic Press.

Squires, D. (1983). *Effective schools and classrooms: Research-based perspective*. Alexandria, VA: Association for Supervision and Curriculum Development.

Sroufe, L.A. (1975). Drug Treatment of children with behavior problems. In F.J. Horowitz (Ed.), *Review of Child Development Research: Vol. 4*. Chicago: University of Chicago Press.

Stainback, W., & Stainback, S. (1984). A rationale for the merger of special and regular education. *Exceptional Children*, *51*, 102–111.

Sternberg, L., & Taylor, R.L. (1982). The insignificance of psycholinguistic training: A reply to Kavale. *Exceptional Children*, *49*(3), 254–256.

Summers, E.G. (1986). The information flood in learning disabilities: AS bibliometric analysis of the journal literature. *Remedial and Special Education*, *7*, 49–60.

Swanson, H.L. (1984). Does theory guide practice? *Remedial and Special Education*, *5*(5) 7–16.

Swanson, H.L. (1988). Toward a metatheory of learning disabilities. *Journal of Learning Disabilities*, *21*, 196–209.

Tarver, S.G., & Dawson, M.M. (1978). Modality preference and the teaching of reading: A review. *Journal of Learning Disabilities*, *11*, 5–17.

Tindal, G. (1985). Investigating the effectiveness of special education: An analysis of methodology. *Journal of Learning Disabilities*, *18*(2), 101–112.

Tuthill, D., & Ashton, P. (1983). Improving educational research through the development of educational paradigms. *Educational Researcher*, *12*, 6–14.

Ulman, J.D., & Rosenberg, M.S. (1986). Science and superstition in special education. *Exceptional Children*, *52*, 459–460.

Walberg, H.J. (1984). Improving the productivity of America's schools. *Educational Leadership*, *41*, 19–30.

Wender, E.H. (1977). Food additives and hyperkinesis. *American Journal of Diseases of Children*, *131*, 1204–1206 .

White, W.A.T. (1988) . A meta-analysis of effects of direct instruction in special education. *Education and Treatment of Children*, *11*, 364–374.

Wong, B.Y.L. (1988a). Basic research in learning disabilities: An introduction to the special series. *Journal of Learning Disabilities*, *21*, 195–196.

Wong, B.Y.L. (1988b). Closing comments on the forum on basic vs. applied research in learning disabilities. *Journal of Learning Disabilities*, *21*, 298.

Wong, B.Y.L. (1988c). An instructional model for intervention research in learning disabilities. *Learning Disabilities Research*, *4*, 5–16.

Worthen, B.R., & Sanders, J.R. (1973). *Educational evaluation: Theory and practice*. Worthington, OH: Charles A. Jones.

Ysseldyke, J.E. (1973). Diagnostic-prescriptive teaching: The search for aptitude-treatment interactions. In L. Mann & D. Sabatino (Eds.), *The first review of special education*. Philadelphia: JSE Press.

Ysseldyke, J.E., & Salvia, J. (1974). Diagnostic-prescriptive teaching: Two models. *Exceptional Children*, *41*, 181–185.

Ysseldyke, J.E., & Salvia, J. (1980). Methodological considerations in aptitude-treatment interaction research with intact groups. *Diagnostique*, *6*, 3–9.

2
Instruction Derived from the Strategy Deficit Model: Overview of Principles and Procedures

H.L. Swanson

There are several studies within the last few years that support the notion that LD children have difficulty accessing and coordinating a number of mental activities. The research in this area may be summarized as follows: LD children experience difficulty with such self-regulating mechanisms as checking, planning, monitoring, testing, revising, and evaluating during an attempt to learn or solve problems (e.g., Bauer & Emhert, 1984; Bos & Filip, 1982; Brown & Palinscar, 1988; Butkowsky & Willows, 1980; Dallego & Moely, 1980; Duffy, Roehler, Meloth, Vavrus, Book, Putnam, & Wesselman, 1986; Grahm, 1985; Palinscar & Brown, 1984; Pressley & Levin, 1987; Short & Ryan, 1984; Wong, Wong, Perry, & Sawatsky, 1986). In addition, these children suffer from deficits in such mental operations as logically organizing and coordinating incoming information that requires carrying out mental operations (e.g., Swanson, 1988). Such children perform poorly on a variety of tasks that require the use of general control processes or strategies for solution (e.g., see Pressley & Levin, 1987, for a review). Under some conditions, well-designed strategy training improves performance (e.g., Borkowski, Weyhing, & Carr, 1988), while at other times some general cognitive constraints prevent the effective use of control processes (Baker, Ceci, & Herrmann, 1987; Swanson, 1986a; see Cooney & Swanson, 1987, for a review). However, when training of information-processing components includes instructions related to self-evaluation (e.g., predicting outcomes, organizing strategies, using various forms of trial and error), enhancing attributions (beliefs) related to effective strategy use (e.g., Licht, Kistner, Ozkaragoz, Shapiro, & Clausen, 1985), and certain subprocesses are relatively familiar or automatized (see Pellegrino & Goldman, 1987; Spear & Sternberg, 1987), training attempts are successful (e.g., Borkowski et al., 1988; Englert et al, in press; McLoone, Scruggs, Mastropieri, & Zucker, 1986; Palincsar & Brown, 1984).

Based on these findings, the disabled learner is viewed as having poor strategies for approaching the complex requirements of academic tasks and so is unable to meet his or her academic potential. The learning disabled student is further described as an inefficient learner—one who either lacks certain strategies or chooses inappropriate strategies and/or generally fails to engage in self-monitoring behavior. A concept theoretically important to strategy instruction is related to *access*. Access refers to the notion that the information necessary for successful task performance resides within the child. Some children are not able to access information flexibility (e.g., the learning disabled), that is, a particular behavior is limited to a constrained set of circumstances (Campione, Brown, Ferrara, & Jones, 1985). In addition, some children (e.g., the learning disabled) are *not* "aware" of their own cognitive processes and/or have difficulty consciously describing and discussing their own cognitive activities that allow them to access information.

The implication from these findings is that the previous research, which has primarily focused on isolated processing deficits (e.g., phonological coding), must now incorporate findings which suggest that LD children suffer from higher-order cognitive processing problems. No doubt, it is possible that isolated or specific processing deficiencies influence higher-order cognitive problems. It may also be argued, however, that a learning disability may be related to the efficient regulation or *coordination* of mental processes that are not related to a specific type of processing deficiency (see Swanson, 1985, for a related discussion). It is not the intent of the above comments to suggest that the domain-specific or process specific models of LD be abandoned, but rather put into perspective. While the "notion of specificity" is a critical assumption to the field of learning disabilities (Stanovich, 1986), this orientation has generated many competing hypotheses. Further, even if a specific deficit is isolated, as suggested by Paris and Oka (1989), the problem is pervasive over time in its influence on cognition and the acquisition of knowledge. Without denying a specific etiology of LD, there are both theoretical and practical benefits to focusing on the higher-order processing difficulties of learning disabled children.

Strategy Instruction as a Continuum

When one attempts to convert some of the assumptions of the strategy deficit model to actual classroom instruction it is usually in terms of inducing LD learners to become aware of their own cognitive processes (i.e., a focus is placed on metacognition). For example, the training mechanisms favored are those that mediate learning via the teacher who provides hints, clues, counter examples, probes, etc. (Borkowski, Weyhing, & Carr, 1988). Adequate learners are those who pose questions to themselves, practice strategies, challenge their assumptions, provide counter strategies, and so on. However, the reader should be aware that strategy instruction must be conceptualized within a broad instructional continuum.

At one part of this continuum, the teacher is viewed as one who acts as a model and interrogator of the child's strategic thinking, as well as one who engineers instructional activities that influence the child's strategic use of mental resources. As the learners' self-regulatory controls eventually become more internalized, the teachers' level of participation diminishes (e.g., Palincsar & Brown, 1987). It is assumed that these instructional activities influence the learners' executive control (monitoring) functions. For example, Palincsar and Brown (1987) suggest the possibility of enhancing the LD students' metacognitive knowledge about learning as a means of further influencing executive control skills that monitor strategies across various tasks. Metacognitive knowledge (i.e., the learners' awareness and knowledge of their own learning processes) is viewed as providing mental input to the executive control system, which in turn organizes and mobilizes relevant information processing skills and subskills.

At the other end of the continuum, a focus is placed on processing skills and subskills that must be performed automatically (Spear & Sternberg, 1987). It is assumed that the ability to perform deliberate and effortful tasks, such as reading, mathematics, and spelling, require the automatic and rapid deployment of relevant subskills (see Goldman & Pellegrino, 1987). Within this context, instruction that includes, for example, computer-based drill and practice is viewed as a possible medium capable of training subskills.

When combining both ends of the continuum, instruction for the LD child may be conceptualized as moving through a metacognitive training phase in which the learning environment consciously directs, encourages, or elicits learning strategies toward a more automatic and less controlled form of processing. This continuum from highly effortful conscious processing to processing that occurs without awareness, effort, or intention appropriately represents the continuum of difficulties experienced by the LD student. In short, improvement in the learning ability of LD children necessitates not only the deployment of strategies, but also an executive mechanism that automatically accesses and combines learning skills (i.e., information-processing components) when they are needed.

With the above qualifications in mind, there are several positive aspects to a strategy-oriented perspective on learning disabilities. Let me briefly list two such advantages.

A focus is placed on what is modifiable. That is, differences between ability groups are conceptualized in terms of cognitive processes that are susceptible to instruction, rather than to fundamental or general differences in ability. Thus, rather than focusing on isolated elementary processing deficiencies, the types of questions that are addressed by strategy research are more educationally relevant. For example, a focus is placed on: What can LD students do without strategy instruction, what can they do with strategy instruction, and what can be done to modify existing classroom materials to improve instruction? For example, in the area of reading, Paris and Oka (1989) argue that although learning disabilities are traditionally conceptualized in terms of "specific" deficits, there are benefits to focusing on strategy instruction because such children's learning has been diminished (possibly because of processing deficits) in terms of the acquisition ,of knowledge in the content areas. Strategy instruction emphasizes what reading strategies are important because they are usually not associated with instruction in the classroom. Understanding how to select, deploy, and monitor appropriate strategies enables learning disabled readers to regulate the quality of their reading performance.

Paris and Oka (1989) see two additional benefits to LD students who receive strategy instruction. First, strategies are enabling skills that promote effective learning because they effectively use the students' existing mental resources. Second, they are constructed by the student to fit their own learning styles and needs. They further state that effective strategy instruction includes: (a) a focus on processes and content, (b) demonstration in the use of particular strategies, (c) recognition of the need to see strategies as useful, (d) dialogues about strategies between the student and teacher, (e) the development of meaningful goals, and (f) instruction that promotes generalization.

Related to our concentration on what is modifiable, Borkowski, Estrada, Milstead, and Hale present a model of metacognition that has relevance to the understanding of problem-solving deficits in learning disabilities. A focus is placed on general learning disability problems, rather than learning impairments. Their analysis of the literature suggests that no matter how extensively strategy specific knowledge is ingrained, the generalization of strategies to a new stimuli and novel situations is difficult for the LD student. While extensive training in strategies is useful, it is not sufficient. Children with LD problems need direct instructions in analyzing task demands, monitoring the effectiveness of strategy use, and developing a personal belief about the effective use of strategies. Their assumptions are that the maintenance and generalization of newly acquired strategies require the presence of higher-order executive processes such as strategy selection and monitoring. In their instructional model, two components are highlighted that are modifiable for instruction. The first focuses on executive processes and they correctly argue that LD students lack the executive processes required for efficient learning, combination, and integration of new information. The second component focuses on the attributional beliefs of LD students and they argue that specific strategy knowledge and executive processing may prove insufficient if such students' attributional beliefs are resistant to change.

A focus is placed on conscious and active rule-creation and rule following. Cognition involves planful activities and a focus on strategies allows one to search for underlying "plans" that influence behavior. Also, a strategy approach allows for a counter perspective of learning disabled children's instructional needs when contrasted with simplistic stimulus response, direct instruction, and/or rote drill and practice approaches to instruction.

As stated by Pressley, Symons, Snyder, and Cariglia-Bull (1989), comprehensive strategy programs are made up of a number of factors that support active rule-creation and rule following. First, it is necessary that one has an understanding of the processing required to do the task. For example, to write an essay the student must plan the essay, translate the plan into a narrative, and review and revise the various steps. Second, one must have a complete model of strategy use. Pressley et al. has identified good strategy users as (a) having a variety of strategies to accomplish a task, (b) integrating specific strategies into high-order sequences that accomplish complex cognitive tasks, (c) using metacognitive factors to regulate competent performance, (d) holding appropriate beliefs about the pay-offs in the strategies they use, and (e) possessing an adequate knowledge base.

In sum, effective strategy instruction must entail: (a) information about a number of strategies, (b) how to control and implement those procedures, and (c) how to gain recognition of the importance of effort and personal causality in producing successful performance. Any of these components taught in isolation is likely to have rather diminished value in the classroom context. Given these important principles related to strategy instruction, let us now briefly outline some points not usually addressed in development of strategy programs for learning disabled youngsters. I will primarily draw upon my own research because these are the studies I know the most about. Drawing upon my own research also controls for any overgeneralization from other's research.

Principles of Strategy Instruction

There are eight principles that must be accented for strategy instruction research to be a major intervention approach in the field of learning disabilities. Some of these principles have been outlined elsewhere, (e.g., Levin, 1986, 1988), but are summarized here with particular application to learning disabilities.

1. *Strategies serve different purposes.* My analysis of the cognitive strategy research suggests there is no single best strategy for LD students within or across particular domains. As can be seen in a number of studies, LD research is in pursuit of the best strategy to teach learning disabled students. A number of studies, for example, have looked at enhancing LD children's performance through the use of advanced organizers, skimming, asking, questioning, taking notes, summarizing, and so on. But apart from the fact that LD students have been exposed to various types of strategies, the question of which strategies are the most effective is not known. We know in some situations, such as remembering facts, the key word approach appears to be more effective than direct instruction models (Scruggs, Mastropieri, & Levin, 1987), but of course the rank ordering of different strategies changes in reference to the different types of learning

outcomes expected. To illustrate this point consider the list of strategies outlined by Moely, Hert, Santulli, Leal, Johnson, Rao, and Burney (1986) shown in Table 2.1. Certain memory strategies are better suited to enhancing students' understanding of academics, such as what they previously read, while other strategies are more appropriate for enhancing students' memory of words or facts. The point in outlining these various strategies is to suggest that there are a number of ways that different strategies can effect different cognitive outcomes.

2. *Strategy instruction must operate on the law of parsimony.*   There are a "number of multiple component packages" of strategy instruction that have been suggested for improving learning disabled children's functioning. These components have usually encompassed some of the following: skimming, imagining, drawing, elaborating, paraphrasing, mnemonics, accessing prior knowledge, reviewing, orienting to critical features, and so on. No doubt there are some positive aspects to these strategy packages in that:

1. These programs are an advance over some of the studies that you see in the LD literature that focus on rather simple or "quick fix" strategies (e.g., rehearsal or categorization to improve performance).
2. These programs promote a domain skill, and have a certain metacognitive embellishment about them.
3. The best of these programs involve (a) teaching a few strategies well rather than superficially, (b) teaching students to monitor their performance, (c) teaching students when and where to use the strategy in order to enhance generalization, (d) teaching strategies as a integrated part of an existing curriculum, and (e) teaching that includes a great deal of supervised student feedback and practice.

The difficulty of such packages, however, at least in terms of instructional intervention, is that little is known about which components best predict student performance, nor do they readily permit one to determine why the strategy worked. The multiple component approaches typically found in a number of LD strategy intervention studies must be carefully contrasted with a *component analysis* approach that involves the systematic combination of instructional activities known to have an additive effect on performance. As stated by Pressley (1986), good strategies are "composed of the sufficient and necessary processes for accomplishing their intended goal, consuming as few intellectual processes as necessary to do so" (p. 140).

Thus, the question arises, what components are necessary for performance improvement and which for maintaining performance? For example, consider a typical effective strategy intervention program used by Swanson (1985). In this study (Swanson, 1985, Experiment 1), the daily instructional treatment followed the verbal modeling procedure outlined by Meichenbaum and Goodman (1971). Training proceeded according to the following five sequential steps: (1) Subject quietly observed the

TABLE 2.1. Classification of memory strategies.

1. Rehearsal

Rote learning strategies are instructed for simple repetitive learning. Children are told to rehearse stimuli verbally or to write, look at, go over, study, or repeat the stimuli in some other way. The children may be instructed to rehearse items just once, a finite number of times, or an unlimited number of times. Rehearsal strategies do not include any explicit activities that would add meaning to the stimulus or cause it to be processed to a deeper level or in terms of more extensive associative relationships.

2. Elaboration

The elaboration strategy is instructed or use with stimulus materials that generally do not have much intrinsic meaning to children, such as the definition or pronunciation of words. Children are instructed to use elements of the stimulus material and assign meaning by, for instance, making up a phrase or sentence, making an analogy, or drawing a relationship based on specific characteristics found in the stimulus material.

3. Orienting (attention)

These strategies are suggested by teachers to direct or maintain children's attention to a task. For example, teachers may instruct children to "follow along" or "listen carefully" during lesions.

4. Specific attentional aids

This strategy is similar to the attention strategy, but children are instructed to use objects, language, or a part of their body in a specific way to maintain orientation to a task. Although these aids are employed in a specific way for the attentional task, they may have other uses ordinarily.

5. Transformation

Transformation is a strategy suggested by teachers for transforming unfamiliar or difficult problems into similar or simpler ones that can then be solved more easily. Transformations are possible because of logical, rule-governed relationships between stimulus elements. Teachers identify these relationships and tell children either that a problem can be rewritten or that it can be reformulated if the method of solution is related or derived from rules and procedures learned previously. Because of the emphasis on logical, rule-governed relationships, this strategy is usually suggested in mathematics.

6. Categorical instruction

Children are instructed to use their general knowledge, in combination with any organizational clue from the material that seems helpful, to recall information. Teachers might direct children to use taxonomic information (e.g., pictures accompanying a category) or to analyze the item into smaller units (e.g., looking for interitem associations).

7. Selective attention

Children are told to eliminate incorrect options systematically. For example, children may do the problems they know first and then try to match questions and answers that are left over or they may try out all possibilities and select the one that seems correct.

8. Imagery

This strategy usually consists of nonspecific instructions to remember by taking a mental picture of them or to maintain or manipulate them in the mind.

9. Specific aids for problem solving and memorizing

This strategy involves the use of specific aids in problem solving or memorizing. Even though these aids may have other uses, the teacher instructs one specific application of them. For example, teachers may tell children to use blocks or other counters to represent addition or subtraction operations in a concrete way.

10. General aids

In contrast to specific aids, teachers recommend the same general aid for a variety of different problems. These aids are designed and used to serve a general reference purpose. Examples include the use of dictionaries or other reference works.

11. Self-checking

Teachers instructing this strategy suggest that children check their work for errors before turning it in. It includes procedures children can use on their own to make sure they are doing a task correctly. Teachers may also suggest that children test themselves or have someone else test them. Or children might be encouraged to keep track of all steps involved in a task so that they can later identify where they made a mistake. The instructions for this strategy are often not specific, but rather a general remark to "check" the work.

12. Metamemory

Teachers using this strategy tell children that certain procedures will be more helpful for studying and remembering than others, and sometimes teachers may also explain why this is so. The strategy frequently includes giving hints about the limits of memory, asking children about the task factors that will influence ease of remembering, or helping them understand the reasons for their own performance. Teachers may ask children how they can focus memory efforts effectively or what they can do to remember. Teachers also tell children that they can devise procedures that will aid their memory or indicate the value of using a specific strategy.

Adapted from Moely et al. (1986)

teacher (model) performing a task as the model talked aloud to herself; (2) subject performed the same task while the teacher instructed; (3) subject performed the task again while instructing themself aloud; (4) subject then performed the task while whispering softly with no experimenter prompting; and (5) finally, the subject was instructed to perform the task quietly.

In the beginning phases, the teacher models (verbalizes) task-specific and general skills statements. Some general skills or strategy statements served to slow down the problem-solving process to assist in error monitoring. ("Yesterday I didn't _____ and I missed the answer"), to self-interrogate ("I need to ask myself. . ."), to make predictions ("If I do that I'll be able to. . ."), and to set the stage for self-reinforcement when the corrected response occurs. The error-monitoring component of instruction included a coping statement from previous sessions (i.e., "I should have asked myself the title of the story, then I would have been able to answer the question"). The specific task self-instruction statement focused on identifying what the child could do (task-specific requirements) to ascertain the appropriate knowledge (i.e., ask the teacher, look up the word in the dictionary, study the word list aloud) to produce the appropriate response (write the answer in the blank). For example, a typical monologue included the following:

Spelling: "Let's see, what is it I have to do today? (Self-interrogation) Later I will need to spell these 10 words correctly. (Identify) I need to study these words slowly by underlining word families. I need to remember this for the spelling test. (Ascertain knowledge) This has the vowel-consonant-silent/e/. From my spelling test yesterday. I missed a word formed like this. (Error monitoring) I need to ask myself how is the best way to do this? (Self-interrogation) If I remember my word families (Ascertain), I won't have to guess on spelling words I'm not sure of. That's easy. (Self-reinforcement) Even if I don't remember each of the letters of the word to spell, I can remember the word family. (Prediction and error monitoring) I need to write my words on this piece of paper." (Produce)

Which components or instructional phases are necessary for instruction? Perhaps one approach to answering this question is to have selected components or steps from the package "dropped out" at various points in the training. Such a procedure would allow the teacher to determine if the previously instructed behavior can be maintained. For example, Swanson (1985; Experiment 2) assessed differential performance of subjects when various instructional stages of Meichenbaum's (1982) self-instruction model were introduced. This manipulation had a certain social validity about it because the components of the training procedure were time-consuming in terms of other skills that must be taught. In order to shorten training periods, it was necessary to separate cognitive-behavioral training steps (e.g., cognitive modeling, subject verbalizes aloud while doing task) across different instructional sessions. That is, the five steps of cognitive-behavioral instruction were separated across sessions.

Steps 1, 2, 3 included the first three steps of the Meichenbaum and Goodman (1971) procedure discussed earlier (modeling, subject performs task while teacher verbalizes, subject does task and verbalizes). For step 3, the modeling and subject performance/teacher verbalization steps were eliminated from the cognitive-behavioral procedure. Instead, the child was instructed to do the task and verbalize aloud. The teacher consistently prompted the child if self-statements did not include task-specific and general task components. For step 4, children were instructed to whisper their self-instructions to themselves. They were provided cue cards with questions to help them remember their self-instructional components. For step 5, children were instructed for each session "to think about what they had been instructed in the past." They were told to do their thinking to themselves.

The dependent measures in the study were correct math computation and spelling. For both math and spelling performance the introduction of the various cognitive-behavioral steps improved academic performance and performance was maintained on a related task. The important finding of this study, however, was that the cognitive-behavioral program was efficiently "spread" across sessions, thus making parsimonious use of the components of intervention as well as the child's time. Another important finding related to strategy intervention is that a major goal of instruction was reached. This relates to the utilization of internal speech as a means for generating control over behavior (Vygotsky, 1962). That is, as environmental manipulations by the teacher lessened, the child assumed major responsibility for using verbal mediation to direct behavior. Children in the present study were instructed to think quietly of all the components of self-instruction and to practice those in their heads before beginning their academic tasks. This covert self-instruction maintained academic task performance.

3. *Good strategies for NLD students are not necessarily good strategies for LD students.*   It is my assumption that strategies that enhance access to procedural and/or declarative knowledge for NLD students will not, in some cases, be well suited for the LD child. For example, in a study by Swanson and Cooney (1987), it was discovered that students who do well in mathematics benefited from strategies that enhanced the access of procedural knowledge, while children poor in math benefited from strategies that enhanced declarative knowledge. To further illustrate, Wong and Jones (1982) trained LD and NLD adolescents in a self-questioning strategy to monitor reading comprehension. Results indicated that although the strategy training benefited the adolescents with learning disabilities, it actually lowered the performance of non-LD adolescents. This concept is also illustrated in a study by Dansereau, McDonald, Collins, Garland, Holly, Diekhoff, and Evans, (1979) in which college students were presented a networking strategy for transforming text material into nodes and links. Control subjects, who were not taught the strategy, showed a typical positive correlation between their grade-point average and achievement; whereas for the experimental subjects, the GPA and achievement scores were negatively correlated. Not only were the strategy instructions ineffective, they were actually damaging to the high GPA subjects.

To illustrate this point further with learning disabled children, Swanson (in press) presented LD, mentally retarded, gifted, and average achieving students a series of tasks that involved base and elaborative sentences. Their task was to recall words embedded in a sentence. For example, one type of sentence consisted of a Base sentence (e.g., the ___ people smiled) and the children completed the sentence by choosing between the word *happy* or *sad*. The other sentence consisted of a Base sentence and a short phrase (e.g., the ___ people smiled at the clown). It was assumed that the elaborative sentence would clarify the significance of the target word and thereby improve recall performance. The results of the first study suggested that learning disabled children differ from the other group in their ability to benefit from elaboration. As shown in Figure 2.1, ela-

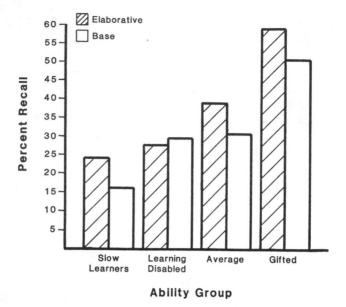

FIGURE 2.1. Recall performance as a function of type of sentence and ability group. From Swanson, 1989. Reprinted with permission.

borative sentences benefited all children, except the learning disabled. The elaboration requirement placed excessive demands on LD children's central processing strategies when compared to the other ability groups. This assumption was supported in a follow-up study (Swanson, 1989, Experiment 2) which suggested that encoding difficulty must be taken into consideration when determining strategy effects. The results also suggest that disabled children may require additional strategies to bring their performance to a level comparable to their cohorts.

In another study (Swanson, Cooney, & Overholser, 1988), learning disabled college students were asked to recall words in a sentence under semantic and imagery instructional condition. The stimulus materials were in the form of common and uncommon sentences. Common sentences depicted ordinary scenes (e.g., The lawyer dropped a magazine in the pond), whereas uncommon sentences depicted unusual scenes that would not be likely to occur (e.g., The lawyer floated across the pond on a magazine). After hearing each sentence, subjects in the imaginal processing condition were instructed to form an interactive image of three underlined word and then to rate the ease of forming that image. For the semantic processing condition, subjects were instructed to form a *category* that tied the sentence's three underlined words together and then rate the ease of categorizing those words. A scale from 1 to 5 (r = very easy, 4 = 1easy, 3 = moderately difficult, 2 = difficult, 1 = very difficult) was used for both conditions. A cued recall task was then administered. Subjects were asked to respond to the cue by recalling the second and third underlined printed words in the order that they originally appeared in the sentence. These cued-recall procedures were followed for each condition.

The results of the above manipulations indicated that disabled readers recall more words for common than uncommon sentences and recall more words under semantic than imagery processing instructions. Similarly, skilled readers recall more targeted words from common than uncommon sentences. In contrast to disabled readers, however, skilled readers preferred imagery over semantic processing. Ability groups were comparable during semantic processing, but recall differences in favor of skilled readers occurred during imagery processing. These results support the notion that self-generated imagery instructions for learning disabled subjects fail to provide a "distinctive" item representation. Further, the results suggest that bizarre images may actually disrupt disabled readers' coding of word information. Of course, one may argue that the effects of imagery recall are not consistent with the extant literature (e.g., Scruggs, Mastropieri, & Levin, 1987). The poor recall effects related to bizarre imagery are consistent, however, with the notion that internally generated representational images result in variable memory traces (e.g., Levin, 1981). Thus, a self-generated bizarre image does not add much to an already meaningfully interpreted text (Levin, 1981). Regardless, the results suggest that disabled readers have difficulty benefiting from instructions that prompt self-generated imagery, while skilled readers do not.

In sum, some studies suggest that strategies that are effective for NLD students may, in fact, be less effective for LD students.

4. *The use of effective strategies does not necessarily eliminate processing differences.* It is commonly assumed that if disabled children are presented a strategy that allows for the efficient processing of information, then improvement in performance results because the strategies are affecting the same processes as nondisabled students (e.g., Torgesen, Murphy, & Ivey, 1979). This assumption has emanated primarily from studies that have imposed organization on seemingly unorganized material. For example, considerable evidence exists that learning disabled readers do not initially take advantage of the organizational features of material (e.g., Dallego & Moely, 1980). When learning disabled children are instructed to organize information into semantic or related categories, some of these studies (e.g., Torgesen et al., 1979) suggest that their performance is comparable to nondisabled students. However, the notion that disabled readers process the organizational features of information in the same fashion as nondisabled students is questionable (Swanson, 1987a). For example, some memory training studies (e.g., Dallego & Moely, 1980; Torgesen, 1977; Wong et al., 1977) have directed disabled readers to sort items (rods, pictures) into separate but multiple categories of superordinate information (e.g., pictures that go with furniture, animals, transportation). Such procedures are assumed to increase learning-disabled superordinate classification of information and thereby enhance their ability to automatically

access information stored in long-term memory (see Worden, 1986, for a review; also see Worden, Mandler, & Chang, 1978, for alternative explanations). Such an interpretation, however, does not adequately explain why residual differences between ability groups still emerge (Wong et al., 1977). It is possible that the sorting of multiple categories as required in previous studies reflects an interactive process between different types of organization. That is, while sorting procedures may produce optimal learning for both ability groups, how the two processes interrelate may determine residual differences in recall. For example, it may be hypothesized that nondisabled readers know that a particular word rhymes with another (intrastructural relation) as well as the fact that a word has meaning between other categories or organizational classes of information (interstructural relation). On the other hand, disabled readers may recognize that a word "fits" within a larger interstructural network, but do not effectively attend to words within an immediate categorical context (i.e., intrastructural organizational deficiency). Thus, recall differences between ability groups as a function of strategy training may be better understood if the organizational dimensions of material during strategy training (i.e., sorting) are isolated. The next study reviewed will address this issue.

In order to determine if recall differences between ability groups during strategy training reflect the dimensions of organizational processing, two experimental phases were implemented in a study by Swanson and Rathgeber (1986). The integrative training phase was presented first because knowledge of the various organizational classes is a prerequisite skill of elaborative organization (Mandler, 1979). During the integrative phase, children sorted separate word lists by either semantic, phonemic, or orthographic classes of word features. The sorting of words into distinct features accents the intrastructural (integrative) characteristics of words within each list. After each sorting condition, a memory task assessed the independent effects of each type of integrate organization on LD readers' recall and clustering performance. In second phase of the study, the elaborative phase was to assess whether individual differences in recall emerge when the three types of integrative organizations (i.e., semantic, phonemic, orthographic) are merged into an interstructural (elaborative) network. Elaborative organization was assessed in two tasks. One task utilized familiar words from the previous integrative phase, while another task used unfamiliar words. When compared to unfamiliar word structures, the more familiar word structures (as presented in the previous integrate phase) were assumed to be more likely to facilitate processes related to elaborative organization.

The results for the study are shown in Table 2.2. The organizational processing of LD readers under conditions that direct the encoding of elaborative dimensions (interstructural relationships) is not qualitatively different from that of their age-related counterparts. That is, under conditions that allow for interstructural organization of word classes, disabled read-

TABLE 2.2. Mean proportion correct recall, clustering and selective attention.

| | Integrative phase | | | Elaborative phase | | | | | |
| | | | | Unfamiliar | | | Familiar | | |
	Semantic	Phonemic	Orthographic	Semantic	Phonemic	Orthographic	Semantic	Phonemic	Orthographic
Younger children									
Learning disabled									
Item recall	.57	.30	.33	.27	.16	.39	.56	.37	.49
Recall organization	.84	.51	.71	.25	.25	.25	.66	.33	.33
Selective attention	.35	.02	.11	.04	−.06	.15	.25	.06	.02
Nondisabled									
Item recall	.74	.45	.41	.47	.27	.33	.56	.33	.16
Recall organization	.75	.75	.73	.91	.50	.50	.54	.27	.18
Selective attention	.10	.08	−.09	.21	.00	.10	.25	.02	−.17
Older children									
Learning disabled									
Item recall	.88	.44	.45	.37	.35	.49	.56	.41	.39
Recall organization	.82	.71	.58	.41	.41	.41	.83	.41	.50
Selective attention	.01	.01	−.10	−.04	−.06	−.02	.02	−.13	−.02
Nondisabled									
Item recall	.80	.57	.49	.50	.47	.47	.75	.33	.50
Recall organization	.91	.78	.64	.66	.41	.41	.91	.25	.50
Selective attention	.08	.14	−.10	−.10	−.13	−.13	.25	−.17	.16

From Swanson, 1986. Reprinted with permission of the Helen Dwight Reid Educational Foundation. Published by Heldref Publications, 4000 Albemarle St., N.W., Washington, D.C. 20016. Copyright © 1986.

ers' recall is like that of nondisabled readers. However, when compared to nondisabled readers, LD readers are inferior in their ability to access a comparable amount of information during integrative or intrastructural organizational processing. These recall differences are related to disabled readers' uneven distribution of attention to the various intrastructural word organizations. Young disabled readers appear to overattend to the intrastructural aspects of words when compared to age-related nondisabled readers, whereas skilled readers process such features without intention or awareness. The diffuse attention (i.e., selective-attention scores below zero) that occurs at the older age for disabled readers reflects the fact that when integrative processing places minimal demands on attention, such children may simply fail to focus on important word features.

Implications related to the results of the study are as follows. First, for the integrative phase, LD readers' clustering scores were similar to their nondisabled counterparts while recall scores differed. This finding does not support current notions suggesting that recall differences between LD and nondisabled readers are eliminated if both groups are taught to use the same encoding strategy (e.g., Torgesen, 1977; Torgesen et al., 1979).

Second, training LD and nondisabled readers to utilize a particular organizational dimension (i.e., integrative) does not necessarily place certain constraints on the other (i.e., elaborative). What constraints that do exist appear to be developmental. The important point is that under some circumstances children take advantage of the integrative and elaborative structure of materials and under other circumstances they do not. The educational issue here is how organizational dimensions at input correspond to mental structures inside the child. Just because LD readers are sensitized to the internal structure of material by sorting activities does not mean they will make use of it in a manner consistent with the expectation of the experiment.

Finally, intrastructural organization (integration) can take place without, or at least with minimal, elaborative organization. Younger LD and nondisabled readers can retrieve words without interrelating superordinate, subordinate, and coordinate classes. As applied to a school setting, younger children can learn to process information without knowing its meaning (e.g., they learn the alphabetic system within an integrative organizational system). These integrative systems may prepare the child developmentally for the acquisition of more complex organizational structures such as elaboration. However, when material is organized by enhancing its hierarchical structure, developmental as well as ability group differences in recall will emerge.

The previous study indicated that LD children can process information in an organizational sense without knowing the meaning of the material. Just because these children are sensitized to internal structure of material via some strategy (e.g., by cognitive strategies that require the sorting of material), it does not mean they will make use of the material in a manner consistent with what was intended from the instructional strategy. To further illustrate this problem let us consider a *pilot* study recently completed in an LD classroom (Swanson, Kosleski, & Stegink, 1987). Two learning disabled adolescents, who had serious memory and reading (i.e., comprehension) problems, were given two tasks. One task required remembering critical details of various stories read daily from a newspaper column. During all sessions, immediately after the subjects listened to passages they freely recalled idea units. After recall was completed their taped verbal responses were played back. For each idea unit recalled subjects were asked, "Now how did you remember that?" Subject responses were tape recorded and their responses subjected to a verbal protocol analysis. The coding of verbal "think aloud" protocols was as follows:

(a) *Nonstrategic.* Subjects recalled idea units but verbalizations were irrelevant or did not reveal an action sequence (e.g., "I must remember it," "It seemed important.")
(b) *Visual imagery.* Verbal response in which the context associated with the idea unit is a nonverbal referent such as an object, a picture, or a mental image (e.g., "I imagined a basketbal court in my mind").
(c) *Access long-term memory.* Verbal responses in which previous experience and/or familiarity with the word or idea is associated with an idea unit (e.g., "I have a friend with the same name").
(d) *Advanced organization.* Verbal responses that refer to the structure of the prose, key words in the prose, or related ideas for logically organizing information. (e.g., "I remember that from when I wrote the words on paper in the beginning").
(e) *Rehearsal.* Verbal responses in which rote repetition or repetitive naming is associated with an idea unit (e.g., "I just keep saying the information over to myself").
(f) *Novel encoding.* Verbal responses that emphasized the salience or unfamiliarity of ideas (e.g., "I remember that because it is so unusual . . . ").

The second task, which assessed any possible generalization of training effect from the primary task, required the retrieval of critical information on a social studies assignment. Students were provided a "a mapping organizer" to enhance their recall of idea units. It was assumed that writing idea units into visual organizational chunks and linking these chunks to the title of the passage would encourage verbatim encoding and thereby improve recall. Strategy training involved teaching the students to map (write) on paper the main idea and the supporting idea units of each passage on the space provided on the sheet. The visual organizer (map) was assumed to guide the learner in building a coherent outline or 'organizer' of the prose material (see Pressley & Levin, 1986, for a review of the literature on this procedure). Students were instructed to "take notes" on the mapping organizer during the tape-recorded presentation of the prose passage. At the end of the prose passage presentation, students were then instructed to turn over the mapping organizer and recall as many idea units as possible. Procedures followed for the taping and playback were the same as baseline.

Two findings were of interest. First, nonstrategic components characterize baseline performance, whereas components related to rehearsal strategies emerge during cognitive training sessions. These results suggest that treatment effects for disabled readers represent a qualitative change in mental processing. Second, and most important, prose recall improved during strategy training, but the student's verbalized strategies were *not* ostensibly related to the treatment condition (i.e., verbalizations related to rehearsal were more frequent compared to verbalizations on imagery). The findings support the notion that isolated or sustaining mental processes may *influence* or *depress* disabled readers' prose performance. These processes are not directly related to specific instruction, and appear to represent a general activation of simple strategies in the child's repertoire (i.e., rehearsal).

5. *Comparable performance does not mean comparable strategies.*   Although the previous principle suggests that different processes may be activated *during* intervention that are not necessarily the intent of the instructional intervention, it is also likely that disabled subjects use different strategies on tasks in which they seem to have little difficulty and it is likely that these tasks will be overlooked by the teacher for possible intervention. It is commonly assumed that although LD children have isolated processing deficits and require general learning strategies to compensate for these processing deficits, they process information comparable to their normal counterparts on tasks they have little trouble with. Yet several authors suggest that there are a number of alternative ways for achieving successful performance (Newell, 1980), and there is some indirect evidence that the disabled may use qualitatively different mental operations (Shankweiler, Liberman, Mark, Fowler, & Fisher, 1979) and processing routes (e.g., Swanson, 1986a) when compared to their nondisabled counterparts.

For example, a recent study (Swanson, 1988) found that disabled children may use qualitatively different processes on tasks they have little difficulty with. Evidence in support of this finding was provided when comparing learning disabled and nondisabled children's "think aloud protocols" on picture arrangement problem-solving tasks. Think aloud responses were divided into heuristics and strategies. Although learning disabled and nondisabled were *comparable* in the total number of mental components used to solve the task and the number of problems solved, disabled children had difficulty in using isolated *heuristics* related to problem representation and deleting irrelevant information. In addition, nondisabled children were superior to LD children in using strategies that relate to evaluation, systematic problem solving, feedback, and pattern extraction.

Further, a stepwise regression analysis suggested that learning disabled children's overall mental processing was best predicted by heuristics, whereas nondisabled children's overall mental processing was best predicted by a specific strategy. Three major implications of this finding apply to strategy intervention research.

First, LD and NLD students have a number of alternative means for achieving successful performance. The idea that a task can be performed with a variety of different mental components is important when designing instructional programs. My findings suggest that disabled children's mental processing is more likely driven by heuristics than by algorithms. No doubt such general methods of problem solving allow them to benefit from general strategy instruction interventions that are not deeply embedded in a particular academic domain. Further, the use of heuristics allows them to perform in the normal range of intelligence. Unfortunately, although these general problem-solving methods have greater generality than algorithms, they also have relatively less power. Support for this assumption is based on the fact that disabled children in my study were comparable to nondisabled children in their ability to verbalize mental components related to the heuristics of acquiring information, evaluation, and pattern analysis. My findings also suggest that learning disabled children may not understand how *explicit* strategies or algorithms can be used in task performance. Thus, instructions that help LD children organize certain mental processes into algorithms may have more applicability to classroom performance than the teaching of heuristics.

Second, my findings are in contrast to current models that view learning disabled children as passive or strategically inactive learners (e.g., Torgesen et al., 1979). The majority of LD strategy research has been conducted within the framework of a *production deficiency* hypothesis. That is, a focus is placed on the failure to use strategies *rather* than on the range of strategies used. So if one is to characterize LD strategy research, it is usually in terms of first demonstrating that the LD child does not adopt a strategy and then after strategy training their performance improves. I would argue, however, that a more accurate characterization of learning disabled children is that they are *actively inefficient* learners. In my study, learning disabled children were able to tag new information and abandon inappropriate algorithms throughout different phases of the task. Likewise, they had relatively little difficulty in accessing various pieces of information to solve a problem. Thus, when compared to nondisabled, it appears that learning disabled children "actively" develop strategic thought patterns, although inefficiently. These inefficiencies appear to be related to their preferred use of heuristics and suggest that such disabled children may be constrained in their ability to use strategies in a flexible manner (see Brown & Campione, 1986, for a related hypothesis).

Finally, the protocols for both ability groups tend to reflect thinking that is "multidirectional" rather than linear. This kind of thinking is in contrast to the *step-by-step* or serial thinking followed in some "strategy training packages." Rather, the natural flow of children's thinking reflects a co-ordination of multiple pieces of information (i.e., subroutines) or multiple operations rather than a step-by-step or component-by-component process. This finding is consistent with other literature on "opportunistic" thinking (e.g., Hayes-Roth & Hayes-Roth, 1979) and suggests that children and adults make decisions related to task performance that do not meet the requirement that each component of their thinking fit into a completely integrated or hierarchical plan. Further, as individuals make decisions, their problem-solving approach may develop by processes that may not be coherently integrated. However, for some learning disabled children, this "opportunistic thinking" may reflect an *excessively* poor coordination or independent functioning of mental components (also see Swanson, 1984, 1985, for a related hypothesis). In terms of strategy intervention, a possible instruction goal is one directed at the executive processing or monitoring of various components so that a smooth coordination of information processing occurs during task performance.

6. *Strategies must be considered in relation to a student's knowledge base and capacity.* Levin (1986) has suggested that there must be a match between strategy and learner characteristics. One important variable that has been overlooked in the LD intervention literature is the notion of processing capacity (Swanson, 1982; 1987b,c; Swanson, Cochran, & Ewers, 1989). Unfortunately, most LD strategy research, either implicitly or explicitly, has considered cognitive capacity to be a confounding variable and made very little attempt to measure its influence.

Swanson (1984c) conducted three experiments related to LD students' performance on a word recall task. In these experiments, an intentional free-recall task (children informed of the secondary memory test) was presented after subjects correctly matched to-be-remembered words to a series of anagrams organized semantically, phonemically, or in an uncategorized fashion. The anagram problem-solving task of the to-be-remembered words involved two degrees of effort. In the low-effort, condition, anagrams were scrambled for only the first and second letters; in the high-effort condition, all letters were rearranged. These conditions are similar to those of current cognitive effort studies (e.g., Ellis, Roger, & Rodriquez, 1984), in which manipulation of primary task difficulty and subsequent performance on a secondary task is used to infer cognitive effort (Tyler et al., 1979). However, task difficulty influences not only how much effort or mental input has been invested but also the various attentional resources necessary for output (recall). In the present study, task difficulty was best conceived as influencing not only the intensity or effort of processing during input, but also the availability of attentional resources to transmit information.

The results related to the first experiment are shown in Figure 2.2. The results are unequivocal in showing the individual variations in the facilita-

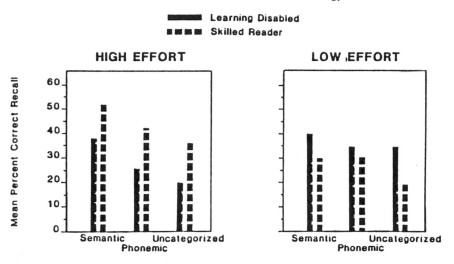

FIGURE 2.2. Recall as a function of encoding effort. From Swanson, 1984. Copyright by the American Psychological Association. Reprinted by permission of the publisher.

tive effects of cognitive effort on later retrieval. It is inferred that learning disabled readers' faulty memory performance is due to limited attentional capacity. This reduced capacity is related to their failure to activate distinctive features of words from among-term memory, to allocate attentional capacity to elaborate those features, and in some instances (as found on anagram solutions that included errors), to activate a critical number of word features to fill the allocated attentional capacity. Skilled readers' successful recall apparently represents some critical number of word features activated during encoding that matched allocated attentional capacity. Therefore, it is clear that any general relationship between cognitive effort and distinctive word encoding must be qualified by the child's capacity.

In subsequent work (Swanson, 1986), I found that skilled readers accessed more usable information from semantic memory for enhancing recall than disabled readers. Disabled children were inferior in the quantity and internal coherence of information stored in semantic memory as well as the means by which it is accessed. The implication of this finding is also noted in the study (Swanson, 1989) discussed earlier comparing learning disabled, mentally retarded, gifted, and normal achieving students' use of elaborative encoding strategies. The results suggested that slow learners, normal, and gifted children improved in performance using elaborative strategies when compared to nonelaborative strategies. In contrast, disabled children were less positively influenced by elaborative strategies, possibly due to excessive demands placed on central processing capacity.

Thus, in some instructional cases, poor strategy use may provide an adequate, but not necessarily, comprehensive explanation of learning disabilities. This is because the learning characteristics, such as deficits in cognitive capacity, have not been taken into consideration. Before a strategy deficit explanation can provide a comprehensive explanation of instructional effects related to learning disabled children's performance, the majority of predictions provided below

1. LD students who use strategies should show minimal variation in their performance across tasks that *demand the use of such strategies*. That is, if the LD child is using a systematic approach, his or her performance should be relatively constant.
2. LD students should be specifically prone to disruption of their performances that make demands on higher-order processes.
3. LD students should be minimally influenced by task parameters that are irrelevant to strategy formation.
4. LD students should be specifically influenced by strategy components of instruction, such as feedback.
5. LD students should show marked-up performance when they discover definite strategies for coping with the task.
6. Residual performance and differences between ability groups should be eliminated when effective strategies are acquired and learned.

The point that is being stressed here is that strategy inefficiencies are not a sufficient explanation of learning disabled children's instructional performance. No doubt, the need for previous studies to explain LD children's instructional deficiencies in terms of strategy use may be, in part, a by-product of the efforts to place learning disabilities within a "production deficiency" framework or some other optimistic instructional model. What is needed, however, is instructional research that provides a framework for considering how both processes and structures interact during instructional interventions.

7. *Comparable strategy use may not eliminate performance differences.* In a production deficiency view of learning disabilities, it is commonly assumed that without instruction, learning disabled students are less likely to produce strategies than their normal counterparts. Several studies have indicated that residual differences remain between ability groups, even when ability groups are instructed/or prevented from strategy use (Gelzheiser, 1984; Swanson, 1983; 1987a; Wong, Wong, & Foth, 1977). For example, in a study by Gelzheiser, Cort, and Sheperd (1987) LD and NLD children were compared on their ability to use organizational strategies. After instruction in organizational strategies, disabled and nondisabled were compared on their ability to recall information on a post-test. The results indicated that disabled children were comparable in strategy use to nondisabled, but were deficient in overall performance.

In another study, Swanson (1983) found that the recall of a learning disabled group did not improve from baseline level when trained with rehearsal strategies. Using disabled and nondisabled children for two age groups (8 and 10 years), he examined the relationship of memory estimation (children estimate performance prior to performing task), and retrieval knowledge for specific rehearsal strategies in the free recall of unrelated words. At each level, a baseline and two instructional conditions were devised to manipulate the child's rehearsal activity to the task. The baseline condition emphasized spontaneous rehearsal, whereas the two instructional conditions emphasized (a) one-item and (b) multi-item rehearsal. All conditions emphasized that children were to recall words. In addition to comparisons of recall performance, children's use of estimated recall ability and retrieval understanding were assessed for all instructional conditions so that links between strategic knowledge and rehearsal activity could be examined. It was expected that if disabled readers are "production deficient" in rehearsal strategy, increased recall would occur on the instructional conditions.

Specifically, the experimenter told the children they would be presented a list of items orally and they were to practice learning the words aloud during the interval following the presentation of each item. For the baseline condition, children were told to practice aloud. No particular rehearsal strategy was suggested since children could practice aloud one item or with any other previous words. Two other trials were given. For one-item instructions, children were told to "say only the presented word once"; for multi-item instructions, children were told to "practice each word with as many of the earlier presented words as possible but say the newly presented word at least once." After rehearsal instructions were given for each word list, children were asked to examine that list and estimate how many words they could remember. After an estimation was made, the experimenter presented the lists of words orally. To determine the extent to which rehearsal instructions would lead to effective metamnemonic behavior, the experimenter asked up to four questions in the order given below for all three instructional conditions (questioning ceased after any unambiguous recall strategy was repeated):

1. How did you remember these words?
2. What did you think about when the word list was given?
3. Some children remember by following my instructions or say or do something different. What did you do?
4. Maybe you did it the way I presented it to you; did you? How did I do it?

The results related to the recall phase are shown in Table 2.3. As seen in the Table-4, learning disabled readers were generally inferior in recall to nondisabled readers even though both ability groups were comparable in rehearsal use. The poor recall performance of the disabled readers, in contrast to nondisabled, suggests these children initially encode individual words to a shallower, weak semantic-elaborative level and the nature of this encoding results in inferior recall. Support for this interpretation comes from the lack of rehearsal activity difference between groups on

TABLE 2.3. Percentage mean recall by rehearsal activity, group, and age.

	Baseline	One-item	Multi-item
Younger			
Disabled	40.83 (16.93)	35.50 (16.58)	40.41 (17.93)
Nondisabled	53.33 (13.94)	46.16 (16.17)	50.00 (24.67)
Older			
Disabled	60.58 (16.15)	54.00 (16.82)	44.61 (19.78)
Nondisabled	70.33 (13.77)	62.83 (14.50)	65.33 (14.48)

Note: Standard deviations in brackets.

baseline and multi-item conditions. An inspection of the retrospective reports suggested that disabled readers analyze words at a more superficial level then skilled readers.

Data on the interrelation of baseline, one-item, and multi-item rehearsal activity, self-estimates of span, and reported strategy provide an interesting interpretation of the inferior recall performance of learning disabled readers. Although these readers did not articulate clearly a plan for recalling words, they did in fact use rehearsal activity comparable to nondisabled readers. Therefore, one cannot say learning disabled children failed to use the appropriate rehearsal activity because they were unaware of the difficulty of the task or cannot articulate a mnemonic strategy. Rather than being production deficient in rehearsal strategies, they may have failed to elaborate, automatically, words for a deeper level of processing. An awareness of the value of word retrieval strategies may have not depended upon previously acquired metamemorial knowledge, but simply that one word can remind us of another and to put words into a sentence is generally easier than frequent repeating.

In summary, an assumption of the "strategy orientation" research to the field of learning disabilities is that accurate memory estimation and strategic awareness lead to strategic behavior, but this is not necessarily true. As suggested from my study (Swanson, 1983) on reported strategies, learning disabled children were less automatic in word elaboration than nondisabled, despite their comparable appraisal. Not surprisingly, span estimation was unrelated to rehearsal activity and actual recall. Perhaps recall differences between disabled and nondisabled readers lie not in their failure to employ rehearsal strategies or self-knowledge of memory, but in automatic word elaboration.

The results of the studies reviewed support the notion that groups of children with different learning histories may continue to learn differently, even when the groups are equated in term of strategy use.

8. *Strategies taught do not necessarily become transformed into expert strategies.*   One mechanism that promotes expert performance is related to strategy transformation (e.g., Chi, Glaser, & Farr, 1988). It often

appears that children who become experts at certain tasks have learned simple strategies and through practice discover ways to modify them into more efficient and powerful procedures. In particular, the proficient learner uses higher-order rules to eliminate unnecessary or redundant steps so as to hold increasing amounts of information. The learning disabled child, in contrast, may learn most of the skills related to performing an academic task and perform appropriately on that task by carefully and systematically following prescribed rules or strategies. Although learning disabled children can be taught strategies, recent evidence suggests that the differences between learning disabled and nondisabled children (experts in this case) is that the latter have modified such strategies to become more efficient (Swanson & Cooney, 1985; Swanson & Rhine, 1985). It is plausible that the learning disabled child remains a novice because he or her fails to transform simple strategies into more efficient forms.

Our recently completed study (Swanson & Cooney, 1985; Swanson & Rhine, 1985) illustrates this point. This study assumed that a possible mechanism that permits superior performance on arithmetic tasks is strategy transformation. The dependent measure is an averaging technique for determining the subject's information "handling" rate for different types of problems. The technique assumes that the information handling rate of the subject remains constant across problems, but the time-requirement for each problem will "be strictly proportional to the information requirements and the constant of proportionally will measure the information handling rate of the system" (Thomas, 1963, p. 174). For example, the information processing load on addition problems (e.g., $7 + 9 = 16$) that were completed in an average of 3.3 seconds (number of problems/total time to complete all problems) was $\log (p + q + r)/t = K$ where p, q represent two one-digit numbers of the addition problem and r is the result. Log $(p + q + r)$ may be considered the information requirement per calculation, t is the time taken to perform a calculation for a variety of problems and k (dependent measure) is the information handling rate of the subject. Computed for a single subject, $K = \log (7 + 9 + 16)/3.3$, we note that $K = 1.04$. Given this rather cursory introduction to the dependent measure let us briefly describe the problems presented to LD and NLD children.

Assuming that strategy transformations occur, each subject was made to perform calculations covering as large a range of arithmetic problems as possible. It was assumed the greater the variety of arithmetical operations encompassed by such calculations, the more comprehensive the test of strategy transformation will be. Problems selected were at least three grade levels below the learning disabled children's current mathematical functioning on standardized math tests. Each transformation condition included a minimum of five problems as numerically diverse as possible, but arithmetically comparable. A discussion of each strategy transformation condition is provided below.

Results to Answers

This strategy transformation focuses on the extent that children rely on memory retrieval rather than computation For example, it is possible that learning disabled students compute simple addition sums, subtraction, and multiplication products while nondisabled retrieve those answers from memory. A critical aspect in making this transformation is the awareness that some problems always have a certain result. Such a transformation was operationalized in the present study as the time necessary to retrieve sums of addition or products of multiplication that were of the form $p + q = r$ or $p \times q = r$, where p and q were any single, nonnegative integers, and solutions (r) contained two digits.

Reduction to Rule

This strategy transformation focuses on the extent to which children identify a set of steps that provide an answer with minimal calculation. These sets of steps require searching for constant relationships across problems. For example, in the sequence of problems 9×1, 14×4, 31×1, 563×1, a child discovers that three of the problems require no calculation since a number multiplied by 1 equals the number. Multiplication problems were organized in two rows of six problems.

Method Replacement

Method replacement consists of replacing one procedure with another that more efficiently accomplishes the same result. For example, the result of an addition problem $10 + 3 + 8 + 10 + 9 + 10$ may be accomplished by sequential processing (e.g., $10 + 3 = 13 + 8 = 21$) or by simply retrieving the answer to $3 \times 10 = 30$ and adding 20 ($3 + 8 + 9$). That is, the alternative method to sequential addition is the multiplication of similar number sets.

Unit Building

Unit building consists of grouping mental operations into a single set. This single set is composed of memorizing consistent sequences that can be clustered together. Consider three arithmetic problems: $1 + 2 + 3 + 4 + 11$; $26 + 1 + 3 + 10 + 2 + 4$. In the first problem, the subject calculates the result by adding in sequence. If the sequence of numbers is examined in problem two, the subject discovers that a reoccurring subsequence has occurred. This subsequence may also be discovered in problem three. These subsequences are clustered into new units or response classes. Unit building has occurred since addition efficiency does not occur on a number-by-number basis for problems two and three.

Saving Partial Results

Saving of partial results is like unit building transformation in that a focus in placed on reducing computation effort. However, saving partial results differs in that a subsequence analysis is not required. Consider the problems 869×4 and 869×40. A subject can save considerable effort on the second problem if one remembers that $4 \times 869 = 3476$ after first computing it. Then, rather than doing additional calculation, one can determine 869×40 simply annexing a zero. The present task had three sets of three multiplication problems. Each set had 1, 2, and 3 multipliers with all problems having a 3 digit multiplication.

Process Elimination

Process elimination is comparable to method replacement, except that a transformation is made of all prior operations. In contrast, method replacement may reuse earlier operations. For example, the subject may be directed to an addition problem of $14 + 14 + 14 + 14 = $ _____. The subject then "scans" upcoming problems and notes that all problems have the same digit sequence within each problem. The subject then discerns that addition is an *unnecessary* process for successful task completion.

Reordering

Reordering refers to the changing of previously learned strategies to reduce task difficulty. Consider the problem $1 + 4 - 5 + (18 \times 3) - 1$. Subjects are taught to calculate such a series of operations from left to right. However, a strategy transformation may involve calculating intermediate values (18×3) first to avoid the nuisance of large calculations.

Learning disabled children are more likely to use strategies they have been taught yielding lower information handling rates than their nondisabled counterparts. Our finding suggests that acquired knowledge must undergo changes in specific processes or operations before proficient performance can be obtained. Three implications of this study related to strategy instruction are important.

First, strategies make varying demands on an individual's processing effort and memory load. These demands can arise either in accessing a strategy (encoding) or in applying (observed) strategy transformation. However, the locus of group differences in transformation ability did not appear to be clearly related to encoding or the rate of functioning. Except for the reduction to rule and the saving of partial results transformation, it appears that learning disabled and nondisabled children may have used a different series of "processing stages" to handle information.

Second, the results raise the question of why some learning disabled children failed to efficiently activate potential available knowledge that could make the tasks less difficult and easier to compute. The results of the study suggest two processing categories: knowledge-based processes and pattern detection processes. We suggest that these two processes are critically linked. The reduction to answer task, which is assumed to be related to stored computation knowledge, correlated positively with all transformation tasks. Likewise, the observed group differences in pattern detection processes were related to stored computation facts. Thus, the answer to the question, how do children acquire knowledge to become experts, appears not only related to children's ability to detect regularities (6 + 7 is always 13) but also to how quickly that information is retrieved.

Finally, the types of strategy transformations presented in the study have broad implications for instructional practice. Instructional procedures that assume that LD children lack the conceptual knowledge necessary to spontaneously use task-relevant strategies must be countered with the notion that in areas where they do have the necessary conceptual and procedural knowledge, they fail to make the necessary transformations to become expert learners. Of course, it is highly probable that some strategies used by nondisabled children are quite complex and not suitable for direct instruction. An instructional alternative for children who continue to exhibit novice behavior, however, is to teach simple strategies as well as to provide direct instruction that promotes such strategy transformation.

Conclusions

The previous principles are consistent with many of the points made by other authors (e.g., Levin, 1988). This chapter highlights some of the major steps and components that enhance effective strategy use. It is clear that LD students' knowledge about and beliefs about the how, where, and why of strategy use are important if they are to take control of their cognitive processing. Such information should be included in an instruction program designed to teach strategy use. However, researchers and teachers must also follow certain guidelines and principles in their selection of strategies to be taught to students. Strategies are never applied in isolation of person, process, and context. Strategies are always applied to specific materials, in a specific context, with a specific student. When these factors are kept in mind, the strategy model of instruction has much to offer the LD field.

References

Baker, J.G., Ceci, S.J., & Herrmann, N.D. (1987). Semantic structure and processing: Implications for the learning disabled child. In H.L. Swanson (Ed.), *Memory and learning disabilities* (pp. 83–110). Greenwich, CT: JAI Press.

Bauer, R.H., & Emhert, J. (1984). Information processing in reading-disabled and nondisabled children. *Journal of Experimental Child Psychology*, *37*, 271–281.

Borkowski, J.G., Estrada, M.T., Milstead, M., & Hale, C. (1989). General problem-solving skills: Relations between metacognition and strategic processing. *Learning Disability Quarterly*, *12*, 57–70.

Borkowski, J.G., Weyhing, R.S., & Carr, M. (1988). Effects of attributional retraining on strategy-based reading comprehension in learning-disabled students. *Journal of Educational Psychology*, *80*, 46–53.

Bos, C., & Filip, D. (1982). Comprehension monitoring skills in learning disabled and average students. *Topics in Learning and Learning Disabilities*, *2*, 79–85.

Brown, A.L., & Campione, J.C. (1986). Psychological theory and the study of learning disabilities. *American Psychologist*, *41*, 1059–1068.

Brown, A.L., & Palinscar, A.S. (1988). Reciprocal teaching of comprehension strategies: A natural history of one program for enhancing learning. In J. Borkowski & J.P. Das (Eds.), *Intelligence and cognition in special children: Comparative studies of giftedness, mental retardation, and learning disabilities*. New York: Ablex.

Butkowsky, I.S., & Willows, D.M. (1980). Cognitive-motivational characteristics of children varying in reading ability: Evidence for learned helplessness in poor readers. *Journal of Educational Psychology*, *72*, 408–422.

Campione, J.C., Brown, A.L., Ferrara, R.A., Jones, R.S., & Steinberg, E. (1985). Breakdown in flexible use of information: Intelligence-related differences in transfer following equivalent learning performance. *Intelligence*, *9*, 297–315.

Chi, M.T.H., Glaser, R., & Farr, M. (1988). *The nature of expertise*. Hillsdale, NJ: Erlbaum.

Chi, M.T.H., & Koeske, R.D. (1983). Network presentation of a child's dinosaur knowledge. *Developmental Psychology*, *19*, 29–39.

Cooney, J.B., & Swanson, H.L. (1987). Memory and learning disabilities: An overview. In H.L. Swanson (Ed.), *Memory and learning disabilities* (pp. 1–40). Greenwich, CT: JAI Press.

Dallego, M., & Moely, B. (1980). Free recall in boys of normal and poor reading levels as a function of task manipulations. *Journal of Experimental Child Psychology*, *30*, 62–78.

Dansereau, D.F., McDonald, B.A., Collins, D.W., Garland, J., Holly, C.D., Diekhoff, G., & Evans, S.H. (1979). Evaluation of a teaching strategy system. In H.F. O'Neil & C.D. Spielberger (Eds.), *Cognitive and affective learning strategies* (pp. 3–43). New York: Academic.

Duffy, G.G., Roehler, L.R., Meloth, M., Vavrus, L., Book, C., Putnam, J., & Wesselman, R. (1986). The relationship between explicit verbal explanation during reading skill instruction and student awareness and achievement: A study of reading teacher effects. *Reading Research Quarterly*, *21*, 237–252.

Duffy, G.G., Roehler, L.R., Sivan, E., Rackliffe, G., Book, C., Meloth, M., Vavrus, L., Wesselman, R., Putnam, J., & Bassiri, D. (1987). The effects of explaining the reasoning associated with using reading strategies. *Reading Research Quarterly*, *22*, 347–368.

Ellis, H.C., Roger, L., & Rodriquez, I. (1989). Emotional mood states and memory. *Journal of Experimental Psychology: Learning, Memory and Cognition*, *10*, 470–482.

Englert, C.S., Raphael, T.E., Anderson, L.M., Anthony, H., Fear, K., & Gregg,

S. (in press). A case for writing instruction: Strategies for writing informational text. *Learning Disabilities Focus*.

Ferrara, R.A., Brown, A.L., & Campione, J.C. (1986). Children's learning and transfer of inductive reasoning rules: Studies of proximinal development. *Child Development, 57*, 1087–1089.

Gelzheiser, L.M. (1984). Generalization from categorical memory tasks to prose in learning disabled adolescents. *Journal of Educational Psychology, 76*, 1128–1138.

Gelzheiser, L.M., Cort, R., & Sheperd, M.J. (1987). Is minimal strategy instruction sufficient for LD children? Testing the production defending hypothesis. *Learning Disability Quarterly, 10*, 267–276.

Goldman, S., & Pellegrino, J. (1987). Information processing and educational microcomputer technology: where do we go from here? *Journal of Learning Disabilities, 20*, 155–165.

Graham, S. (1985). Effects of direct instruction and metacomprehension on finding main ideas. *Learning Disability Research, 1*, 90–100.

Hayes-Roth, B., & Hayes-Roth, F. (1979). A cognitive model of planning. *Cognitive Science, 3*, 275–310.

Kant, E., & Newell, A. (1984). Problem solving techniques for the design of algorithms. *Information Processing & Management, 20*, 97–118.

Levin, J.R. (1981). On the function of pictures in prose. In F.J. Pirozzola & M.C. Wittrock (Eds.). Neuropsychological and cognitive processes in reading (pp. 203–220). New York: Academic Press.

Levin, J.R. (1986). Four cognitive principles of learning strategy instruction. *Educational Psychologist, 21*, 3–17.

Levin, J.R. (1988). Elaboration-based learning strategies: Powerful theory = powerful application. *Contemporary Educational Psychology, 13*, 191–205.

Licht, B.G. (1983). Cognitive-motivational factors that contribute to the achievement of learning disabled children. *Journal of Learning Disabilities, 16*, 483–490.

Licht, B.G., Kistner, J.A., Ozkaragoz, T., Shapiro, S., & Clausen, L. (1985). Causal attributions of learning disabled children: Individual differences that implications for persistence. *Journal of Educational Psychology, 77*, 208–216.

Mandler, G. (1979). Organization and repetition: Organization Principles with special reference to rote learning. In L. Nilsson (Ed.) Perspective on memory research (pp. 293–315). Hillsdale, N.J.: Erlbaum.

McLoone, B.B., Scruggs, T.E., Mastropieri, M.A., & Zucker, S.F. (1986). Memory strategy instruction and training with learning-disabled adolescents. *Learning Disability Research, 2*, 45–53.

Meichenbaum, D. (1982). *Teaching thinking: a cognitive behavioral approach*. Austin, TX: Society for Learning Disabilities and Remedial Education.

Meichenbaum, D., & Goodman, J. (1971). Training impulsive children to talk to themselves: A means of developing self-contol. *Journal of Abnormal Psychology, 77*, 115–126.

Moely, B., Hart, S., Santulli, K., Leal, L. Johnson, I., Rao, N. & Burney, L. (1986). How do teachers teach memory skills. *Educational Psychologist, 21*, 55–71.

Newell, A. (1980). Reasoning, problem solving and decision processes: The problem space as a fundamental category. In R. Nickerson (Ed.), *Attention and performance VIII*. Hillsdale, NJ: Lawrence Erlbaum.

Oka, E.R., & Paris, S.A. (1987). Patterns of motivation and reading skills under-achieving children. In S.J. Ceci (Ed.), *Handbook of cognitive, social, and neuropsychological aspects of learning disabilities* (pp. 115–145). Hillsdale, NJ: Erlbaum.

Palincsar, A.S., & Brown, A.L. (1984). Reciprocal teaching of comprehension-fostering and monitoring activities. *Cognition and Instruction, 1*, 117–175.

Palincsar, A.M., & Brown, A. (1987). Enhancing instructional time through atten-tion to metacognition. *Journal of Learning Disabilities, 20*, 66–76.

Paris, S.G., & Oka, E.R. (1989). Strategies for comprehending text and coping with reading difficulties. *Learning Disability Quarterly, 12*, 32–42.

Pellegrino, J., & Goldman, S. (1987). Information processing and math. *Journal of Learning Disabilities, 20*, 23–34.

Pressley, M., Johnson, C.J., & Symons, S. (1987). Elaborating to learn and learn-ing to elaborate. *Journal of Learning Disabilities, 20*, 76–91.

Pressley, M., & Levin, J.R. (1986). Elaborative learning strategies for the in-efficient learner. In S.J. Ceci (Ed.), *Handbook of cognitive. social and neuro-psychological aspects of learning disabilities*, Vol. 1. Hillsdale, NJ: Erlbaum.

Pressley, M., Symons, S., Snyder, B., & Cariglia-Bull, T. (1989). Strategy instruc-tion research comes of age. *Learning Disability Quarterly, 12*, 3–15.

Scruggs, T.E., Mastropieri, M.A., & Levin, J.R. (1987). Transformational mne-monic strategies for learning disabled students. In H.L. Swanson (Ed.), *Memory and Learning Disabilities* (pp. 225–244). Greenwich, CT: JAI Press.

Shankweiler, D., Liberman, I., Mark, L., Fowler, C., & Fisher, F. (1979). The speech code and learning to read. *Journal of Experimental Psychology: Human Learning and Memory, 5*, 531–545.

Short, E.J., & Ryan, E.B. (1984). Metacognitive differences between skilled and less skilled readers: Remediating deficits through story grammar and attribution training. *Journal of Educational Psychology, 76*, 225–235.

Spear, L.C., & Sternberg, R.J. (1987). An information-processing framework for understanding reading disability. In S. Ceci (Ed.), *Handbook of cognitive, social and neuropsychological aspects of learning disabilities* (pp. 3–32). Hillsdale, NJ: Erlbaum.

Stanovich, K. (1986). Matthew effects in reading: Some consequences of individual differences in the acquisition of literacy. *Reading Research Quarterly, 21*, 360–387.

Sternberg, R.M. (1987). A unified theory of intellectual exceptionality: In Day, J.D., & Borkowski, J.G. (Eds.), *Intelligence and exceptionality: New directions for theory, assessment, and instructional practices* (pp. 135–172). Norwood, NJ: Ablex.

Swanson, H.L. (1982). Strategies and constraints—A commentary. *Topics in Learning and Learning Disabilities, 2*, 79–81.

Swanson, H.L. (1983). Relations among metamemory, rehearsal activity and word recall in learning disabled and nondisabled readers. *British Journal of Education-al Psychology, 53*, 186–194.

Swanson, H.L. (1984a). Process assessment of intelligence in learning disabled and mentally retarded children: A multidirectional model. *Educational Psychologist, 19*, 149–162.

Swanson, H.L. (1984b). Semantic and visual memory codes in learning disabled readers. *Journal of Experimental Child Psychology, 37(1)*, 124–140.

Swanson, H.L. (1984c). Effects of cognitive effort and word distinctiveness on learning disabled and nondisabled readers' recall. *Journal of Educational Psychology*, 76, 894–908.

Swanson, H.L. (1985). Effects of cognitive-behavioral training on emotionally disturbed children's academic performance. *Cognitive Therapy and Research*, 9, 201–216.

Swanson, H.L. (1986a). Do semantic memory deficiencies underlie disabled readers encoding processes? *Journal of Experimental Child Psychology*, 41, 461–488.

Swanson, H.L. (1986b). Learning disabled readers' verbal coding difficulties: A problem of storage or retrieval? *Learning Disability Research*, 20, 3–7.

Swanson, H.L. (1987a). Organization training and developmental changes in learning disabled children's encoding preferences. *Learning Disability Quarterly*, 8, 1–18.

Swanson, H.L. (1987b). Verbal-coding deficits in the recall of pictorial information by learning disabled children: The influence of a lexical system for input operations. *American Educational Research Journal*, 24, 143–170.

Swanson, H.L. (1987c). What learning disabled readers' fail to retrieve: A problem of encoding, interference or sharing of resources? *Journal of Abnormal Child Psychology*, 15, 339–351.

Swanson, H.L. (1988). Learning disabled children's problem solving: Identifying mental processes underlying intelligent performance. *Intelligence*, 12, 261–278.

Swanson, H.L. (1989). Central processing strategy difference in gifted, normal achieving, learning disabled and mentally retarded children. *Journal of Experimental Child Psychology*, 47, 378–397.

Swanson, H.L., Cochran, K., & Ewers, C. (1989). Working memory and reading disabilities. *Journal of Abnormal Child Psychology*, 17, 145–156.

Swanson, H.L., & Cooney, J. (1985). Strategy transformations in learning disabled children. *Learning Disability Quarterly*, 8, 221–231.

Swanson, H.L., & Cooney, J. (1987). Individual differences in mental arithmetic: Procedural or declarative knowledge. Paper presented at the American Educational Research Association, Washington, D.C.

Swanson, H.L., & Cooney, J.D., & Overholser, J.D. (1989). The effects of self-generated visual mnemonics on adult learning disabled readers' word recall, *Learning Disabilities Research*, 4, 26–35.

Swanson, H.L., Kozleski, E., & Stegink, P. (1987). Effects of cognitive training on disabled readers' prose recall: Do cognitive processes change during intervention? *Psychology in the Schools*, 24, 378–384.

Swanson, H.L., & Rathgeber, A. (1986). The effects of organizational dimensions on learning disabled readers' recall. *Journal of Educational Research*, 79, 155–162.

Swanson, H.L., & Rhine, B. (1985). Strategy transformation in learning disabled children's math performance: Clues to the development of expertise. *Journal of Learning Disabilities*, 18, 596–603.

Thomas, H.B. (1963). Communication theory and the constellation hypothesis of calculation. *Quarterly Journal of Experimental Psychology*, 15, 173–191.

Torgesen, J.K., Murphy, H., & Ivey, G. (1979). The effects of an orienting task on the memory performance of reading disabled children. *Journal of Learning Disabilities*, 12, 396–401.

Vygotsky, L. (1962). *Thought and language*. New York: Wiley.

Wong, B.Y.L., & Jones, W. (1982). Increasing metacomprehension in learning-disabled and normally-achieving students through self-questioning training. *Learning Disability Quarterly*, *5*, 228–240.

Wong, B.Y.L., & Sawatsky, D. (1984). Sentence elaboration and retention of good, average and poor readers. *Learning Disability Quarterly*, *6–7*, 229–236.

Wong, B.Y.L., Wong, R., & Foth, D. (1977). Recall and clustering of verbal materials among normal and poor readers. *Bulletin of the Psychonomic Society*, *10*, 375–378.

Wong, B.Y.L., Wong, R., Perry, N., & Sawatsky, D. (1986). The efficacy of a self-questioning summarization strategy for use by underachievers and learning-disabled adolescents. *Learning Disability Focus*, *2*, 20–35.

Worden, P.E. (1986). Comprehension and memory for prose in the learning disabled. In S.J. Ceci (Ed.) Handbook of Cognitive, Social and Neuropsychological aspects of learning disabilities (pp. 106–112). Hillsdale, N.J.: Erlbaum.

Worden, P.E., Mandler, J.M., & Chary, F.R. (1978). Children's free recall: An explanation of sorts. *Child Development*, *49*, 835–844.

Commentary
Foundations of Intervention Research

Thomas E. Scruggs

The preceding chapters by Kavale and Swanson set the stage for this whole volume, one devoted entirely to research on interventions in learning disabilities. As noted by Kavale, intervention is the reason for the existence of the field of learning disabilities. While other disciplines, such as psychology and paleontology, can establish and develop themselves by virtue of their ability to explain existing phenomena relevant to those disciplines, learning disabilities is a viable and worthwhile field of inquiry only to the extent that it is able to actuate positive change in the lives of those so characterized. Without reliably effective interventions, all our abilities to document and explain the learning disabilities phenomenon are of little value.

Effective research aimed at the amelioration of learning disabilities, to be of consequence, must be systematic, rule-governed, and closely tied to existing characterizations of disabled learning. The chapters by Kavale and Swanson offer substantial contributions toward an overriding framework for the progress of intervention research.

In spite of the compelling need for more and better intervention research in learning disabilities, the nature and purposes of intervention research are subject to a variety of interpretations. Important concerns in intervention research include (a) defining intervention research in learning disabilities, (b) clarifying the purposes of such research, (c) accommodating the role of theory, and (d) resolving issues in the practice of intervention research. In this chapter, I will comment on the chapters by Kavale and Swanson within the context of these four major issues.

Definitions

Defining Intervention Research

It is generally agreed that intervention research refers to scientifically based efforts to document specific techniques whose intention is to improve, in some socially acceptable way, the functioning of individuals characterized as learning disabled (LD) (see also Wong, 1987). Nevertheless, such a characterization allows for different interpretations, not the least of which involve the intentions of the researcher and considerations for the external validity of the research methods and materials. For example, consider a paper by Swanson (1987) describing the relative inability of learning disabled students to benefit from the provision of verbal labels to facilitate memory of nonmeaningful geometric figures. Swanson concluded that LD students, unlike their nondisabled counterparts, have functionally independent visual and verbal coding systems. Stated thus, the research can rightly be characterized as oriented toward uncovering the characteristics of learning disabilities. Nevertheless, could it not also be argued that such research is intervention-oriented in that it specified differential conditions under which retrieval for nonverbal information (i.e., shapes) could be facilitated? In his chapter, Swanson maintains that LD students may have greater difficulty than nondisabled students in benefiting from prompted imagery instructions. Again, such information seems to augment our knowledge of the characteristics of learning disabilities, as well as provide us with intervention-relevant information.

Swanson (1988a) indicated that basic and applied research can be largely differentiated with respect to the *motive* of the researchers as well as the obtained *results* of the research. Ideally, research should provide us with important information about the characteristics of LD students as they respond to interventions on their social, academic, or affective functioning.

Kavale, in his chapter, carefully distinguishes between research and evaluation, noting that evaluation is "parochial rather than universal in scope" in that it serves immediately to provide information about the merits of a particular program, rather than increasing knowledge and understanding of learning disabilities. Without the theoretical underpinnings so evident in, for example, Swanson's own research, evaluation studies provide more limited, though certainly useful, information on learning disabilities. Kavale argues that much of the misdirection of the past has resulted from the substitution of program evaluation for systematic intervention research, which addresses systematically specific, theoretically grounded components of such programs.

Defining Learning Disabilities

Neither Swanson nor Kavale offered specific definitions of learning disabilities, although each of these researchers has extensively discussed LD definitions in previous works (e.g., Cooney & Swanson, 1987; Kavale & Forness, 1985). Certainly, the issue of definitions of learning disabilities has been addressed in detail over the past decade, perhaps beginning with the important paper of Keogh, Major, Omori, Gandara, and Reid (1980), and discussed more recently in volumes edited by Vaughn and Bos (1987) and Ceci (1986).

With respect to intervention research, there are several issues of importance regarding definitions of learning disabilities. Prominent among these
is the choice between the use of broadly versus narrowly defined samples of
learning disabled students. Skilled researchers frequently subject their
samples to rigorous screening for specific characteristics prior to their inclusion in the study. While it is important that as much subject information
as possible be included to facilitate later replication or synthesis efforts
(Keogh, 1987), it is also true that more narrowly defined samples will
necessarily be less representative of, and perhaps less valid for, the more
heterogeneous classroom samples the learning disabilities teacher is faced
with. Broadly defined samples, on the other hand, may provide greater
external validity for intervention effectiveness, while sacrificing precision
in sample definition. While each choice appears to entail disadvantages,
these may not be as consequential as feared. Kavale, in his chapter,
provides information on the application of meta-analytic techniques to
examine relative intervention effectiveness across a variety of individual research reports. Although a number of these meta-analyses have been conducted, I am unaware of any that have uncovered any differences in intervention effectiveness for LD students as a function of sample definition.

Nevertheless, it does seem of importance that all included students in
intervention studies be shown to exhibit some deficit in the area targeted
for intervention. It makes little rational sense, for example, for a broad
sample of LD students to be included in a social skills training intervention,
if many of the targeted students exhibit no social skills deficits. Although
there have been calls for greater homogeneity in sample selection, perhaps
is would be well for intervention researchers to employ samples that bear
logical relation to the intervention target, and be as precise as possible in
providing sample information. As intervention results are replicated,
perhaps with somewhat different samples, external validity of the treatment could be enhanced.

Defining Effectiveness

Since a major goal of intervention research is to develop "effective"
treatments for learning disabilities, it is important that researchers pursue
criteria for determining treatment effectiveness. It has been stated that
intervention research often aims at improving, in some socially acceptable way, the functioning of learning disabled individuals. However, given
such an admittedly subjective guideline, it seems unlikely that "effectiveness" could be operationalized in such a way that would satisfy all researchers.

Kavale argued that effectiveness is not the same as "cure" or "leading toward a cure" for learning disabilities; in fact, he maintained that
"cure" orientations have inhibited the development of highly effective
intervention techniques which nonetheless do not qualify as "cures" for

learning disabilities. From Kavale's perspective of meta-analysis, relative effectiveness of an intervention can be quantified by use of the "effect size," a standardized difference score between experimental and control conditions. Effectiveness can be conceptualized across domains as the comparability of the average (50th percentile) experimental and control students. For example, Kavale reported the average student receiving perceptual-motor training as performing at the 53rd percentile of the control group.

Although attempts have been made to standardize an effect size of, for example, .33 as "educationally significant" (Tallmadge, 1977), such a consideration depends greatly on the dependent measure being considered. For example, while a mean effect size of .39 for psycholinguistic training (Kavale & Forness, 1985) could receive a qualified judgment of "effective," it is important to note that those effects were obtained largely on the Illinois Test of Psycholinguistic Ability (ITPA), and do not necessarily reflect any concomitant effect on such skill domains as reading or spelling. Whether such an effect on ITPA scores can be regarded as "effective" depends on the attitude of the individual toward the value of ITPA scores.

While Swanson does not discuss the issue of relative effect sizes, he does raise several important points regarding intervention effectiveness. He argues that effective interventions may not necessarily eliminate performance differences between LD and nondisabled students, and that specific cognitive interventions may or may not have differential effects on LD and nondisabled students. Swanson concurs, indirectly, that effectiveness does not necessarily indicate "cure," and that a specific treatment may or may not be effective for all targeted learner types (LD, normal, gifted).

In evaluating "effectiveness," however, it may be wise to avoid an insistence on "big" effects, as often voiced by some behaviorists (e.g., Parsonson & Baer, 1978). All other things being equal, larger positive effects are to be valued over smaller effects; however, it is also true that "small" effects may provide important information about learner characteristics and interventions that may otherwise be overlooked. It is also true that treatment variations that produce small effects can later be combined with other treatments to produce effects of major consequence. Given the magnitude of the challenges presented to the field of learning disabilities interventions, it may be a mistake to overlook any obtained reliable effect, however small.

The Purposes of Intervention Research

The Purpose of Remediation in Research

It has been stated that intervention research is intended to improve the functioning of LD students in some socially acceptable way. Such a statement, however, is open to different interpretations. Should intervention research focus on remediation of specific academic or social skills, or should it concentrate on "remediation" of underlying cognitive processes? In the former case, the researcher could be accused of treating symptoms, rather than causes; of "patching the cracks in the plaster" rather than attending to the major structural problems of which cracks are only the apparent manifestation. On the other hand, researchers focusing on underlying processing deficits can be accused of faulty theorizing; of reviving techniques of nineteenth-century faculty psychology intended to "train the brain," techniques that have largely failed in intervention research in learning disabilities.

In part, both sets of criticism are true. Kavale's previous research syntheses have conclusively documented the failures of previous attempts to remediate learning disabilities by training such processes as perceptual-motor functioning and modality strengths and weaknesses. Likewise, Swanson (1988b) has noted that previous learning disability "process" research has suffered from faulty theorizing. Additionally, both authors have acknowledged that skill and strategy-based training have resulted in effects that are consistently positive, but more limited in their generalizability. Swanson, among others, has demonstrated that supplying LD students with task-specific cognitive strategies typically improves their performance, but not to the level of normally achieving students. This suggests that there may be "structural" deficits, not addressed by the treatment, which continue to inhibit academic learning. It could also be argued that "process" training is potentially effective, but to date simply has not been properly conducted (or measured). Such an argument, however, will only appear substantial in light of new empirical findings.

In spite of the apparent opposition of process versus skill orientations, there may be some area in which these perspectives overlap. For example, most LD teachers agree that their students exhibit serious deficits in the area of memory; however, failures in the training of memory as a process have been documented since the work of William James (1890). Nevertheless, it has been seen that specific memory (mnemonic) strategies can improve recall of specific units of information, and when combined effectively can greatly improve recall of larger domains of content (see Mastropieri & Fulk, this volume). Furthermore, if learners can effectively generalize the use of these strategies to further independent learning, their domain of recall can be even more greatly extended. Thus, it can be seen that skill or task-specific training can build to the remediation, or certainly improvement, of specific cognitive processes.

Intervention Research as a Test of LD Theory

An additional purpose of intervention research is to test specific theories of learning disabilities. Indeed, the reader of Swanson's chapter will note that many of his interventions tell us as much about theoretical conceptualizations as they do about individual treatments. In fact, most conceptualizations of learning disabilities presuppose some aspect of disabled learning that could presumably be remediated. Kavale lists a number of treatments that have not been demonstrably effective, and consequently detract from the theoretical perspectives that underlie such treatments. Although the consistent success of specific interventions can be used as evidence to lend support to corresponding theories of learning disabilities (see, e.g., Scruggs, Mastropieri, & Levin, 1987), and, consequently, detract from competing theories, this does not mean that basic research which attempts only to test LD theory is not valuable. In fact, the final arbiter of the adequacies of LD theories would appear to be direct, planned tests of those theories.

Intervention Research and Teacher Training

Once specific interventions are determined to be effective, it is assumed they will be disseminated widely for the purpose of improving practice. Initially, validated practices may be published in special education journals where they are read by university special education faculty and classroom teachers. However, a major forum for the dissemination of teaching practice is in college and university level teacher training programs. This is an important forum for dissemination because many pre-service or in-service teachers will use such information throughout their teaching career.

For the above reasons, it is important to consider when specific intervention research findings are sufficiently documented for inclusion in teacher education programs. It is critical for new findings to be included in such programs; yet it is important for these findings to be "accepted" as practices before they are disseminated in teacher education programs. Kavale (1989) and Mastropieri (1989) have provided some guidelines on these issues. Ideally, positive findings will have been replicated by different researchers, and the classroom implications empirically tested before students are strongly encouraged to use such methods. Furthermore, pre-service teachers will have been trained to implement formative evaluation procedures to test the efficacy of all interventions employed in their future classrooms, and will have been encouraged to maintain membership in professional organizations, to keep current with new developments in the field.

Theoretical Issues

The Relationship Between Basic and Intervention Research

In most cases, basic researchers do not conduct intervention research, and intervention researchers do not conduct basic research. Basic researchers are not primarily concerned with practical applications, and intervention researchers do not necessarily wait for the latest basic research findings on which to base interventions; to a certain extent, the two groups can function independently (Scruggs & Mastropieri, 1988b; but see Swanson, 1988a). Nevertheless, the best intervention research should be influenced by theory; as the best basic research should be mindful of the results of intervention research.

In response to the issue of the independence of basic and applied research, Swanson (1988a) has previously described basic research as the initial source of questions regarding interventions, and the means by which problems in need of intervention can be identified. If basic research cannot contribute at least a large share of this information, other sources are likely to be unsystematic, anecdotal, and therefore suspect. Kavale (1988) suggested that basic research in learning disabilities has had insufficient impact on practice, due to the "faddish and episodic" nature of much basic research in learning disabilities (p. 216). Nevertheless, Kavale (1988, this volume) argued for a stronger link between high quality basic and intervention research.

Theories of Learning Disabilities Versus Theories of Learning

Most introductory educational psychology courses include the study of different theories of learning. It soon becomes apparent that there is no one universally agreed-upon theory of what learning is and how it is facilitated. Often distinctions are made among behavioral, developmental/constructivist, cognitive, and information-processing theories; but within each of these general subdivisions are many different competing theories. How, then, are we to generally agree upon a theory of learning disabilities? Need there be as many theories of learning disabilities as there are theories of learning?

Swanson makes a compelling case for intervention research based upon strategy deficit models of learning disabilities. Nevertheless, he points out that strategy-based interventions may not completely "normalize" the functioning of LD students, and that basic research should continue to expand our knowledge of learning disabilities. For extensive discussion on the role of theory in learning disabilities, the reader is referred to Swanson (1988b).

Kavale addresses the suggestion that multiple models may be necessary to address the efficacy of LD interventions. Nevertheless, some generally agreed-upon standards will be necessary to develop the field. Kavale argues that unchecked relativism is to be avoided, or it will be impossible to favor any treatment over any other treatment. In most cases, age-appropriate skill at reading, language, and computation; a well-developed knowledge base; and sufficient verbal and mathematical reasoning skills to employ with that knowledge base are considered desirable for LD students. Any theoretical orientation that intends to drive practice should consider such outcomes and accommodate systematic means for their attainment.

Aptitude-Treatment Interactions

To a certain extent, special education is based upon assumptions of aptitude-treatment interactions, in that "special" treatment is intended to differentially elevate the functioning of certain students identified as having need for such treatment. However, many if not most nondisabled students could be expected to benefit from the smaller classes, additional teacher attention, and individualized instruction found in most special education classes. Need instruction be shown to be *ineffective* for nondisabled students for it to be characterized a "learning disabilities intervention"?

Previous "process" attempts at intervention appeared qualitatively different from the type of instruction typically provided in regular classrooms. Practices derived from intervention models such as modality training, perceptual-motor training, or multi-sensory training, including sandpaper writing and the use of balance beams and trampolines, represented radically different alternatives. For these types of education, special class instruction and specially trained teachers seemed particularly appropriate. Unfortunately, as documented by Kavale, such practices have been largely ineffective, and never resulted in the anticipated aptitude-treatment interaction, whereby qualitatively different treatments result in strong effects for specifically defined subgroups of the population.

Nevertheless, it seems overly simplistic to assert that "all students benefit from systematic instruction" (Ysseldyke, Algozzine, & Thurlow, 1983, p. 146) and that therefore systematic, skill-based instructional procedures for learning disabled students are not "special." Although this statement may have aspects of truth in it, especially for basic skills acquisition, it cannot be construed to suggest that all students benefit from the *same* systematic instruction. Phonetically regular materials seem to be of special benefit to students experiencing persistent reading difficulties; however, most students seem to learn to read quite easily using standard basal materials and benefit from the diversity of focus they represent. Additionally, students differ with respect to the skills they need to be taught, and the pace at which they can be taught these skills. Many of the strategies covered by Swanson in his chapter could be helpful to "normal" students, if they are not already using such strategies. In some of my own research, it has been seen that mnemonic strategies, under somewhat different administration conditions, can be of benefit to normally achieving, or even gifted students (Scruggs & Mastropieri, 1988a). Nevertheless, such students may have less need for these strategies, may have different ability to incorporate them into their own learning, and may require them for different learning activities. In short, specific intervention strategies for

LD students may also be beneficial to nondisabled students. However, the specific circumstances under which they need to be applied may have direct relevance on how and when they are differentially used.

The Practice of Intervention Research

Laboratory Research Practices

Many of the empirical investigations described by Swanson refer to laboratory research practices. In such investigations, students are typically seen individually, in an isolated setting free of distractions and removed from the conditions of the regular classroom. Although such practices may be limited in their external validity (i.e., the extent to which they reflect actual school conditions), they are ideally suited for the evaluation of individual instructional strategies. Pressley, Scruggs, and Mastropieri (1989) have argued that, once specific cognitive deficits have been identified through basic research, laboratory settings are ideal for documentation that specific applied learning strategies are actually effective, as statistical power and experimental control can be optimized in these settings. Any obtained positive findings, however, must be tempered by the fact that the actual potential of such classroom strategies is untested. Nevertheless, as Swanson argues, such research designs can provide important information on more basic research questions, and offer explicit implications for classroom-based research.

Classroom Research Practices

Actual classroom implementations, administered over extended time periods by regularly assigned learning disabilities teachers using school-relevant materials, certainly appear to have greater implications for practice than the previously described laboratory practices, in which university researchers administer brief treatments, using experimental materials, to individual students in isolated settings. Nevertheless, in order to be externally valid, research must first be internally valid, and it is in this area that many potential problems are found in classroom-based research. Among the many potential threats to the internal validity of classroom-based research are (a) administrative limitations on random assignment, (b) "unit of analysis" problems of non-independence when treatments are administered in groups, (c) classroom-by-treatment confounding, (d) attrition, and (e) fidelity of implementation problems when cooperating teachers are not consistently observed and monitored.

In addition, classroom-based research can suffer from threats to external validity, even though a major purpose of classroom research is to *improve* external validity. For instance, individual classrooms and subjects may exhibit idiosyncracies that have little to do with learning disabilities per se, and limit representativeness of the sample to the parameter. Likewise, the use of existing classrooms implies that the researcher will be compelled to employ school-identified samples of learning disabled students, which may or may not fit the individual researcher's definition.

It can be seen that classroom-based research, although superficially more externally valid, is subject to a variety of threats that can seriously limit its utility (see also Wong, 1987). An often overlooked threat is that the treatment of choice actually *was* effective, in that students so engaged learned more that they ordinarily would have learned, but the power lost in conducting an "ecologically valid" intervention study resulted in the documentable effectiveness of the treatment being obscured. Kavale, in his chapter, and in other writings (e.g., Kavale & Forness, 1990), has argued that the scientific difficulties in conducting classroom-based research have resulted, in part, in the conflicting intervention findings found for most interventions. He points out that the results of his meta-analyses indicate that in most cases the variability of individual treatments exceeds the average effect of those treatments. In other words, given the research bases he has synthesized, it is difficult to predict whether an individual treatment will be effective, since the obtained results have been so variable.

Both laboratory and classroom-based procedures are of critical importance in learning disability intervention research. Rather than viewing them as competitors, it may be of value to examine the complementary role played by each of these procedures. Pressley, Scruggs, and Mastropieri (1989), and Scruggs and Mastropieri (1990) have described how laboratory-based research can be used to determine whether specific instructional strategies are effective, while classroom-based research can provide instructional implications of such instruction. Laboratory research is necessary to provide the systematic, tightly controlled designs that can argue very strongly for the effectiveness of a particular treatment. If the findings of classroom-based interventions are supported by laboratory findings, any experimental design flaws found in the classroom research may appear to be of less significance. Conversely, if classroom research based on successful laboratory applications does not yield positive effects, the researcher will know that the difficulty to be overcome lies either in the classroom experimental design, or the actual application of the strategy in classroom situations. If, on the other hand, there are no supporting laboratory research findings, the researcher is left to wonder whether the failure lay in the classroom application of the strategy, or if in fact the strategy is simply ineffective, under any circumstances.

In sum, the most powerful conclusions seem to be realized by the implementation of theoretically based interventions, validated under tightly controlled, laboratory conditions, and finally extended and replicated in classroom settings. Such conclusions, of course, require the implementation of many different, interconnected experiments conducted over extended periods of time, but have the advantage of providing the most valuable information for special education.

Ethical Issues

Since the overall purpose of intervention research in learning disabilities is to improve the functioning of this population, it should be assumed that intervention research is doing some tangible good. However, good intentions on the part of researchers do not guarantee positive results, and it is critical that researchers assure that their efforts will not have negative consequences. It is important, for instance, that students who participate do not lose valuable instructional time, or that this time be made up to them; that control condition students who receive instruction on less-than-optimal strategies be informed, after the experiment, on the use of more efficient strategies; and that students are not made to feel incompetent if they are unable to learn under the constraints of their particular experimental condition.

Nevertheless, it should be acknowledged that *no* treatment can be considered effective until it has been demonstrated to be effective. Without the efforts of the countless researchers in the field of learning disabilities, there would have been little progress beyond the relatively ineffective interventions of the past, and little promise that more progress will be made in learning disabilities in the future. Although researchers should be very aware of any potential harm their research might do, and take corresponding action, we should also consider the level of harm that is done by *not* conducting research on more effective teaching methods for disabled students. The best hope for the future improved functioning of LD students lies in the efforts of individuals to develop and validate ever better instructional procedures, and in the ability of our society to put such procedures into practice.

References

Ceci, S. (Ed.) (1986). *Handbook of cognitive, social, and neuropsychological aspects of learning disabilities* (Vol. 1). Hillsdale, NJ: Erlbaum.

Cooney, J.B., & Swanson, H.L. (1987). Memory and learning disabilities: An overview. In H.L. Swanson (Ed.), *Memory and learning disabilities: Advances in learning and behavioral disabilities* (pp. 1–40). Greenwich, CT: JAI.

James, W. (1890). *Principles of Psychology*. New York: Holt.

Kavale, K.A. (1989). Addressing individual differences in the classroom: Are we up to the job? *Teacher Education and Special Education, 12*, 179–182.

Kavale, K.A., & Forness, S.R. (1990). Substance over style: A rejoinder to Dunn's animadversions. *Exceptional Children, 56*, 357–361.

Kavale, K.A., & Forness, S.R. (1985). *The science of learning disabilities*. Boston: College Hill.

Keogh, B.K. (1987). A shared attribute model of learning disabilities. In S. Vaughn & C. Bos (Eds.), *Research in learning disabilities: Issues and future directions* (pp. 3–12). Boston: College-Hill.

Keogh, B.K., Major, S.M., Omori, H., Gandara, P., & Reid, H.P. (1980). Proposed markers in learning disabilities research. *Journal of Abnormal Child Psycholooy*, *8*, 21–31.

Mastropieri, M.A. (1989). Using general education teacher effectiveness literature in the preparation of special education personnel. *Teacher Education and Special Education*, *12*, 170–172.

Parsonson, B.S., & Baer, D.M. (1978). The analysis and presentation of graphic data. In T.R. Kratochwill (Ed.), *Single subject research: Strategies for evaluating change*. New York: Academic.

Pressley, M., Scruggs, T.E., & Mastropieri, M.A. (1989). Memory strategy research in learning disabilities: Present and future directions. *Learning Disabilities Research*, *4*, 68–77.

Scruggs, T.E., & Mastropieri, M.A. (1988a). Acquisition and transfer of learning strategies by gifted and non-gifted students. *Journal of Special Education*, *22*, 153–166.

Scruggs, T.E. & Mastropieri, M.A. (1988b). Legitimizing the field of learning disabilities: Does research orientation matter? *Journal of Learning Disabilities*, *21*, 219–222.

Scruggs, T.E., & Mastropieri, M.A. (1990). The case for mnemonic instruction: From laboratory investigations to classroom applications. *Journal of Special Education*, *23*, 7–29.

Scruggs, T.E., Mastropieri, M.A., & Levin, J.R. (1987). Implications of mnemonic strategy research for theories of learning disabilities. In H.L. Swanson (Ed.), *Memory and learning disabilities: Advances in learning and behavioral disabilities* (pp. 225–244). Greenwich, CT: JAI.

Swanson, H.L. (1987). Verbal coding deficit in learning disabled readers: Remembering pictures and words. In H.L. Swanson (Ed.), *Memory and learning disabilities: Advances in learning and behavioral disabilities* (pp. 263–304). Greenwich, CT: JAI.

Swanson, H.L. (1988a). Comments, countercomments, and new thoughts. *Journal of Learning Disabilities*, *21*, 289–298.

Swanson, H.L. (1988b). Toward a metatheory of learning disabilities. *Journal of Learning Disabilities*, *21*, 196–209.

Tallmadge, G.K. (1977). *The joint dissemination review panel idea book*. Washington, DC: National Institute of Education and U.S. Office of Education.

Vaughn, S., & Bos, C. (Eds.). (1987). *Research in learning disabilities: Issues and future directions*. Boston: College Hill.

Wong, B.Y.L. (1987). Conceptual and methodological issues in interventions with learning disabled children and adolescents. In S. Vaughn & C. Bos (Eds.), *Research in learning disabilities: Issues and future directions* (pp. 185–196). Boston: College Hill.

Ysseldyke, J., Algozzine, B., & Thurlow, M. (1983). On interpreting institute research: A response to McKinney. *Exceptional Education Quarterly*, *4*(1), 145–147.

Part II   Academic Interventions

3
Strategy Instruction Is Often Insufficient: Addressing the Interdependency of Executive and Attributional Processes

ANDREA K. GROTELUSCHEN, JOHN G. BORKOWSKI, AND CATHERINE HALE

For several decades, research on the amelioration of learning disabilities (LD) has focused on the training of learning and memory strategies (Ceci, 1987). The intent was to reduce or eliminate performance deficits in LD children by developing learning skills that, for many reasons, had failed to emerge as normal development would predict. Alhough this research focus met with some success (Borkowski, Johnston, & Reid, 1987), problems of strategy maintenance and generalization have remained an obstacle for in-laboratory research and its classroom applications: Learning disabled children who have acquired study strategies generally do not deploy these strategies without prompting on new tasks or with materials different from those used during training (Borkowski et al., 1987).

In this chapter, we argue that the focus of strategy-based training needs to be expanded to include *executive processes* that *direct strategy use* as well as *the attributional processes* that *energize strategic routines*. Since the context for these suggestions is our model of metacognition, we first present a sketch of that model. Next, we review data showing that detailed instruction is necessary but not sufficient for strategy generalization. Finally, we support the case for including both executive and attributional processes in training packages in order to maximize strategy maintenance and generalization.

A Model of Metacognition

Pressley, Borkowski, and O'Sullivan (1985) and Borkowski, Milstead, and Hale (1988a) have formulated a theory of metacognition that outlines a sequence of events that must occur for students to deploy strategies consciously. The model has particular implications for understanding problems of strategy generalization encountered by adolescents with LD as well as for assisting their teachers in developing instructional procedures for classroom use.

Our model of metacognition, presented in Figure 3.1, centers on improv-

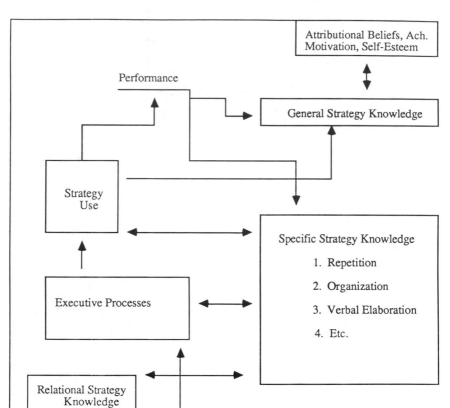

FIGURE 3.1. A model of metacognition.

ing performance through the deliberate use of a strategy. In this chapter we focus on three important components: Specific Strategy Knowledge, Executive Processes, and General Strategy Knowledge (especially beliefs about self-control). The first component, Specific Strategy Knowledge, is a prerequisite for strategic behavior. This basic aspect of metacognition contains background information about, and understanding of, a range of strategies that might be used to solve a learning or problem-solving task. Although we have referred to the sum total of the information that a learner has about a strategy as Specific Strategy Knowledge (Pressley et al., 1985), others have labeled this aspect of metacognition as meta-memorial knowledge (cf. Schneider, 1985). Whatever the terminology used, this component has been the primary focus for strategy-based research with LD children (Borkowski & Kurtz, 1987; Ceci, 1987). As we shall argue, however, a restricted focus on inculcating specific strategy knowledge will likely prove insufficient in developing generalizable strategies.

Two other components of the model—executive processes and attributional beliefs—are critical for understanding strategy generalization problems often encountered by LD students. Prior to the time when the use of a strategy becomes automated or habitual, a deliberate, evaluative decision is required for strategy implementation. That is, a decision to deploy a specific strategy rather than another is always based on an evaluation of the demands of the tasks and a contrast of these demands with the learner's past history of strategy use as well as with all relevant and available strategies. This is the major role of Executive Processes in our metacognitive model. Other important functions include monitoring a strategy's effectiveness and substituting strategies when an initial selection proves ineffective. In short, a child with mature executive processes in place is highly planful—in the sense that he or she has the capacity to select strategies appropriate for the task or problem at hand.

Another important component of the metacognitive model is General Strategy Knowledge: the understanding that effort is required to apply strategies and that well-chosen strategies improve performance. We believe that General Strategy Knowledge and its major motivational correlate, *attributional beliefs about the causes of success and failure*, are bidirectionally related, each contributing to the development of the other. The tendency to attribute success to effort is the consequence of a history of consistent, successful, strategy-based habits of responding. Good performance following strategy use strengthens General Strategic Knowledge which, in turn, promotes positive self-esteem and attributions of success to effort rather than to uncontrollable factors such as ability or luck (Borkowski, Carr, Rellinger, & Pressley, in press). Positive self-esteem and effort-related attributional beliefs enhance the likelihood of strategy generalization by energizing the executive processes necessary for strategy selection. Thus, motivational factors (such as attributional beliefs) play a critical role in what appears as eventual "spontaneous" strategy use by providing incentives necessary for selecting and deploying strategies, especially on challenging tasks.

The model we have advanced provides a heuristic framework that sketches the interacting factors we believe promote generalized strategic behaviors in the laboratory, in the home, and in the classroom. From this perspective, knowledge about the attributes of specific strategies, self-regulating (executive) mechanisms, and general beliefs about self-efficacy are three components that interact to determine the likelihood of strategy generalization. We turn now to the major focus of this chapter: demonstrating the insufficiency of the first of these components—narrowly based strategy training—especially since LD students have major deficits in executive and attributional processes that are also necessary for successful strategy-based learning. If our theory is tenable, the eventual outcome will be an integrated approach to strategy-based instructions that utilizes the multiple components of metacognitive theory.

"Enriched" Strategy Instructions

A recurrent research finding is that LD children and adolescents fail to utilize appropriate strategies on academic and laboratory tasks (Ceci, 1987). An objective of a recent study conducted by Hale, Milstead, Turner, and Borkowski (1988) was to observe whether enriched instructions during strategy acquisition would be sufficient to alleviate strategy transfer deficits commonly found with LD children. To overcome this deficit, LD children were provided with extensive feedback about strategy utility, as well as direct practice using strategies in different learning situations. It was assumed that feedback and practice would be sufficient to enhance their understanding of a strategy's appropriateness and would lead directly to its successful generalization.

In this study, the performance of elementary school-aged learning disabled children, who were at least two years behind in their reading achievement scores, was contrasted across three conditions: traditional strategy training, enriched strategy training, and a non-instructional control. Children in the two strategy conditions were trained to use two dissimilar strategies, categorization and method of loci. The two training groups differed in the extensiveness of the strategy instructions and feedback provided, with the enriched strategy training group receiving more practice and feedback than the traditional group. Learning disabled children in the control condition did not receive strategy training or feedback concerning their performance. All children were seen for four sessions during the course of a two-week period.

In the first session, all children were administered a metamemory battery (Belmont & Borkowski, 1988) that assessed their initial understanding of, and knowledge about, strategies. The five subtests in the battery measured (1) understanding that categorization facilitates learning; (2) flexibility in prospective recall; (3) ability to specify appropriate study time distribution for memorizing pairs of words; (4) allotment of study time in a circular recall task; and (5) memory estimation ability.

In Session 2 children in the two experimental groups received two types of strategy training: categorization and method of loci. For categorization, a series of semantically related pictures was shown. Children were instructed to use three steps when presented with categorizable items: (1) arrange items according to semantic categories; (2) rehearse the items within each category; and (3) at the time of recall, generate the category label and recall the items within each category. Three practice trials were given during which children were prompted, if necessary, to use the three-step procedure.

Next, children were instructed how to use the method of loci whenever presented with a series of unrelated pictures that must be recalled in a specified order. First, they were shown a cutaway model of a house drawn on a large posterboard and were instructed to memorize the room locations in the house. Children were then told the method of loci required three steps: (1) form an interactive image associating each item to be remembered with a different room in the house; (2) construct images in a specified order utilizing the layout of the house; and (3) at the time of recall, take a mental walk through the house in order to remember the items. Again, children were given three practice trials using the method of loci. During Session 2 children in the control condition were given a series of eight recall trials without benefit of strategy instruction.

At the beginning of Session 3, all children were presented with two strategy maintenance tests, one containing unrelated items to be remembered in a specified order, and the other with semantically related items. Children in the enriched strategy condition received feedback concerning their performance on the maintenance tasks if they did not choose to use the appropriate strategy (categorization or method of loci). In addition, children in the enriched strategy condition were given examples of how to use categorization and the method of loci if asked to learn similar tasks in the future (prospective feedback), as well as how to use these techniques to remember items in the past (retrospective feedback). More specifically, the prospective feedback manipulation gave children the opportunity to imagine situations in the future in which they would be required to remember a number of items such as pretending to spend a night at a friend's house.

Retrospective feedback consisted of asking the children to recall when they had to remember items in the testing situation and what they did to recall the items. Feedback in both the prospective and retrospective cases focused on the effectiveness of the newly learned mnemonics. Two practice trials were provided for each type of feedback. Finally, children were presented with two memory situations in which they had to choose the appropriate strategy which was either the method of loci or categorization. In contrast to the children in the enriched strategy condition, those in the traditional strategy and control groups received recall practice on the two tasks without feedback concerning the utility or appropriateness of their strategic behavior.

Children's attributional beliefs about the reasons for their own performance were assessed in Session 4. For each of eight hypothetical situations (four with success and four with failure outcomes), children were asked to make attributional choices about the causes of various performance outcomes in terms of effort, ability, luck, and task difficulty. For instance, they might be asked to explain why they did well on a math test last week or what best explains poor performance on next week's spelling test.

Children also received two generalization tests. For the near generalization task, two tests were administered, one containing categorizable words and one containing unrelated words that had to be remembered in sequence. The far generalization task was a variation of a common children's game called "Ten Questions." In this task children were informed that the experimenter was thinking of a strategy that could be used to remember items. They were then given three questions, each of which contained a characteristic of categorization, the method of loci, or an irrelevant strategy. The series of questions was presented until children chose the target strategy. For example, if the target strategy was categorization, children were first presented the following three alternatives: "Do the things go together?; Are the things different and do I have to remember them in order?; Should I think of something new to do?" Children then selected one of the alternatives which they thought represented the target strategy. If they selected the correct alternative, three more alternatives were presented. If children chose an incorrect alternative (i.e., one that was not characteristic of the target strategy), they were asked to select one of the two remaining alternatives. The series of questions was continued until children indicated the correct target strategy. Three sets of questions were given with each series corresponding to categorization, the method of loci, and an irrelevant strategy (making a rhyme of a string of items).

Results indicated significant differences between the strategy trained groups and the control condition on strategy use and recall for both the near and far generalization tests of categorization, and recall on the far generalization task for method of loci. What needs emphasis, however, is the fact that no reliable differences were found between the two strategy training groups on measures of recall or strategy use. The results of this study are similar to those found by Gelzheiser (1984) who concluded that the extensiveness of specific strategy knowledge does not appear to be a major determinant of generalization with learning disabled children. A similar conclusion, that extensive training of strategy use is necessary but not sufficient, for strategy generalization has been reached by Borkowski and Cavanaugh (1979).

What other condition must be met in order to train learning disabled children to maintain strategies and to use them wisely on new tasks? One influential factor is self-attributions. In the Hale et al. study, children's attributions about the role of effort were found to be related to recall performance on the categorization and method of loci tasks. In particular, attributions for failure situations were predictive of performance on the method of loci maintenance tasks. Attributional beliefs, and the executive for success were correlated with recall on both the categorization and method of loci maintenance task. Attributional beliefs, and the executive processes driven by these beliefs, provide a partial answer to the problem of strategy generalization in LD students. We turn now to a discussion of these important components of metacognition.

Higher-Order Metacognition: Attributional and Executive Processes

From the perspective of our metacognitive model (see Figure 3.1), two aspects of metacognition are critical for the development of good strategy use: General Strategy Knowledge (especially its motivational properties) and Executive Processing. Ideally, these components interact during the course of cognitive-social development so as to produce efficient and effective learners who possess a vast repertoire of strategic skills and firmly-held beliefs about their ability to control academic outcomes (Borkowski et al., in press). Beliefs in the value of strategic behavior and in the role of effort in producing success are hypothesized to result from a history of strategy-based actions in multiple settings. These forms of General Strategy Knowledge, in turn, spur the development of Executive Processes by encouraging the selection and monitoring decisions needed to deploy strategies successfully in new situations (Borkowski & Turner, 1988). Unfortunately, the complex interactions between these metacognitive components do not always work to promote independent strategy-based learning. It is to the nature of this interdependence between motivational, personal, and cognitive processes that we now turn.

Attributions, the Self-System, and Metacognition

It has been argued that general knowledge about the utility of strategies has motivational properties (Borkowski et al., 1988a). The motivational correlates of metacognition include high self-esteem, an internal locus of control, and effort-related attributions about the causes of success and failure (Borkowski et al., in press). We believe that Specific Strategy Knowledge and its associated motivational factors are bidirectionally related, each contributing to the development of the other. Both motivational and personality states are the consequences of a wide variety of successful or unsuccessful experiences with strategy-based learning. Additionally, stronger beliefs in self-efficacy engender a greater willingness to experiment with strategies. Such personal experimentation is necessary for the development of self-regulatory processes needed to select, modify, and generalize specific strategies.

Self-esteem, locus of control, and attributional beliefs are parts of a larger self system that seems to influence, directly and indirectly, on many different levels, the course of metacognitive development and the quality of academic performance (McCombs, 1986). Motivational and attitudinal constructs included within the self-system are interrelated via complex developmental pathways. For instance, affective responses, following success and failure—such as pride and happiness or guilt and shame—have been linked to the development of the metacognitive system (Borkowski et al., in press) and to achievement expectancies (Covington & Omelich, 1979a). The processes by which these emotions are evoked, however, are mediated by attributional beliefs (Covington & Omelich, 1979b; Weiner & Kukla, 1970). Indeed, attributional beliefs have been tied to a number of aspects of the self-system, including self-esteem (Carr & Borkowski, 1987), intrinsic motivation (Deci & Ryan, 1985), and beliefs about ability (Dweck & Leggett, 1988). Self-esteem and other self-system constructs, in turn, predict performance (Borkowski et al., in press; Elliott & Dweck, 1988; Marsh, 1986a; Oka & Paris, 1987). This sequence of events squares with McComb's model (1989) of metacognitive-motivational development.

While the self-system provides the general motivational mechanisms needed for strategic learning and performance to take place, recent research and theory suggest that attributional beliefs (especially effort-related attributions) are the key catalyst. In a sense, the active role of the learner in metacognitive development assures that attributions play formative roles. For instance, the development of higher-order executive processes such as strategic monitoring and modifying requires much effort, and strategic effort is initiated and sustained by beliefs in its utility (Borkowski et al., 1988a). Kurtz and Borkowski (1984) found that, among strategy-trained children, those who attributed success to effort were both more strategic and higher in metamemory than those who attributed task outcomes to uncontrollable factors such as ability or task characteristics. Likewise, LD children who attributed failure to insufficient effort made greater academic progress and received more favorable teacher ratings of their classroom behaviors, whereas LD children who made ability-attributions progressed less (over a two-year period) and were viewed by teachers as overly dependent in the classroom (Kistner, Osborne, & LeVerrier, 1988). Attributional difference scores, which reflect the importance of effort beliefs of the child relative to the child's estimation of the importance of effort for others, have yielded better predictions of strategy use than either IQ or knowledge of memory processes (Hale, Turner, Rellinger, Bados, & Borkowski, 1988). A plausible interpretation of these findings is that children who believed that effort determined the quality of their performance were more likely to pursue learning opportunities independently and to engage in the executive functioning needed to deploy strategies successfully. In this way, the self-system becomes essential for metacognitive development via the emergence of effort-related attributional beliefs.

Development of Attributional Beliefs

We assume that there is a causal bidirectionality between attributional beliefs and other metacognitive processes, with the former evolving from lower-level skills and later energizing higher-level executive processes. In understanding the development of attributions, it is useful to distinguish between program-specific and antecedent attributions (Reid & Borkowski,

1987). *Program-specific attributions* are causal explanations for success or failure that are restricted to specific learning situations. These domain-restricted attributions are believed to arise from children's learning experiences as they acquire Specific Strategy Knowledge and apply it in isolated settings. As children accumulate successes from behaving strategically, they begin to understand the benefits of expending effort and to believe in their personal control over learning outcomes. These general, more transsituational beliefs are *antecedent attributions*.

Antecedent attributions are the referents of terms such as "attributional style," which capture the long-standing, cumulative nature of children's tendencies to favor certain causal explanations over others across situations. These pervasive beliefs about the causes of success can either inhibit or enhance the likelihood of strategy generalization and experimentation, thus establishing a bidirectional route between attributions and the rest of the metacognitive system (Borkowski & Turner, 1988). In short, children who see effort as the key to success and believe in their ability to channel it constructively are more likely to seek and acquire higher-order metacognitive skills.

Attributional styles are strongly influenced by familial and cultural factors (Kurtz, Schneider, Carr, Borkowski, & Turner, 1988) and develop early. By the time children enter elementary school they already possess a well developed self-system including self-esteem, attributional beliefs, and intrinsic motivation (McCombs, 1986). This underscores the need, often ignored in short-term instructional research, to focus on antecedent attributions as well as program-specific attributions in intervention programs. In addition, learning impaired children may benefit from having their own attributional retraining supplemented by parental retraining (see Ames & Archer, 1987), a point to be discussed later.

Attributions of LD Students

Children who encounter repeated failures in the classroom do not have the same opportunities to experience personal control over learning outcomes as other children. Attribution theory (Weiner, 1979) maintains that the consequences of a history of failure include a sense of helplessness and low self-worth, which, through "reciprocal interaction," increase the likelihood of, and are reinforced by, new failures (Bandura, 1977). Thus, the low-achieving child is hypothesized to enter a self-perpetuating failure cycle in which self-perceptions become increasingly negative and debilitating.

Research on the self-systems of LD children has generally supported this rather depressing outlook. Children with LD disorders have been found to possess a number of cognitive-motivational problems, including negative academic self-concepts, low self-esteem, and maladaptive attributions (Butkowsky & Willows, 1980; Chapman, 1988; Licht, 1983; Licht, Kistner, Ozkaragoz, Shapiro, & Clausen, 1985). In particular, LD children do not seem to employ the self-serving attributional bias that is associated with normal self-esteem (Jacobsen, Lowery, & DeCette, 1986). This bias is the tendency to attribute success to internal causes and failure to external factors; that is, to take more personal responsibility for one's triumphs than for one's defeats (Marsh, 1986b).

Not only do LD children assume responsibility for their failures, they attribute failure to *uncontrollable internal factors*, such as insufficient ability, more often than NLD children, and are less likely to blame failure on insufficient effort, an internal factor within their control (Butkowsky & Willows, 1980; Kistner et al., 1988; Licht et al., 1985). While LD children choose effort as the most common explanation for their successes, they still externalize success more often than their NLD peers (Chapman, 1988; Jacobsen et al., 1986; Kistner et al., 1988) and use a greater variety of explanations, such as luck and task ease (Jacobsen et al., 1986). Given the important role of attributions in stimulating the development of executive processes, it is likely that this de-emphasis on effort has far-reaching negative consequences for the development of the entire metacognitive system.

Although the dysfunctional nature of LD children's attributional beliefs has been reliably demonstrated, recent longitudinal work suggests that these belief patterns do not become increasingly maladaptive, as some have predicted (e.g., Bandura, 1977). Chapman (1988) discovered that the cognitive-motivational characteristics of LD children, including attributional beliefs, remained negative yet stable over a two-year period. Kistner et al. (1988) also tracked LD children's achievement attributions for two years and found that, while LD children lagged behind NLD children in their use of effort explanations, the developmental pattern for LD children's attributions paralleled that of NLD children. Thus, there is a gap between the attributional belief patterns of LD and NLD students, but it does not appear to increase with age. Chapman (1988) argues that the negative motivational characteristics of LD children develop early in their school careers but reach a level of stability that is maintained through high school. These findings offer a preliminary challenge to the notion of a self-perpetuating failure cycle and have positive implications for intervention programs that are needed if LD children are to gain a stronger sense of control over their development and achieve their full metacognitive potential.

Attributional Retraining

For students to become active, independent learners they must see their own efforts as the determinants of their success. Numerous studies have shown that providing students with effort-related feedback results in greater feelings of self-efficacy, increased motivation, and improved performance (e.g., Dweck, 1975; Licht et al., 1985; Schunk & Cox, 1986). The combination of attribution and executive skill training has been particularly successful in producing strategy maintenance and generalization among hyperactive, underachieving, and learning disabled students (Borkowski, Weyhing, & Carr, 1988b; Borkowski et al., in press; Reid & Borkowski, 1987). Learning disabled students in strategy training programs with no motivational component have shown discouragingly little improvement in performance (e.g., Borkowski et al., 1988b; Gelzheiser, 1984). Understandably, program-specific attributions have been found to be easier to alter than long-standing antecedent attributions (Borkowski et al., 1988b). Nevertheless, retraining that addresses both types of attributions can be effective (Reid & Borkowski, 1987), and, we argue, plays a critical role in the remediation of strategy deficits.

Given the long histories of educational failures experienced by LD students, the challenge of altering their general beliefs about the inevitability of failure is a serious one. However, the finding that children's attributional beliefs are somewhat domain-specific (Marsh, 1986a) is encouraging, as it suggests children with a negative attributional system are less likely to discount or dismiss the experience of effort-related success on a new task than they might if attributions were more global and pervasive. Borkowski et al. (1988b) propose intense retraining of program-specific attributions across multiple domains as the best method to influence the general antecedent attributional beliefs of LD students. Other suggestions emerging from research include the use of children's correct and incorrect responses during strategy training to initiate success-oriented and failure-coping dialogues, thereby concretely linking attributions to behavior (Reid & Borkowski, 1987), and encouraging parents of LD children to adopt achievement goals for their children that focus on mastery rather than on performance, as the latter emphasis may foster a sense of helplessness in less-able children (Ames & Archer, 1987).

While the goal of attribution retraining is to generate and strengthen effort-related beliefs about the causes of success, careful consideration of the nature of LD students' attributional belief systems and sensitivity to their specific motivational problems (e.g., low self-esteem) are needed in designing success- and failure-oriented interventions. As mentioned earlier, LD children tend to attribute failure to internal uncontrollable factors, especially insufficient ability. Caution must be taken in delivering effort-related feedback so that LD children do not assume too much personal responsibility for failure (Jacobsen et al., 1986). Learning disabled children need to give themselves a break when failure occurs, but they also need to understand that they have some control over whether they succeed or fail. The need to maintain some degree of personal responsibility for failure cannot be ignored.

Barker and Graham (1987) found that children develop an understanding of a compensatory relation between effort and ability by the age of 11 or 12. Children of this age who observe a child being praised for trying hard when success occurs but not being blamed for lack of effort when failure occurs will infer that the child has low ability. Further, as LD children learn successful strategies and increase their problem-solving abilities, they complete academic tasks with less perceived effort (Schunk & Cox, 1986). Pride is maximized when success is perceived as the result of a combination of high ability and effort (Covington & Omelich, 1979b). Thus, simply teaching a belief in effort is not sufficient; LD children also need to be taught how to cope with failure constructively and how to try hard (i.e., to use strategies) so that their efforts pay off in increased skills. The most important payoff of all is the potential for the accelerated development of executive skills.

Executive Processes and Strategy Generalization

Executive processing is at the core of metacognition, in that decisions about how and when to use cognitive strategies are based on knowledge about how the mind operates (Borkowski & Turner, 1988). Executive processes enhance the development of Specific Strategy Knowledge by supplying students with missing information when strategy instructions are incomplete. More important, they provide the self-regulatory routines that guide strategy use (Borkowski et al., in press). This second function is integral to the maintenance and generalization of newly acquired strategies. Upon encountering a new problem, the successful strategy user must (1) identify and define the problem, (2) select an appropriate strategy, (3) monitor the strategy's effectiveness, and (4) revise the strategy or change strategies altogether if progress is not being made. Although these procedures become automatic for expert problem-solvers, there is a need to make them explicitly conscious in less mature strategy users to promote the development of the "executive." In particular, teaching children with metacognitive deficits to guide themselves through processes such as strategy selection and monitoring increases the likelihood of strategy maintenance within a domain and, eventually, strategy transfer across dissimilar domains and problem settings.

Deficits in Executive Processing

No matter how extensive a child's knowledge about specific strategies, successful strategic behavior demands higher-order rules that govern the use of subordinate strategy knowledge. These executive rules inform decisions about how and when to use (or not use) strategies. They are the self-regulatory mechanisms that give metacognitive knowledge its transsituational applicability (Borkowski & Turner, 1988). And they are, we believe, a major factor in accounting for the differences in ability that are observed between LD and NLD children.

To date, most strategy training programs designed for LD students have been unidimensional, focusing on the instruction, practice, and testing of specific strategies (e.g., Schunk & Cox, 1986; Scruggs, Mastropieri, McLoone, Levin, & Morrison, 1987; Wong, 1979). This type of research has generally indicated that LD children acquire simple strategies for specific tasks, as long as they receive detailed, repeated instructions and corrective feedback during practice (Borkowski & Cavanaugh, 1979; Schunk & Cox, 1986). That is, while some LD children may possess neurologically based decoding deficits that hamper their ability to learn strategies, most children with *general learning disabilities* (cf. Borkowski, Estrada, Milstead, & Hale, 1989) have the information-processing capacities to use mnemonics and other strategic devices (Veit, Scruggs, & Mastropieri, 1986). Unfortunately, even when instructors enrich training by explicitly teaching strategy attributes, such as the effectiveness of a strategy or the range of its appropriate applications, reliable maintenance and generalization effects are difficult to obtain (e.g., Gelzheiser, 1984; Milstead et al., 1988). The consistent failure of LD children to use available strategies and exhibit planful behavior on new learning tasks has been well documented (cf. Torgesen & Kail, 1980). Given the demonstrated ability of LD children to learn specific strategies, it is likely that the causes of these strategy deficits are rooted in motivational factors (i.e., disbelief in the importance of effort and perceived lack of control over learning outcomes, as discussed earlier) and in higher-order executive routines, such as undeveloped problem identification and strategy selection skills.

Research on problem-solving variables suggests a developmental delay of approximately two years in the strategic skills of LD children (Barton, 1988). While this temporal estimate illustrates the existence of a metacognitive gap between LD children and their NLD peers, it understates the qualitative differences in executive processing that are observable between the two groups. Learning disabled students often fail to use strategies spontaneously (Torgesen & Kail, 1980), and experience difficulty in selecting appropriate problem-solving techniques for a variety of tasks, such as reading comprehension (Kavale, 1980), analytical reasoning (Barton, 1988), and arithmetic story problems (Fleischner & Garnett, 1987). They are also deficient in comprehension monitoring (Kotsonis & Patterson, 1980) and performance monitoring (Slife, Weiss, & Bell, 1985), two other salient components of mature executive processing. Interestingly, Slife et al. (1985) found group performance differences in mathematical skill were paralleled by differences in metacognition, with LD students demonstrating less skill and possessing a less extensive metacognitive knowledge base than NLD students; yet there were no group differences in the amount of time needed to complete the task. These findings led to the conclusion that differences in metacognitive skills offered a more plausible explanation for the math performance differences than appeals to the inattentiveness, inactivity, or indifference of LD students.

In sum, LD students seem to possess an overall deficit in executive processing, as manifested by their inability to select, implement, monitor, transfer, and generalize available strategies. The persistence of this deficit in the presence of extensive strategy instructions suggests that LD children may need explicit training of executive skills, in combination with attributional retraining that stresses the importance of strategic effort, across multiple learning domains, in order to become good strategy users.

Training Executive Processing

Despite the observation that feedback about a strategy's utility facilitates strategy use (e.g., Kennedy & Miller, 1976; Paris, Newman, & McVey, 1982), educators often fail to explain the goals and purposes of strategy training to their students (Brophy, Rohrkemper, Rashid, & Goldberger, 1983). Even more rare is the teaching of self-regulatory skills that would guide strategy use, such as strategy selection and modification. However, research on viable methods of training executive processes has grown over the last decade, and some encouraging findings have emerged. In particular, methods that have employed highly interactive, explicit teaching techniques, such as reciprocal teaching (Palincsar & Brown, 1984), direct instruction (Borkowski et al., in press), and self-instruction (Reid & Borkowski, 1987) have been successful with learning-impaired students. The self-instructional method of training executive processes (cf. Meichenbaum & Goodman, 1971) will be the focus of the discussion here, as it has been used effectively with LD students, and seems to have potential as a method of generating and consolidating internal executive routines.

The self-instructional techniques for LD children described in the studies below originated with Meichenbaum and Goodman's (1971) classic work with impulsive children. Meichenbaum and Goodman argued that self-instructions foster more independent problem-solving and sophisticated thinking than do lower level techniques, such as teaching students how to implement a single strategy. In short, the rationale behind the self-instructional approach is that providing students with internal cues allows them to initiate executive processes when they are confronted with new tasks (Asarnow & Meichenbaum, 1979). As self-regulatory skills are acquired, the student gains control in areas previously externally directed by others. That is, the transfer of control from teacher to child allows higher-order processes to become internally directed (Day & Hall, 1987).

While the specific self-instructional sequence that is taught may vary, a student must perform some or all of the following steps in order to use self-instructions: analyze task demands; select a strategy that has been successful with similar tasks in the past; accommodate the strategy to the new task; monitor its effectiveness; devise a more efficient or viable strategy if necessary; and judge when the problem has been adequately solved or is unsolvable for the time being (Borkowski & Turner, 1988). For instance, in a study with hyperactive children, Reid and Borkowski (1987) used a five-step self-instructional sequence (cf. Padawer, Zupan, & Kendall, 1980) that was trained on multiple exemplars via modeling and direct practice. Self-control statements included (1) "find out what I am supposed to do," (2) "consider all answers," (3) "stop and think," (4) "mark my answer," and (5) "check my answer." Students were shown how to shift from overt to covert performance in carrying out the five steps of the sequence. When this instructional method was combined with attribution retraining, impulsivity was reduced and strategy maintenance and generalization effects were obtained.

Leon and Pepe (1983) had similar success with a self-instructional format used to teach LD and educable mentally handicapped students. Their training program contained the following elements: modeling, feedback, self-administration of reinforcement, coping instructions, and a self-instructional dialogue. Children in the self-instruction condition outperformed their control group peers on both posttest and generalization measures. Other researchers (e.g., Barton, 1988; Schunk & Cox, 1986) have suggested the inclusion of prolonged self-regulatory training in strategy instruction programs for LD students. Thus, while research on the self-instructional method of instilling executive routines is just beginning, there are positive preliminary indications of its potential for mediating the process of strategy transfer.

Considerations of viable methods of teaching executive processes raise an important issue regarding strategy generalization. Generalization can occur on two levels. "Near" generalization requires the availability of higher-order processes to augment the use of specific skills (such as reading summarization or paraphrasing) across tasks (e.g., social studies and literature) and settings (e.g., lab, classroom, or living room) but *within a domain.* "Far" generalization, in contrast, demands general executive processes (e.g., problem orientation and adaptation) that augment performance on tasks *across domains* (Borkowski et al., 1989). While both types of generalization involve executive functioning and both are part of the good strategy user's repertoire, very few studies have attempted to teach the latter type. Instead, researchers have provided specific strategy instruction and, sometimes, metacognitive training and then tested for generalization to the classroom. Strategy transfer across learning domains has rarely been assessed, let alone taught. An exception to this pattern is the Process-Based Instruction program (PBI), recently developed by Ashman and Conway (1988) in Australia. Because of the general deficits LD children demonstrate in executive processing and the likelihood of their need for explicit training in both types of strategy generalization, the PBI model is presented here as an exemplar of the kind of training we believe would promote the development of executive processes and the facilitation of strategy use in LD students.

An Applied Example: Process-Based Instruction (PBI)

Processed-based instruction is a classroom-based instructional framework designed to help teachers incorporate metacognitive training into their curricula (Ashman & Conway, 1988). Originally intended for mildly disabled learners, PBI has since been developed for use in diverse classrooms (regular to learning disabled) and grouping (individual to whole class). It consists of five stages: Assessment, Orientation, Strategy Development, Intra-Task Transfer, and Consolidation and Generalization. All but the first stage are relevant to our discussion of executive processes.

At the beginning of the second phase, Orientation, the teacher initiates a structured discussion on how the mind works and introduces the concept of planning. The importance of having a plan when one is solving problems (e.g., trying to win a football game or tackling a difficult math problem) is stressed to the students. During Strategy Development, the third phase, the instructor presents the students with an appropriate plan for approaching the particular curriculum topic that is being taught. The students use the planning strategy, receive feedback on their performance, and then restate the plan in their own words. The restating of the plan in each individual's own words is done to encourage students to "own" the strategy (i.e., to facilitate the transition from externally directed plans to internally generated strategies). Phase four, Intra-Task Transfer, involves practice of the strategy within the same learning domain. Here students refine their skill in using the strategy (i.e., Specific Strategy Knowledge is enriched) and become further convinced of the benefits of using the strategy (i.e., General Strategy Knowledge is cultivated). Finally, during Consolidation and Generalization, the specific strategy is modified into a more general, concise form that will be more easily accessible for transfer within and across the domain. Under the teacher's supervision, the students actively search for other academic tasks for which the strategy would be appropriate. In this way independence in problem solving is encouraged and strategy generalization is reinforced.

Throughout this chapter we have seen that training LD students to become more mature, strategic learners is a complex and challenging task that must occur at both cognitive and motivational levels. The Process-Based Instruction program does not explicitly teach the importance of effort, but it is not difficult to imagine how this component might be added to make the training more comprehensive and effective. For example, during Orientation, the importance of exerting strategic effort can easily be stressed and, subsequently, during the practice phases of Strategy Development and Intra-Task Transfer, strategic effort can be reinforced (e.g., "Good job! You did well because you tried hard and used the strategy.").

The need for attributional retraining in metacognitively-based instruction cannot be overlooked. As discussed earlier, enriched strategy instruction without motivational training generally fails to produce reliable gains in strategic performance (Borkowski et al., 1988b; Reid & Borkowski, 1987). LD students must come to believe in their ability to control learning outcomes if they are to use strategies on their own initiative. Similarly, attribution retraining alone is insufficient (Borkowski et al., 1988b; Short

& Ryan, 1984). Learning disabled students need to be taught how to make their efforts pay off and to deploy strategies successfully. Increased success following strategy use should strengthen feelings of personal control, which should, in turn, fuel future executively governed strategic behavior. And so goes the emergence of a good strategy user.

Integrating the Components of Metacognition: Implications for the Classroom

The amount of attribution retraining needed to alter beliefs about personal control and to inspire strategic behavior among LD children is probably situation-specific and depends on learner characteristics, task difficulty, and specific strategy knowledge prior to training (Borkowski et al., 1988b). However, the technique of combining attribution retraining with executive skill training (e.g., teaching selection and monitoring routines) offers the most promise for initiating the mutually enhancing relationship between positive self-attributions and the rest of the metacognitive system. Reid and Borkowski (1987) designed an intervention in which hyperactive children received antecedent and program-specific attribution retraining, as well as self-control training, which included self-regulatory techniques and strategy instruction. Children in the attribution plus self-control condition showed greater strategy maintenance and generalization, obtained higher personal causality scores endorsing effort, and displayed less impulsivity than children in the self-control-only and strategy training-only conditions. Ten months later, children in the combined condition remained more strategic, maintained effort-related attributional beliefs, and demonstrated more mature metamemories. The inclusion of a motivational, affective component in an otherwise cognitive treatment program not only improved strategic performance but also enhanced metacognitive knowledge about the general importance of using strategies.

Other research with LD students (Borkowski et al., 1988b) and underachieving students (Borkowski et al., in press) has also found that attribution retraining that focused on the importance of effort was a potent addition to traditional strategy training. Borkowski et al. (1988b) discovered that LD students in attributional-strategy trained groups outperformed LD students in attribution-only and strategy-only conditions on tests of strategy maintenance and generalization. In addition, only attributional-strategy trained students demonstrated reliable improvement in strategic reading skills on a final posttest.

A similar study conducted with underachieving children (Borkowski et al., in press), revealed that supplementing strategy training with instructions about the need for effort, particularly in the form of attentiveness to the strategy, produced significant gains in strategic performance, effort attributions, and reading grades. The improvement in grades is rather remarkable, as classroom performance has been found to be relatively stable and difficult to alter.

It appears, then, that positive effort-related attributions and their concomitant motivational properties increase the likelihood of successful strategy-based performance, given prerequisite specific strategy knowledge. Increased successes, in turn, reinforce beliefs about personal control and hasten the emergence of executive processes. By possessing internal incentives and general knowledge about the efficacy of strategies, the developing strategy user is prompted to acquire the executive processes that will allow further selectivity, deliberation, and skill in deploying strategies across domains—a worthy but elusive goal for most special education students

Acknowledgment. The writing of this chapter was supported, in part, by NIH grant HD-21218.

References

Ames, C., & Archer, J. (1987). Mothers' beliefs about the role of ability and effort in school learning. *Journal of Educational Psychology*, *79*, 409–414.

Asarnow, J., & Meichenbaum, D. (1979). Verbal rehearsal and serial recall: The mediational training of kindergarten children. *Child Development*, *50*, 1173–1177.

Ashman, A.F., & Conway, R.N.F. (1989). *Cognitive strategies for special education*. New York: Routledge.

Bandura, A. (1977). *Social learning theory*. Englewood Cliffs, NJ: Prentice-Hall.

Barker, G.P., & Graham, S. (1987). Developmental study of praise and blame as attributional cues. *Journal of Educational Psychology*, *79*, 62–66.

Barton, J.A. (1988). Problem-solving strategies in learning disabled and normal boys: Developmental and instructional effects. *Journal of Educational Psychology*, *80*, 184–191.

Belmont, J.M., & Borkowski, J.G. (1988). A group test of children's metamemory. *Bulletin of the Psychonomic Society*, *26*, 206–208.

Borkowski, J.G., Carr, M., Rellinger, E., & Pressley, M. (in press). Self-regulated cognition: Interdependence of metacognition, attributions, and self-esteem. In B. Jones & L. Idol (Eds.), *Dimensions of thinking and cognitive instruction*. Hillsdale, NJ: Erlbaum.

Borkowski, J.G., & Cavanaugh, J.C. (1979). Maintenance and generalization of skills and strategies by the retarded. In N. Ellis (Ed.), *Handbook of mental deficiency* (2nd ed., pp. 569–617). Hillsdale, NJ: Erlbaum.

Borkowski. J.G., Estrada, M.T., Milstead, M. & Hale, C. (1989) General problem-solving skills: Relations between metacognition and strategic processing. *Learning Disabilities Quarterly*, *12*, 57–70.

Borkowski, J.G., Johnston, M.D., & Reid, M.K. (1987). Metacognition, motivation, and controlled performance. In S. Ceci (Ed.), *Handbook of cognitive, social, and neurological aspects of learning disabilities* (Vol. 2, pp. 147–174). Hillsdale, NJ: Erlbaum.

Borkowski, J.G., & Kurtz, B.E. (1987). Motivation and executive control. In J.G.

Borkowski & J.D. Day (Eds.), *Cognition in special children* (pp. 123–150). Norwood, N.J.: Ablex.

Borkowski, J.G., Milstead, M., & Hale, C. (1988a). Components of children's metamemory: Implications for strategy generalization. In F.E. Weinert & M. Perlmutter (Eds.), *Memory development: Universal changes and individual differences* (pp. 73–100). Hillsdale, NJ: Erlbaum

Borkowski, J.G., & Turner, L.A. (1988). *Transsituational characteristics of metacognition.* Paper presented at the Symposium on the Interaction of Knowledge States and Strategy Use, July, Munich.

Borkowski, J.G., Weyhing, R.S., & Carr, M. (1988b). Effects of attributional retraining on strategy-based reading comprehension in learning-disabled students. *Journal of Educational Psvchology, 80,* 46–53.

Brophy, J., Rohrkemper, M., Rashid, H., & Goldberger, M. (1983). Relationships between teachers' presentations of classroom tasks and students' engagement in those tasks. *Journal of Educational Psychology, 75,* 544–552.

Butkowsky, I.S., & Willows, D.M. (1980). Cognitive motivational characteristics of children varying in reading ability: Evidence for learned helplessness in poor readers. *Journal of Educational Psychology, 72,* 408–422.

Carr, M., & Borkowski, J.G. (1987). *The importance of attributional retraining for the generalization of comprehension strategies.* Paper presented at the annual meeting of the American Educational Research Association, April, Washington, D.C.

Ceci, S.J. (1987). *Handbook of cognitive, social and neurological aspects of learning disabilities* (Vol. 2). Hillsdale, NJ: Erlbaum.

Chapman, J.W. (1988). Cognitive-motivational characteristics and academic achievement of learning-disabled children: A longitudinal study. *Journal of Educational Psychology, 80,* 357–365.

Covington, M.V., & Omelich, C.L. (1979a). Are causal attributions causal? A path analysis of the cognitive model of achievement motivation. *Journal of Personality and Social Psychology, 37,* 1487–1504.

Covington, M.V., & Omelich, C.L. (1979b). It's best to be able and virtuous too: Student and teacher evaluative responses to successful effort. *Journal of Educational Psychology, 71,* 688–700.

Day, J.D., & Hall, L.K. (1987). Cognitive assessment, intelligence, and instruction. In J.D. Day & J.G. Borkowski (Eds.), *Intelligence and exceptionality* (pp. 457–80). Norwood, NJ: Ablex.

Deci, E.L., & Ryan, R.M. (1985). *Intrinsic motivation and self-determination in human behavior.* New York: Plenum Press.

Dweck, C.S. (1975). The role of expectations and attributions in the alleviation of learned helplessness. *Journal of Personality and Social Psychology, 31,* 674–685.

Dweck, C.S., & Leggett, E.L. (1988). A social-cognitive approach to motivation and personality. *Psychological Review, 95,* 256–273.

Elliott, E.S., & Dweck, C.S. (1988). Goals: An approach to motivation and achievement. *Journal of Personality and Social Psychology, 54,* 5–12.

Fleischner, J.E., & Garnett, K. (1987). Arithmetic difficulties. In K. Kavale, S. Forness, & M. Bender (Eds.), *Handbook of learning disabilities Vol. 1: Dimensions and diagnosis* (pp. 189–209). Boston: Little, Brown & Co.

Gelzheiser, L. (1984). Generalization from categorical memory tasks to prose by learning disabled adolescents. *Journal of Educational Psychology, 76,* 1128–1138.

Hale, C., Milstead, M., Turner, L., & Borkowski, J.G. (1988). *Transfer of learning skills in LD children: Are enriched instructions sufficient?* Paper presented at the Gatlinburg Conference on Research and Theory in Mental Retardation, March, Gatlinburg, TN.

Hale, C., Turner, L., Rellinger, E., Bados, M., & Borkowski, J.G. (1988). *The development of memory processes in retarded and nonretarded adolescents.* Paper presented at the Gatlinburg Conference on Research and Theory in Mental Retardation, March, Gatlinburg, TN.

Jacobsen, B., Lowery, B., & DuCette, J. (1986). Attributions of learning disabled children. *Journal of Educational Psychology, 78*, 59–64.

Kavale, K.A. (1980). The reasoning abilities of normal and learning disabled readers on measures of reading comprehension. *Learning Disability Quarterly, 3*, 34–45.

Kennedy, B.A., & Miller, D.J. (1976). Persistent use of verbal rehearsal as a function of information about its value. *Child Development, 47*, 566–569.

Kistner, J.A., Osborne, M., & LaVerrier, L. (1988). Causal attributions of learning-disabled children: Developmental patterns and relation to academic progress. *Journal of Educational Psychology, 80*, 82–89.

Kotsonis, M.E., & Patterson, C.J. (1980). Comprehensive monitoring skills in learning disabled children. *Developmental Psychology, 16*, 541–542.

Kurtz, B.E., & Borkowski, J.G. (1984). Children's metacognition: Exploring relations among knowledge, process, and motivational variables. *Journal of Experimental Child Psychology, 37*, 335–354.

Kurtz, B.E., Schneider, W., Carr, M., Borkowski, J.G., & Turner, L.A. (1988). Sources of memory and metamemory development: Societal, parental, and educational influences. In M. Gruneberg, P. Morris, & R. Sykes (Eds.), *Practical aspects of memory.* Vol. 2. New York: Wiley.

Leon, J.A., & Pepe, H.J. (1983). Self-instruction training: Cognitive behavioral modifications for remediating arithmetic deficits. *Exceptional Children, 50*, 54–60.

Licht, B.G. (1983). Cognitive-motivational factors that contribute to the achievement of learning disabled children. *Journal of Learning Disabilities, 16*, 483–490.

Licht, B.G., Kistner, J.A., Ozkaragoz, T., Shapiro, S., & Clausen, L. (1985). Causal attributions of learning disabled children: Individual differences and their implications for persistence. *Journal of Educational Psychology, 77*, 208–216.

Marsh, H.W. (1986a). Verbal and math self-concepts: An internal-external frame of reference model. *American Educational Research Journal, 23*, 129–150.

Marsh, H.W. (1986b). Self-serving (bias) in academic attributions: Its relation to academic achievement and self-concept. *Journal of Educational Psychology, 78*, 190–200.

McCombs, B.L. (1986). *The role of the self-system in self-regulated learning.* Paper presented at the annual meeting of the American Educational Research Association, April, San Francisco.

McCombs, B.L. (1989). Self-regulated learning and academic achievement: A phenomenological view. In B.J. Zimmerman and D.H. Schunk (Eds.), *Self-regulated learning and academic achievement* (pp. 51–82). New York: Springer-Verlag.

Meichenbaum, D., & Goodman, J. (1971). Training impulsive children to talk to themselves: A means of developing self-control. *Journal of Abnormal Psychology, 77*, 115–126.

Milstead, M., Hale, C., Turner, L., Dutka, S., & Borkowski, J.G. (1988). *Meta-*

cognitive training for learning disabled students: Investigation of metacognitive feedback on near and far generalization tasks. Paper presented at the Gatlinburg Conference on Research and Theory in Mental Retardation, March, Gatlinburg, TN.

Oka, E.R., & Paris, S.A. (1987). Patterns of motivation and reading skills in underachieving children. In S.J. Ceci (Ed.), *Handbook of cognitive, social, and neuropsychological aspects of learning disabilities* (pp. 115–145). Hillsdale, NJ: Erlbaum.

Padawer, W.J., Zupan, B.A., & Kendall, P.C. (1980). *Developing self-control in children: A manual of cognitive-behavioral strategies.* Minneapolis: University of Minnesota.

Palincsar, A., & Brown, A.L. (1984). Reciprocal teaching of comprehension fostering and monitoring activities. *Cognition and Instruction, 1,* 117–175.

Paris, S.G., Newman, R.S., & McVey, K.A. (1982). Learning the functional significance of mnemonic actions: A microgenetic study of strategy acquisition. *Journal of Experimental Child Psychology, 34,* 490–509.

Pressley, M, Borkowski, J.G., & O'Sullivan, J. (1985). Children's metamemory and the teaching of memory strategies. In D.L. Forrest-Pressley, D. MacKinnon, & T.G. Waller (Eds.), *Metacognition, cognition, and human performance* (pp. 111–153). San Diego: Academic Press.

Reid, M.K., & Borkowski, J.G. (1987). Causal attributions of hyperactive children: Implications for training strategies and self-control. *Journal of Educational Psychology, 76,* 225–235.

Schneider, W. (1985). Developmental trends in the metamemory-memory relationship: An integrated review. In D.L. Forrest-Pressley, G.E. MacKinnon, and T.G. Waller (Eds.), *Metacognition. cognition and human performance Vol. 1: Theoretical perspectives* (pp. 57–109). San Diego: Academic Press.

Schunk, D.H., & Cox, P.D. (1986). Strategy training and attributional feedback with learning disabled students. *Journal of Educational Psychology, 78,* 201–209.

Scruggs, T.E., Mastropieri, M.A., McLoone, B.B., Levin, J.R., & Morrison, C.R. (1987). Mnemonic facilitation of learning disabled students' memory for expository prose. *Journal of Educational Psychology, 79,* 27–34.

Short, E.J., & Ryan, E.B. (1984). Metacognitive differences between skilled and less skilled readers: Remediating deficits through grammar and attribution training. *Journal of Educational Psychology, 76,* 225–235.

Slife, B.D., Weiss, J., & Bell, T. (1985). Separability of metacognition and cognition: Problem-solving in learning disabled and regular students. *Journal of Educational Psychology, 77,* 437–445

Torgesen, J.K., & Kail, R.V. (1980). Memory processes in exceptional children. In B.K. Beogh (Ed.), *Advances in special education.* Vol. 1: *Basic constructs and theoretical orientations* (pp. 59–99). Greenwich, CT: JAI Press.

Veit, D.T., Scruggs, T.E., & Mastropieri, M.A. (1986). Extended mnemonic instruction with learning disabled students. *Journal of Educational Psychology, 78,* 300–308.

Weiner, B. (1979). A theory of motivation for some classroom experiences. *Journal of Educational Psychology, 71,* 3–25.

Weiner, B., & Kukla, A. (1970). An attributional analysis of achievement motivation. *Journal of Personality and Social Psychology, 15,* 1–20.

Wong, B.Y.L. (1979). Increasing retention of main ideas through questioning strategies. *Learning Disabilities Quarterly, 2,* 42–47.

4
Enhancing Academic Performance with Mnemonic Instruction

MARGO A. MASTROPIERI AND BARBARA J. MUSHINSKI FULK

This chapter describes recent advances in mnemonic (memory enhancing) instruction with learning disabled populations. Particular emphasis is given to several long-term classroom interventions in which we have adapted classroom materials to incorporate the use of specific mnemonic strategies in the science and social studies areas. In these classroom-based interventions, a wide variety of dependent measures have been employed including: immediate and long-term recall tests, interviews regarding strategy usage, students' and teachers' attitudes toward mnemonic instruction, students' ability to generate such strategies independently, and students' overall weekly assigned class grades. All results to date indicate that: (a) students' academic performance on immediate and delayed recall measures increased significantly under mnemonic instructional conditions; (b) students reported enjoying instruction more under mnemonic instructional conditions; (c) mnemonically instructed students accurately reported the specific strategies used to retrieve the information; (d) students reported wanting to use similar mnemonic instructional procedures for other academic areas; (e) teachers reported enjoying the use of the mnemonic materials; (f) teachers stated that students appeared more motivated to learn under mnemonic instructional conditions; and (g) teachers reported that students participated more during instruction under mnemonic instructional conditions.

First, some initial mnemonic instruction investigations that occurred in laboratory-type settings using experimental materials are described. The results of these investigations were promising and provided the foundation for further investigations, although they themselves provided little information for long-term classroom applications of these strategies. Second, the development and expansion of the model, "reconstructive elaborations," for adapting all content areas to mnemonic instruction is presented. Third, long-term classroom implementation studies in social studies and in science are described. Finally, assumptions regarding the underlying theoretical support for the explanations of the success of mnemonic instruction with learning disabled populations are provided.

Initial Investigations

Interest in memory-enhancing devices has existed for centuries. Some historians report that training in specific mnemonic techniques was common practice before the invention of the alphabet and printing press (see Yates, 1966, for a review). Even empirical investigations in mnemonics have been conducted for several decades (e.g., Bower, 1970), although much of this initial work was aimed at differentiating between verbal and imaginal processes, rather than at increasing learning per se. Simultaneously, some researchers investigated the use of mnemonic techniques involving simple verbal elaborations with retarded populations (e.g., Jensen & Rohwer, 1963). More recently, however, Pressley and his colleagues employed mnemonic techniques in investigations with school-age populations with the primary intent of determining the effects on learning (e.g., Pressley, Levin, & Delaney, 1982). Results of these investigations provided some of the initial directions for research with learning disabled students that followed. The latter investigations are described below, first under vocabulary studies, then under attribute studies.

Vocabulary Studies

Some early investigations using specific mnemonic procedures to teach learning disabled (LD) students vocabulary words were conducted by Mastropieri, Scruggs, Levin, Gaffney, and McLoone (1985). In a study containing two experiments, junior high school LD students were taught English vocabulary words using experimenter-provided illustrations (Exp. 1), or student-generated elaborative images (Exp. 2). Results of both experiments indicated that mnemonically instructed students outperformed students in a directed instruction control condition. Additionally, students in the condition with the experimenter provided illustrations recalled more than those in the condition with student generated images.

In a followup investigation McLoone, Scruggs, Mastropieri, and Zucker (1986) examined the transfer of these mnemonic strategies across lists of English and Italian vocabulary words. Junior high school LD students were taught to use the mnemonic strategy or to use a directed rehearsal approach. The results paralleled those of the earlier vocabulary studies in that mnemonically instructed students successfully transferred the strategy and recalled more than their control counterparts. Veit, Scruggs, and Mastropieri (1986) added evidence that LD middle school-aged students significantly outperformed their control subjects in learning the roots of Greek words. In that investigation, students successfully maintained the learning on surprise delayed recall measures.

In a more recent study, Mastropieri, Scruggs, and Fulk (in press) extended the results of the previous studies. In this study, abstract vocabulary words were selected as target materials, and comprehension as well as recall measures were employed. Again, junior high school LD students in the mnemonic condition not only recalled more abstract words, but also "comprehended" more words than control students. Taken together, the results of the vocabulary studies indicated that: (a) LD students could achieve superior performance on vocabulary tasks using the keyword method on both immediate and delayed recall measures; (b) LD students generated elaborative interactions and transfered the strategy to similar task; and, (c) LD students' comprehension of abstract vocabulary was enhanced using these strategies.

Attribute Studies

Simultaneous with the series of vocabulary studies, we conducted parallel studies to examine the instruction of information that contained multiple attributes, rather than only a single definition as in vocabulary tasks. Mastropieri, Scruggs, and Levin (1985a), for example, taught ninth-grade LD students the hardness levels of minerals using a combined keyword-pegword strategy. Mnemonically instructed students outperformed students in the control conditions of free-study control and direct questioning on both an immediate and a surprise delayed recall test. In a followup study, it was found that this type of instruction could be delivered successfully in small group instructional formats (Mastropieri, Scruggs, & Levin, 1986).

Although these results provided positive findings, it was unknown whether or not LD students could learn more than one or two pieces of information mnemonically. In other words, would LD students begin to confuse the mnemonic images as more and more information was presented to them? In a series of followup studies designed to address this question, LD students were taught multiple attributes of minerals (color, hardness, and use) in three instructional conditions: a combined mnemonic strategy, free study, or direct instruction. Results indicated that mnemonically instructed students significantly outperformed those in the two control conditions. In a followup study, Mastropieri, Scruggs, McLoone, and Levin (1985) used dichotomies (e.g., hard vs. soft mineral, pale in color vs. dark in color, used in the home vs. used in industry) of the same information and found that mnemonically instructed students outperformed students in the control conditions. Several additional studies were conducted to answer the following questions: (a) the extent to which visual-spatial display treatment would compare with mnemonic conditions (Scruggs, Mastropieri, Levin, McLoone, Gaffney, & Prater, 1985); (b) whether prose passages that were embedded with mnemonic illustrations could facilitate learning (Mastropieri, Scruggs, & Levin, 1987a; Scruggs, Mastropieri, McLoone, Levin, & Morrison, 1986); and (c) whether several days of related instruction using mnemonic strategies could enhance learning (Veit, Scruggs, & Mastropieri, 1986). In all cases, students who were instructed with mnemonic strategies consistently outperformed their control counterparts. All findings indicated: (a) increases on immediate and delayed recall measures; (b) increases on application and comprehension measures; (c) ability to benefit from multiple attributes; (d) ability to generate elaborative images; (e) ability to transfer strategy to a similar tasks; and (f) ability to independently read and execute the strategic information (see Mastropieri, Scruggs, & Levin, 1985a; 1987b; and Scruggs, Mastropieri, & Levin, 1987 for previous reviews). These cumulative results provide the empirical foundation necessary for the development of a comprehensive model for adapting content area information in which mnemonic strategies can be engaged.

Development of the Reconstructive Elaborations Model

The findings from the vocabulary studies and the multiple attribute studies show that although many fruitful applications could be drawn from the cumulative data, almost as many limitations could be listed regarding actual research implementations in classrooms over time involving actual school content. These limitations included the following: (a) materials were developed by researchers; (b) materials were implemented by researchers; (c) materials were typically limited to single, short lessons, with the exception of the Veit, Scruggs, and Mastropieri (1986) study.

In an effort to address the ultimate utility of this type of mnemonic instruction with actual school content, it became apparent that further extensions would have to be made. Toward this end, Scruggs and Mastropieri (1989b) examined a variety of U.S. history textbooks at several grade levels and completed a content analysis of those materials. It soon became obvious that the information presented in those textbooks contained many types of pieces of information that need to be learned as associates. For example, names of famous people were presented, along with their respective accomplishments. Second, names of places and events that were associated with those places were frequently emphasized. This was especially apparent in the chapters that presented information on wars and those that covered explorations of new lands. Third, descriptions of novel items and their respective associates were presented, as in the case of new weapons and their associated uses and effects. Fourth, conditions of life during specific time periods were described, such as life during the pioneer days, the roaring twenties, the depression, or even the sixties. Finally, it appeared that sometimes several pieces of information needed to be recalled together, such as the names of the northern states versus the names of the southern states during the Civil War, or the products associated with specific cities, states, or regions, or the countries in the Allied Powers during World War I.

Along with this analysis, two points soon became very obvious. First, much of the information presented in the textbooks did not lend itself to the keyword type reconstructions that we had used in our earlier studies. Second, much of the to-be-learned information was already familiar, meaningful, and concrete to the target learners. In contrast, in the previous investigations, much of the information taught to LD students had been totally unfamiliar and nonmeaningful. In fact, we found that we could reliably classify target information along "meaningfulness" and "concreteness" dimensions, ranging from totally nonmeaningful to partially meaningful, and from abstract to meaningful and concrete with respect to a particular target population.

In an attempt to validate the reconstructive elaborations model, Scruggs and Mastropieri (1989b) designed an investigation in which the chapter on World War I from the locally adopted U.S. history textbook (Rawls & Weeks, 1985) was adapted to incorporate the various types of mnemonic systems based upon the level of meaningfulness and concreteness for the target population. Junior and senior high school LD and mildly mentally handicapped (MiMh) students were selected as the target population. Then, the to-be-learned content was classified as: (a) meaningful/concrete, (b) partially meaningful/abstract, or (c) not meaningful and neither concrete nor abstract. Descriptions of the specific reconstructions that were made to accommodate each of those classifications in the validation study are described below.

Acoustic Reconstructions

Acoustic reconstructions were employed whenever the content was totally unfamiliar to the target population. For example, in the World War I chapter, numerous famous people are introduced with concomitant associated events for which they were considered famous or important. Some of the many unfamiliar names include: William Jennings Bryan, Pancho Villa, Woodrow Wilson, Gavrilo Princip, Archduke of Austria-Hungary, Eddie Rickenbacker, George M. Cohan, General Pershing, the Zimmerman incident, the *Lusitania*, Central Powers, Allied Powers, and Alliance System, just to name a few. The associated important information for each of the above unfamiliar names was also unique to each name. For example, William Jennings Bryan was President Woodrow Wilson's Secretary of State. Bryan was also considered a pacifist at the beginning of World War I. We assumed that the name Bryan was totally unfamiliar to our LD and MiMh students, so the name Bryan was reconstructed to an acoustically similar, but familiar and concrete term, "lion," as in the manner that the earlier keyword vocabulary studies were conducted (see Mastropieri et al., 1985). The lion was portrayed interacting with the to-be-remembered information of "Secretary of State and Pacifist" by showing a picture of a lion sitting at a secretary's desk saying please "no fighting" to two other animals who were starting to fight in front of the secretary's desk. In the present example "opposed to fighting" was depicted rather than pacifist, because the word pacifist was unfamiliar to the target learners.

Acoustic reconstructions similar to the Bryan example were developed for any piece of information that was considered to be important to learn and totally unfamiliar to the learners. Notice that in using the acoustic reconstruction, we were relying upon the "acoustic" properties of the word that *are familiar* to the target population. In other words, the only thing familiar about this word is *its acoustic resemblance to something that is familiar and easily pictured* to the target population. Following that, an elaboration was constructed in which stimuli and response information were depicted interacting in an illustration.

Symbolic Reconstructions

We also encountered information in the World War I chapter that was familiar but abstract to our target population. For example, the notion of U.S. policy was meaningful, but abstract. U.S. policy was symbolized as "Uncle Sam," a more concrete instantitation of U.S. policy, and then Uncle Sam was shown interacting with the to-be-associated information. In the present example, the U.S. policy at the beginning of World War I was neutrality. Therefore, a picture of Uncle Sam standing on the U.S. side of a globe while saying: "It's not my fight!" (to Europe who was fighting) was shown.

Similarly, we symbolized the "League of Nations" as a baseball league, who assembled to "provide protection, independence, and security for all nations involved." We found that the most critical element of the symbolic reconstructions to be the notion of prerequisite "partial knowledge" about the relevant concept being symbolized. If, for instance, the target population were unfamiliar with the initial concept, an acoustic reconstruction, rather than the symbolic reconstruction might be more appropriate.

Mimetic Reconstructions

We also encountered information that was already meaningful and concrete for our target population. During World War I, for example, many types of new weapons were introduced, including poison gas, gas masks, airplanes, tanks, trench warfare, submarines, and various types of naval ships. This type of information is probably meaningful and concrete to most LD and MiMh junior and senior high school populations. What is unknown to them, however, is the specific to-be-associated information. In the case of trench warfare, for example, the textbook authors stressed that much of the war was fought from the trenches and that the conditions of life in those trenches became so unhealthy that many soldiers contracted illnesses and died from the unhealthy conditions. However, the illustrations in the textbooks were pictures of soldiers in trenches looking healthy and posing for the photograph, rather than looking ill. We therefore, reconstructed that information into an elaborative illustration depicting "sick soldiers in the trenches." Similarly, we depicted soldiers putting on gas masks as protection from the poison gas that was being shot at them. Likewise, we reconstructed mimetic interactions of "tanks" going from trench to trench and providing protection from gunshot for the soldier inside, in order to associate the relevant information with tanks.

Validation Study

To assess the potential usefulness of each type of reconstruction, we developed eight acoustic reconstructions, eight symbolic reconstructions, eight mimetic reconstructions, and two first letter strategies using acoustic reconstructions as described above. The first letter strategies were designed to teach the names of the countries in each alliance system. For example, to learn that Turkey, Austria-Hungary and Germany were the countries in the Central Powers, a first letter strategy TAG (*T*urkey, *A*ustria-Hungary, *G*ermany) was made and children playing TAG in *Central Park* was shown. Central Park was the acoustic reconstruction for Central Powers. Similarly, a FIRE in an *Allied Van* was shown to represent the countries *F*rance, *I*taly, *R*ussia, and *E*ngland in the Allied Powers. These reconstructions represented the major content presented in the World War I chapter. Each reconstruction was presented on a page that contained the textual information and interactive illustration depicting the strategic information. We also developed a set of control condition materials that contained identical textual information, and representational illustrations similar to the ones found in the textbooks, rather than the interactive reconstructive elaborations. We then randomly assigned special education students to either a mnemonic instruction or a representational picture control condition and taught those students the information on World War I. Students were taught individually the information for equivalent amounts of time, and were tested immediately upon completion of the instruction and after delay intervals of three or four days.

The results indicated that students learned significantly more information under the mnemonic instructional condition than under the control condition. We further found, as we had originally hypothesized, that the greatest effect sizes were for the acoustic reconstructions, followed by the symbolic, and finally mimetic reconstructions. In other words, as the information became less meaningful, students in the control condition learned less information.

These findings were encouraging for several reasons. First, they demonstrated that specific mnemonic strategies could be developed from textbook content. These mnemonic strategies were based upon a model of meaningfulness and concreteness to the target population, and relied upon using interactive elaborations for linking the stimulus and response information.

Second, the findings demonstrated that LD and MiMh students' performance could be significantly enhanced with instruction that utilized these mnemonic strategies on both immediate and delayed recall measures. Finally, the findings suggested a framework for research and direction for efforts to extend the model. The immediate extensions of the model involve implementation studies of mnemonic instruction in social studies and science.

Social Studies Research Implementation Studies

We began our research implementation studies by examining materials such as textbooks, teachers' guides, resource materials, and curricular guides adopted by several school districts in Indiana in the areas of U.S. history and state and local history. We also met with teachers and social studies specialists of the participating school districts and solicited input regarding "what's taught" in those content areas. We then targeted specific "eras" of history for our research implementation projects. The next phase of the research involved "identifying" the most important information to be mastered in those "eras" by the special education students. In identifying this content, we selected information presented from all available sources, and attempted to prioritize the information. This step involved making decisions regarding the elimination of some information that others might select as "important," but in our collective judgment was "not as important" as other information. Approximately 20 to 35 pieces of information per textbook chapter from the targeted U.S. history and state history areas were selected. We then proceeded, as described above, to determine the levels of meaningfulness and concreteness of that information for the targeted populations. Following that, the reconstructive elaborations to assist in teaching that important information were developed (see Mastropieri & Scruggs, 1989a, 1989b for specific procedures). The specific social studies' implementation studies are now described.

U. S. History

The first research implementation study involved the teaching of several chapters of U.S. history content to inner-city junior high school aged special education students (Scruggs & Mastropieri, 1989). We developed mnemonic illustrations for another chapter of U.S. history content, and added several illustrations to the World War I chapter. Therefore, mnemonic materials for the content on World War I and the Great Depression or the 1930s were developed. We then trained a special education teacher to use the mnemonic materials and the teacher effectiveness variables, as described in Mastropieri and Scruggs (1987), to teach the traditional and mnemonic instruction. This teacher was the U.S. history teacher for three classes of special education students. She then delivered the content in the following way: The first two weeks were mnemonic instruction covering the World War I information. The next two weeks were traditional instruction covering the Roaring Twenties. The following two weeks were mnemonic instruction covering the Great Depression. The final two weeks were traditional instruction covering World War II. At the end of each instructional unit the teacher administered multiple choice tests covering the content that had been instructed. The teacher also assigned grades to all students based upon their class participation, as well as their class and homework assignments completed throughout the eight weeks of instruction. Additionally, we asked the teacher to complete Behavioral Inventory Rating Scales (BIRS) (Von Brock & Elliott, 1987) for each student under each type of instructional procedures, and to complete a survey on her opinions and attitudes toward both types of instruction.

Overall, students' test scores were significantly higher under mnemonic instructional conditions on chapter tests as well as class grades. In fact, the students' class grades went from D+ to B using the mnemonic instruction. Additionally, the teacher reported that the mnemonic instructional procedures were more appropriate to the students' needs than the traditional instruction. She felt students enjoyed instruction more and were much more motivated to learn when she employed the mnemonic instructional procedures than when she employed the traditional procedures. She also reported that the students were more actively engagd in class discussions when she employed the mnemonic instructional procedures.

These findings extend our previous research in several ways. First, a special education teacher implemented mnemonic instruction. Second, the instruction took place in the students' regularly assigned U.S. history classes, delivered by the assigned teacher. Third, mnemonic materials using the reconstructive elaborations model had been developed for two chapters in the U.S. history content area from their adopted textbook. Fourth, the mnemonic instruction occurred over four weeks time. Finally, all results paralleled those of the previously conducted investigations.

Second U. S. History Implementation Study

The results of the first study were promising, however, several questions remained unanswered. First, in that investigation only one special education teacher implemented the instructional procedures. She reported liking the materials, but would other special education teachers have the same opinion? Second, since only two chapters of mnemonic materials were developed and used, the question of chapter difficulty was unclear. Third, students' cumulative performance was not assessed in the earlier investigation. In other words, after several units of mnemonic instruction, would LD students begin to confuse all the previously learned information and perform more poorly on a delayed cumulative examination? Fourth, in the previous investigation, the classroom teacher administered all the tests.

Would students perform as well on the testing situation if experimenters who were "blind" to experimental condition conducted some of the testing? Finally, in the previous study, students were not questioned regarding the use of specific strategies during recall. Therefore, it was unknown whether or not students were actually relying upon the reconstructive elaborations for retrieving the information. In order to attempt to extend the ecological validity of the model and to answer the above questions, the second research implementation study was undertaken.

In this investigation, we (Mastropieri & Scruggs, 1988) added two chapters of mnemonic materials to the U.S. history content described above. Mnemonic materials were therefore developed for the Roaring Twenties and World War II, in addition to World War I and the Depression. We trained three special education teachers in a different inner city school to use both types of materials, and set up a counterbalanced design. In one classroom, the teacher implemented mnemonic instruction for World War I, then traditional instruction for the Roaring Twenties, mnemonic instruction for the Depression, and traditional instruction for World War II. In a second classroom, the reverse order of treatments were delivered by a different teacher. In that classroom, traditional instruction was presented for World War I and the Depression, while mnemonic instruction was delivered for the Roaring Twenties and World War II. In a third classroom, another teacher delivered mnemonic instruction for the first three chapters, and traditional instruction for the final chapter. While in the fourth classroom, traditional instruction was implemented for the first three chapters, and mnemonic instruction for the final chapter. With this type of within-subjects design, we could control for several potential internal validity threats, including attrition. Additionally, in the present design two classrooms always received mnemonic instruction, while two received traditional instruction, so the question of chapter difficulty could be examined.

As in the previous investigation, instruction for each chapter occurred over a two-week period. Following each chapter, students were administered multiple choice tests covering the content taught. Additionally, teachers were observed throughout the implementation project and given feedback regarding the level of their fidelity of implementation. At the end of the eight weeks of instruction all students were given a delayed cumulative recall test that sampled content from World War I through World War II by project staff who were unaware of experimental condition. All students were also questioned regarding the strategies they used to answer the items, and given a consumer satisfaction survey regarding the mnemonic instruction. Teachers were also asked to complete the BIRS for all of their students on both traditional and mnemonic instruction, and to complete a consumer satisfaction interview.

The results of this investigation replicated the findings of the earlier investigation. When students were instructed under mnemonic procedures, their performance was consistently and significantly higher. This finding was true even for their performance in the delayed recall test after eight weeks, which covered content from all four units of instruction. Students also reported using the strategies to retrieve their responses on the delayed recall test, and their successful retrieval of strategies was significantly related to their recall scores. Students also reported enjoying mnemonic instruction more than traditional instruction, and learning more when teachers used those procedures. In other words, students were attributing their success to the use of mnemonic instructional procedures.

Teachers reported enjoying the mnemonic materials and thinking that such instructional procedures were more appropriate for LD students than the currently employed traditional instruction, or other procedures of which they were currently aware. Teachers reported that the strategies facilitated the learning of the targeted information better than other instructional procedures. Teachers also reported that their students appeared more "motivated" to learn and participated in class under mnemonic instructional procedures. We also found that there was no apparent confusion with the mnemonic strategies on the eight-week delayed recall test. Not surprisingly, we also found no spontaneous transfer on the part of students during traditional instruction. In other words, after as much as six weeks of mnemonic instruction, students did not generate any mnemonic strategies independently.

Elementary Level Social Studies Study

A third research implementation study was undertaken to replicate and extend the results of the two U.S. history studies (Mastropieri & Scruggs, 1989). First, we wanted to determine whether or not the reconstructive elaborations model could be adapted to state and local history materials. Second, we were interested in determining whether elementary aged special education students could benefit from mnemonic instruction. Third, we wanted additional information from teachers and students regarding the efficacy of mnemonic instruction.

We selected chapters from the adopted state history text on natural resources and transportation, and developed two sets of materials as in the previous investigation. This time, however, our target population was an elementary and middle school aged group of LD and MiMh learners. Three special education teachers were trained in both sets of instructional procedures, and each teacher implemented two instructional groups. One group received mnemonic instruction first, while the other group received traditional instruction first, for the natural resources information, and the instructional procedures were reversed for the second chapter. This within-subjects design again allowed us to control for order effects, teacher effects, chapter difficulty, and attrition. Instruction occurred over several weeks and teachers were monitored by project staff and given feedback regarding the fidelity of treatment implementation.

The results again paralleled those found in the previous investigations. Elementary aged LD and MiMh students learned significantly more content when their teachers used mnemonic instruction than when they employed traditional instructional procedures. This finding held for both the immediate and delayed recall tests. Again, teachers and students reported enjoying the mnemonic instruction, and requested additional mnemonic materials for other content area classes.

Taken together, the results of the social studies investigations extended previous studies substantially. First, the ecological validity of the model of reconstructive elaborations was considerably advanced. Second, social studies content from adopted textbooks was adapted to incorporate the use of specific mnemonic instructional strategies. Third, long-term investigations using mnemonic instruction were implemented in schools by regularly assigned special education teachers. Fourth, statistically significant performance increases were found for immediate and long-term retention whenever mnemonic instruction was implemented. Fifth, both teachers and students reported liking the mnemonic instruction.

Science Investigations

Although the investigations in the social studies area were very successful, several questions remained. Would the model of reconstructive elaborations also work in the science content area? Science content typically contains more abstract concepts and tends to be more conceptually laden than social studies content. Although Mastropieri, Scruggs, and Fulk (in press) successfully taught abstract science concepts using acoustic reconstructions, the materials for that investigation consisted of lists of vocabulary terms, rather than materials adapted from a specific textbook. Very little work to date had examined the issue of concept teaching in the context of entire curricular area, such as science. Additionally, mnemonic materials had typically been developed by researchers, not teachers. Consequently, the following questions remained: (a) Could teachers analyze their own curricular areas in science, and develop mnemonic materials to facilitate instruction? (b) If materials were developed by teachers and implemented by them, would the findings parallel results of previous investigations? (c) Could the model of reconstructive elaborations be applied to science content area as successfully as it was with social studies curriculum? (d) Could special education students be trained to generate these strategies, rather than have teachers supply them? Investigations intended to answer the above questions are described separately below.

Teacher-made Science Materials

In the first science research implementation study several of the above questions were addressed (Mastropieri, Emerick, & Scruggs, 1988). First, a special education teacher volunteered to attempt to develop mnemonic materials in science for her special education students. Second, to assess the efficacy of these instructional materials and procedures as compared with her traditional instructional procedures, she implemented these mnemonic materials in a crossover design to two groups of students. Third, she assessed immediate and delayed recall, as well as consumer satisfaction of her elementary aged behaviorally disordered students.

Prior to developing the materials, this teacher participated in training designed to acquaint her with the previously conducted mnemonic investigations, as well as procedures designed to assist her with the development of the materials (e.g., Mastropieri, 1988; Mastropieri & Scruggs, 1989a). She selected the students' regularly assigned textbook in science as the content area in which her students were experiencing the most difficulty, and proceeded to develop mnemonic materials for several of those chapters. First, she identified the most important concepts in each chapter. Next, she generated reconstructive elaborations for each identified piece of information. Because all of the targeted information was totally unfamiliar to her students, she developed "acoustic" reconstructions for each unit. She relied totally upon available resources, and since the services of an artist were unavailable, she drew "stick figures" as line drawings, and utilized cut-outs from magazines whenever possible. For example, to develop the mnemonic illustration for the word "herbivore," she used the acoustically similar word "herd" and used a picture from a magazine of a "herd of animals eating grass" to teach that herbivores are animals that eat only plants. She also developed specific instructional procedures to teach students in both mnemonic and control conditions. After the science instruction, students were tested immediately following each lesson, and with delay intervals of one day, three days, and one week.

The results of this investigation paralleled and extended the previous investigations in that under mnemonic instructional conditions, students' performance significantly outperformed their performance in control instruction. Interestingly, students' performance decreased from the high 70's to the 40's in the control condition over a week, while their performance maintained in the 90's for the mnemonic condition, over the same delay interval. Students also reported enjoying the mnemonic materials. The teacher reported enjoying using the mnemonic materials, even though she reported that it was very difficult and very time consuming to develop them.

This investigation added several important findings to the accumulating evidence surrounding mnemonic instruction. First, a teacher successfully developed her own mnemonic materials to accompany the adopted textbook materials. Second, she implemented this instruction over two weeks of school in a counterbalanced experimental design. Third, her elementary aged behaviorally disordered students' performance was significantly higher under mnemonic conditions on both immediate and delayed recall tests. Finally, both teacher and students reported a preference for mnemonic materials.

Second Science Research Implementation

The first science study offered some positive findings, but left additional unanswered questions. First, because only acoustic reconstructions were employed, the issue of applications of the reconstructive elaborations models was not assessed in the Mastropieri, Emerick, and Scruggs (1988) study. Second, the implementation period lasted only approximately two weeks in the above study, and the question remained of longer-term implementation. Third, the question of student-generated mnemonic elaborations remained untested. Fourth, little attributional retraining had been conducted with mnemonic strategy instruction. Scruggs and Mastropieri's (in press) investigation was proposed to address some of these remaining questions.

In this study, science content from the adopted textbooks was adapted using the reconstructive elaborations model. Two chapters covering life science and two chapters covering the earth's history and geology were adapted using specific acoustic, symbolic, and mimetic reconstructions. It was found that the science content could successfully be adapted via the reconstructive elaborations model. For example, many of the terms introduced were unfamiliar to the target population, and those terms were reconstructed into acoustically similar, easily pictured, familiar terms, and then shown in interactive elaborations with the to-be-associated information. An example of one acoustic reconstructions that was made included teaching the meaning of "extinct." The word was unfamiliar to the target population, whereas the acoustically similar word "stink" was. Stink was shown interacting in an elaboration, for example, by depicting dead dinosaurs starting to stink, with someone saying: "These dinosaurs sure stink, that's because they are extinct!"

Concepts such as warm-blooded and cold-blooded were reconstructed symbolically, by presenting animals who were sweating while in a summer scene (warm-blooded), or wearing scarves in a cold winter-like scene (cold-blooded). Mimetic reconstructions were employed whenever the target information was considered totally familiar and concrete—for example, in learning the attributes associated with earthworms (they have many hearts, are roundworms, and live in the earth). Earthworms were pictured in an interactive elaboration containing a round worm with many hearts who was living in the earth. All the important content fit into the reconstructive framework and materials were developed accordingly. Similarly, parallel materials that identified the important information, but did not provide any strategic information were prepared for the control condition. Additionally, all students had practice activities designed to accompany the appropriate set of instructional materials and extra practice at learning the target information.

The target population was middle school learning disabled and mildly mentally handicapped youngsters who were receiving science instruction from their regularly assigned special education teachers. A crossover design was implemented in which each of two self-contained special education classrooms received mnemonic and traditional instruction for the various units. Additionally, three phases were implemented in this design. The first phase was the training phase, during which time classrooms received either mnemonic for one chapter or traditional instruction for another. The second phase was referred to as the maintenance phase. During this phase each group received mnemonic instruction on another chapter. The third and final phase was referred to as the generalization training phase. During this phase, students were taught to generalize the strategies during their class for another new chapter of science content.

During the generalization phase, teachers identified the important information for students, but then prompted and elicited strategies from the class as a whole. For example, instead of providing the strategy for remembering that the earth's core is made of iron and nickel, teachers said something like the following: "We know that the earth's core is made of iron and nickel now. But we need to have a good way to remember that information. Remember how we used the strategies and pictures to help us learn and remember information last week? Let's try to come up with our own strategies for this information. What might be a good way to think of "core"? Then the teachers wrote all of the brainstormed ideas from the students on the blackboard. Students elicited responses like: core sounds like door, ore, cord, or apple core reminds me of core. Following that, teachers said: "We need to select the best one for us as a class to use," and proceeded to select the one that seemed optimal for the class. In the case of the present example, one class used "door," while the other class used "apple core." Teachers then said that they would draw a good interactive illustration like the ones they had used last week. Teachers drew pictures and then asked students to draw good interactive pictures on the study booklets, just like the ones they had provided in previous lessons. The resulting pictures contained either "doors with nickel and iron on them" or "apple cores made out of nickels and irons." Teachers provided students with feedback regarding their illustrations and asked students to label their drawings. Ample time was provided for students to draw and review their strategies. Additionally, all classes were videotaped for examination of specific verbal interactions that occurred throughout the instructional sessions.

Testing was completed at several times throughout this study. First, students' recall was assessed following the instruction of the two chapters that were taught either mnemonically or traditionally. Second, students were tested immediately following the week of mnemonic instruction. Students were also tested at the end of the generalization unit, and at that time given a surprised delayed recall test on all information covered to date. Students were always questioned regarding the specific strategies that they used to retrieve responses, and they were questioned regarding their preference for all three types of instruction that had occurred: provision of mnemonic strategies, generation of mnemonic strategies, and traditional instruction.

The results of the training phase replicated all previous investigations in that mnemonic instruction resulted in statistically higher performance for both classrooms, on both the immediate recall test and the delayed recall measure. During the maintenance phase of mnemonic instruction only, both classrooms maintained high levels of performance. During the generalization phase, the mean recall performances were slightly lower than the mean performances of mnemonic instruction delivered by the classroom teachers. However, this time, only one-third the amount of content was covered during the same amount of instructional time, as when teachers presented the mnemonic strategies that were already prepared. These results indicate that although students as a group could effectively generate their own "reconstructive elaborations," they proceeded significantly slower throughout the content than when the pace was held constant by teachers. Results from the student survey were mixed. Students were asked what they enjoyed the most, learned the most, tried the hardest, and would use again. They were also asked to rank the three instructional procedures accordingly. Mnemonic instruction (where teachers supplied the materials) was reported as the instructional condition enjoyed the most by 68% of the sample, followed by generalization training by 26% of the sample. Similarly 74% and 63% of the students reported "learning the most" and "would use again" for the teacher-supplied mnemonic materials. Interestingly, 58% of the students reported trying the hardest during the generalization training, while between 21% and 26% of the students reported generalization training as the method of "learning the most," "enjoying the most," and "would use again." Students consistently reported (between 68% and 74%) that traditional instruction was not only the "least preferred method," but also one on which they "learned the least" amount of information. Perhaps even more interesting was the fact that 42% of the students reported that they had to try the least during mnemonic instruction, but still performed very well. Taken together, the results of this and the previously described research implementation studies provide some interesting evidence on the utility of mnemonic instruction as a component of instruction for special education students. First, positive and consistent academic gains have been found across content areas, across age groups, and across handicapping conditions. Second, these positive gains have been consistently maintained over delayed recall intervals. Third, students have reported liking such instruction, and in the recent initial generalization training study, some students actually preferred this method over teacher-supplied mnemonics. Fourth, teachers have reported liking the materials, and have consistently asked for additional mnemonic materials for use in their classrooms. Although results of an initial investigation demonstrate that a teacher can develop such materials, it was difficult and time consuming. Finally, although this generalization information is promising on one hand, the findings are negative on the other. Although these students could successfully generate, in group formats, strategies that were successful at increasing their learning, the costs were evident in the amount of time expended to complete this activity. Teachers must carefully weigh the costs associated with training for generalization versus covering content. If the objective is to teach generalization, then the amount of time necessary is adequate. If, however, the objective is to cover content, then teachers must decide how much time is allocated throughout the year and make careful decisions regarding how that time is spent. One-third the content was covered in the present investigation, and that appears to be a significant decrease in the amount of information presented to these special education students. Additional generalization studies should be undertaken to clarify this, and to determine how well individual students might be able to generate such mnemonic strategies in the content area. This work is currently being undertaken (Fulk, 1990), as well as research to test the efficacy of these procedures when implemented in mainstream settings (e.g., Mastropieri, Plummer, & Scruggs, 1989). The final section presents some background information describing the theoretical support for mnemonic instruction with learning disabled students.

Theoretical Support for Reconstructive Elaborations

It has been widely reported that learning disabled populations exhibit serious deficits in memory (see a recent volume edited by Swanson, 1987, for a review). Some researchers have argued that these memory deficits may be language based (e.g., Swanson, 1987; Vellutino & Scanlon, 1982), while other researchers have argued that these deficits occur as a result of word-finding problems (e.g., Kail & Leonard, 1986), or semantic memory problems (e.g., Baker, Ceci, & Hermann, 1987). Baker et al. posited that deficits in the structure and the process of semantic memory are related to learning problems in this population. Similarly, Ceci (1985) suggested that LD students lack purposive semantic processing, which then interferes with their ability to encode information efficiently. Ceci further argues that LD students might be helped by specific training in elaborative strategies to assist in ameliorating these deficiencies (Ceci, 1985), while Kail and Leonard have also argued that research should focus on finding effective instructional procedures. In light of these documented deficiencies, as well as the inadequacies of previous explanations of LD (see also Kavale, this volume), it seems likely that strategies that directly intervene on semantic processing would be highly beneficial.

The research cited in this chapter tends to confirm that elaborative strategies facilitate LD students' performance on school tasks for both immediate and delayed recall tests. A potential explanation as to why such strategies are so beneficial incorporates the work from psychology on elaboration learning (e.g., Jensen & Rohwer, 1963), meaningfulness and learning (e.g., Glover & Bruning, 1987), concreteness and learning (e.g., Paivio, 1971), and effective encoding of information (e.g., Underwood & Schulz, 1960). As stated earlier, it is known that effective elaborative techniques facilitate the recall of information. Moreover, it has been seen that when information is more meaningful, it is more memorable. Additionally, when information is made concrete, it is more memorable than when it is abstract. Finally, it has been seen that when information is encoded effectively, direct retrieval routes are established and thus new information is more readily recalled.

Each of these variables—elaboration, meaningfulness, concreteness, and effective encoding—contributes toward a theoretical framework for explaining why mnemonic instruction described herein facilitates the performance of LD students. The reconstructive elaboration model utilizes each variable in presenting information to LD students and seems to be ideally suited to help these students succeed on academic tasks that have high information-processing demands.

Acknowledgements. Preparation of this chapter was supported in part by grants (G008730144-89 and H029D80034) from the U.S. Department of Education, Special Education Programs. The authors thank Tom Scruggs and Bernice Wong for their feedback on an earlier version of this chapter and Cate Violanti for her assistance in the preparation of the manuscript.

References

Baker, J.G., Ceci, S.J., & Herrmann, D. (1987). Semantic structure and processing: Implications for the learning disabled child. In H.L. Swanson (Ed.), *Memory and learning disabilities: Advances in learning and behavioral disabilities* (pp. 83–109). Greenwich, CT: JAI.

Bower, G.H. (1970). Analysis of a mnemonic device. *American Scientist, 58,* 496–510.

Ceci, S.J. (1985). A developmental study of learning disabilities and memory. *Journal of Experimental Child Psychology, 39,* 202–221.

Fulk, B.J.M. (1990). *An investigation of mnemonic generalization training including attribution retaining with learning disabled adolescents.* Dissertation in progress. Purdue University: West Lafayette, IN.

Glover, J.A., & Bruning R.H. (1987). *Educational psychology: Principals and applications.* Boston: Little Brown.

Jensen, A.R., & Rohwer, W.D. Jr. (1963). The effect of verbal mediation on the learning and retention of paired-associates by retarded adults. *American Journal of Mental Deficiency, 68,* 80–84.

Kail, R., & Leonard, L.B. (1986). Sources of word-finding problems in language-impaired children. S.J. Ceci (Ed.), *Handbook of cognitive. social. and neuropsychological aspects of learning disabilities* (Vol. 1, pp. 185–202). Hillsdale, NJ: Erlbaum.

Mastropieri, M.A. (1988). Using the keyword method. *Teaching Exceptional Children, 21*(20), 4–8.

Mastropieri, M.A., Emerick, K., & Scruggs, T.E. (1988). Mnemonic instruction of science concepts. *Behavioral Disorders, 14*, 48–56.

Mastropieri, M.A., & Scruggs, T.E. (1987). *Effective instruction for special education*. Boston: Little Brown/College Hill.

Mastropieri, M.A., & Scruggs, T.E. (1988). Increasing the content area learning of learning disabled students: Research implementation. *Learning Disabilities Research, 4*, 17–25.

Mastropieri, M.A., & Scruggs, T.E. (1989a). Mnemonic social studies instruction: Classroom applications. *Remedial and Special Education, 20*(3), 40–46.

Mastropieri, M.A., & Scruggs, T.E. (1989b). Reconstructive elaborations: Strategies for adapting content area information. *Academic Therapy, 24*, 391–406.

Mastropieri, M.A., Scruggs, T.E., & Fulk, B.J.M. (in press). Teaching abstract vocabulary with the keyword method: Effects on recall and comprehension. *Journal of Learning Disabilities*.

Mastropieri, M.A., Scruggs, T.E., & Levin, J.R. (1985a). Maximlzing what exceptional students can learn: A review of keyword and other mnemonic strategy research. *Remedial and Special Education, 6*(2), 39–45.

Mastropieri, M.A., Scruggs, T.E., & Levin, J.R. (1985b). Memory strategy instruction with learning disabled adolescents. *Journal of Learning Disabilities, 18*, 94–100.

Mastropieri, M.A., Scruggs, T.E., & Levin, J.R. (1986). Direct vs. mnemonic instruction: Relative benefits for exceptional learners. *Journal of Special Education, 20*, 299–308.

Mastropieri, M.A., Scruggs, T.E., & Levin, J.R. (1987a). Facilitating LD students' memory for expository prose. *American Educational Research Journal, 24*, 505–519.

Mastropieri, M.A., Scruggs, T.E., & Levin, J.R. (1987b). Mnemonic instruction in special education. In M.A. McDaniel & M. Pressley (Eds.), *Imagery and related mnemonic processes: Theories, individual differences, and applications* (pp. 358–376). New York: Springer-Verlag.

Mastropieri, M.A., Scruggs, T.E., Levin, J.R., Gaffney, J., & McLoone, B.B. (1985). Mnemonic vocabulary instruction for learning disabled students. *Learning Disability Quarterly, 8*, 57–63.

Mastropieri, M.A., Scruggs, T.E., McLoone, B.B., & Levin, J.R. (1985). Facilitating the acquisition of science classifications in LD students. *Learning Disability Quarterly, 8*, 299–309.

McLoone, B.B., Scruggs, T.E., Mastropieri, M.A., & Zucker, S. (1986). Mnemonic instruction and training with learning disabled adolescents. *Learning Disabilities Research, 2*, 45–53.

Paivio, A. (1971). *Imagery and verbal processes*. New York: Holt, Rinehart, & Winston.

Pressley, M., Levin, J.R., & Delaney, H.D. (1982). The mnemonic keyword method. *Review of Educational Research, 52*, 61–91.

Rawls, J.J. & Weeks, P.W. (1985). *Land of liberty*. New York: Holt, Rinehart, & Winston.

Scruggs, T.E., & Mastropieri, M.A. (1989a). Mnemonic instruction of learning disabled students: A field-based evaluation. *Learning Disability Quarterly, 12*, 119–125.

Scruggs, T.E., & Mastropieri, M.A. (1989b). Reconstructive elaborations: A model for content area learning. *American Educational Research Journal, 26*, 311–327.

Scruggs, T.E., & Mastropieri, M.A. (in press). Classroom applications of mnemonic instruction: Acquisition, maintenance, and generalization. *Exceptional children*.

Scruggs, T.E., Mastropieri, M.A., & Levin, J.R. (1987). Implications of mnemonic strategy research for theories of learning disabilities. In H.L. Swanson (Ed.), *Advances in learning and behavioral disabilities: Memory and learning disabilities* (pp. 225–244). Greenwich, CT: JAI.

Scruggs, T.E., Mastropieri, M.A., Levin, J.R., & Gaffney, J. (1985). Facilitating the acquisition of science facts in learning disabled students. *American Educational Research Journal, 22*, 575–586.

Scruggs, T.E., Mastropieri, M.A., Levin, J.R., McLoone, B.B., Gaffney, J., & Prater, M. (1986). Increasing content area learning: A comparison of mnemonic and visual-spatial direct instruction. *Learning Disabilities Research, 1*, 18–31.

Scruggs, T.E., Mastropieri, M.A., McLoone, B.'B., Levin, J.R., & Morrison, C.R. (1987). Mnemonic facilitation of learning disabled students' memory for expository prose. *Journal of Educational Psychology, 79*, 27–34.

Swanson, H.L. (Ed.). (1987). *Memory and learning disabilities: Advances in learning and behavioral disabilities*. Greenwich, CT: JAI.

Underwood, B.J., & Schulz, R.W. (1960?. *Meaningfulness and verbal learning*. Philadelphia: Lippincott.

Veit, D.T., Scruggs, T.E., & Mastropieri, M.A. (1986). Extended mnemonic instruction with learning disabled students. *Journal of Educational Psychology, 78*, 300–308.

Vellutino, F.R., & Scanlon, D.M. (1982). Verbal processing in poor and normal readers. In C.J. Brainerd & M. Pressley (Eds.), *Verbal processes in children: Progress in cognitive development research* (pp. 189–254). New York: Springer-Verlag.

Von Brock, M.B., & Elliott, S.N. (1987). The influence of treatment effectiveness information on the acceptability of classroom interventions. *Journal of School Psychology, 25*, 131–144 .

Yates, F.A. (1966). *The art of memory*. Chicago: University of Chicago Press.

5
Content Enhancement: A Model for Promoting the Acquisition of Content by Individuals with Learning Disabilities

B. Keith Lenz, Janis Bulgren, and Pamela Hudson

Introduction

In evaluating the educational progress of students with learning disabilities, it becomes clear that educators face several challenges related to intervention. The first is to find good models of instruction that can be effectively and efficiently applied to instructing individuals with learning disabilities. Indeed, it can be argued that successful pedagogy may be the highest stage of learning in a discipline; a stage that deserves a place as the seventh level on Bloom's taxonomy (Shulman, 1989). Such a view of pedagogy challenges all researchers in the field of learning disabilities to carefully evaluate intervention research to identify pedagogy that is consistent with the information-processing characteristics of the individual with learning disabilities. A second challenge is to understand and make instructional decisions related to the interactive nature of teaching and learning. Research on how to teach students to acquire more efficient and effective strategies and how to become more strategic learners and performers should go hand in hand with research on how the teacher can *induce* more strategic processing of information. Students' strategic processing of information can be enhanced by teacher expositions and actions during the processes of planning to teach, teaching, and selecting and using appropriate curriculum materials. In light of these two challenges, the purpose of this chapter is to present an instructional model on promoting the acquisition of content by individuals with learning disabilities. The model has been designed to focus on the assumptions and components potentially required to assist content-area teachers in planning and presenting content in a manner that is sensitive to the information-processing characteristics of students. Within the context of this model, this chapter presents a theoretical rationale for the use of specific instructional procedures, describes the dimensions of the procedures, and discusses how teachers might begin to think about organizing and implementing this type of instruction for individuals with learning disabilities.

Information Processing and Pedagogy for Students with Learning Disabilities

A learning disability is usually identified within the context of instruction. Children are referred for learning disability services only when they do not respond to traditional instruction commensurate with their ability and comparable to the rate of their peers. As a result, the construct of learning disabilities is a contextualized one that requires an examination of the characteristics of the individual in terms of the demands present in the environment. An information-processing orientation to intervention research consistent with the construct of learning disabilities, therefore, must include an examination of the information-processing abilities and responses of the individual in the context of related instructional demands and pedagogy. Such a perspective may advance our understanding of the overall construct of learning disabilities. In fact, a number of individuals have raised the same point. For example, Farnham-Diggory (1986) has argued that the issue of definition and identification of learning disabilities will only be fully addressed once "the processes identified in the laboratory enter into the performance of school tasks" (p. 134), and Swanson (1987) has argued that a full understanding of learning disabilities will only take place when we take into consideration the interaction between the student's information-processing abilities, experiential history, and environmental context. Clearly, student performance at complex information-processing stages must be studied within the educational context so that appropriate pedagogical procedures can be developed to promote the use of strategies within that context.

Instructional Implications of Information-Processing Theory for Students with Learning Disabilities

Consideration of the instructional implications of information processing has not been the traditional focus of information-processing research. Most of the research has focused on the identification of dysfunctions rather than on appropriate pedagogy. For example, some information-processing research has focused on dysfunctions in isolated mental components as an explanation for a learning disability. Consequently, a number of researchers have concluded that many children with learning disabilities do not differ from other children on elementary processes related to perceptual identification or discrimination, serial ordering, cross-modality integration, selective or sustained attention, and basic short-term memory capacity (e.g., McNellis, 1987; Morrison, 1987; Morrison & Manis, 1982; Samuels, 1987; and Vellutino, 1979).

Other researchers have investigated higher-order processes as an explanation for learning disability (e.g., Torgesen, 1977, Wong & Jones, 1982). These studies have often focused on whether or not students can be instructed to use the higher-order processes or strategies. While research on instruction in discrete strategies has demonstrated dramatic improvements in the performance of individuals with mental retardation or learning disabilities (see Butterfield & Belmont, 1977 and Campione & Brown, 1977, for reviews), evidence from the early studies indicated that these subjects had difficulty generalizing the use of strategies to situations different from the training conditions (e.g., Borkowski & Cavanaugh, 1979; Brown, 1978; Ellis, Lenz, & Sabomie, 1987). Based on these findings, subsequent studies were conducted in which instruction on strategies included the delivery of metacognitive information about the strategy that related to characteristics and identification of situations where the strategy might be useful. These studies demonstrated transfer of the strategy to related tasks (e.g., Brown, Bransford, Ferrara, & Campione, 1983) but not to academic tasks such as reading, writing, and arithmetic.

Instruction for Students with Learning Disabilities

Problems in the generalization of specific strategies to other situations have prompted the design of interventions which, in turn, has led to research on "strategy systems." Research on such strategy systems has focused on instruction of students in strategy interventions that relate to general sets of academic demands and contexts (see Brown & Palinscar, 1987, and Deshler & Schumaker, 1988, for a review of two lines of research in this area). These researchers have identified specific strategies related to academic tasks and then have carefully defined specific pedagogy about how the strategies were to be taught within the context of academic demands. Their studies have demonstrated that well-designed instruction can result in a dramatic increase in the acquisition and generalization of strategies for both elementary and secondary school-age students with learning disabilities.

Nevertheless, most research on instruction of individuals with learning disabilities has focused on pedagogy as only a secondary area of interest while the primary area has been on the nature of the strategy learned by students. Ideally, as replications of instructional methodologies across academic areas continue to be conducted, opportunities for analytical comparisons of instructional procedures will increase. These types of replications are most notable in the programmatic research on "direct instruction" procedures developed by Doug Carnine and his colleagues, the "reciprocal teaching" model developed by Ann Brown and Annemarie Palinscar and their colleagues at the University of Illinois Center for the Study of Reading, and the "stages of strategy acquisition and generalization" developed by Don Deshler and his colleagues at the University of Kansas Institute for Research in Learning Disabilities. While there are distinct differences in these methodologies (e.g., in the role and degree of specificity in teacher actions and talk), all the models adopt the idea that "expert support" is provided by the teacher during the early stages of learning but is faded as instruction proceeds and as the student becomes successful and assumes the primary responsibility for learning.

It appears that general steps or patterns of instruction have been found to be more effective than others. However, instruction of individuals with learning disabilities has not always been successful when these general procedures have been utilized, especially in the regular classroom environment. In other words, even when specialized and intensive instructional procedures especially designed to promote the learning of individuals with learning disabilities have been utilized, some students within the population still have difficulty. For example, while Palincsar (1986a) reported that 78% of the experimental group met the established criterion (versus 19% in the control group) when reciprocal teaching was applied, it is evident that not all the experimental group met the criterion. In addition, in studies on the strategy instruction conducted at the University of Kansas Institute for Research in Learning Disabilities, student success has often been controlled by the careful selection of students who have demonstrated mastery of specified prerequisites essential for the intervention (e.g., reading at the fourth grade reading level). While this may be a harsh evaluation of very successful and powerful instructional methodologies, it highlights the outstanding lack of knowledge about the qualitative features of instruction, the interaction that these features have with prior knowledge, and the ability of teachers to make instructional decisions about learners within general sets of instructional procedures.

Information-Processing Theory and Pedagogy

Clearly, not all information-processing research has concentrated on instruction for students with learning disabilities; other researchers have focused their work upon the critical dimensions of instruction for all students and the role of the teacher as instructor. Turnure (1985, 1986) has suggested that research on cognitive development should examine the interaction among a number of dimensions including: (a) the characteristics of the learner (skills, knowledge, attitudes); (b) the learning activities (e.g., attention, discrimination, rehearsal); (c) the nature of the criterion task (e.g., recognition, recall, transfer); (d) the nature of the materials (e g., sequencing, structure, appearance, difficulty), and (e) the instructional agent (e.g., how he or she describes, questions, sequences instruction, models). Turnure suggested that the teacher is the central organizer of the various dimensions of instruction. A model that emphasizes the teacher's role as the primary "learning situation organizer" places great responsibility on the teacher. Inherent in such a model is the assumption that the teacher has sufficient knowledge and experience to enhance learning and to successfully make decisions that provide for an appropriate balance among the dimensions Turnure described.

Description of Teacher's Planning and Teaching Routines

Many teachers appear to be inflexible once a teaching plan has been made. In a review of research, Clark and Peterson (1986) found that the structure of the "problem space" within which teachers and students operate is defined early in the year and changes little throughout the year (as cited from Anderson & Evertson, 1978; Buckley & Cooper, 1978; Brown, 1988; Shultz & Florio, 1979; Tikunoff and Ward, 1978). Clark and Peterson (1986) concluded from their extensive review of research on teachers' thought processes that ineffective teaching may stem, in part, from the inability of a teacher to efficiently process the variety and quantity of information that emerges during ongoing classroom interaction. Their review of the research on teacher planning indicates that teachers tend to enter the classroom with specific plans and expectations about the flow of activities and responses of students. Once teaching has begun, very little conscious decision making occurs. In fact, teachers often utilize routines for simplifying their decision making within the class as much as possible. For example, Shavelson and Stern (1981) noted that teachers often used heuristics (implicit rules used without conscious awareness) that, in effect, helped them simplify the complexities of teaching. Lundgren (1972) found that teachers often pinpointed "steering groups" in deciding when a point had been understood sufficiently and the class could move on. The steering group usually consisted of the group of students performing in a range between the 10th and 25th percentile in achievement. The assumption appears to be that if the steering group understands the concept, so will the majority of the students in the group. This general view of the pervasiveness of preestablished routines is supported by Morine-Dershimer (1979) who indicated that teachers generally make only minor changes in their plans.

Many complex elements are, obviously, incorporated into the typical plan and flow of activities for a given teacher. However, the extreme complexity of teachers' lesson plans may be an explanation for the inability of teachers to easily deviate from these plans. Morine-Dershimer (1979) noted that teachers' plans were seldom fully reflected in written lesson plans, but that written details were nested within more comprehensive planning structures labeled "lesson images." Joyce (1978–1979) indicated that these lesson images were nested within a still larger construct called the "activity flow," and Yinger (1977) found that "routines" were established early in the year. Brophy (1984) indicated that teachers seem reluctant to change their routines even if they are not working well. One reason suggested is that established routines serve to provide predictability and structure in the lesson for both teachers and students. As a result, abandoning these established routines can increase the chances for disruption in the classroom and may impose greater cognitive demands on the teacher for making new decisions about the lesson. Therefore, these "routines" may serve to reduce the complexity of teacher planning and teaching and increase the predictability of classroom activities.

Despite the potential value of set routines, overreliance on these routines may constitute another instructional problem: Some studies have indicated that when teachers are forced to move out of their preplanned routine, very few alternatives seem to be considered. For example, in a case study, Wodlinger (1980) found that most of the interactive decisions of the studied teacher were made after consideration of only one alternative. Wodlinger suggested that many decisions may become routinized, based on previous experience in which alternatives may be considered and then rejected. Thus, when dramatic discrepancies between lesson plans and the realities of the situation do occur, teachers rarely know how to reduce the discrepancy. Shroyer (1981) pointed out that teachers can respond to these situations in one of three ways: They can exploit the possible advantages to expand their teaching plans; they can respond briefly to the problem but return quickly to their original plan; or they can avoid responding at all. Teachers in this type of situation apparently do not have acceptable alternatives readily available. Morine-Dershimer (1979) described the teaching strategy used by teachers in this situation as "postponement," that is, either aborting the lessons or moving ahead with their original routine even though it is not working efficiently.

Suggestions for Improving Teacher's Planning and Teaching Routines

The value of being able to be flexible and to move out of these routines has also been described. Shroyer (1981) depicted the teacher as working on "automatic pilot" when things are going well but moving to a more active stance when unanticipated events occur. The thought processes that emerge from this "more active stance" may result in "teachable moments" which may provide teachers with opportunities to depart from their planned routines to take advantage of a chance to expand on a learning point. However, Shroyer found that only 8% of the teachers studied actually took advantage of these "teachable moments" to move outside a preestablished teaching plan. This is an ominous finding given Brophy's (1984) argument that effective teaching occurs most when teachers seek out and exploit these critical "moments of teaching" rather than sticking to a preconceived plan.

Given the wide range of student abilities in many classrooms and the likelihood that unplanned responses and situations will occur in a classroom setting, teachers need to become aware that positive results can occur when they move outside their preplanned teaching routines. When Morine-Dershimer (1979) explored the changes that occurred in pre- planned routines at various decision points in teacher lessons, she found that most decision points were handled by previously established routines. Furthermore, most of the teachers' information processing involved responding to their own preformed "images" of the flow of the lesson. Morine-Dershimer concluded that minor deviations from expected rou- tines resulted in positive teaching decisions and hypothesized that when teachers were forced to deal with minor deviations from their expectations, their information processing on these decisions became more "reality oriented" than "image oriented." Essentially, the teachers had to respond to and interact with what the students were actually doing rather than to their own preformed images of the teaching routine. Apparently, this was more productive than a totally uninterrupted flow in the preplanned teaching because the teachers were receiving information about the stu- dents' learning as a result of the many interruptions (e.g., student queries and comments). This may be particularly important for teaching indi- viduals with learning disabilities because McNair (1978–1979) found a trend toward the need for more teacher decision making when teaching groups of students likely to be at risk for school failure.

A number of conclusions can be drawn from this research on the critical attributes of instruction. First, teaching is a very complex task that requires a great deal of planning and decision making. Unfortunately, as Brophy (1984) contended, very few teachers become expert enough to function as effective decision-makers, particularly since decisions cover a wide range of content and method selection, adaptation, supplementation, evaluation, remediation, and adjustment of plans. The instructional task becomes even more complex when, in addition to content decisions, the teacher must also consider the needs of individuals with learning disabilities. Second, since classroom processes are clearly preformed and envisioned in the mind of the teacher before teaching begins, teachers are not always responsive to the unexpected problems and needs of students in the class. Individuals with learning disabilities may often present unexpected instructional prob- lems and further complicate the instructional process; it is therefore unlike- ly that the teacher will be prepared to make the required adjustments during the teaching session. Third, teachers already tend to teach using routines and structures. Therefore, instructional procedures that address the needs of individuals with learning disabilities may best be conceptual- ized through the development of structured routines and instructional de- vices. These are specifically designed to promote effective and efficient in- formation processing that can be incorporated into the teacher's planning and teaching processes. Fourth, since one goal of instruction is to make students independent learners, instructional practices should include pro- cedures that promote student ownership and control of the instructional process. That is, the teacher may find that some of the decision-making responsibilities can be assumed by the learner if teaching is viewed as a collaborative process. This notion of a collaborative instructional process is also consistent with the "active" and "independent" learner orientation of an information-processing model. Fifth, teachers must be instructed in pedagogy based upon information processing and decision making and in the appropriate use of this type of pedagogy. In essence, teachers must be instructed in how to effectively and efficiently plan lessons that incorporate information about their students and the pedagogy that is suitable to them.

Information-Processing-Sensitive Pedagogy for the Content Areas

If teachers are asked to incorporate methods based on information-processing theory into their planning and teaching, then teachers must be supported in this process. This can be accomplished, in part, by helping teachers understand the characteristics of pedagogy that is sensitive to the information-processing ability of students and how information-processing theory can be translated into practice.

Characteristics of Information-Processing-Sensitive Pedagogy

For our purposes, "information-processing-sensitive pedagogy" refers to instruction, that:

a. Is fashioned and differentially delivered based on the teacher's knowledge of the range of information-processing and communication abilities of students (e.g., Deshler, Alley, Warner, & Schumaker, 1981; Lenz & Bulgren, in press).
b. Promotes student attention or reception of incoming information (e.g., Lenz, Alley, & Schumaker, 1987; Mayer, 1975, 1984, 1987).
c. Facilitates the activation of strategies that enable the student to access and integrate prior knowledge with to-be-learned information (e.g., Ausubel, 1960; Lenz, Alley, & Schumaker, 1987; Mayer, 1983).
d. Promotes the activation of strategies that enable the student to build logical or structural connections between and among incoming ideas and ideas already in memory (e.g., Bulgren, Schumaker, & Deshler, 1988; Mayer, 1987).
e. Encourages the active participation of the student in the learning process as a planner, implementor, and evaluator (e.g., Brown, 1978; Hughes, Schumaker, Deshler, & Mercer, 1988; Van Reusen, Bos, Schumaker, & Deshler, 1987).
f. Instructs the student in the "why, when, and where" aspects of information related to the use of knowledge (e.g., Brown, Day, & Jones, 1983; Lenz & Hughes, 1990).

g. Informs the student of progress and provides appropriate feedback in a manner that improves learning (e.g., Kline, 1989; Palincsar & Brown, 1984).
h. Leads the student in the learning process through expert scaffolding and proleptic teaching (e.g., Deshler & Schumaker, 1988; Vygotsky, 1978; Wertsch & Stone, 1979).
i. Takes advantage of the developmental and social contexts of learning by gradually moving from adult guidance and modeling to peer and student guidance and modeling (Allington, 1984; Palincsar & Brown, 1984; Lenz, Schumaker, Deshler, & Beals, 1984; Vygotsky, 1978).
j. Plans for and promotes the acquisition and integration of semantic, procedural, and strategic knowledge throughout all phases and types of instruction (Mayer, 1987).

However, simply identifying the characteristics of such pedagogy does little to assist in the translation of theory into practice.

Translating Theory into Practice

The process of translating theory into practice must focus on how instructional principles can be organized to affect classroom practice in a systematic and reliable manner. Consequently, the identification of pedagogy sensitive to an information-processing perspective requires a practical interpretation of information-processing theory. Ideally, such an interpretation would set the stage for the teacher to monitor and adjust the teaching process as necessary. That is, a teacher's instructional procedures must be designed to interrupt an existing information-processing sequence, if necessary, and then to externally guide or prompt the student's strategic processing of information in a more effective and efficient manner than would be possible if the learner proceeded alone. As a result, while the learner is processing information, the teacher is attempting to *hypothesize* how the learner is processing information. This, in turn, can lead to the modification of instruction in an attempt to alter how the learner is learning and performing.

To further accomplish the translation of theory into practice, it is necessary to reduce the complex nature of information-processing theory into a simpler framework while retaining the essential and powerful elements of the information-processing model. It is possible to think of pedagogy as accomplishing three primary purposes. These purposes deal with the student's awareness that learning is about to occur, the student's active and personal involvement in the learning process, and the student's willingness to use this new knowledge. First, the learner must orient himself or herself to the instructional situation by: (a) becoming aware that a learning situation or opportunity exists, (b) attending to the new information, and (c) drawing upon appropriate prior knowledge to contextualize or make logical associations with the new information. The major purpose of instruction at this stage of learning can be conceptualized as promoting an orientation to content learning. Second, the learner begins to understand the information by: (a) identifying concepts, (b) identifying similarities between different examples that indicate that they belong or do not belong to the same concept class, (c) making appropriate associations with prior knowledge regarding these concepts, and (d) distinguishing between important and unimportant pieces of information in the reconstruction of his or her knowledge base. The major purpose of instruction is promoting the understanding of content. Third, the learner must start acting on the new information by: (a) testing knowledge and the impact of this knowledge in the real world, (b) exploring the various dimensions of knowledge across situations, settings, and conditions, (c) applying knowledge to solve problems, and (d) ensuring that the knowledge is available for later access through self-practice and memorization activities. The major purpose of instruction at this stage is promoting independent activation of content. In short, three distinct instructional phases appear to emerge about which the teacher should be concerned: (a) Orientation, (b) Understanding and (c) Activation.

These three general elements have been supported by various instructional researchers. For example, Roth, Smith, and Anderson (1984) suggested that the phases of science instruction consist of: (a) preparation; (b) exploration; (c) acquisition; (d) application/practice; and (e) synthesis. Palincsar (1986b) described the stages of reciprocal teaching as including: (a) initial group review of strategies, importance, and contexts for use; (b) presentation of the task and cueing of the goal to be met and strategies to be used; (c) interactive and cooperative completion of the task with students taking turns as "teacher;" (d) "teacher" summary and group elaboration and clarification on what was learned; and (e) prediction about future learning and the appointment of a new "teacher." In addition, Rosenshine and Stevens (1986), from a review of "teaching functions," presented a synthesis of research on effective instruction that included these key instructional stages and aspects of presentations from research in the regular classroom environment. Therefore, the challenge in developing a model to improve content area instruction based on information-processing theory requires the researcher to consider how the conditions listed above can become part of the the teacher's approach to the teaching process.

Overview of the Content Enhancement Model

Wong (1985) has pointed out the importance of promoting content learning for individuals with learning disabilities. A model for promoting effective content learning through the careful *organization* and *delivery* of information by the teacher is currently being developed by researchers at the University of Kansas Institute for Research in Learning Disabilities (e.g., Bulgren, Schumaker, & Deshler, 1988; Deshler & Schumaker, 1988; Lenz, Alley, & Schumaker, 1987; Lenz & Bulgren, in press; Schumaker, Deshler, & McKnight, in press). While only portions of the model have been completely validated, the concepts that serve as the foundation for the model are based on findings from research across the areas of curriculum, instruction, educational and cognitive psychology, and special education. Therefore, this model can potentially serve as a guide to teacher thinking, planning, and teaching in the content areas.

Definition and Assumptions of the Content Enhancement Model

The model is based on the idea of "content enhancement." Content enhancement is defined as the process of teaching scientific or cultural knowledge to a heterogeneous group of students in which: (a) both group and individual learning needs are met; (b) the integrity of the content is maintained; (c) critical features of the content are selected, organized, manipulated, and complemented in a manner that promotes effective and efficient information processing; and (d) the content is delivered in a partnership with students in a manner that facilitates and enriches learning for all students. In order to accomplish this, six major assumptions have been made. First, it is the responsibility of the content teacher to present information in a manner that will promote student understanding and remembering of information to all students. Second, the processes of planning, teaching, and evaluating for learning should be based on careful consideration of the information-processing demands placed on the teacher as well as the student. Third, enhancements, consisting of carefully planned instructional routines and devices, should be utilized to enhance the delivery of content information. Fourth, the teacher must inform students of the enhancements that are to be used to enhance the delivery of information and, as a result, student learning. Fifth, the teacher must cue students when specific enhancements are being used to promote learning. Sixth, the teacher must purposely implement the enhancement in a partnership with students. And, seventh, the teacher should induce both himself or herself and the students to reflect on the enhancement and to evaluate its roles in learning and whether it has been an effective teaching/learning experience. Therefore, great responsibility is placed on the teacher to become the primary instructional organizer.

The Content Enhancement Model

The model is made operational through the recognition of at least three major components. The first component of the Content Enhancement

Model includes specific teaching routines that might be used to enhance or guide the delivery of major chunks of a content lesson, (e.g., routines designed to orient the students to information that will be learned, routines designed to help students understand concepts, or routines to promote active learning of new material). The second component consists of instructional devices that might be embedded in a routine to further enhance the delivery of content (e.g., devices designed to help the student to understand, remember, or organize information). The third component consists of procedures for planning instruction and organizing the content enhancement process daily and over time under both planned and spontaneous circumstances, (e.g, guidance in identifying important information, analyzing prior knowledge requirements of the students, etc.).

The integration of the major concepts involved in the teaching process that have been incorporated into the Content Enhancement Model are depicted in the diagrams in Figure 5.1. These diagrams illustrate what might be conceptualized as the unit of instruction. For our purposes, we will call this "the lesson," although the unit of instruction under consideration might be the entire course, a specific unit or a chapter as well as a daily lesson. The boxes represent the actual lesson that occurs. The portion inside the box not covered by the oval represents those aspects of the lesson not predicted in the preparation of the lesson. This is the portion of the lesson that is potentially not under the control of the teacher, for which the teacher does not know if he or she is influencing students or adequately imparting information, and for which desired outcomes are not achieved. The oval inside the box represents the *planned* portion of the lesson that is implemented. This is the part of the lesson that is predicted, is actually under the control and influence of the teacher, yields ongoing information regarding whether or not the students are understanding the information in the lesson, and results in the desired outcomes.

As shown in Figure 5.1, Diagram A, lessons typically consist of a beginning, a middle, and an end. The diagram also represents various areas of expertise that all teachers bring to the lesson, including subject matter knowledge and teaching methods. However, in certain lessons, if the teacher's knowledge and methods are not supplemented by an adequate repertoire of techniques to deal with the variety of responses that may occur in a classroom, a less than optimal portion of the lesson may be available for efficient delivery of content information. This is represented by the relatively large area of gray in Figure 5.1, Diagram A, indicating those portions of the lesson that did not evolve as the teacher had planned and over which the teacher did not have the control he or she would have wished. As a result, less than optimal levels of content is acquired by the students.

Diagram B, in Figure 5.1, indicates that the area inside the oval representing more efficient and effective instruction can increase when the teacher is sensitive to the information-processing characteristics of stu-

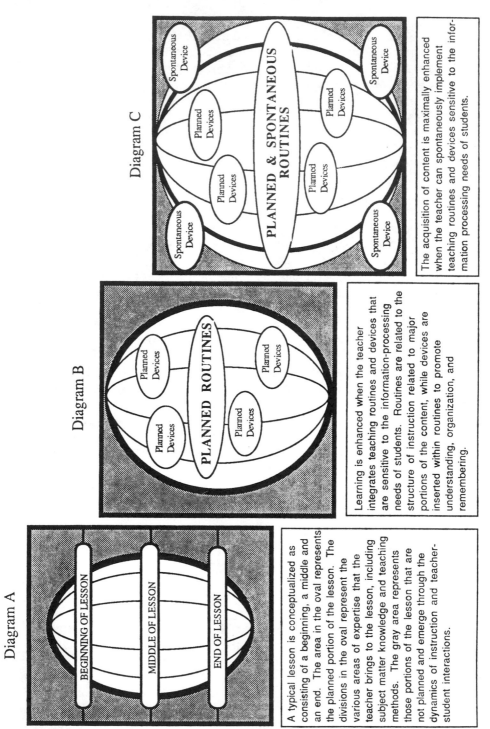

Diagram A

BEGINNING OF LESSON

MIDDLE OF LESSON

END OF LESSON

A typical lesson is conceptualized as consisting of a beginning, a middle and an end. The area in the oval represents the planned portion of the lesson. The divisions in the oval represent the various areas of expertise that the teacher brings to the lesson, including subject matter knowledge and teaching methods. The gray area represents those portions of the lesson that are not planned and emerge through the dynamics of instruction and teacher-student interactions.

Diagram B

Planned Devices

Planned Devices

PLANNED ROUTINES

Planned Devices

Planned Devices

Learning is enhanced when the teacher integrates teaching routines and devices that are sensitive to the information-processing needs of students. Routines are related to the structure of instruction related to major portions of the content, while devices are inserted within routines to promote understanding, organization, and remembering.

Diagram C

Spontaneous Device

Planned Devices

Planned Devices

Spontaneous Device

PLANNED & SPONTANEOUS ROUTINES

Spontaneous Device

Planned Devices

Planned Devices

Spontaneous Device

The acquisition of content is maximally enhanced when the teacher can spontaneously implement teaching routines and devices sensitive to the information processing needs of students.

FIGURE 5.1. The content enhancement model.

dents. This diagram indicates the addition of teaching routines that are related to major portions of the content and/or teaching devices that are utilized within the routines to promote understanding, organization, and remembering. This facilitation of the processing of information for students with learning disabilities is the central thrust of the content enhancement process; it is accomplished by the infusion into the lesson of a variety of these teaching routines and devices. As demonstrated in Figure 5.1, Diagram B, this infusion of planned routines and planned devices increases the size of the oval and, theoretically, the success of instruction within the lesson.

It is naive to believe, however, that teachers can predict and plan for everything that takes places in a classroom setting. In reality, the teacher must be well-prepared before the lesson but must also be prepared for the unexpected that might occur during the lesson. Therefore, the teacher must be able to skillfully break out of planned routines and spontaneously initiate contextually appropriate routines that are not dependent on advanced preparation and refinement. It is the ability of the teacher to gain control, monitor student understanding and achieve the desired outcomes in the exceptionally difficult moments of teaching that may result in the greatest gains in teaching students with learning disabilities. This aspect of the Content Enhancement Model is represented in Figure 5.1, Diagram C. Here, those aspects of the lesson that fall into the gray area are further reduced by the use of additional, appropriate, and spontaneous teaching routines and teaching devices that are sensitive to the information-processing needs of students. Therefore, at the heart of the content-enhancement process is the use of specific routines and devices that can be used to enhance or enrich content learning. Other components in the model simply support or guide the effective use of these procedures.

Components of the Content Enhancement Model

In general, the routines and devices all appear to support or promote instruction consistent with three major goals. First, the teacher must become aware of the relationship between the various types of information that the student must learn and how this information can best be presented. This awareness would include the presentation of important concepts, delivery of background knowledge, discussion of textbook formats, descriptions of methods or processes, explanation of facts or themes, exploration and discovery of information or ideas, and promoting methods for generalization of information to other areas. Second, there must be an awareness of the problems that many students have in processing information. For example, the teacher must determine if there is a lack of background experiences, a gap in the understanding of key conceptual information, an unfamiliarity with processes or methods of inquiry, a difficulty with the written word or textual formats, or an inability to generalize a specific skill from one area to another. Third, there must be an awareness of ways to make information more meaningful to the student. Such methods could include verbal expansions, verbal and concrete illustrations, graphics, or extended interactive routines that have been explained to the students. Each of the routines and devices discussed in the next two sections seeks to achieve these purposes.

The Teaching Routines

The teaching routines have been divided into areas relating to orientation, understanding, and activation. Each of these three areas will be discussed in terms of goals associated with routines, the background theory and research, and special needs of students with learning disabilities that may be addressed with each type of routine.

The Content Orientation Routines

Orientation is the process of preparing and directing a student's attention to what has been learned and then identifying its relationship to what is to be learned. The orientation process might include the following: gaining student attention and cueing the use of a specific orientation routine, identifying or reviewing previously learned information that is critically related to forthcoming information, identifying the key elements of the to-be-learned information, explaining learning goals, discussing specific instructional activities of how the information will be learned, personalizing learning through effective rationales, and identifying expectations. The teacher might think about preparing for the orientation process by reviewing what has potentially been learned by students, previewing what should be learned, and then making decisions about how students can be guided to learn the content. The teacher must rely on her (a) previous experiences with the content, (b) knowledge of the structure of the textbook or materials, (c) knowledge of the actual content, and (d) knowledge of how students will process the information. The teacher also must make judgments about the relative importance of the information to which students will be exposed. In general, the orientation process must place the current learning goals, at whatever level, in the context of what the student already knows and what outcomes are desired.

Brainin (1985) has presented the work of Feuerstein in the context of the orientation process. According to Brainin, Feuerstein's instructional mediation includes instruction for the teacher to: (a) explicitly explain purpose and predict what will occur, (b) interpret events in light of background knowledge, and (c) relate events to the student's prior knowledge and identify relationships between problems. This orientation process takes place within the overall context of scaffolding (Wood, Bruner, & Ross, 1987). Scaffolding is defined as the process of prompting a student to complete a task that could not be completed by the student unassisted. Palincsar (1986b) has argued that scaffolding takes place at the very edge of the student's ability to perform and within what Vygotsky (1978) has called the "zone of proximal development." The purpose of the orientation process is to bring the student to the edge of this zone in an effective and efficient manner and to prepare the learner for information integration and understanding.

Most of the time, the orientation process is viewed as an activity that is initiated at the beginning of the lesson. However, the orientation process should continue throughout the content learning process. For example, at the beginning of a lesson, a teacher may present information related to the previous lesson and then integrate what the student knows with the topics that will be covered. The teacher may also explain the topic that will be covered, how it is organized, and what she considers to be most important. During the lesson, the teacher may continue to refer to the previously learned information as an anchor, note when specific topics are being covered, and then emphasize and review the organization of the information. Finally, at the end of the lesson (not necessarily at the end of the instructional period), the teacher may review the key elements and then check to see if students understand the key concepts and the organization of the information. Furthermore, the orientation process should be implemented at various instructional levels. For example, the teacher may spend one or more days providing an orientation to an entire subject area or course. The introduction of a new unit or chapter may also require the teacher to orient the student to a new area of information. In fact, it may be that the manner in which the overall conceptual umbrellas of a course, unit, and chapter are introduced, set up, and then reinforced are really the foundations to the orientation process and related routines.

The concept of orientation has emerged primarily from research in cognitive psychology in the area of "organizers." Interest in organizers initially centered on the use of "advance organizers" (Ausubel, 1960; Ausubel, Novak, & Hanesian, 1968). Ausubel et al. described the advance organizer as a tool to "provide ideational scaffolding for the stable incorporation and retention of more detailed and differentiated material that follows" (1968, p. 148). However, differential results from various research studies have indicated that the effects of the advance organizer are contingent on the circumstances under which it is used. Research on the advance organizer has indicated that it is most likely to promote learning when students do not have the background knowledge for a particular task, do not make the connection between prior knowledge and the to-be-learned information, and do not make the connections between relationships in the to-be-learned information (Mayer, 1979). Mayer (1987) concluded that advance organizers are successful and should be used when: (a) students lack the background knowledge necessary to understand to-be-learned information, (b) the goal of instruction is for the student to transfer or apply learned information to new problems or circumstances, (c) a simplified or concrete model can be constructed that will be easy for students to learn and organize the information. Therefore, it is clear that the teacher's predications about the state of the learner and how the learner is processing information is a critical aspect of the use of the advance organizer.

Researchers have also explored the benefits of signaling important information, directing attention during lectures, using cues related to note-taking, and using post organizers to help a student process information (see review in Mayer, 1987). The results of various studies indicate that how a teacher cues information, pauses, and prompts review can significantly affect attention to important information (Aiken, Thomas, & Sheenum, 1975; Faw & Waller, 1976; Peters, 1972; Carter & Van Matre, 1975; Bretzing & Kulhavy, 1981). Simultaneously, the results of these same studies indicate that learning can be inhibited if students attempt to appropriately process information through notetaking, but the teacher does not adjust the presentation when information-processing demands begin to overwhelm the student.

While research on the orientation process indicates that the use of specific routines can promote learning, application of these routines with individuals with learning disabilities indicate that many of these individuals (a) do not independently recognize these routines when they are used by teachers (Lenz, Alley, & Schumaker 1987), (b) do not independently use lesson organizers and cues to promote learning during a lesson (Robinson, Deshler, Denton, & Schumaker, in prep.), and (c) can usually only benefit from the application of these routines when these routines are made explicit prior to, during, and after a lesson (Bulgren, Schumaker, & Deshler, 1988; Lenz, Alley, & Schumaker, 1987; Robinson, Deshler, Denton, and Schumaker, in prep.). Therefore, the key to making the "organizer" work to enhance learning appears to be related to the degree to which learners learn about the presence and use of these routines to enhance learning and are then prompted by the teacher to become actively involved in using organizers (Lenz, Alley, & Schumaker, 1987).

A study that directly examined the application of these concepts to the process of teaching content to individuals with learning disabilities was conducted by Lenz, Alley, and Schumaker (1987). In this study the investigators matched regular classroom content teachers with an individual identified as having a learning disability who was already in their class. Components associated with organizer use (beginning of a lesson, during a lesson, and after a lesson) were identified and the teachers were observed over a period of days to determine how they typically used organizers. Measures of student learning were also obtained. Teachers were then trained to use advance organizers and their implementation of the teacher-constructed advance organizers were then observed. While teachers implemented the teaching routines, very little change was observed on the measures of student learning. Students were then informed of the presence of the advance organizer and were prompted to take notes and begin to use the advance organizer to organize learning. Improvement on the student measures was then observed. A key factor in the success of this routine was the student's awareness of the routine and the knowledge of how it could be used to facilitate learning.

In another study, Schumaker, Deshler, and McKnight (1989) investigated how student learning might be influenced when the advance organizer construct was expanded to include an entire lesson designed to orient students to an entire chapter. In this study, the teacher interactively went through a textbook chapter and discussed how the chapter fit with other chapters, hypothesized what the chapter was about, and paraphrased and discussed chapter titles and subtitles. Schumaker et al. reported that the results of the routine on student learning were promising but inconsistent. While test scores of individuals with learning disabilities improved an average of 10 percentage points in some classes, the same effect was not observed in all classes. In addition, the students never learned to internalize the routine. When the teacher stopped using the routine, students stopped engaging in the survey behaviors despite the positive effects on learning. Therefore, while it appears that surveying the chapter may be valuable, it may be that, for individuals with learning disabilities, in the absence of intensive strategy instruction in how to use a textbook, the teacher may need to be responsible for overt prompting of the orientation process. Moreover, specific teacher variables and content variables may also need to be considered in the development of a chapter survey routine.

While it may be possible to identify appropriate orientation routines, it is unclear what types of orientation routines are needed or will be used by teachers. For example, after Lenz, Alley, and Schumaker (1987) trained teachers to begin using advance organizers, the use of post organizers decreased. Teachers simply ran out of time at the end of the class period. Likewise, it is important to understand which types of orientation routines are most important to the learning of individuals with learning disabilities (e.g., the chapter survey or the lesson level advance organizer), which aspects of specific orientation routines are necessary and which are unnecessary (e.g., daily implementation, preview, review, rationales), and which form of delivery is most beneficial (e.g., graphic organizer, verbal organizer, student generated organizer).

The Understanding Routines

Before discussing the understanding routines, it is necessary to first consider the content understanding process itself. Although the process of "understanding" is certainly a fundamental and pervasive part of all learning, the demands of understanding involved in content area learning, as it exists in the middle and secondary school years, involves higher-order processing strategies. Whereas the primary purpose of the orientation process is to promote awareness and readiness to learn, the primary purpose of the understanding process is the acquisition of new information *through* the integration of the new information with prior knowledge. Therefore, as the teacher moves from orientation to understanding, the teacher shifts the *focus* of the lesson from reviewing and predicting to integrating and storing.

Although researchers have not yet empirically derived the various types of content learning demands placed on students, a number of key demands can be identified for instructional planning. The major types of demands related to promoting the understanding of content area information appear to minimally include: (a) learning concepts; (b) applying or generalizing learned concepts to novel situations; (c) comparing and contrasting concepts; (d) learning rules and propositions (which specify the relationship between concepts); (e) learning and integrating main ideas and details; (f) learning procedures, processes, or sequences of actions; (g) learning cause-and-effect relationships; and (h) exploring problems and arriving at solutions. Therefore, the role of the teacher is to determine if one of these content learning demands is present (induced by either the text or the learning objectives and goals), to organize and manipulate the content in a manner that highlights the demands of the content, and to promote content acquisition in a manner consistent with learning goals. These general demands must, of course, be considered in light of specific course requirements. Indeed, the nature or characteristics of the content set the stage for the type of instructional procedures that are most likely to facilitate learning. Instruction that neglects to take this relationship into consideration may prove to be unsuccessful. Therefore, the first task of the teacher is to identify the content learning demands that are placed on students, then identify methods that help the student to meet these demands.

Theory and research on the understanding process provide the foundations needed for the development of the understanding routines. Research in the area of concept teaching is an area that has been investigated in promoting understanding in the content classroom, and a clear understanding of concepts and how to explain concepts often serves as a vehicle for clarifying understanding. Numerous researchers agree that, in essence, a concept is the category of class into which events, ideas, or objects are grouped (Bruner, Goodnow, & Austin, 1956; Gagne, 1965; Ausubel, Novak, & Hanesian, 1968; and Klausmeier & Associates, 1979). This grouping is done according to decisions made through the application of at least four different components (Klausmeier & Ripple, 1971). These components are (1) the attributes, properties, or characteristics by which things are placed in a specific category; (2) the rules by which these attributes are joined in a concept class; (3) the hierarchical patterns of supraordinate, coordinate, and subordinate concepts into which a concept fits; and (4) the instances or examples of a concept. For example, the concept of "democracy" has several attributes; among these are that it is a form of government, citizens are equal, the individual is valued, the people hold the power, and compromise is necessary. Second, these attributes are joined by a rule which states that all these attributes must be present in an example of the concept of "democracy." Third, "democracy" is a concept that fits into a hierarchical pattern in which the supraordinate concept is "political systems"; the instances that are coordinate with "democracy" are "socialism, "dictatorship," or "monarchy." Fourth, an instance or example of "democracy" is the government of the United States of America, and a nonexample is the government of China. A similar application of the same four analytical components to concepts in various classes allows the teacher to utilize a similar pattern that can guide student thought processes.

Emphasis upon the teaching of concepts has been widely emphasized in the development of classroom materials. Taba's (1971) teaching model for concept attainment incorporates these elements of a definition, and Becker, Engelmann, and Thomas (1971) used this definition in developing a programmed learning text. Specifically, it has been applied to science (Voelker, 1972) and social studies (Martorella, 1972), two important content areas. Another area of research that incorporates many aspects of concept teaching has been the research on semantic mapping and semantic feature analysis. These strategies encourage the placement of concepts into categories and relationships based upon students' prior knowledge. Research conducted by Johnson, Toms-Bronowski, and Pittelman (1982) has found that these two strategies positively affect students' acquisition of vocabulary. These are interactive teaching strategies that encourage student involvement through exploration of what the students already know about a word, other words related to that word, and relationships.

The needs of students with learning disabilities in the understanding process must also be considered. Based on current research and theoretical proposals in cognitive psychology (e.g., Gagné, 1985; Mayer, 1987) the role of the learner in the process of understanding content includes (a) receiving the content that is to be learned, (b) recognizing and organizing the relationships in the content, (c) retrieving knowledge already known that is related to the new content, (d) deciding the relevance of the prior knowledge and either deciding that the new information must be learned or must not be learned, (e) translating the content into networks of prior knowledge, and (f) making conclusions based on the integration of prior knowledge with new information. Therefore, if the student has difficulties at any point in the processing of information, the teacher must begin to prompt understanding through information-processing-sensitive pedagogy. Indeed, there may be a particular demand for this pedagogy when the class contains students with learning disabilities. Students with learning disabilities often enter secondary educational settings with deficits that make acquisition of content information difficult. A major problem is that students with learning disabilities often lack required prior knowledge and concepts necessary to benefit from secondary curricula (Schumaker & Deshler, 1984). As Wong (1985) pointed out, lack of prior knowledge of facts and concepts that teachers tend to presume as foundations for advanced presentations become critical in secondary content areas such as science and social studies which build on students' previous knowledge. She indicated that the lack of content knowledge on the part of many students with learning disabilities must be addressed because students benefit from an optimal amount of prior content knowledge when they are attempting to learn new information of the same topic. As teachers explore the concepts they presume that students will know, find ways to assess students' knowledge of those concepts, and acquire techniques for delivering information about concepts in which the students are deficient, lack of prior knowledge will be addressed for all students.

Drawing on the research on concept teaching from across a variety of disciplines, Bulgren (1987) developed a method designed to promote concept acquisition in regular content classrooms that contained students identified as having learning disabilities as well as students considered normally achieving. Bulgren demonstrated that a given concept can be taught to low-achieving students by providing students with good examples of members in a concept class, then moving on to matched presentations of examples and nonexamples to allow the students to practice discrimination of members of a concept class. Students were also guided by the teacher to identify the critical features of each concept. For example, all "automobiles" have wheels and an engine, but may vary widely in color and design and may still be considered an automobile. Careful attention to a given concept would necessarily include a well-constructed definition and a careful naming of the concept. Ideally, the teacher should use concept teaching to extend the interaction between the teacher and student to insure that the student becomes an active participant in exploring critical characteristics of a concept and evaluating various examples for membership or nonmembership in a concept class.

While there are probably many sets of procedures that can be used to promote the understanding of low-achieving students in the content areas, few have been validated. Therefore, the need exists to explore other procedures that could potentially enhance understanding. In addition to concept teaching, a few of the important content learning demands for which specific procedures must be developed include (a) applying or generalizing learned concepts to novel situations, (b) learning procedures, processes, or sequences of actions, (c) demonstrating knowledge of cause and effect relationships, and (d) identifying problem/solution relationships.

The Activation Routines

Activation is the process whereby the student is induced by the teacher to assume primary responsibility for learning the content. In the basic academic skill areas of reading and mathematics, the activation process is usually thought of as the practice phase of instruction. During the skill practice phase, the teacher controls the early stages of practice to insure accuracy, guides students through the various aspects of skill mastery, and finally leads the student to an independent practice level. However, in the content areas, the activation process is usually achieved through assignments in which the student must independently find, manipulate, memorize, and then express information. The focus is not on the acquisition of skills; the focus is on the acquisition of content. A number of general guidelines can be identified across studies that suggest how a teacher can induce students to become active in learning. In general, these guidelines prompt the teacher to: (a) apply principles of information-processing theory to task construction; (b) induce learning and task completion by compensating for a student's ineffective or inefficient strategies by the way assignments are structured and delivered; and (c) apply principles of social learning theory to increase the probability of facilitating meaningfulness of information.

Theory and research on the activation process are available to provide support for the development of the activation routines and the incorporation of the guidelines presented above. Support for the concept of activation can be found in cognitive psychology. Craik and Lockhart (1972) conceptualized information processing as a continuum of levels of processing. The range of superficial processing to deeper level processing is purported to affect *how well* material is learned and *how durable* that learning proves to be. When difficult information is processed, a deeper level of comprehension is required. In addition, the more deeply the information is processed, the more durable is the memory trace and thus the learning (Houston, 1981). Teachers facilitate deeper level processing when they provide students with opportunities to practice content knowledge previously presented. The role of practice in the acquisition and retention of new knowledge has also been studied over the years. In a review of research related to practice, Joyce and Weil (1986) identified six principles of effective practice: (a) systematically move students from structured and guided practice to independent practice or homework; (b) provide short, intense, highly motivated practice periods; (c) monitor the initial stage to prevent students from practicing errors; (d) require an 85 to 90% level of accuracy at each level of practice, (e) distribute practice sessions over a period of time; and (f) provide practice sessions immediately after new content has been presented and continue frequently until independence is achieved. These principles must, of course, be viewed in light of actual classroom practices.

In addition to research related to an individual's ability to process information, other theory and research has focused on the value of activities based upon interaction among individuals. It may be particularly important to be aware of students who do not have skills that enable them to successfully complete assignments on their own. In such cases, the teacher may need to structure assignments in a manner that will compensate for the student's lack of effective and efficient strategies. Based on Vygotsky's (1978) position that much of learning is mediated through social interaction, peers can be a valuable resource in the activation process. Many researchers have found the cooperative learning model to be an effective means of promoting skill and content practice. In this model, students work together in heterogeneous ability groups of three to six members. Through the pooling of skills, knowledge, and resources, students complete the assignment in a cooperative fashion. In a review of more than three dozen methodologically adequate experiments, various cooperative learning methods were found to have more positive effects than traditional control methods on student achievement, time on task, and other social outcomes (Madden & Slavin, 1983). Similarly, the effectiveness of peer tutoring is strongly supported by research. For example, Maheady, Sacca, and Harper (1988) found classwide peer tutoring to enhance the acquisition of social studies content knowledge.

While it is possible to categorize the types of assignments required of students, the effect of these assignments on the success of students in the content learning setting has been more difficult to determine. Nevertheless, we will review literature that addresses the active involvement of students in the learning process through a variety of procedures including homework assignments, seatwork assignments, assignment completion procedures, segmentation of content and cooperative learning procedures; where available, research specifically related to students with learning disabilities will also be addressed.

From a broad perspective, research in the area of "homework" indicates that the more time a student spends working on homework, the higher his or her achievement (e.g., Austin, 1979; Fredrick & Walberg, 1980; Keith & Page, 1985; Walberg, 1984), even when researchers have controlled for such variables as socioeconomic status and ability (e.g., Coleman, Hoffer, & Kilgore, 1981; Page and Keith, 1981; Wolf, 1979). Harnischfeger (1980) found that this relationship was consistent across subject-matter areas even as early as fourth grade. Polachek, Kniesner, and Harwood (1978) also found that less able students can compensate for their lower ability by increasing the amount of homework completed. However, these findings have almost always been tempered by qualifying statements on the positive effects of homework such that as made by Keith and Page (1985) who completed their review of the research on the benefits of homework with the statement, "Of course, care should be taken that the assignments are appropriate for the child's ability and achievement levels" (p. 356). As a result, teachers have often been left with the challenge of assigning more homework with little direction related to appropriate means of accomplishing this in the content areas.

In addition to homework, some research on assignments related to seatwork has been conducted at the elementary school level. For example,

Anderson (1984) found that the most important part of assigned seatwork, for both high and low achievers, was to "get it done." She found that: (a) presentation of assignments seldom included statements about the purpose of learning or relationships with other types of information; (b) teacher attention during seatwork was not directed toward monitoring understanding and accuracy but on maintaining a quiet, busy classroom atmosphere; (c) explanations of the assignment usually focused on the procedural elements of the task and neglected to cue the use of strategies such as checking; and (d) teacher feedback on seatwork focused on correctness and neatness rather than on explanations of processes leading to correct answers. Anderson reported that when low-achieving students did not understand the assignment they appeared to revert to an emphasis on inappropriate "getting-finished" strategies. Anderson contended that students may have been learning to equate success on seatwork with completion rather than with understanding.

It would seem that since students spend a large amount of time both in and out of school completing assignments, there would be a wealth of information related to assignment completion in the mainstream professional literature. However, relatively little research has been conducted on assignments in the content areas, and even less research has been completed on assignments and their effect on mildly handicapped and other low-achieving students. Lenz, Ehren, and Smiley (in press) argued that assignment completion is often the test of how independent a learner has become in an academic setting. They organized assignment completion into completion knowledge and completion management. Completion knowledge involves the academic skills and background knowledge required to actually get the assignment done. Completion management involves the planning, integration, and organization of time, interests, and resources that facilitate the use of academic skills and knowledge. Applied to the activation process, the teacher would need to take into consideration or predict the student's completion knowledge in an attempt to guide the student's skills in completion management.

Lenz, et. al. identified three basic types of assignments: (1) study, (2) daily work, and (3) project. *Study* assignments require the student to prepare for a test or some type of class activity. The focus of the assignment is usually on a process, not on a permanent product. *Daily work* consists of assignments that are routine followup activities of content covered in class. They are designed to promote practice and understanding of the content. Completion of chapter questions and worksheets are usually considered daily work assignments. Whereas many daily work assignments usually take a day or two to complete, they can sometimes take as long as a week. *Project* assignments require more than one or two days to complete and often require student extension or application of content in the form of a report, theme, visual, product, or presentation. All three assignment types can be completed in the classroom setting (seatwork) or out of the classroom setting (homework) and can be completed individually or in a group, depending on the expectations of the teacher.

A number of studies related to assignments in the content areas have been completed with mildly handicapped and other low-achieving students. Many of these studies have focused on the effect of segmenting the content and prompting peer assistance to enhance learning. The effects of segmenting content was explored by Nagel, Schumaker, and Deshler (1986) who validated a first-letter mnemonic strategy intervention in which the students are taught a memorization strategy, but are also induced to segment the chapter into parts as part of a study assignment. Students are instructed in how to segment the book during class time, identify the to-be-memorized information, create mnemonics, and go through a series of self-test procedures to prepare for a test. While the focus of the intervention procedures was to teach the student to use specific memorization techniques, the manner in which the teacher required students to study using the strategy was found to be a key factor in promoting successful content learning. In another study related to segmenting content to enhance learning, Hughes, Hendrickson, and Hudson (1986) described a lecture-pause procedure in which the instructor paused for three to five minutes during a content lecture. During the "pause" in the lecture, students worked in groups in activities designed by the teacher to enhance learning. The process of grouping students was similar to the procedures described and implemented by Slavin, Leavey, and Madden (1982) in which heterogeneous groups of students work together cooperatively toward a common goal such as completing a worksheet or finding information in a text and agreeing upon the answers to a set of questions. In addition to studies on the value of segmenting content, many researchers have also explored models of cooperative learning (Johnson & Johnson, 1975; Slavin, 1983) and peer tutoring (Delquadri, Greenwood, Whorton, Carta, & Hall, 1986; Maheady, Sacca, & Harper, 1987).

Teaching Devices

A content enhancement device is an instructional procedure or tactic designed to achieve a singular goal in promoting learning and is associated with facilitating the understanding, remembering, and organization of information. A teaching device usually covers a very small segment of a lesson and is frequently embedded in a teaching routine. For example, within a routine designed to teach a broad concept, a device might be embedded in the routine to help students memorize a list of features salient to the concept. Therefore, the teaching devices can almost be conceptualized as instructional "tricks" used to enhance the learning of content.

The teaching devices are employed when specific elements of a lesson appear to present learning demands for the student that require more manipulation than the teacher predicts can effectively or efficiently be handled by the student. According to Schumaker, Deshler, and Mc-Knight (in press) the Content Teaching Devices are used to: (a) make abstract information more concrete; (b) connect new knowledge with familiar knowledge; (c) enable students who cannot spell well to take useful notes; (d) highlight relationships and organizational structures within the information to be presented, and (e) draw unmotivated learner's attention to the information. There are three types of instructional devices: (a) devices for understanding; (b) devices for remembering; and (c) devices for organizing.

Devices for Understanding

Devices for understanding are specifically used to either make a complex or abstract concept more concrete for students or to link new information to something within the student's realm of experience or interest. Some devices for understanding have been explored by Schumaker et al. (in press) in terms of a wide range of verbal and visual devices designed to promote student understanding. These devices may be explored to enhance understanding of examples, comparisons, and cause-and-effect relationships. A further refinement may involve structuring the devices into specific areas representing concrete examples, verbal comparisons, or active demonstrations. These devices may be inserted at any point in a lesson where the teacher anticipates difficulty in understanding or when students have failed to respond to the presentation of some information.

Rationales for the development of specific devices for understanding come from educators such as Gagné (1985) who indicated that the acquisition of declarative knowledge occurs when new knowledge stimulates the activation of the student's prior knowledge. This leads to storing the new knowledge with the relevant prior knowledge. She suggested that some procedures that can be used by teachers to encourage elaboration include the use of analogies, instructions to the learners to form images, or instructions to generate elaborations. Many of the devices for understanding build on just such links to prior knowledge.

Devices for Remembering

Devices for remembering are techniques that teachers specifically use to guide students in how to memorize important pieces of information that may be part of a class presentation. These devices may consist of a variety of tactics including creating mental images, making familiar associations, or using keyword strategies. Devices for remembering can be inserted at any point in the lesson when the student is expected to memorize factual information.

Research on memory devices suggests that these can be powerful tools that teachers can use to help students remember certain types of information. Bellezza (1981) noted that mnemonic devices are learning strategies that can often enhance the learning and later recall of information. He further noted that the basic distinction between various types of mnemonic devices is whether the purpose is to organize information or encode information. An organizing operation is one that associates or relates units of information that may appear to be unrelated. An encoding operation, on the other hand, transforms a unit of information into some other form so that it can fit into some organizational scheme.

According to Bellezza, mnemonic devices involve two types of organizational mnemonic devices and three types of encoding mnemonic devices. In the first category of organizational mnemonic devices, Bellezza lists the following: (1) "peg type" devices which are extrinsic cueing devices such as linking lists of items to locations in a sequential manner, linking items to mental images cued by a "peg-word," or remembering lists of items by using the first letter of each item to form another single word that cues memory; and (2) intrinsic cueing devices, referred to by Bellezza as "chain type" devices, include devices as story mnemonics, link mnemonics, and rhymes. In the second category, encoding mnemonic devices include: (a) concrete word encoding such as visual imagery; (b) abstract word encoding such as linking together words that have similar sounds or meanings; and (3) number encoding in which digits are changed into consonants to facilitate a memory pattern.

Several pieces of research support the use of various types of these mnemonic devices in the classroom. For example, Pressley, Levin, and McDaniel (1987) noted that if the teacher's objective is to maximize vocabulary remembering, then a mnemonic approach is an ideal instructional strategy because vocabulary-remembering research has proven mnemonic strategy instruction to be consistently superior to other strategies. They noted that no one strategy, of course, represents a single answer to all needs for facilitating vocabulary-learning objectives. Therefore, teacher and student alike benefit from a wide range of choices among memory devices which can be applied to differing content demands.

There is, indeed, a wide range of research directed toward facilitation of memorization. Various research has explored types of mnemonics such as the keyword device, rhymes, and first letter-mnemonics. For example, Mastropieri, Scruggs, Levin, Gaffney, and McLoone (1985) found that when learning disabled junior-high school students were taught definitions using a pictorial mnemonic strategy called the "keyword method," instruction was more effective than when students were taught definitions using direct instruction. This was true whether the teacher presented the mnemonic or students generated their own mnemonic images. Elliott and Gentile (1986) found that students who were taught the peg-word rhyme "one-bun, two-shoe . . . ten-hen" to remember how to associate numbers with images remembered facts about the to-be-remembered information significantly better than without the mnemonic. In a study involving the

FIRST-Letter Mnemonic Strategy, Nagel, Schumaker, and Deshler (1986) indicated that students performed significantly better on both ability level and grade level material when the students were taught to memorize lists of information through a FIRST-letter mnemonic strategy. Students used a wide variety of mnemonic devices on grade level tests; mnemonic devices consisted of both single-word mnemonics and sentence or phrase mnemonics.

Devices for Organizing

Devices for organizing are techniques that teachers specifically use to make the organization of and relationships between information in a presentation explicit. These devices may include explicit use of lists, words to cue sequence or importance, use of graphic organizers, and study or lecture guides that are used as adjuncts to a class presentation. Devices to help the student organize information can be inserted throughout and at any point in the lesson when the structure of the lesson or the relationship between information needs to be drawn to the student's attention. These devices serve the same purpose as the advance and post organizer orientation routines discussed earlier. However, devices for organizing are inserted in the actual lesson. Therefore, once the organizing structure has been made explicit in the advance organizer, the organizer devices in the main part of the lesson serve to reinforce and guide the student's attention to the structure of the information. Study or lecture guides and graphic organizers serve a similar function. Therefore, the three primary types of devices for organizing include organizing: (a) cues; (b) guides; and (c) illustrators.

Devices for organizing may take the form of verbal cues, written study sheets to guide student understanding, or graphics designed to present information in an alternative manner to verbal lecture presentation. Verbal cues to facilitate acquisition of information from lecture have been presented by Robinson, Deshler, Denton, and Schumaker (in prep.). Study sheet adaptations and graphic organizers are two areas that teachers can employ to facilitate learning. For example, Lovitt, Rudsit, Jenkins, Pious, and Benedetti (1985) found that students with learning difficulties showed better performance on chapter tests when teachers supplemented the text with textbook adaptations such as vocabulary practice sheets and framed outlines than in a lecture-discussion format. Furthermore, Lovitt, Stein, and Rudsit (1985) introduced charts and diagrams with direct instruction and found that this combination led to improved scores on chapter tests. Similarly, the use of visual depictions has been shown to improve the performance of both students with and without learning disabilities on tests given after the teacher incorporated visual depictions in lecture presentations when compared to lectures presented without use of the visual enhancers (Crank, in prep.).

Teacher Planning

The challenge in developing routines to *improve teacher planning* based on an information-processing model for instruction requires the researcher to consider how the characteristics of information-processing oriented instruction can become part of the teacher's orientation to the teaching process. This requires that both the tangible and intangible aspects of the teaching and learning processes be considered. This approach to teaching also challenges educators to reconsider the notion that teachers effectively use information related to the characteristics of students to change their teaching behavior in order to promote student mastery of the stated curriculum. An alternate approach to teaching that is consistent with an information-processing orientation would be to view the teacher as a thinker responsible for potentially organizing situations for learning that promote effective and efficient information processing.

The use of an information-processing approach to study the role of the teacher in the teaching and learning process becomes more difficult as research attention shifts to focus on the performance of the student with learning disabilities. It is made more difficult because the focus of research is on judging the effects of the intervention based on changes in a small segment of the student population in the mainstream classroom. This places unique demands on the planning and teaching process. In essence, the teacher must be a good information processor to accomplish this task. A "Good Teacher Thinker Model" (depicted in Figure 5.2) has been proposed by Lenz, Bulgretz, Deshler, and Schumaker (in press) to serve as a conceptual framework for examining teacher thinking. This model is based on three principles. First, the teacher must have sufficient command of the subject matter and its organization. Therefore, the focus of teacher planning and thinking should be based on transforming, manipulating, organizing, and communicating information that is already part of the teacher's background knowledge rather than on teacher acquisition of knowledge (i.e., trying to learn the content that must be taught to students). Second, the teacher must have a repertoire of successful teaching routines that reduce the complexity of decision making and take into consideration the maximum amount of student variance in learning. These routines should focus on planning, content teaching, management, and strategy instruction, although other routines may also be useful and necessary. Third, the teacher should be encouraged and prompted to be a "good thinker" related to the integration of routines in the delivery of subject matter and in the spontaneous decision making required during the events of classroom instruction when the teaching-learning process breaks down. Figure 5.2 depicts a visual model of how these three elements might be associated in a simplified fashion. As shown, "Good Teacher Thinking" must take into account and is dependent on knowledge of teaching and management

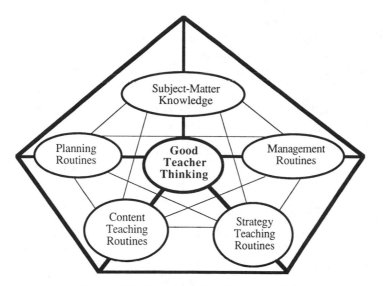

FIGURE 5.2. Good teacher thinker model.

routines; it must also take into account how these routines can be integrated so that student learning and performance is optimally enhanced.

Teacher planning is addressed in the Content Enhancement Model in two ways. First, each teaching routine specifies a specific planning process that is consistent across each of the routines. In general, the process includes: (a) specification of the to-be-learned content, (b) mapping of the critical features of the content, (c) analysis of prior-knowledge requirements, (d) decision making related to appropriate types and levels of content enhancement options, (e) delivery of the content using specific routines and devices through the enlistment of students as key agents in the teaching-learning process, (f) evaluation of the success of the instruction and the use of the routines and devices, and (e) evaluation of content potentially not yet learned. Second, the model incorporates specific routines for course, unit, and daily planning designed to focus teacher attention on the potential information processing characteristics of students in relation to the content that must be learned. Third, the implementation process will be grounded in the context of a teacher's personal development. Potentially, a Personal Development Strategy could be developed that could assist the regular education content teacher to identify what is personally gratifying about teaching and evaluate how student response to instruction affects their satisfaction and belief systems concerning teaching. This area of research has been initiated to address teacher motivations related to planning and teaching for individuals who potentially comprise a small subset of the total instructional group. Research directed toward understanding a teacher's willingness to change may be the most critical factor in understanding and influencing the processes of planning and teaching for individuals with learning disabilities.

Ongoing and Future Research on Instructional Routines and Devices

Future research on the content-enhancement process will continue to focus on the development of planning and teaching procedures that can have a positive impact on the learning and performance of individuals with learning disabilities. In the area of teacher planning, future research efforts by the staff of the University of Kansas Institute for Research in Learning Disabilities will focus on how specific planning routines can affect content-area teachers' consideration of the information-processing characteristics of students before, during, and after direct contact with students. In addition, studies on the various levels of planning are currently being implemented. Future research on planning will focus on how teachers think about making modifications for individuals with learning disabilities and whether both general and specific routines for planning at the course, unit, chapter, and lesson levels can be successful.

The ongoing research on teaching routines will focus on the relationship between teaching routines and devices and will attempt to identify which of these have the most potential for promoting student success. An overview of current and future research efforts related to the development of those teaching routines that appear to have some potential for enhancing content acquisition is presented in Figure 5.3. The areas targeted for potential research have been generated from an analysis of the learning demands commonly placed on students in the content areas. For example, Explanation Routines may specify a set of instructional procedures that a teacher might use for successfully presenting objective information about a process, a series of events, a set of steps, a procedure, or a specific cause-and-effect relationship. In addition, it may be found that several routines may be required to enable the teacher to present specific information effectively and efficiently. An overview of current and potential research efforts related to teaching devices is presented in Figure 5.4. It is likely that these research areas will expand and be modified as the relationships between and among routines and devices become more clearly defined.

Model-Related Research Issues and Perspectives

The term "model' being used in this chapter is consistent with the conceptualization of "model' used by Wong (1988). According to Wong (1988), an intervention research model for learning disabilities should: (a) provide

Orientation Routines	Understanding Routines	Activation Routines
Current research areas Advance Organizer Routines (e.g. Lenz, Alley, & Schumaker, 1987) Chapter Survey Routines (e.g., Schumaker & McKnight, 1989)	*Current research areas* Concept Teaching Routines (e.g., Bulgren, Schumaker, Deshler, 1988)	*Current research areas* Assignment Completion Routines (e.g., Hudson, 1987)
Potential research areas Post Organizer Routines	*Potential research areas* Analogical Anchoring Routines Explanation Routines Exploration Routines Case-making Routines Listing Routines Problem-Solution Routines	*Potential research areas* Assignment Construction Routines Assignment Instruction Routines

FIGURE 5.3.   Teaching routines potentially related to enhancing content acquisition.

	Current research areas	Potential research areas
Devices for Organizing	Verbal cues (e.g., Robinson, Deshler, Denton, & Schumaker, in prep) Illustrators/graphics (e.g. Crank, in prep)	Lecture/Study guides
Devices for Understanding	Verbal devices such as synonyms and analogies (e.g., Schumaker & McKnight, 1989)	Concrete devices such as manipulatives Active devices such as role play
Devices for Remembering	FIRST-Letter mnemonics (e.g., Nagel, Schumaker, & Deshler, 1986) Paired Associates (e.g., Bulgren & Schumaker, in prep.)	"Big Picture" Technique

FIGURE 5.4. Teaching devices potentially related to enhancing content acquisition.

a theoretical rationale related to how information-processing differences are addressed in the intervention, (b) be based on sound theory and prior research, and (c) utilize sound theory and prior research to identify powerful methods of instruction. Utilizing these basic assumptions as an umbrella, Wong has further argued that the model should include components that emphasize: (a) the acquisition of knowledge, (b) how students process and misprocess information, and (c) how motivation is or can be affected. While this chapter has attempted to demonstrate that these conditions have been considered in the development of this model, current and future research efforts are being planned with these assumptions and components in mind. In addition to these dimensions, Wong has identified a number of model-related issues that might be considered in the implementation of intervention research. These issues include: (a) distinguishing between content-specific strategies (e.g., obtaining history information from a history textbook), versus task-specific strategies (reading for important information from any textbook), (b) deciding how the comparison group for the validation effort is comprised, (c) distinguishing between teaching a strategy and teaching a student to be strategic, and (d) considering how strategy generalization and maintenance are ensured and measured. These represent very important issues in the validation process, and a few comments related to how these issues are related to the intervention research described in this chapter are necessary.

First, the teaching routines and devices have been conceptualized, proposed, and developed by examining the learning outcomes and processes involved in specific content domains. The completed and ongoing research has focused primarily on teacher implementation of the routines in the areas of science and social studies, and some exploratory research of the routines has been accomplished in the areas of language arts and mathematics. While there seems to be a demand for more frequent use of some routines in some areas, the same learning outcomes and processes appear to be prevalent across the domains. That is, the basic goals of the routines such as concept learning, understanding a process, remembering, understanding cause-and-effect relationships, taking and defending a position, etc. seem to be required across the disciplines, and the use of the routines in these areas appears to be an attractive instructional alternative for teachers. Simultaneously, there definitely are matching learning strategies for these same outcomes. Therefore, the potential exists for the teacher to be inducing strategic learning in an area while the student is attempting to acquire and apply more efficient and effective learning strategies in the same area. However, domain-specific instructional routines have not emerged. In fact, in the chapter reviews of the research on domain-specific teaching procedures included in Wittrock's *Handbook of Research on Teaching* (1986), a strong case for instructional uniqueness of the various content areas does not emerge. However, domain-specific learning strategies appear to be a possibility. For example, understanding and using "motive" as a way of interpreting world events or literary works might be considered a specific learning outcome unique to the areas of social studies and literature. However, the teaching routine for teaching students to evaluate "motive" in history events or stories is likely to be based on general procedures for teaching students about cause-and-effect relationships or teaching students how to understand and apply a process or procedure. While the power of teaching general learning strategies in the context of subject matter that must be immediately mastered by the student has been repeatedly demonstrated (e.g., Deshler & Schumaker, 1988; Lenz & Hughes, in press; Palinscar & Brown, 1984; Schumaker, Deshler, Alley, Warner, Clark, & Nolan, 1982), the relative power of instruction in potentially distinct domain specific learning strategies has yet to be determined. Clearly, further research must be conducted to determine the relationship between domain specific and task specific routines and and strategies.

Second, the initial studies in the development of specific content enhancement procedures have focused on: (1) whether teachers could learn to use the routine successfully (i.e., effectively and efficiently), (2) whether the content learning of students identified as learning disabled and who had repeatedly failed to learn and apply content could be improved, and (3) whether teachers and students have found the intervention to be socially valid and have continued to use the routine to promote learning. These questions have been addressed by replicating multiple-baseline single-subject research designs pairing one or more students with learning disabilities with a teacher and then observing student learning and performance in relation to teacher implementation of the specific teaching routine or device. A variety of grade levels, ranging from seventh grade through twelfth grade across the content areas, have been involved in the research effort. In addition, peer comparisons on learning have been included in some of the studies.

While these studies have provided an enormous amount of information about the effectiveness of the intervention on individual students, current studies have been arranged to examine the learning and test performance of all students involved in each class. However, as Wong has suggested, it is still unclear as to whether the individuals identified as learning disabled are qualitatively different from other subjects in the way they process information. Such a distinction is important since the underlying construct of the model is based on the assumption that qualitative differences in the way that individuals with learning disabilities process information can be addressed through differentiated instruction. As a result, planning has begun for a series of experimental studies using both an approximate chronological age control group and an approximate reading age control group. The control groups have been labeled "approximate" because the range of reading in a regular fourth grade class varies. Fourth grade was selected because fourth grade reading performance appears to be a minimum criterion for success in secondary content area classes. The application of this approach to the problem should functionally address the problem of discerning the uniqueness of the sample of individuals with learning disabilities within the context of regular classroom research. In addition, if qualitative differences are not observed, the intervention research can continue, but as line of intervention research with a broader intervention mission.

Third, Wong has argued that intervention research efforts should distinguish between teaching a strategy and promoting strategic behavior. Rightly, many researchers have argued that a great deal of strategy instruction taking place over a long period of time is required to teach a student how to be strategic (e.g., Pressley, Goodchild, Fleet, Zajchowski, & Evans, 1989; Wong, 1988; Deshler & Schumaker, 1988). However, the development of strategic problem solvers also rests on the degree to which agents in the total educational environment cue, prompt, model, demand, and reinforce strategic performance. That is, long-term programmatic efforts in strategy instruction should also enlist the support of key agents in settings in which strategic performance is required. As a result, while it cannot be said that the Content Enhancement Model induces strategic problem solving, it can be said that the development of strategic problem solvers is a goal of this model and measures should be taken to make this a part of the long-term evaluation of its success.

Fourth, the important role of generalization in intervention research has been discussed by a number of authors (Ellis, Lenz, & Sabornie, 1987; Pressley, Woloshyn, Lysynchuk, Martin, Wood, & Willoughby, in press; Wong, 1988). However, most of the generalization related research has focused on whether students can learn a strategy or a skill and then generalize its use to specific situations outside of the training setting. To accomplish this, researchers have proposed various paradigms for promoting strategy generalization and maintenance (e.g., Wong, 1985 and 1988; Ellis, Deshler, Lenz, Schumaker, & Clark, in press). However, how knowledge transfer and generalization in the content areas are accomplished is another area worthy of research attention. While research in cognitive psychology and reading has focused attention on flexibility and transfer in the content domains (e.g., Spiro, Vispoel, Schmitz, Samarapungavan, & Boerger, 1987), few researchers in the field of special education have considered the problem presented by the types of generalization involved in the nonskill areas of content learning for individuals with learning disabilities. That is, can students take information learned in science and or history class and apply this information in new situations and integrate it with new information when appropriate? While generalization of learning strategies to content learning situations is certainly a goal of the content enhancement model, the identification of content knowledge and then the automatic retrieval and use of this information as background knowledge to draw appropriate relationships to solve problems is the logical extension of the strategy generalization process.

Conclusion

As a conclusion to this chapter, it is important to discuss two key points about the Content Enhancement Model and its development. First, the constructs discussed in this chapter are the focus of a series of research studies that is part of a programmatic research effort and fits within a comprehensive set of research efforts involved in the development of the Strategies Intervention Model (Deshler & Schumaker, 1988). The key components of the Content Enhancement Model have evolved from the findings and observations of many completed and ongoing studies. In addition, future studies will probably alter the model and the relationships described here. Therefore, it is unwise to interpret this model as fixed, and it should be viewed as one proposal for thinking about content-area instruction for individuals with learning disabilities. As a result, it can be viewed as both a conceptual and a development model. Second, while the interpretation and application of information-processing theory has played a critical role in the development process, it has always served as a rather broad umbrella for development decisions and has been subject to interpretation in light of successful practice. Therefore, if there is a debate as to the role of theory in intervention research, it may be that the debate rests on how theory and how much of theory can be translated into effective and efficient practice. This is an important consideration because some lines of intervention research that have proven to be effective and have had a powerful impact on performance have not yet met the test of efficiency and replicability in practice. Thus, on one hand, we might agree with Kurt Lewin's (1935) suggestion that there may be nothing more interesting than practice that emerges from good theory. On the other hand, we may prefer to endorse Walter Doyle's (1989) suggestion that there is nothing more theoretically interesting than good practice.

References

Aiken, E.G., Thomas, G.S., & Sheenum, W. (1975). Memory for lecture: Effects of notes, lecture rate, and information density. *Journal of Educational Psychology*, *67*, 439–444.

Allington, R.L. (1984). So what is the problem? Whose problem is it? *Topics in Learning and Learning Disabilities*, *3*(4), 91–99.

Anderson, L. (1984). The environment of instruction: The function of seatwork in a commercially developed curriculum. In G.G. Duffy, L.R. Roehler, & J. Mason (Eds.), *Comprehension instruction: Perspectives and suggestions*. New York: Longman, 93–103.

Anderson, L.M., & Evertson, C.M. (1978). *Classroom organization at the beginning of school: Two case studies*. Paper presented to the American Association of Colleges for Teacher Education, Chicago.

Austin, J.D. (1979). Homework research in mathematics. *School Science and Mathematics*, *79*, 115–121.

Ausubel, D.P. (1960). The use of advance organizers in the learning and retention of meaningful verbal material. *Journal of Educational Psychology*, *51*, 267–272.

Ausubel, D.P., Novak, J.D., & Hanesian, H. (1968). *Educational psychology: A cognitive view*. (2nd ed.) NY: Holt, Rinehart, and Winston.

Becker, W.C., Englemann, S., & Thomas, D.R. (1971). *Teaching: A course in applied psychology*. Chicago: Science Research Associates.

Bellezza, F.S. (1981). Mnemonic devices: Classification, characteristics, and criteria. *Review of Educational Research*, *51*(2), 247–275.

Borkowski, J.G., & Cavanaugh, J. (1979). Maintenance and generalization of skills and strategies by the retarded. In N.R. Ellis (Ed.), *Handbook of mental deficiency: Psychological theory and research*. Hillsdale, NJ: Erlbaum.

Brainin, S. (1985). Mediating learning. Pedagogical issues in the improvement of cognitive functioning. In E.W. Gordon (Ed.), *Review of research in education* (*Vol. 12*). Washington, DC: American Educational Research Association.

Bretzing, B.H.,& Kulhavy, R.W. (1981). Note-taking and passage style. *Journal of educational Psychology*, *73*, 242–250.

Brophy, J. (1984). The teacher as thinker. In G.G. Duffy, L. A. Roehler, & J. Mason (Eds.), *Comprehension instruction: Perspectives and suggestions*. New York: Longman.

Brown, A.L. (1978). Knowing when, where, and how to remember a problem of metacognition. In R. Glaser (Ed.), *Advances in instructional psychology (Vol. 1)*. Hillsdale, NJ: Erlbaum.

Brown, A.L., & Palincsar, A.S. (1987). Reciprocal teaching of comprehension strategies: A natural history of one program for enhancing learning. In J. Borkowski & J.D. Day (Eds.), *Intelligence and cognition in special children: Comparative studies of giftedness, mental retardation, and learning disabilities*. New York: Ablex.

Brown, A.L., Bransford, J.D., Ferrara, R.A., & Campione, J.C. (1983). Learning, remembering, and understanding. In J.H. Flavell & E.M. Markman (Eds.), *Handbook of child psychology: Vol 3 Cognitive development*. New York: Wiley.

Brown, A.L., Day, J.D., & Jones, R.S. (1983). The development of plans for summarizing texts. *Child Development*, *54*, 968–979.

Brown, D.S. (1988). Twelve middle-school teachers' planning. *The Elementary School Journal*, *89*(1), 69–87.

Bruner, J.S., Goodnow, J.J., & Austin, G.A. (1956). *A study of thinking*. New York: Wiley

Buckley, P.K., & Cooper, J.M. (1978). *An ethnographic study of an elementary school teacher's establishment and maintenance of group norms*. Paper presented at the annual meeting of the American Educational Research Association, Toronto.

Bulgren, J.A. (1987). The development and validation of instructional procedures to teach concepts in secondary mainstream classes which contain students with learning disabilities. Unpublished doctoral dissertation, University of Kansas, Lawrence, K.S.

Bulgren, J.A., & Schumaker, J.B. (in prep.). *The learning strategies curriculum: The paired-associates strategy*. Lawrence: The University of Kansas Institute for Research in Learning Disabilities.

Bulgren, J.A., Schumaker, J.B., & Deshler, D.D. (1988). Effectiveness of a concept teaching routine in enhancing the performance of LD students in secondary-level mainstream classes. *Learning Disability Quarterly*, *11*, 3–17.

Butterfield, E.C., & Belmont, J.M. (1977). Assessing and improving the cognitive functions of mentally retarded people. In I. Bailer & M. Steinlicht (Eds.), *Psychological issues in mental retardation*. Chicago: Aldine.

Campione, J.E., & Brown, A.L. (1977). Memory and metamemory development in educable retarded children. In R.V. Kail & J.W. Hagen (Eds.), *Perspectives on the development of memory of cognition*. Hillsdale, NJ: Erlbaum.

Carter, J.F. & Van Matre, N.H. (1975). Notetaking versus note having. *Journal of Educational Psychology*, *67*, 900–904.

Clark, C.M. & Peterson, P.L. (1986). Teacher's thought processes. In M.C. Wittrock (Ed.) *Handbook of research on teaching (3rd ed.)*. (pp. 225–296) New York: MacMillan.

Coleman, J.S., Hoffer, T., & Kilgore, S. (1981). *Public and private schools*. Washington DC: U.S. Department of Education.

Craik, F.I.M., & Lockhart, R.S. (1972). Levels of processing: A framework for memory research. Journal of Verbal Learning and Verbal Behavior, *11*, 671–684.

Crank, J. (in prep.) *Post-doctoral fellowship final report: Visual depiction develop-*

ment and validation for content teachers. Lawrence: University of Kansas Institute for Research in Learning Disabilities.

Delquadri, J., Greenwood, C.R., Whorton, D., Carta, J.J., & Hall, R.V. (1986). Classwide peer tutoring. *Exceptional Children, 52*(6), 535–542.

Deshler, D.D., Alley, G.R., Warner, M.M., & Schumaker, J.B. (1981). Instructional practices for promoting skill acquisition and generalization in severely learning disabled adolescents. *Learning Disabilities Quarterly, 4*(4), 415–421.

Deshler, D.D., & Schumaker, J.B. (1988). An instructional model for teaching students how to learn. In J.L. Graden, J.E. Zins, & M.J. Curtis (Eds.), *Alternative educational delivery systems: Enhancing instructional options for all students.* Washington, DC: National Association of School Psychologists.

Deshler, D.D., Schumaker, J.B., Lenz, B.K., & Ellis, E.S. (1984). Academic and cognitive interventions for LD adolescents: Part II. *Journal of Learning Disabilities, 17* (3), 170–187.

Deshler, D.D., Kass, C.E., & Ferrell, W.R. (1978). Monitoring of schoolwork errors by LD adolescents. *Journal of Learning Disabilities, 11*(7), 10–23.

Doyle, W. (1989). *Classroom knowledge as a foundation for learning.* Paper presented at the national conference on Foundational Studies in Teacher Education: A Re-examination. May. University of Illinois at Urbana-Champaign.

Elliott, J.L., Gentile, J.R. (1986). The efficacy of a mnemonic technique for learning disabled and nondisabled adolescents. *Journal of Learning Disabilities, 19*(4), 237–241.

Ellis, E.S., Deshler, D.D., Lenz, B.K., Schumazker, J.B., & Clark, F.L. (in press). An instructional model for teaching learning strategies. *Focus on Exceptional Children.*

Ellis, E.S., Deshler, D.D., & Schumaker, J.B. (in press). Teaching adolescents with learning disabilities to generate and use task-specific strategies. *Journal of Learning Disabilites.*

Ellis, E.S., Lenz, B.K., & Sabornie, E.J. (1987). Generalization and adaptation of learning strategies to natural environments: Part 1: Critical agents. *Remedial and Special Education, 8*(1), 6–20.

Farnham-Diggory, S. (1986). Commentary: Time, now, for a little serious complexity. In S.J. Ceci (Ed.), *Handbook of cognitive, social, and neuropsychological aspects of learning disabilities.* Hillsdale, NJ: Erlbaum.

Faw, H.W. & Waller, T.G. (1976). Mathemagenic behaviors and efficiency in learning from prose. *Review of Educational Research, 46,* 691–720.

Fredrick, W.C., & Walberg, H.J. (1980). Learning as a function of time. *The Journal of Educational Research, 73,* 183–204.

Fullan, M. (1982)/ *The meaning of educational change.* New York: Teachers College Press.

Gagné, E.D. (1985). *The cognitive psychology of school learning.* Boston: Little Brown.

Gagné, R.M. (1965). *The conditions of learning.* New York: Holt, Rinehart, & Winston.

Goodlad, J.L. (1984). *A place called school.* New York: McGraw Hill.

Graff, H.J. (1987). *The legacies of literacy: Continuities and contradictions in western culture and society.* Bloomington, IN: Indiana University Press.

Hansen, J. (1984). The role of prior knowledge in content area learning. *Topics in Learning and Learning Disabilities, 3*(4), 66–77.

Harnischfeger, A. (1980). Curricular control and learning time: District policy, teacher strategy, and pupil choice. *Educational Evaluation and Policy Analysis*, *2*(6), 19–30.

Hazel, J.S., Schumaker, J.B., Sherman, J.A., Sheldon-Wildgen, J. (1981). *ASSET: A social skills program for adolescents*. Champaign, IL: Research Press.

Holmes Group (1986). *Tomorrow's teachers: A report of the Holmes Group*. East Lansing, MI: Holmes Group.

Hord, S.M., Rutherford, W.L., Huling-Austin, L. & Hall, G. (1987). *Taking charge of change*. Alexandria, VA: Association of Supervision and Curriculum Development.

Houston, J.P (1981). *Fundamentals of learning and memory*, 2nd ed. New York: Academic Press.

Howe, H. Edlelman, M.W. (1985). *Barriers to excellence: Our children at risk*. Boston: National Coalition of Advocates for students.

Howell, S.B. (1986). *A study of the effectiveness of TOWER-A theme writing strategy*. Unpublished masters thesis. University of Kansas, Lawrence.

Huberman, A.M. & Miles, M.B. (1984). *Innovation up close: How school improvement works*. New York: Plenum Press.

Hudson, P.J. (1987). The pause procedure: A technique to help mildly handicapped students learn lecture context. Unpublished doctoral dissertation, University of Florida, Gainesville.

Hughes, C. (1985). A test taking strategy for learning disabled and emotionally handicapped adolescents. Unpublished dissertation, University of Florida, Gainesville

Hughes, C.A., Hendrickson, J.M., & Hudson, P.J. (1986). The pause procedure: Improving factual recall from lectures of low and high achieving middle school students. *International Journal of Instructional Media*, *13*, 217–226.

Hughes, C.A., Schumaker, J.B., Deshler, D.D., & Mercer, C.M. (1988). *The learning strategies curriculum*: *The test-taking strategy*. Lawrence, KS: Edge Enterprises.

Johnson, D.D., Toms-Bronowski, S., & Pittelman, S.D. (1982). *An investigation of the effectiveness of semantic mapping and semantic feature analysis with intermediate grade level children. Program Report 83-3*. Madison: The University of Wisconsin, Wisconsin Center for Education Research.

Johnson, D.W., & Johnson, R.T. (1975). *Learning together and alone*. Englewood Cliffs, NJ: Prentice-Hall.

Joyce, B.R. (1978–79). Toward a theory of information processing teaching. *Educational Research Quarterly*, *3*(4), 66–77.

Joyce, B., & Weil, M. (1986). *Models of teaching*, 3rd ed. Englewood Cliffs, NJ: Prentice-Hall.

Keith, T.Z., & Page, E.B. (1985). Homework works at school: National evidence for policy changes. *School Psychology Review*, *14*(3), 351–359.

Klausmeier, H.J., and Associates (1979). *Cognitive learning and development: Information-processing and Piagetian perspectives*. Cambridge, MA: Ballinger Publishing.

Klausmeier, H.J., & Ripple (1971). *Learning and human abilities: Educational psychology*. New York: Harper & Row.

Kline, F. (1989). *The development and validation of feedback routines for use in special education settings*. Unpublished dissertation. The University of Kansas, Lawrence.

Lenz, B.K., Alley, G.R., & Schumaker, J.B (1987). Activating the inactive learner: Advance organizers in the secondary content classroom. *Learning Disability Quarterly*, *10*(1), 53–67.

Lenz, B.K. & Bulgren, J.A. (in press). Promoting learning in the content areas. In P.A. Cegelka and W.H. Berdine (Eds.), *Effective instruction for students with learning problems*. Needham Heights, MA: Allyn & Bacon.

Lenz, B.K., Bulgren, J.A., Deshler, D.D., & Schumaker, J.B. (in prep). Planning in the face of academic diversity: The good teacher thinker model. The University of Kansas, Institute for Research in Learning Disabilities, Lawrence, KS.

Lenz, B.K., Ehren, B.J., & Smiley, L.R. (in press). A goal attainment approach to improve completion of project-type assignments by learning disabled adolescents. *Learning Disability Focus*, *23*(3), 149–159.

Lenz, B.K., & Hughes, C.A. (1990). A word-identification strategy for learning disabled adolescents. *Journal of Learning Disabilities*.

Lenz, B.K., Schumaker, J.B., Deshler, D.D., & Beals, V.L. (1984). *The learning strategies curriculum: The word identification strategy*. Lawrence: The University of Kansas Institute for Research in Learning Disabilities.

Lewin, K. (1935). *A dynamic theory of personality: Selected papers*. Translated by Donald K. Adams & Karl E. Zener. New York: McGraw-Hill.

Lovitt, T., Rudsit, J., Jenkins, J., Pious, C., & Benedetti, D. (1985). Two methods of adaptive science materials for learning disabled and regular seventh graders. *Learning Disability Quarterly*, *8*, 275–285.

Lovitt, T.C., Stein, M., & Rudsit, J. (1985). *The use of visual spatial displays to teach science facts to learning disabled middle school students*. Unpublished manuscript, Experimental Education Unit, University of Washington, Seattle.

Lundgren, U. (1972). *Frame factors and the teaching process*. Stockholm: Almquist and Wiksell.

Madden, N.A., & Slavin, R.E. (1983). Mainstreaming students with mild handicaps: Academic and social outcomes. *Review of Educational Research*, *53*, 519–560.

Maheady, L., Sacca, M.K., & Harper, G.F. (1987). Technology for persons with severe disabilities: Practical and ethical considerations. *The Journal of Special Education*, *21*(3), 107–121.

Maheady, L., Sacca, M.K,.& Harper, G.F. (1988). Classwide peer tutoring with mildly handicapped high school students. *Exceptional Children*, *55*, 52–59.

Martorella, P.H. (1972). Teaching concepts. In J.M. Cooper (Ed.), *Classroom teaching skills*, 2nd ed. Lexington, MA: D.C. Heath.

Mastropieri, M.A., Scruggs, T.E., Levin, J.R., Gaffney, J., & McLoone, B. (1985). Mnemonic vocabulary instruction for learning disabled students. *Learning Disability Quarterly*, *8*(1), 57–64.

Mayer, R.E. (1975). Information processing variables in learning to solve problems. *Review of Educational Research*, 45, 525–541.

Mayer, R E. (1979). Twenty years of research on advance organizers: Assimilation theory is still the best predictor of results. *Instructional Science*, *8*, 133–167.

Mayer, R.E. (1983). *Thinking, problem solving, cognition*. New York: Freeman.

Mayer, R.E. (1984). Aids to prose comprehension. *Educational Psychologist*, *19*, 89–130.

Mayer, R.E. (1987). *Educational psychology: A cognitive approach.* Boston: Little Brown.

McNair, K. (1978-1979). Capturing inflight decisions. *Educational Research Quarterly, 3*(4), 26–42.

McNellis, K.L. (1987). In search of the attentional deficit. In S.J. Ceci, (Ed.), *Handbook of cognitive, social, and neuropsychological aspects of learning disabilities.* Hillsdale, NJ: Lawrence Erlbaum.

Morine-Dershimer, G. (1979). *Teacher plan and classroom reality: The South Bay Study, Part IV.* Research Series No. 60. Lansing: Institute for Research on Teaching, Michigan State University.

Morrison, F.J. (1987). The nature of reading disability: Toward on integrative framework. In S.J. Ceci, (Ed.), *Handbook of cognitive, social, and neuropsychological aspects of learning disabilities.* Hillsdale, NJ: Lawrence Erlbaum.

Morrison, F.J., & Manis, F.R. (1982). Cognitive processes and reading disability: A critique and proposal. In C.J. Brainerd & M.I. Pressley (Eds.), *Verbal processes in children.* New York: Springer-Verlag.

Nagel, D.R., Schumaker, J.B., & Deshler, D.D. (1986). *The FIRST-letter mnemonic strategy: Instructor's manual.* Lawrence, KS: Edge Enterprise.

Page, E.B., & Keith, T.Z. (1981). Effects of U.S. private schools: A technical analysis of two recent claims. *Educational Researcher, 10*(7), 7–17.

Palincsar, A.S. (1986a). The role of dialogue in providing scaffolded instruction. *Educational Psychologist, 21*, 73–98.

Palincsar, A.S. (1986b). Metacognitive strategy instruction. *Exceptional Children, 53*, 118–124.

Palincsar, A.S., Brown, A.L. (1984). Reciprocal teaching of comprehension fostering and comprehension monitoring activities. *Cognition and Instruction, 1*(2), 117–175.

Peters, D.L. (1972). Effects of note taking and rate of presentation on short-term objective test performance. *Journal of Educational Psychology, 63*, 276–280.

Polachek, S.W., & Kniesner, T.J., & Harwood, H.J. (1978). Education production functions. *Journal of Educational Statistics, 3*, 209–231 .

Pressley, M., Goodchild, F., Fleet, J., Zajchowski, R., & Evans, E. (1989). The challenges of classroom strategy instruction. *The Elementary School Journal, 89*, 301–342.

Pressley, M., Levin, J.R., & McDaniel, M.A. (1987). Remembering versus inferring what a word means: Mnemonic and contextual approaches. In M.G. McKeown & M.E. Curtis (Eds.), *The nature of vocabulary acquisition.* Hillsdale, NJ: Lawrence Erlbaum.

Pressley, M., Woloshyn, V., Lysynchuk, L.M., Martin, V., Wood, E., & Willoughby, T. (in press). *Cognitive strategy instruction: The important issues and how to address them.* Submitted for publication.

Robinson, S., Deshler, D.D., Denton, P., & Schumaker, J.B. (in prep.). *The learning strategies curriculum: The listening and notetaking strategy: Instructor's manual.* Lawrence, KS: Edge Enterprises.

Rosenshine, B., & Stevens, R. (1986). Teaching functions. In M.E. Wittrock (Ed.), *Handbook of research on teaching,* 3rd ed. (pp. 376–91) New York: Macmillan.

Roth, K.J., Smith, E.L., & Anderson, C.W. (1984). Verbal patterns of teachers: Comprehension instruction in the content areas. In G.G. Duffy, L.R. Roehler,

& J. Mason (Eds.), *Comprehension instruction*. New York: Longman.

Samuels, S.J. (1987). Infommation-processing abilities and reading. *Journal of Learning Disabilities*, *20*, 18–22.

Schmidt, J.L., Deshler, D.D., Schumaker, J.B., & Alley, G.R. (in press). Effects of generalization instruction on the written language perfommance of adolescents with learning disabilities in the mainstream classroom. *Journal of Reading, Writing, and Learning Disabilities*.

Schumaker, J.B., & Deshler, D.D. (1984). Setting demand variables: A major factor in program planning for LD adolescents. *Topics in Language Disorders*, *4*(2), 22–140.

Schumaker, J.B., Deshler, D.D., Alley, G.R., Warner, M.M., Clark, F.L. & Nolan, S. (1982). Error monitoring: A learning strategy for improving adolescents'academic performance. In W.M. Cruickshank & J.W. Lemer (Eds.), *Coming of age: Vol. 3: The best of ACLD*. Syracuse, NY: Syracuse University Press.

Schumaker, J.B., Deshler, D.D., & McKnight, P.C. (in press). *Teaching routines for content areas at the secondary level*. Washington, DC: National Association for School Psychologists.

Schumaker, J.B. & McKnight, P.C. (1989). *Final report: The development and validation of a set of teaching routines for enhancing the performance of low-achieving students in secondary mainstream classes*. Submitted to the United States Department of Education, Division of Innovation and Development.

Shavelson, R.J., & Stern, P. (1981). Research on teachers' pedagogical thoughts, judgments, decisions, and behavior. *Review of Educational Research*, *51*, 455–498.

Shroyer, J.C. (1981). *Critical moments in the teaching of mathematics: What makes teaching difficult?* Unpublished doctoral dissertation. Michigan State University, East Lansing.

Shulman, L. (1989). *Reconnecting the foundations to the substance of teacher preparation*. Paper presented at the national conference on Foundational Studies in Teacher Education: A Re-examination. May. University of Illinois at Urbana-Champaign, Champaign.

Shultz, J., & Florio, S. (1979). Stop and freeze: The negotiation of social and physical space in a kindergarten/first grade classroom. *Anthropology and Education Quarterly*, *10*, 166–181.

Slavin, R.E. (1983). *Cooperative learning*. New York: Longman.

Slavin, R.E., Leavey, M., & Madden, N.A. (1982). *Effects of student teams and individualized instruction on student mathematics achievement, attitudes, and behaviors*. Paper presented at the annual convention of the American Education Research Association, New York.

Spiro, R.J., Vispoel, W.P., Schmitz, J.G., Samarapungavan, A., & Boerger, A.E. (1987). *Knowledge acquisition for application: Cognitive flexibility and transfer in complex content domains*, (Technical report #409). University of Illinois at Urbana-Champaign, Center for the Study of Reading, Champaign.

Swanson, H.L. (1987). Information-processing theory and learning disabilities: An overview. *Journal of Learning Disabilities*, *20*, 3–7.

Taba, H. (1971). *A teacher's handbook to elementary social studies*, 2nd ed. Reading, MA; Addison-Wesley.

Tikunoff, W.J., & Ward, B.A. (1978). *A naturalistic study of the initiation of students into three classroom social systems* (Report A-78-11). San Francisco: Far West Laboratory.

Tollefson, N., Tracy, D.B., Johnsen, E.P., Buenning, M., & Farmer, A. (1981). *Implementing goal setting activities with LD adolescents.* (Research Report No.48). The University of Kansas Institute for Research in Learning Disabilities, Lawrence, K.S.

Torgesen, J.K. (1977). Memorization processes in reading-disabled children. *Journal of Educational Psychology, 79*, 571–578.

Turnure, J.E. (1985). Communication and cues in the functional cognition of the mentally retarded. In N.R. Ellis & N.W. Bray (Eds.), *International review of research in mental retardation.* New York: Academic Press.

Turnure, J.E. (1986). Instruction and cognitive development: Coordinating communication and cues. *Exceptional Children, 53*(2), 109–117.

Van Reusen, A.K., Bos, C.S., Schumaker, J.B., & Deshler, D.D. (1987). *The learning strategies curriculum: The educational planning strategy.* Lawrence, KS: Edge Enterprises.

Vellutino, F.R. (1979). *Dyslexia: Theory and research.* Cambridge, MA: MIT Press.

Voelker, A. (1972). Concept learning in the science curriculum, K–12: Issues and approaches. In P.H. Martorella (Ed.), *Concept learning: Designs for instruction.* Scranton, PA: Intext.

Vygotsky, L.S. (1978) *Mind in society: The development of higher psychological processes.* M. Cole, V. John-Steiner, S. Scribner, & E. Souberman, Eds. & Trans. Cambridge: Harvard University Press.

Walberg, H.J. (1984). Improving the productivity of America's schools. *Educational Leadership, 41*(8), 19–30.

Wertsch, J.V., & Stone, C.A. (1979). *A social international analysis of learning disabillties remediation.* Paper presented at the International Conference of the Association for Children with Learning Disabilities. May. San Francisco.

Wittrock, M.C. (1986). Handbook of research on teaching, (3rd ed.). New York Macmillan.

Wodlinger, M.G. (1980). *A study of teacher interactive decision making.* Unpublished doctoral dissertation, University of Alberta, Edmonton, Canada.

Wolf, R.M. (1979). Achievement in the United States. In H.J. Walberg (Ed.), *Educational environments and effects: Evaluation, policy, and productivity.* Berkeley, CA: McCutchan.

Wong, B.Y.L. (1985). Potential means of enhancing content skills acquisition in learning disabled adolescents. *Focus on Exceptional Children, 17*(5), 1–8.

Wong, B.Y.L. (1988). An instructional model for intervention research in learning disabilities. *Learning Disabilities Research, 4*(1), 5–16.

Wong, B.Y.L., & Jones, W. (1982) Increasing comprehension in learning disabled and normally achieving students through self-questioning training. *Learning Disability Quarterly, 5*, 228–240.

Wood, D.J., Bruner, J.S., & Ross, G. (1987). The role of tutoring in problem-solving. *Journal of Child Psychology and Psychiatry, 17*, 89–100.

Yinger, R.J. (1977). *A study of teacher planning: Description and theory development using ethnographic and information-processing methods.* Unpublished doctoral dissertation, Michigan State University, East Lansing.

6
Interactive Teaching and Learning: Instructional Practices for Teaching Content and Strategic Knowledge

CANDACE S. BOS AND PATRICIA L. ANDERS

Students with learning disabilities face challenging reading and learning demands as they move beyond the primary grades. While many of these students continue to encounter difficulties with basic reading skills, moving into the intermediate and secondary grades means they also need to use a cadre of cognitive and metacognitive strategies for negotiating informational text. Within the content areas, they are expected to deepen and broaden their knowledge through reading. However, with regard to reading and learning in the content areas, learning disabled students seem to be in jeopardy for several reasons. First, these students spend much of their in-school time learning how to read in materials that are either narrative or do not require purposeful learning of the content (Snider & Tarver, 1987). Second, at the elementary level it is not unusual for learning disabled students to miss content instruction within the regular classroom due to the time spent in resource rooms (Allington & McGill-Franzen, 1989; Richardson, Casanova, Placier, & Guilfoyle, 1988). Consequently, they miss opportunities to develop rich knowledge structures on which to build content knowledge and domain-specific strategies for comprehending content texts. Third, current teaching techniques used for teaching content knowledge often do not provide the scaffolding necessary for interacting with the concepts presented in texts (Durkin, 1978–79; Roth, Smith, & Anderson, 1984). The compounding of limited strategic knowledge plus limited content background knowledge on the part of the students and limited use of content scaffolding on the part of the teachers places learning disabled students at risk for comprehending content area texts and for concept learning. This situation compels us as teachers and researchers to ask questions concerning effective models for teaching text comprehension and content learning.

An Interactive Model of Teaching and Learning

Based on these concerns, we have been working for the past five years to develop and validate an interactive instructional model for text comprehension and content area learning focused specifically on learning disabled students (Bos & Anders, in press–a). In developing the model we have attempted to deal with two issues critical for intervention research with learning disabled populations (Wong, 1987; 1988). First, the model is theoretically grounded in several related theories of reading and learning (Goodman, 1984; Klausmeier & Sipple, 1980; Rumelhart, 1980; Vygotsky, 1978). Second, the model incorporates instructional theories that guide the intervention (Vygotsky, 1978).

Schema Theory and the Knowledge Hypothesis

One theory of cognition that has been used by reading comprehension researchers to explain the importance of prior knowledge for learning new information is schema theory (Anderson, 1984; Rumelhart, 1980). Schema theory explains how knowledge is structured in memory and how these structures affect incoming information. Schemata provide an organizational framework or scaffolding on which new information can be integrated. "Schemata are employed in the process of interpreting sensory data (both linguistic and nonlinguistic), in retrieving information from memory, in organizing actions, in determining goals and subgoals, in allocating resources, and generally, guiding the flow of processing in the system" (Rumelhart, 1980, pp. 33–34). Assumptions from schema theory have also been used to explain the powerful and consistent correlation between vocabulary or concept knowledge and reading comprehension. Anderson and Freebody (1981) referred to this as the knowledge hypothesis: understanding a concept or knowing a vocabulary word implies that one knows not only the definition but also its relationships to other concepts and its semantic characteristics. Instructional principles derived from schema theory and the knowledge hypothesis to develop an interactive instructional model for text comprehension and content learning are:

1. The richness of a reader's related schemata and the degree to which a reader activates these schemata should affect both content learning and text comprehension.
2. The degree to which the instructional intervention provides opportunities for developing relationships between and among concepts should affect conceptual learning and reading comprehension.
3. The degree to which the instructional intervention allows for analysis of the semantic features of a concept should affect content learning and reading comprehension.

Psycholinguistic Theory of Reading

According to the psycholinguistic theory of reading (Goodman, 1984), readers utilize three language cuing systems when comprehending texts: graphophonic, syntactic, and semantic system. The reader uses cognitive strategies to engage these language systems. Key among the cognitive strategies are sampling or selecting, predicting, confirming, integrating, and justifying. Goodman argues that these processes are engaged at every level of discourse, from letters to entire texts, as readers construct meaning. Drawn from this model is the strong emphasis on strategic reading and teaching which focuses on the flexible use the full range of language systems and strategies for interacting with text. Although the psycholinguistic model is compatible with schema theory, it is different in that Goodman's model explains comprehension while schema theory explains knowledge acquisition and memory. Thus, additional instructional principles are derived from the psycholinguistic model:

1. The degree to which the instructional intervention allows for opportunities to access the language cuing systems affects the quality of comprehension.
2. The degree to which the instructional intervention explicates cognitive strategies such as selecting, predicting, confirming, integrating, and justifying affects the quality of comprehension and content learning.

Concept Learning and Development Theory

Research and theories about concepts and conceptual attainment are rich, drawing on the field of cognitive psychology and information-processing theory. Klausmeier and his colleagues (Klausmeier & Sipple, 1980) have developed a model to describe the attainment of concepts within content area curricula that corresponds well with the schema theorists and Goodman's model of the reading process. This concept learning and development theory hypothesizes four levels of attaining a concept: concrete, identity, classification, and formal. Concepts are attained when a learner engages the concept at all four levels. Evidence suggests that students learn concepts when opportunities are provided to identify and name defining attributes and when examples and non-examples of a concept are presented and used (Klausmeier & Sipple, 1980).

Hierarchically organized and related concepts are remembered best when taught in ways that explicate the organization (Klausmeier, 1984). An author or teacher's conceptual presentation of the content can be organized into concept levels (e.g., superordinate, coordinate, and subordinate) that when obvious and available to readers, enhances comprehension. Concepts, then, are the substance of schemata and are accessed and manipulated by readers using cognitive strategies to construct meaning. Instructional implications from this theory include:

1. Instruction that explicates the attributes of a concept will affect understanding and remembering of that concept.
2. Instruction that provides examples and non-examples of a concept will affect understanding and remembering of that concept.
3. Concepts found within content disciplines are organized in hierarchical structures that may serve as metaphors of schema(ta).

Sociocultural Theory of Cognitive Development

The sociocultural theory of cognitive development assumes that cognitive functioning grows out of social interactions during problem solving and practical activity (Vygotsky, 1978). It is based on the premise that learning occurs during interactions or events between experts and novices who developmentally move from the level of social experience to individual experience (Moll & Diaz, 1987). This learning occurs in the "zone of proximal development" which Vygotsky (1978) describes as "the distance between the actual developmental level as described by independent problem solving and the level of potential development as determined through problem solving under adult guidance or in collaboration with more capable peers" (p. 86).

Characteristic of instruction using this model is scaffold instruction. The metaphor of a scaffold captures the idea of an adjustable and temporary support that can be removed when no longer necessary. Another characteristic is the emphasis on interactive dialogue related to content and strategy instruction. Such dialogue between the teacher and learners provide language models and tools for guiding one's inner talk about learning (Moll & Diaz, 1987). Initially, the expert models the self-talk and vocabulary related to the cognitive processes. However, this monologue gives way to a collaborative or social dialogue in which the learner assurnes increasing responsibility. This type of teaching allows for the instruction of cognitive and metacognitive strategies within purposeful, meaningful discussions and also provides a means for selecting, organizing, and relating subject-matter discourse. The strategies themselves provide a tool, much like a scaffold, to be used while meaning is constructed. Thus, the sociocultural theory of learning implies the following for instruction:

1. Instruction that is designed to facilitate scaffolding and cooperative knowledge sharing among students and teachers within a context of respect and critical acceptance of each others' knowledge and experiences will affect comprehension and content learning.
2. The degree to which content is presented as a meaningful, socially embedded activity affects the quality of comprehension.

3. Instruction that provides opportunities for mediated learning with the teacher or expert guiding instruction within the students' zones of proximal development should enhance strategic learning on the part of the students.

Toward an Interactive Model

The instructional principles derived from each of these theories has led us to develop an interactive, instructional model for text comprehension and content learning. The term "interactive" is associated with this model for two reasons. First, the comprehension process is assumed to be interactive in nature. In other words, reading is not merely gaining meaning from the text and does not proceed in a strict order from perceiving the visual information in letters to the overall interpretation of the text (Anderson, 1984). Rather, reading comprehension is a constructive process in which readers use cognitive strategies to combine information presented in the text with their hypotheses about the text meaning and their current schemata. Thus, instructional strategies compatible with this model provide students opportunities for developing and employing those cognitive strategies.

Second, the term "interactive" assumes that learning will be enhanced if the teacher and students utilize an interactive dialogue to discuss and organize concepts and to discuss and demonstrate strategic knowledge. This interactive dialogue encourages cooperative knowledge sharing because the instruction calls for both the teacher and students to share their knowledge concerning content and strategies. Thus, the teacher serves as a mediator for learning (Goodman, 1984; Vygotsky, 1978).

Characteristics of the Model

The model has been designed to focus on both teaching and learning of content knowledge and strategic knowledge. In the model content knowledge refers to the concepts and relationships among concepts that form the discourse of a domain. Experts in any domain are facile with the content discourse. When asked, they produce organized maps of their knowledge, providing broad, inclusive superordinate concepts along with major categories of ideas that serve a coordinating function between the subordinate concepts and the superordinate ideas (Naveh-Benjamin, McKeatchie, Lin, & Tucker, 1986). As with any discourse system, the organization is flexible and subject to manipulation; however, experts are likely to agree upon a conventional organization scheme when asked to evaluate one. Thus, when experts read a text within a particular content domain, they are likely to predict with some measure of confidence the author's ideas and the organization of those ideas. On the other hand, readers who are novices in a field are at a disadvantage because they do not share the discourse structure with the author. Expert readers who are novices in the content domain work to engage the discourse by relating what is being read to prior knowledge, typically using analogies, elaborating on ideas, specifying examples of concepts, and linking attributes with concepts. The strategies associated with our interactive model provide opportunities for naive students to do the same sort of thinking. A scaffold is provided that encourages students to use their prior knowledge to predict the ideas that may appear in a text. Further, questions are posed that prepare the student to select worthwhile examples and attributes to pay attention to in the text. These strategies provide opportunities to engage content domain discourse in productive and scholarly ways that are analogous to the language used by experts.

Strategic knowledge refers to the cognitive and metacognitive strategies that students employ when learning. Reading comprehension research has highlighted the strategic nature of reading (e.g., Baker & Brown, 1984; Garner, 1987). Paris and his colleagues (e.g., Cross & Paris, 1988; Paris, Lipson, & Wixson, 1983) have highlighted three types of strategic knowledge related to reading: declarative, procedural, and conditional knowledge. Declarative knowledge refers to the knowledge students have of different cognitive and metacognitive strategies associated with reading and factors that influence reading. For example, learning disabled students participating in our research discussed "how brainstorming was looking inside your head for ideas you have about the topic." Procedural knowledge refers to students' understanding and ability to perform cognitive and metacognitive strategies. For example, the same learning disabled students demonstrated how they used the headings, pictures, and highlighted words to generate "clues" about the content of the text. Conditional knowledge refers to knowing when and why to select different cognitive and metacognitive strategies. Students told us they could use the interactive learning strategies when they were studying science as well as social studies, the content in which the strategy was taught. Recent research with reading/learning disabled students has focused on teaching strategic knowledge in reading (e.g., Billingsley & Wildman, 1988; Graves, 1986; Palincsar & Brown, 1984; Wong, Wong, Perry, & Sawaktsky, 1986) with the implication that teachers who work with learning disabled students will engage in such cognitively oriented instruction.

This interactive model for text comprehension and content learning assumes that both content and strategic knowledge should be taught. When teachers' instructional goals focus on students acquiring content knowledge and concepts through reading, then instructional emphasis is appropriately placed on content knowledge and the use of interactive teaching strategies. When teachers' instructional goals are directed toward having students acquire strategic knowledge within content learning, then the emphasis is appropriately placed on strategic knowledge and the use of interactive learning strategies within content materials. Different but related teaching methodologies characterize interactive teaching and interactive learning strategies.

Interactive Teaching Strategies

Interactive teaching strategies employ interactive discussions and content-enhancing activities to facilitate students' construction of content knowledge and text comprehension. In our research we have incorporated both the use of semantic feature analysis (SFA) (Anders & Bos, 1986; Johnson & Pearson, 1984) and semantic mapping (SM) (Pearson & Johnson, 1978). While semantic feature analysis uses a relationship chart or matrix as the key instructional tool (Figure 6.1), semantic mapping uses a relationship map or web (Figure 6.2).

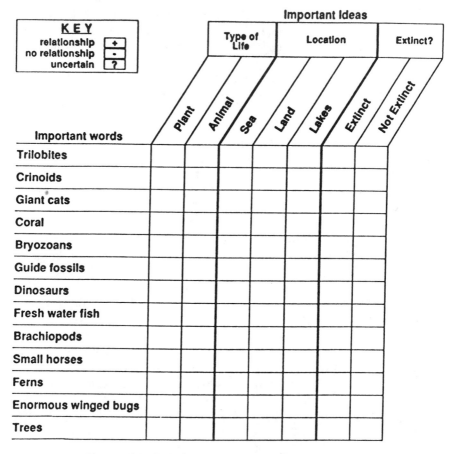

FIGURE 6.1. Relationship chart for chapter on fossils.

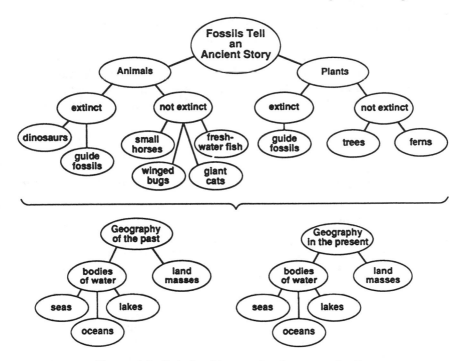

FIGURE 6.2. Relationship map for chapter on fossils.

Conducting a Content Analysis

To use interactive teaching strategies teachers first complete a content analysis on the chapter or unit being studied (Frayer, Frederick, & Klausmeier, 1969). The content analysis provides an opportunity for teachers to think about the concepts associated with the unit to be taught. To assist in this process the text is reviewed with attention given to the textual cues (e.g., titles, headings, subheadings, highlighted words, margin notes). Potential key concepts and supporting concepts are selected and listed. By examining the list and asking oneself what seems to be the all-inclusive idea, the superordinate concept (topic of the chapter) is determined. The superordinate concept then beomes the name for the relationship chart or map (Figures 6.1 and 6.2). Next, the teacher organizes the concepts into categories to determine the coordinate level concepts. These categories may be based on a variety of criteria such as steps in a process or characteristics, functions, or examples of the main concept. The subordinate concepts are also specified, and the concepts arranged onto a chart or map. This process assists the teacher in determining which ideas are relevant to an overall understanding of the content and which are isolated details that can be deleted. It also highlights ideas not in the text that may need to be added instructionally to facilitate comprehension and learning.

In the case of a relationship chart (Figure 6.1), an open-ended matrix is created to be used as a tool for predicting and justifying the relationships among the coordinate and subordinate concepts. In the case of the map (Figure 6.2), the ideas are presented as a list of concepts to be discussed and arranged onto a map. The discussion allows students to add relevant terms and requires students to predict and justify meaning of the conceptual vocabulary.

Employing Interactive Teaching Strategies

Interactive teaching strategies (Bos & Anders, 1990a; 1990b) engage the students and the teacher in mediated discussions that entail the following:

Activating prior knowledge
Utilizing cooperative knowledge sharing
Tying new knowledge to old knowledge
Predicting and justifying meanings and relationships among concepts
Confirming and integrating understanding
Learning concepts in relation to content contexts

Using the relationship chart or map, the teacher and students activate their prior knowledge concerning the superordinate concept and add related ideas to the map or chart. They also, on the basis of prior knowledge, discuss and predict meanings of the concepts and relationships among the various ideas. Students are encouraged to justify their predictions. Before reading and using the map or chart as a guide, students set purposes for reading. During reading, students are encouraged to confirm or disconfirm the predictions made on the map or chart and clarify their understanding of the key concepts. After reading, the teacher and students again discuss the map and chart to integrate prior knowledge and predictions with information gained from text. Often, students will make changes to correct the map or chart and will make new predictions that go beyond the text. The map and chart serve as study tools since they represent the major concepts highlighted in the chapter and their relationships. They also serve as blueprints for writing essays concerning the unit.

Interactive Learning Strategies

Interactive learning strategies are employed when the goal of instruction involves the acquisition of strategic knowledge in relation to text comprehension and content learning. The teaching methodology is based on cognitive and metacognitive strategy instruction (see Paris, Wasik, & Van der Westhuizen, 1988, for a recent review) and Vygotskian notions of teaching and learning (1978). Teaching of strategic knowledge is couched within content learning, thereby establishing inherent purposes for learning the strategic knowledge.

Completing a Content Analysis

When using interactive learning strategies, it is important to complete a content analysis. As with the interactive teaching strategies, the content analysis provides the teacher with a framework for structuring the content knowledge and allows the teacher to serve as an informed mediator during instruction. Whereas with interactive teaching the relationship chart or map was developed by the teacher, these organization frames are developed by the students as they employ the interactive learning strategies.

Employing Interactive Learning Strategies

Interactive learning strategies are based upon the same theoretical notions as interactive teaching strategies, except that students learn the strategic knowledge needed to cooperatively generate their own chart or map and use it to learn the content (Bos & Reyes, 1989). The steps in the strategies include:

Make a Brainstorm List using what you know about the topic.
Make a Clue List using what the text tells you about the topic.
Make a Relationship Map or Relationship Chart to predict how the concepts are related.
Read to confirm and ingrate your understanding and the relationships.
Review and revise the map or chart.
Use the map or chart to study or write about what you learned.

Using interactive learning strategies, students work in cooperative groups to develop a Brainstorm List based on their prior knowledge about the topic. They activate prior knowledge by encouraging each other to discuss what made them think of different ideas. Students write each idea on a post-it and place it on the Brainstorm List. Second, students survey the text to develop a Clue List of key concepts presented in the text. Again students are encouraged through discussion to justify their selections. Meanings are also discussed and clarified through selected reading. Ideas that are found in the text that have already been listed on the Brainstorm List are simply incorporated into the Clue List by moving the post-its. Third, students organize the concepts from the Clue List and related ideas from the Brainstorm List into a chart or map predicting the relationships among the concepts. Again, predictions and justifications of the relationships are encouraged through discussion. These three steps serve as prereading activities.

During the fourth step, the students read the text to confirm and integrate their understanding of the terms and the relationships among the concepts. In the fifth step, the students work together making changes on the map or chart based on information obtained from the text. For the sixth step, the students use the map or chart as a tool for studying the content information and writing essays.

To teach interactive learning strategies, the teacher models the behaviors and cognitive processes associated with developing a brainstorm,
clue list, and map or chart as well as the using the map or chart to guide
reading, studying, and writing. The teacher also models and encourages
the students to predict, justify, clarify, and confirm their understandings.
Thus, the declarative and procedural knowledge associated with learning
the strategy is emphasized. The teacher also provides feedback concerning
the students' use of the strategy, clarifies ideas related to the content knowledge they are studying, and encourages students to regulate and employ
the strategies flexibly. Thus, conditional knowledge is emphasized.

As students become adept at using the interactive learning strategies, the
role of the teacher moves from that of a "mediator" who provides and
maintains the scaffold to that of a "facilitator" with the students providing
and maintaining the scaffold in cooperative learning groups.

Evidence Toward the Model

After conducting several initial studies employing interactive teaching
strategies to teach American government to high school learning disabled
students (e.g., Bos, Anders, Filip, & Jaffe 1985; Bos, Anders, Filip, &
Jaffe, 1989), we developed a programmatic research agenda to learn more
about this interactive model for text comprehension and content learning.
In planning the research, we conceptualized the model and our research as
dynamic, with change occurring as more is understood about the nature of
student and teacher interactions.

The research agenda was three-staged. During the first stage the goal
was to investigate the effectiveness of the interactive teaching strategies
with researchers serving as the teachers. We assumed that when innovative
practices are tested for effectiveness by researchers who serve as teachers,
the researchers would enter the classroom with the major agenda of up-
holding the integrity of the research design. Thus, they manipulate the
participatory structure, the management system, and the content of the
classroom to facilitate the implementation of the practices under study.
When they assume the role of teacher or instructional leader, the context
of the classroom changes to better match the requirements of the research
and the researcher. Findings from these studies hold implications for practice in that they study instructional practices in controlled environments.

However, critical to the application of systematic intervention research
is the capacity to generalize instructional principles from research to practice. It is naive of both researchers and practitioners to assume that those
interventions investigated under controlled classroom conditions will perform in a similar manner when utilized by classroom teachers (Bos &
Anders, 1989; Duffy, Roehler, & Wesselman, 1985). By the nature of the
job role and responsibilities, researchers and teachers uphold differing

agendas and beliefs concerning the implementation of innovative practices (Richardson, Anders, Tidwell, & Lloyd, 1989). Therefore, the goal of the second stage of this programmatic research was to investigate teacher's use of these interactive teaching strategies.

The third stage of the research focused on the interactive learning strategies with instructional emphasis on strategic knowledge. This orientation provides for the bridge between teaching and learning and between content and strategic knowledge that is necessary if students are to employ effective strategies for content learning and text comprehension.

Across the three stages of research two populations and content areas were studied: upper elementary, bilingual students with reading/learning disabilities studying social studies content, and middle school students with reading/learning disabilities studying science content. Six studies were designed and conducted across the three stages with two studies conducted at each stage.

Interactive Teaching Strategies and Content Knowledge

During the first two stages, the focus was on interactive teaching strategies and emphasized content knowledge. For the four studies conducted during these stages, the research design was the same. Students participated in one of three interactive teaching strategies—semantic mapping, semantic feature analysis, or semantic/syntactic feature analysis—or in a contrast instructional condition—definition instruction. Semantic/syntactic feature analysis (SSFA) (Allen, 1985) was similar to semantic feature analysis in that the students and teachers completed the relationship chart; however, students also completed cloze sentences which required them to use the chart to complete the sentences. The definition instruction (DI) consisted of directly teaching the content-related definitions for the concepts generated from the content analysis using teaching techniques that emphasized high student engagement through oral recitation, the correct and automatic pronunciation of each concept, the memorization of concise content-related definitions, and teacher monitoring and feedback (Engelmann & Carnine, 1982; Pany, Jenkins, & Schreck, 1982).

In the first stage, researchers were trained in the different instructional interventions and they instructed the students. In the second stage, responsibility for the instruction was transferred from the researcher to the teacher. A systematic program of staff development was provided for the participating teachers who were the special education teachers for the participating students (Scanlon, Gallego, & Reyes, 1989).

Instructional Materials

For each study, two or three chapters were selected from either a social studies or science text and analyzed using the content analysis procedures.

The identified concepts and their context-grounded definitions served as the focus of instruction in the four instructional conditions. In the DI condition, the instructional materials consisted of a written list of the concepts and their definitions presented in groups of five concepts. In the SM condition, the concepts were listed and the teacher and students generated a relationship map. In the SFA condition, a relationship chart was constructed for use during instruction. In the SSFA condition, the chart was provided along with cloze-type sentences based on the relationships among the coordinate and subordinate concepts. In the upper elementary, bilingual studies, the instructional materials were prepared in both Spanish and English. Teaching guidelines, scripts, and instructional videotapes were also developed for each instructional condition.

Procedures

In the Stage One studies, the researchers served as teachers. They were trained members of the project team and familiar with the methodology for interactive teaching strategies and definition and direct instruction. They were randomly assigned to instructional groups with each researcher teaching at least two different instructional conditions. In the Stage Two studies, the students' special education teachers served as the teachers and were randomly assigned to instructional conditions. To prepare the teachers to use the different instructional interventions, staff development over a five-week period was provided that included videotaped feedback during practice sessions (Bos & Anders, 1989; Scanlon, Gallego, Reyes, 1989).

During intervention, students were given a prior knowledge test and topic interest inventory. Two to three weeks later, students and the researcher/teacher participated in three 50-minute practice sessions and approximately two weeks later, they participated in three 50-minute experimental sessions. At the first session, students were introduced to the study and engaged in the prereading activity using the specified instructional materials. During the second session, the researcher/teacher and students reviewed their respective instructional materials and read to confirm their predictions and learning. Following reading, students again reviewed their instructional materials and offered changes. In the third session, students again reviewed their materials and then completed 20- to 30-item multiple-choice tests over the content. This test served as a posttest measure of content knowledge. Students also completed the same tests one month after instruction to obtain a long-term learning measure of content knowledge. These tests consisted of two types of items: vocabulary items measuring students' understanding of the key concepts and comprehension items measuring students' understanding of the content and their ability to apply the concepts in novel situations. For the bilingual studies, the researchers/teachers used the students' preferred language for instruction using the second language as support during instruction. Students read the passage and took the multiple-choice tests in the language in which their reading was most proficient.

Results

To measure effectiveness of the interactive teaching strategies across studies, simple effect sizes were generated for each study on the vocabulary and comprehension scores (adjusted for students' scores on the pretests) for posttest and long-term learning by comparing the interactive strategies to the definition instruction. Results indicate that across the four studies, the effect sizes for the interactive teaching strategies in comparison to the definition instruction at short- and long-term learning were substantial (Bos & Anders, 1989). Furthermore, comparisons between researchers (Stage 1) and teachers (Stage 2) indicate that effect sizes were similar.

Interactive Learning Strategies

During Stage Three, we investigated whether the interactive teaching strategies could be successfully modified so that students would employ interactive learning strategies in cooperative learning groups. As in the previous two stages, we studied the use of interactive learning strategies with upper elementary, bilingual learning disabled students and middle school learning disabled students. Intervention lasted five weeks with the students and teachers completing one chapter or chapter section each week. Rather than using a contrast condition, student content learning was compared to a content based pretest on the chapter for the fifth week and to the performance of a normative comparison group of average achieving students from the same schools who read and studied the chapter for the fifth week. Content learning for the fifth week was also measured at long term (one month later).

Results from both studies on the multiple-choice tests indicate that the students gained a significant amount of content knowledge (pretest versus posttest) using these strategies and that they continued to maintain this knowledge one month after instruction (long term measure). In addition, their performance both on the multiple-choice tests and holistic ratings of written recalls (Irwin & Mitchell, 1983) at the end of instruction and one month after instruction resembled the performance of the normative groups (Bos & Reyes, 1989).

To measure strategic knowledge, subsamples of students were given a metacognitive interview approximately one month after completing the intervention. In this interview they were asked to demonstrate and explain the interactive learning strategies, rate and justify their ratings for strategy ease and helpfulness, and discuss applications and adaptations of the strategies. Each interview was audiotaped, transcribed, and rated for the quality of declarative, procedural, and conditional knowledge evident. The rating scale consisted of four quality levels as adapted from the procedures used by Englert and her colleagues (Englert, Raphael, Fear, & Anderson, 1988).

Results from the analyses of the metacognitive interviews indicate that as a group the students' procedural and declarative knowledge was at a level of surface understanding. In other words, they described the characteristics of each of the strategy steps and procedures, and in some instances provided rich, elaborated descriptions of the strategies; however, conditional knowledge was rated as limited. This lower rating was confirmed by reviewing the videotapes of instruction, neither students nor teachers placed much importance on conditional knowledge during instruction.

Conclusions and Implications

A major goal of our work has been to embark upon a line of theory-driven research with learning disabled students. What conclusions can we draw from the series of studies described in this chapter that have investigated the same theory-derived methodology across different contents, different age levels of students, bilingual and monolingual students, different persons serving as teachers, and different emphases with regard to interactive teaching and learning strategies? At the most general level, there is support that this methodology is promising for facilitating learning disabled students' text comprehension and content learning.

Our work dovetails well into the growing body of research that has highlighted the importance of using conceptual frames for teaching content knowledge to disabled readers (e.g., Bulgren, Schumaker, & Deshler, 1988; McCormick, 1989). The instructional principles derived from schema theory and concept development theory including activating background knowledge, highlighting relationships among concepts, and describing concepts in terms of attributes and examples/nonexamples seem well supported by our findings.

Similarly, our research integrates well with the work of those intervention researchers who have employed instructional principles related to the psycholinguistic model of reading and sociocultural theory of cognitive development with learning disabled and low achieving students focusing on expository instructional materials (Palincsar & Brown, 1984; Englert, Raphael, Anderson, Stevens, & Anthony, 1989). Instructional principles from these theories highlight the importance of interactive dialogues and the scaffolding of instruction around content knowledge as well as the cognitive and metacognitive processes associated with strategic knowledge.

In reviewing our program of research and comparing it to other intervention research with learning disabled students, we find two characteristics that provide insights worth further exploration. First, this research assumes a strong interaction between content knowledge and strategic knowledge. The assumption is that students' level of content knowledge will affect how students employ strategic knowledge, and the sophistication of the strategic knowledge will affect how students operate on the content. Success cannot be attributed to either strategic or content knowledge alone (Glaser, 1984). Although this interaction has been demonstrated in the developmental and novice-expert literature, limited research has taken this focus in the field of learning disabilities (Wong & Wong, 1988) or embedded programmatic cognitive strategy instruction in the teaching of content knowledge. In the third stage of our research, which focused on interactive learning strategies, strategic knowledge was closely tied to content knowledge. In the interactive learning strategies, students first focused on their background knowledge for the content and then used this knowledge along with the text information to support their strategic actions. Such coupling of content and strategic knowledge invites students to set purposes for learning that are both strategy and content based.

Second, the interactive teaching and learning strategies incorporated content knowledge as an intrinsic motivation for learning and teaching. Cognitive strategy research has been criticized for neglecting the motivational aspects of intervention particularly as it relates to academic achievement (Schunk, 1989; Wong, 1988; Zajonc, 1980). However, much of this research has focused only on the teaching of strategic knowledge with little consideration for the intrinsic motivation that learning content knowledge and developing expertise in specific content domains may hold for students. Evidence of long-term content learning in our research and that of Mastropieri and Scruggs (1988) should encourage future researchers to study the effects that purposeful content learning can play on achievement motivation and acquisition of strategic knowledge.

Although implications from our research are promising, several cautions need to be considered. First, interactive teaching and facilitating interactive learning is a "different" kind of teaching for many teachers (Duffy & Roehler, 1989). The strategies are dependent on teachers' willingness to interact with students' prior knowledge and to link students' prior experience and interest to the content domain being studied, the strategies are also dependent on the teachers' abilities to explicate the cognitive and metacognitive processes associated with text comprehension and content learning. Ongoing staff development is necessary for adequate implementation of these teaching and learning strategies.

Second, the strategies assume some facility with the content being learned. When the content is outside teachers' expertise, teachers are sometimes overly dependent on the text. This results in a superficial approach to the text and content that may affect students' willingness to enthusiastically engage the text. Third, students, particularly learning disabled and low achieving students, are not accustomed to this sort of instruction. In school, they seem more comfortable with not being challenged to think or to construct meaning in content domains. They initially complain that learning this way is "too much work." Thus, demands on the teacher are increased as students need cajoling and encouraging to try.

Finally, an issue we have come to realize as being a next question to address is who should teach content area interactive instruction so that both content and strategic knowledge can be pervasive and generalized throughout the curriculum and the school? Can it be delivered efficiently and effectively in the content classroom for all students, including and especially mainstreamed LD students, or do LD students need interactive strategy instruction in a resource type environment with support for its application in the content area classroom? Are collaborative methodologies an effective alternative? Whatever the delivery model, attention must be placed on integrating generalization and transfer throughout the learning process.

One idea of which we are certain is: helping heretofore unsuccessful students engage and learn content area concepts is an activity well worth the effort. We look forward to the insights this research and the research presented in this book will contribute to those who are interested in carrying on this work, both as researchers and as teachers.

Acknowledgment. The research described in this chapter was supported in part through the Interactive Teaching Project (G008630125) from the Office of Special Education and Rehabilitative Services, U.S. Department of Education.

References

Allen, A. (1985). *Semantic syntactic feature analysis: A reading writing strategy for ESL learners.* Paper presented at the Southwest Regional meeting of the national Council of Teachers of English, March, Phoenix, Arizona.

Allington, R.C., & McGill-Franzen, A. (1989). School responses to reading failure: Chapter one and special education students in grades 2, 4, & 8. *Elementary School Journal, 89,* 529–542.

Anders, P.L., & Bos, C.S. (1986). Semantic feature analysis: An interactive strategy for vocabulary development and text comprehension. *Journal of Reading, 29,* 610–616.

Anderson, R.C. (1984). Role of the reader's schema in comprehension, learning and memory. In R.C. Anderson, J. Osborn, & R.J. Tierney (Eds.), *Learning to read in American schools: Basal readers and content texts* (pp. 243–258). Hillsdale, NJ: Erlbaum.

Anderson, R.C., & Freebody, P. (1981). Vocabulary knowledge. In J.T. Guthrie (Ed.), *Comprehension and teaching: Research reviews* (pp. 77–117). Newark, DE: International Reading Association.

Anderson, R.C., Reynolds, R.E., Schallert, D.L., & Goetz, E.T. (1977).

Frameworks for comprehending discourse. *American Educational Research Journal, 14*, 367–382.

Baker, L., & Brown, A.L. (1984). Metacognitive skills and reading. In P.D. Pearson (Ed.), *Handbook of reading research* (pp. 353–394). New York: Longman.

Billingsley, B.S., & Wildman, T.H . (1988) . The effects of prereading activities on the comprehension monitoring of learning disabled adolescents. *Learning Disabilities Research, 4*, 36–44.

Bos, C.S., & Anders, P.L. (1989). *The effectiveness of interactive instruction practices on the content area reading comprehension.* Paper presented at the annual meeting of the American Education Research Association, April, San Francisco.

Bos, C.S., & Anders, P.L. (1990a). Toward an interactive model: Teaching text-based concepts to learning disabled students. In H.L. Swanson and B. Keogh (Eds.), *Learning disabilities: Theoretical and research issues* (pp. 247–261). Hillsdale, NJ: Erlbaum.

Bos, C.S. & Anders, P.L. (1990b). Effects of interactive vocabulary instruction on the vocabulary learning and reading comprehension of junior-high learning disabled students. *Learning Disability Quarterly, 13*, 31–42.

Bos, C., Anders, P.L., Filip, D., & Jaffe, L.E. (1985). Semantic feature analysis and long term learning. In J.A. Niles & R.V. Lalik (Eds.), *Issues in literacy: A research perspective* (Thirty-fourth yearbook, pp. 42–46). Rochester, NY: The National Reading Conference.

Bos, C., Anders, P.L., Filip, D., & Jaffe, L.E. (1989). The effects of an interactive instructional strategy for enhancing learning disabled students' reading comprehension and content area learning. *Journal of Learning Disabilities, 22*, 384–390 .

Bos, C.S., & Reyes, E.I. (1989). *Knowledge, use, and control of an interactive cognitive strategy for learning from content area texts.* Paper presented at the annual meeting of the National Reading Conference, December, Austin, Texas.

Bulgren, J., Schumaker, J.B., & Deshler, D.D. (1988). Effectiveness of a concept teaching routine in enhancing the performance of LD students in secondary-level mainstream classes. *Learning Disability Quarterly, 11*, 3–17.

Cross, D.R., & Paris, S.G. (1988). Developmental and instructional analyses of children's metacognition and reading comprehension. *Journal of Educational Psychology, 80*, 131–142.

Duffy, G.G. & Roehler, L.R. (1989). Why strategy instruction is so difficult and what we need to do about it. In C.B. McCormick, G.E. Miller, & M. Pressley (Eds.). *Cognitive research: From basic research to educational applications* (pp. 133–156). New York: Springer-Verlag.

Duffy, G.G., Roehler, L.R., & Wesselman, R. (1985). Disentangling the complexities of instructional effectiveness: A line of research on classroom reading instruction. In J.A. Niles & R.V. Lalik (Eds), *Issues in literacy: A research perspective* (Thirty-fourth yearbook, pp. 244–250). Rochester, NY: National Reading Conference.

Durkin, D. (1978–79). What classroom observations reveal about comprehension instruction. *Reading Research Quarterly, 14*, 481–533.

Engelmann, S., & Carnine, D.W. (1982). *Theory of instruction: Principles and applications.* New York: Irvington.

Englert, C.S., Raphael, T.E., Anderson, L.M., Stevens, D.D., & Anthony, H.M. (1989). *Making writing strategies and self-talk visible: Cognitive strategy instruc-*

tion in writing. Paper presented at the annual meeting of the American Educational Research Association, April, San Francisco.

Englert, C.S. & Raphael, T.E., Fear, K.L., & Anderson, L.M. (1988). Students' metacognitive knowledge about how to write informational texts. *Learning Disability Quarterly*, *11*, 18–46.

Frayer, D.A., Frederick, W.C., & Klausmeier, H.J. (1969). *A schema for testing the level of concept mastery* (Working Paper No. 16). Madison: The University of Wisconsin, Wisconsin Research and Development Center for Cognitive Learning.

Glaser, R. (1984). Education and thinking: The role of knowledge. *American Psychologist*, *39*, 93–104.

Garner, R. (1987). *Metacognition and reading comprehension*. Norwood, NJ: Ablex.

Goodman, K.S. (1984). Unity in reading. In A.C. Purves & O. Niles (Eds.), *Becoming readers in a complex society* (Eighty-third yearbook, pp. 79–114). Chicago: The National Society for the Study of Education.

Graves, A.W. (1986). Effects of direct instruction and metacomprehension training on finding main ideas. *Learning Disabilities Research*, *1*, 90–100.

Irwin, P.A., & Mitchell, J.N. (1983). A procedure for assessing the richness of retellings. *Journal of Reading*, *26*, 391–396.

Johnson, D.D., & Pearson, P.D. (1984). *Teaching reading vocabulary* (2nd ed.). New York: Holt, Rinehart, & Winston.

Klausmeier, H.J. (1984). Conceptual learning and development. In R. Corsini (Ed.), *Encyclopedia of Psychology*, (Vol. 1, pp. 266–269). New York: Wiley.

Klausmeier, J.H., & Sipple, T.S. (1980). *Learning and teaching process concepts: A strategy for testing applications for theory*. New York: Academic Press.

Mastropieri, M.A., & Scruggs, T.E. (1988). Increasing content area learning of learning disabled students: Research implementation. *Learning Disabilities Research*, *4*, 17–25.

McCormick, S. (1989). Effects of previews on more skilled and less skilled readers' comprehension of expository text. *Journal of Reading Behavior*, *21*, 219–240.

Moll, L.C.,& Diaz, R. (1987). Teaching writing as communication: The use of ethnographic findings in classroom practice. In D. Bloome (Ed.), *Literacy and schooling* (pp. 193–221). Norwood, NJ: Ablex.

Naveh-Benjamin, M., McKeatchie, W., Lin, Y., & Tucker, D. (1986). Inferring students' cognitive structures and their development using the "ordered tree technique." *Journal of Educational Psychology*, *78*, 130–140.

Palincsar, A.S., & Brown, A.L. (1984) . Reciprocal teaching of comprehension-fostering and comprehension-monitoring activities. *Cognition and Instruction*, *1*, 117–175.

Pany, D., Jenkins, J.J., & Schreck, J. (1982). Vocabulary instruction: Effects on word knowledge and reading comprehension. *Learning Disability Quarterly*, *5*, 202–215.

Paris, S.G., Lipson, M.Y., & Wixson, K.K. (1983). Becoming a strategic reader. *Contemporary Educational Psychology*, *8*, 293–316.

Paris, S.G., Wasik, B.A., & Van der Westhuizen, G. (1988). Meta-metacognition: A review of research on metacognition and reading. In J. Readence & R.S. Baldwin (Eds.), *Dialogues in literacy research* (Thirty-seventh yearbook, pp. 143–166). Chicago: National Reading Conference.

Pearson, P.D., & Johnson, D.D. (1978). *Teaching reading comprehension.* New York: Holt, Rinehart, & Winston.

Richardson, V., Anders, P.L., Tidwell, D., & Lloyd, C. (1989). *The relationship between teachers' beliefs and practices in reading comprehension instruction.* A paper presented at the National Reading Conference, Austin, Texas.

Richardson, V., Cassanova, U., Placier, M., & Guilfoyle, K. (1988). *School children at-risk.* Bristol, PA: Falmer.

Roth, K.J., Smith, E.L., & Anderson, C.W. (1984). Verbal patterns of teachers: Comprehension instruction in the content areas. In G.G. Duffy, L.R. Roehler, & J. Mason (Eds.), *Comprehension instruction: Perspectives and suggestions* (pp. 281–293). New York: Longman.

Rumelhart, D.E. (1980). Schemata: The building blocks of cognition. In R.J. Spiro, B.C. Bruce, & W.F. Brewer (Eds.), *Theoretical issues in reading comprehension* (pp. 33–58). Hillsdale, NJ: Erlbaum.

Scanlon, D., Gallego, M., & Reyes, E. (1989). *Developing teacher's repertoire: The effectiveness of an interactive staff development model.* Paper presented at the annual meeting of the American Educational Research Association, San Francisco.

Schunk, D.H. (1989). Self-efficacy and cognitive skill learning. In C. Ames & R. Ames (Eds.), *Research on motivation in education: Goals and cognitions* (Vol. 3, pp. 13–44). San Diego: Academic Press.

Snider, V.E., & Tarver, S.G. (1987). The effect of early reading failure on acquisition of knowledge among students with learning disabilities. *Journal of Learning Disabilities, 20,* 351–356.

Vygotsky, L.S. (1978). *Mind in society.* Cambridge, MA: Harvard University Press.

Wong, B.Y.L. (1987). Conceptual and methodological issues in interventions with learning-disabled children and adolescents. In S. Vaughn & C. Bos (Eds.), *Research in learning disabilities: Issues and future directions* (pp. 185–196). San Diego: College-Hill.

Wong, B.Y.L. (1988). An instructional model for intervention research in learning disabilities. *Learning Disabilities Research, 4,* 5–16.

Wong, B.Y.L., & Wong, R. (1988). Cognitive interventions for learning disabilities. In K. Kavale (Ed.), *Learning disabilities: State of the art and practice* (pp. 141–160). Boston: College-Hill Publication, Little, Brown.

Wong, B.Y.L., Wong, R., Perry, N., & Sawaktsky, D. (1986). The efficacy of a self-questioning summarization strategy for use by underachievers and learning disabled adolescents in social studies. *Learning Disabilities Focus, 2,* 20–35.

Zajonc, R.B. (1980). Feeling and thinking: Preferences need no inferences. *American Psychologist, 35,* 151–175.

7
Unraveling the Mysteries of Writing Through Strategy Instruction

CAROL SUE ENGLERT

Mildly handicapped students experience serious difficulties in expository writing. Although researchers have documented the difficulties these students have with the mechanics of writing (Myklebust, 1973; Poplin, Gray, Larsen, Banikoski, & Mehring, 1980), there are more formidable and less visible difficulties in their abilities to construct well-formed prose and in the thinking processes that underlie text composition.

In this chapter, several aspects important in shaping the writing curriculum are examined. First, the writing characteristics and problems of students with writing difficulties are considered. Second, we examine the match between students' writing needs and teachers' instructional practices. Third, we describe an instructional program that was developed to provide a framework for constructing classroom dialogues about writing. Cognitive Strategy Instruction in Writing (CSIW) was formulated based on our research team's best knowledge about the writing problems of students and the instructional needs of teachers.

Writing Problems of Learning Disabled Students

The research literature in expository writing suggests three important areas of concern. First, students' knowledge of the various ways that texts are organized affects writing performance. Second, the literature suggests that students' knowledge of the writing process, and the acquisition of a vocabulary for talking about writing, are related to the quality of their written compositions. Third, writers must internalize the perspective of the reader and perceive themselves to be informants to become successful expository writers.

Text Structure

Texts can be organized in a number of ways, although the more common expository text structures include (a) explanations (i.e., sequence), (b) compare/contrast, (c) descriptions, and (d) enumeration or expert text form (Meyer, 1975; Meyer, Brandt, & Bluth, 1980).

Text structure knowledge acts as a frame for generating, organizing, and editing ideas since each text structure answers a different set of questions and is cued by different key words. For example, explanation text structures answer the questions "What is being explained? What materials are needed? What happens first? second? third? . . . last?" and is cued by key words such as "first, second, then." On the other hand, the comparison contrast text structure answers a different set of questions, such as "What is being compared and contrasted? On what? How are they alike? How are they different?," and is signaled by key words such as "in contrast to, alike, different from." Finally, there is a more abstract and general text structure that contains categories of superordinate and subordinate ideas. For example, superordinate categories such as "what it looks like, where it lives, what it does, what it eats" might be employed for an animal topic; whereas superordinate ideas such as "geography, climate, population, customs" might be used for a social studies topic. This latter type of text structure, referred to as "expert" writing, is instantiated by questions such as "What are the categories related to the topic? What are the details that explain each category?," and key words such as "first, second, then, and finally." Knowledge of these text structures (questions, key words) can help writers brainstorm and generate ideas, organize their ideas into well-formed expository texts, and monitor the completeness and coherence of their texts during editing.

Comparative research suggests that learning disabled students have difficulty with the text structures in expository text, affecting the quality of their compositions (Englert & Thomas, 1987; Englert, Raphael, Anderson, Gregg, & Anthony, 1989). Learning disabled students are less aware of, and less successful, in employing the text structure questions and key words to organize their expository papers.

These difficulties are visibly apparent in students' own expository papers. For example, Heather, a typical fourth-grade performer, was asked to write an explanation, comparison/contrast and expert paper on topics of her own choosing (Englert, Raphael, Anderson, Anthony, Stevens, & Fear, 1989). These papers are shown in Figures 7.1 and 7.2.

An examination of Heather' papers reveals serious difficulties in her knowledge of text structures. Her explanation, shown in Figure 7.1, reveals a lack of understanding of the types of questions and key words (first, second, third, finally) that signal the explanation text structure. She does not clearly identify "What is being explained?" and she does not provide a detailed explanation of the steps her readers would need to follow to locate her home. In fact, Heather not only fails to provide directions to her house, she simply lists literal information related to her home address and phone number. She does seem to realize this is a paper, however, and finishes her paper with a flourishing "The End."

I have two friend. to get to my house 6262 Shreser a road.

my telephone number is 393-6902.

The End

FIGURE 7.1. Heather's explanation on the pretest.

I have a brother (and) two sisters. To day is my Dad Birthday.

My sister is going to babysit a boy. My mom babysits the boy

I hate. My dog and I help Mol with her dogs and rabbit.

FIGURE 7.2. Heather's comparison/contrast pretest.

Heather's comparison/contrast also is poorly organized (see Figure 7.2). Her paper does not contain any comparison/contrast information, and she seems unable to focus on the concepts she has chosen to write about. Her paper rambles, moving jerkily from talking about her brother and two sisters, her dad's birthday, and her sister and mother babysitting a boy. She concludes her paper by suddenly interjecting that she helps someone named Mol(ly) with her dogs and rabbit. Even though Heather could have described how she and her brother or sister are alike and different, or how her mother and sister are different babysitters, or how taking care of rabbits and dogs is similar and different, she entirely omits information that answers these comparison/contrast questions.

Heather's strategy for both her explanation and comparison/contrast seems to be to "mention" ideas rather than explain them. For example, she mentions her street address in her explanation, and she mentions a number of people and events in her comparison/contrast paper, but neither paper provides sufficient detail to enable her readers to understand her topics. Although mentioning is an effective response when the audience already possesses the required information and merely needs to be cued by reference to the topic, this attenuated writing style seriously hampers writers' abilities to communicate with a less knowledgeable and naive audience.

Heather also displays an immature writing strategy typical of many disabled writers. She generates a string of associative ideas related to the initial topic without attention to how she should organize those ideas for her readers. For example, when she mentions that her sister babysits, this idea associatively triggers information about her mother. It appears as though Heather's composition is driven by a concern for "What can I say next?" rather than by a concern for how each idea ties back to her writing goal and purpose (Scardamalia & Bereiter, 1986). This knowledge-telling strategy has been described by Scardamalia and Bereiter (1987) as a process in which writers simply put down their ideas in whatever order they come to mind. Seemingly, these writers perceive their goal as getting their ideas down on paper to finish the task rather than to communicate meaningfully with their audience.

Knowledge and Self-regulation of the Writing Process

In addition to knowledge of text structure, students must acquire an understanding of the writing process and the self-regulatory talk that might direct them in their writing activites. Effective expository writers are not only knowledgeable about the writing process, they have internalized the self-talk related to the regulation of writing performance. Writers talk themselves through the writing process, and even skilled writers can be heard muttering aloud as they begin to direct themselves through a particularly difficult problem (Daiute, 1985; Dyson, 1987). Research suggests that this self-talk relates to several writing subprocesses, such as planning (determining purpose, identifying audience, activating background knowledge), organizing (organizing background knowledge into text structure categories and ordering the categories), drafting (translating plans into text), and editing or revising (monitoring text for the achievement of purpose and text structure plans, checking the meaningfulness of text) (Flower & Hayes, 1981; Hayes & Flower, 1987). The acquisition of this self-talk and the language tools for talking about the writing process is an important aspect of self-regulation (Daiute, 1985; Lemke, 1982; Englert, Raphael, & Anderson, 1989).

That learning disabled students are deficient in their knowledge about writing and writing self-regulation is apparent from several studies. Wong, Wong and Blenkisop (1989) examined eighth-grade learning disabled and nonlearning disabled students' performance on a questionnaire designed to probe their metacognition about the writing process. They reported significant qualitative differences in learning disabled and normally achieving students' knowledge about writing. Whereas, normally achieving students showed an awareness that writing is a purposeful activity involving planning and reflection, learning disabled students tended to give answers that reflected a knowledge-telling strategy in which they told their ideas in whatever order the ideas came to mind. Rather than focus on higher-order cognitive processes in writing such as idea generation, planning, organization, writing, and revising, learning disabled students concerned themselves with the lower-order cognitive processes of spelling, punctuation, sentence formation, and neatness. In comparison to normally achieving students, they were less articulate in describing the writing process and their own cognitive and metacognitive processes.

Englert, Raphael, and Anderson (Englert, Raphael, Fear & Anderson, 1988; Englert, Raphael, & Anderson, 1989) examined learning disabled students' and nonlearning disabled students' talk about writing in an interview format. They found that LD students were less aware than normally achieving students of writing strategies (e.g., planning, generating, organizing, editing, and revising), and lacked awareness of how to control and regulate the writing process. Learning disabled students resorted to the use of external cues (e.g., teacher, length of paper, mechanical features) to help them direct, monitor, and regulate the writing process. Although the results strongly suggested that LD students' talk about writing was inferior to nomally achieving students, the quality of students' dialogue was most apparent in the actual interview transcripts. For example, Emily, a fifth-grade LD student, was typical of most LD students. In the interview, she was asked to give advice to hypothetical children (named Sally, Pamela, Mary) with writing problems. Her responses to these questions and the interviewers' prompts are shown below. They reflect her difficulties in naming specific strategies (other than the nonspecific act of thinking), and her dependence on other agents or cues (e.g., teacher, friends, paper length, mechanics) to direct and regulate the writing process.

I: Sally was asked by her teacher to write a report about anything she wanted. But after the teacher gave the directions, Sally just sat there. She didn't know what to write, or how to begin. What advice can you give her?

E: You can indent it. And then write it. Take a pencil and start writing what you want to write.

I: And how would she come up with those ideas that she would write about?

E: By thinking.

I: What kinds of things should she think about?

E: Playing with her friends at lunchtime.

I: Why do you think that would be an important topic to think about?

E: Because she would want to have some friends to play with.

I: Is there anything else that Sally can do to help her find ideas for her paper?

E: By asking the teacher?

I: How would she ask the teacher?

E: I need some help on my work.

I: Is there any other way she can get help?

E: Yeah, by asking someone else, like one of her friends.

I: Well, Sally's teacher has asked her to write a report on a wild animal . . . . Since we know that the report is about animals, we can help Sally plan and write her report! Sally is really excited that you are going to help her. Can you tell Sally the steps she can follow in writing her report? What can she do first? second? third?

E: Follow the directions from the teacher. Ask somebody to help her. Think about writing the story about animals or something. First I would write about animals. Second, I would probably write about the people in the United States.

I: What kinds of things would you do first?

E: I'm going to talk about this dog.

I: (Slightly later in the interview after asking Emily to brainstorm ideas and order the cards in sequence): How will Sally know when her paper is finished?

E: If she goes to the bottom of the page and shows the teacher and see if she is all done.

I: What can Sally do when she is finished writing her ideas?

E: Draw a picture about it.

I: Do you think Sally might try putting her ideas on cards like we did?

E: Yes.

I: Why don't you tell her in your own words, how she might use cards like we did to write a report?

E: Write her sentence on a piece of paper.

I: After she is finished writing the sentence, what can she do?

E: She can read them and show the teacher what she did.

Emily's talk suggests little awareness of the writing process, the strategies for performing the process, or insight into the self-regulating dialogue that directs the writing process. Emily is largely teacher-dependent, relying solely on teacher directives or feedback to write. She lacks the inner dialogue, vocabulary, and writing labels that might prompt her to engage in specific cognitive activities and self-regulatory functions. She shows little awareness that writing involves subprocesses of planning, organizing, drafting, editing, and revising, and that writers write for meaningful purposes and audiences. In fact, Emily's talk suggests that writing is a one-step process. She believes that if writing involves more than one step, it must involve the writing of two separate papers. Emily is unable to monitor her own paper's completion and, similar to other LD students in the study, relies upon mechanical or external criteria to direct and monitor the writing process, such as page length (if she goes to the bottom of the page), teacher (show the teacher what she did), procedures (follow the directions of the teacher), or extraneous finishing routines (she can draw a picture about it). Like the students described by Wong, et al. (1989), Emily shows limited assumptions about writing, with a heavy focus upon procedures or mechanics rather than internal cognitive and metacognitive processes to control and regulate the writing process.

Writers' Sensitivity to Audience

Finally, writers must internalize the perspective of the reader. Writers who are successful in expository writing perceive themselves to be informants who are writing for naive audiences. They are clear about the purposes for which they are writing and seek to engage the reader through a variety of tricks (e.g., questions, personal examples, statement of purpose, etc.). Their sensitivity and concern for their audience is apparent in their skill in reading and rereading their texts with the voice and thoughts of the reader in their minds. They are successful in identifying the ambiguities and information gaps in their own texts, and in predicting the obstacles to their readers' comprehension. In essence, effective writers can distance themselves from their own texts in assuming the perspective of the reader in planning, drafting, and evaluating their texts. Nevertheless, these successful writers still maintain ownership and their voice in the writing process to the extent their own personality and wit are present in their papers.

Learning disabled writers are less sensitive to the needs of their audience and less successful in projecting their own personality and author's voice compared to normally achieving students (Englert, Raphael, Anderson, Anthony et al., 1989). That is, their writing does not convey a purpose for writing, and they lack insight into the needs and questions of their audience. For example, when Mary, a fourth-grade LD student, was asked to write an explanation she wrote, "Now (you) know how to play Sorry. Do you want to know how to play Sorry if you want to know" Mary's text provides little information to her readers. Her purpose is unclear, she does not seek to engage her readers other than through the use of the "you" pronominal, and she is unable to identify the ambiguities and information gaps in her own text that are obstacles to her readers' comprehension. Mary has not internalized the perspective of her readers in planning, drafting, monitoring and evaluating her text.

Summary

In summary, the results of studies suggest that LD writers are seriously deficient in their knowledge about text structures, self-talk related to the regulation of the writing process, and their ability to assume their readers' perspective in directing and monitoring their written texts. These results suggest that LD writers need instruction that (a) promotes awareness and mastery of the text structures that underlie expository texts, (b) immerses students in the subprocesses of writing (e.g., planning, organizing, drafting, editing, and revising) with opportunities for them to hear the self-talk and see the strategies of skilled writers, and (c) promotes the internalization of their readers' perspective.

Problems in Current Practice

Although the literature provides direction for the design of the writing curriculum and instruction, writing instruction in special education is often ill-matched for the writing needs of students with learning disabilities. Isaacson (1987) suggests that the teaching of written expression suffers from three problems. First, he suggests that educators often give insufficient attention to writing and assume that writing is an outgrowth of oral language and reading development. That is, educators mistakenly assume that writing does not need to be taught, or that it needs to be delayed until oral and reading skills are mastered. Second, writing language instruction often suffers because educators possess an incomplete model of written language that leads them to focus on surface aspects of writing related to the instruction of mechanics rather than account for the entire writing process and the purposeful nature of writing. Finally, writing instruction suffers from the lack of information available to teachers about validated teaching approaches and techniques.

Our preliminary research suggests that special education teachers often possess a limited view of writing and the writing process, as well as their learning disabled students that leads them to employ less effective teaching methods. When our research team interviewed twelve special education teachers, we found that the large majority of teachers emphasized the importance of mechanics in writing instruction, and felt that their LD students did not have the maturity to handle expository writing, or even the processes of writing such as peer editing. In the following comments extracted from one interview with a special education teacher, we see the assumption that writing mechanics must be mastered before students can advance to higher order writing skills, and that upper-elementary LD writers are not ready for peer editing or for expository writing. The focus of her comments on teacher-selected writing topics, and the emphasis on student copying of modeled forms suggests a more passive view of LD writers and learning.

I: Have you attended any inservices on writing this year or last year which influenced the way you now teach writing?

T: Last year I had an inservice on process writing and that's where I was coming from mainly with what I had learned last year, although we didn't do the peer conferencing and the teacher conferencing. My students aren't up to that type of format. They get silly or they really don't understand what's going on so I just keep it pretty much as a total class. I'd give them something to begin with, an idea, and they had to write on that idea.

I: What specific skills in writing do you think your students should learn before they leave your room?

T: Punctuation, capitalization mainly, at least the first letter in every sentence and then for them to understand when you use a question mark and a period. Many of them don't understand that. By the time they finish, they do understand to capitalize the first letter in your sentence and when to use the question mark or period. Then, making sure that they . . . use a full thought for a sentence. I think those are about the three things, the only things I can really hit on in the fourth or fifth grade if they haven't had it too much by this time.

I: Do your students do any informational writing, such as reports?

T: Nothing like that. We read informational things and discuss it as a whole and there might be some questions I've written up at the end and put on the board and we do that together as a whole group. But as far as anything on their own, they haven't done that.

I: What kind of instruction do you think good writers benefit from the most?

T: Oh, I'm sure the demonstration. Not so much lectures from a teacher. Well, you'd have to lecture a little bit as you demonstrate but then getting them up and hands on type of situations, too. You might write a paragraph or think of something to show, I'm thinking right now of paragraphs and sentence structure, to write a good sentence or a good paragraph. Then you might have them, now they would write it down on paper. Then I'll get you up here to write it on the board and compare and contrast that way. Lecturing, with a lot of hands on type of things to see exactly what's what you want. But then I also sometimes just tell them just go ahead and do whatever you want. There's no guidance; nothing, and many of them get frustrated.

This interview suggests a possible mismatch between LD writers' needs and the special education writing curriculum. Although the performance data suggests that LD writers need instruction that focuses on expository writing and the development of students' cognitive and metacognitive processes, special education teachers tend to emphasize mechanics and teacher control of writing topics and tasks. Unfortunately, the absence of an instructional emphasis on modeling self-talk and self-regulation and the failure to provide students with greater insight into the cognitive processes and strategies that underlie writing is likely to perpetuate their learning difficulties.

CSIW Curriculum

Cognitive Strategy Instruction in Writing (CSIW) was a curriculum that was designed to support both LD students and teachers in arriving at a better understanding of all facets of the writing process. There were two important premises that undergirded the development of the CSIW curriculum. First, CSIW was intended to support teachers in teaching the entire writing process, including the cognitive and metacognitive strategies for planning, organizing, drafting, editing, and revising. Second, CSIW was designed to make the expository text structures visible to students and assist them in their planning, organizing, drafting, editing, and revising activities.

To accomplish these goals, the CSIW curriculum provided students with strategies corresponding to each facet of the writing process, as well as organizational frameworks that were intended to guide students as they produced explanations, comparison/contrast, and expert papers. The strategies in the program are cued by the mnemonic "POWER," which stands for Plan, Organize, Write, Edit/Editor, and Revise.

Figure 7.3 outlines the cognitive strategies that are taught in CSIW for the planning, organizing, writing, editing, and revising subprocesses. For planning, students consider their audience, purpose, and activate their background knowledge. For organizing, students categorize their ideas by grouping them into superordinate or subordinate ideas, and then ordering their ideas in the order in which they would appear in their papers. They

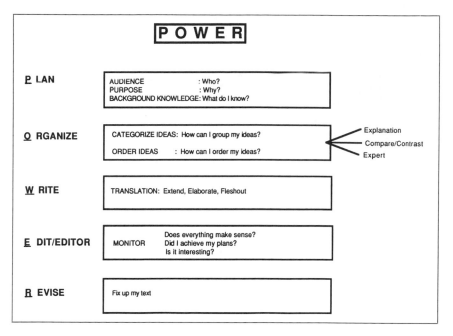

FIGURE 7.3. Strategies in CSIW.

also consider which text structure might be used to organize and order their ideas (e.g., explanation, compare/contrast, expert). To write their first drafts, students translate and extend their planned ideas as they generate text, with careful attention to the information and interest needs of their audience. During editing, students both self-edit (Edit) and peer edit (Editor) text, as they consider whether the paper makes sense to themselves and their audience, monitor their text to ensure that text structure plans and questions had been accomplished, consider the interestingness of their paper to their audience, and make plans to revise their text. Finally, students revise their text by reviewing both their own and their editor's suggestions for their papers (e.g., edit and editor think-sheets), and implementing suggestions.

Think-sheets in the Writing Curriculum

The strategies listed in Figure 7.3 are those that skilled writers employ (Flower & Hayes, 1981; Bruce, Collins, Rubin, & Gentner, 1982). However, the strategies of skilled writers are very complex, and LD students need a temporary support to employ them successfully. This support must not only make the strategies visible to students, but guide both teachers and students in the self-talk and vocabulary related to writing to make tacit knowledge about strategies and procedures more accessible.

```
                                      PLAN

        Name _____     Date _____

                      TOPIC: _____


WHO:   Who am I writing for?

       _____

       _____


WHY:   Why am I writing this?

       _____

       _____
```

FIGURE 7.4. Plan think-sheet. From Englert & Raphael, 1989. © Jai Press. Reprinted with permission.

To provide this temporary support, the CSIW curriculum uses strategy think-sheets. Think-sheets serve to activate writing strategies that LD students do not normally employ and foster metacognition by making cognitive processes more overt. Furthermore, think-sheets provide a basis for teachers to lead classroom dialogues about writing strategies, and give both teachers and students labels for writing actions to make strategies and procedures more visible and, therefore, attainable.

Each think-sheet in CSIW corresponds to a particular subprocess in writing, such as Plan, Organize, Write, Edit/Editor, and Revise. Each is also color-coded to cue students to where they are in the general writing process and remind them of the specific strategies appropriate to each subprocess. In the following sections, the learning and strategies for each subprocess are described in greater detail.

Plan

The *Plan* think-sheet cues students to consider their writing purpose or goals, their intended audience, and their background knowledge related to their selected topic by having them answer the questions "Who am I writing for?" (audience), "Why am I writing this?" (purpose), "What do I know?" (background knowledge), and "How can I group my ideas?" (organization of background knowledge). Figure 7.4 shows the think-sheet

Name _____

WHAT: What do I know?   (Brainstorm)

1.   _____
2.   _____
3.   _____
4.   _____
5.   _____
6.   _____
7.   _____
8.   _____

HOW: How can I group my ideas?

FIGURE 7.4. *continued*

used to guide students in planning their papers for an explanation text structure.

In modeling planning strategies, teachers model several writing strategies. Teachers can begin by modeling how to choose a topic, including such writing actions as struggling with the topic, brainstorming topics, selecting and dropping topics, and considering reasons why particular topics are good topics (e.g., I know something about this topic; I don't know very much about this topic; This topic would be interesting to my readers). For example, Mary Jones, a teacher of fourth and fifth grade students, had her LD students discuss their topics and explain why they had selected particular topics.

T: Who has picked a writing topic?
S1:   I don't have a topic.

T: Well, let's listen to other students. Maybe someone else's idea will help you. Who has picked a topic?

S2: I picked shopping.

T: Why did you pick that?

S2: I do it everyday.

T: What kinds of shopping do you do?

S2: All kinds—grocery, clothing, shoes. Every kind!

T: Good! You're an expert at it. You know a lot about different kinds of shopping and you do it often.

S3: I'm writing about medieval knights.

T: How do you know a lot about that topic?

S3: I read a lot about knights.

T: So we got our information in different places. S3, you got your information from books. S2, you got your information from doing it. S1, do you know what you are writing about?

S1: Computers!

T: Why did you choose that?

S1: I know a lot about it.

T: How do you know about it?

S1: I read a lot about them.

In this example, Mary Jones reinforces the notion that all students can be experts about a topic, an important assumption for the development of expository writing ability. Furthermore, she communicates the sources of information that students can use to become experts in their topics as she reviews why they have chosen particular topics. Not surprisingly, the student who did not originally have a topic rapidly learns from the ideas of his peers and easily provides both a topic and a reason for selecting his topic when Mary returns to him.

In modeling "Who am I writing for?" and "Why am I writing this?" teachers can talk about the role of audience and purpose in deciding what information to include and how to organize the ideas. They lead students to consider how the information they include in their papers is different when they write for different audiences (e.g., writing for a younger child, peers, parent, principal), and make public their own reasons and purposes for writing, as shown in the following example from the lesson taught by Mary Jones.

T: When I write a report, I have to stop and think. I ask myself, "Am I writing for the parents, children, myself, or the principal?" I have to think who I'm writing for. It makes a difference because I include different kinds of information for different people. I want you to think who you are writing for and write that information on your think-sheet.

S1: I don't know how to spell a word.

T: Remember, this is just part of planning. Is this the finished product? (Students say "no"). Is this going to be graded? (Students say "no"). (Teacher sits down and writes, too. After a few minutes, she continues the lesson). I'm going to share my topic with you. My topic is "how to take care of AJ, my infant son."

The reason I'm writing about this topic is that my husband and I are going out of town and AJ's grandmother is going to take care of him. So my topic is important because she will need to know the steps for taking care of AJ. So my topic is "taking care of AJ." My audience is AJ's grandmother. Who else could be my audience? (surveys group members). The reason I'm writing this is "Why?" My reason for writing this paper is to explain how to take care of AJ. Does anyone want to share why you are writing your papers? (Surveys each member of the group). So most of our papers are for the purpose of informing other people about our topics by explaining how to do something. There are other reasons we could give for writing papers that are not explanations—we can entertain, compare/contrast two things, or tell a story.

After writers choose a topic and audience, writers activate background knowledge and ask themselves, "What do I know?" In modeling brainstorming, teachers talk about the various strategies they use to retrieve and gather information (e.g., "I make a picture in my mind," "I let one idea trigger another idea," "I talk to others to get their ideas," "I look at books," "I imagine the whole scene in my mind and play it again like a camera running in my head"). Questions should be presented to students as they brainstorm ideas, such as "What made you think of that idea?" or "Why did you include that idea?" to help them become more metacognitively aware of the strategies they use to retrieve ideas, and the types of information that are important for the reader to know (Langer, 1981). Particular emphasis is placed on the purposes of brainstorming (e.g., brainstorming helps writers remember all their ideas before they are forgotten, and making notes can help us remember information when we find it in many different places). Thus, teachers emphasize that the purpose of planning is to gather information and make notes, while deemphasizing the importance of using complete sentences, correct punctuation, and spelling. In fact, teachers purposefully model for students how to use phrases rather than sentences, and modify the plan sheet to make it an effective note-taking tool (e.g., writing additional notes or questions in the margins, drawing arrows to show relationships). Procedurally, the most efficient way to model these writing processes is by actually putting the think-sheet(s) on overhead transparencies so that students can see the coordination of thought, self-talk, and the actual writing actions.

To prepare students for the organize step and to help them learn to anticipate categories of superordinate and subordinate ideas, students also group their brainstormed ideas into categories as they consider the planning question "How can I group my ideas?" For explanations, these categories are usually related to materials, setting, and categories related to the steps. For example, a teacher modeling how to play a game developed categories related to "materials," "how to start the game," "how to play the game," and "how to win." Another teacher who was explaining baby-sitting had categories related to "how to feed the baby," "safety steps," "playing with the baby," and "putting the baby to bed." To guide this

process, teachers can model how to consider which ideas might go together
in groups. For example, Mary Jones led her students in this discussion in
the following manner.

T: "I'm wondering which of my ideas might go together? I'm sort of thinking that
    the baby's juice, giving the baby milk, and giving the baby some food might go
    together. What do you think?"
S1: I think they go together. They are all things the baby takes in his mouth.
T: Good thinking! But sometimes AJ puts toys in his mouth. Should we put that
    idea with these others?
S2: No, because juice, milk, and food are all things that he eats. But he can't eat
    toys.
T: So what you are telling me is that some of our ideas go together, but not all of
    our ideas can go together. That's a very important strategy in writing. We stop
    and look back at our brainstormed ideas and ask ourselves, "Do any of my
    ideas go together?" Some of the ideas will go together and make sense, but
    others do not. We call this part of planning "organizing our brainstormed
    ideas." I'm wondering what would happen if we didn't stop and organize our
    brainstormed ideas.
S1: It wouldn't make sense. It would be all jumbled up.
S3: It would be like the story about making pizza you showed us. The steps would
    be out of order and we wouldn't know how to make the pizza.
T: That's right! When we brainstorm our ideas, we put them down in any order
    that we think of them. But that's not how we write our paper because our
    paper would not make sense to someone else. We have to organize our ideas
    and put them in groups so it makes good sense . . . . Once we put our ideas in
    groups, I'm also thinking that I have to label my ideas by thinking of a word or
    phrase that tells what the ideas in the group are all about—what they have in
    common. Can anyone help me think of a word or phrase that tells me what
    'juice, milk, and giving the baby food' are all about?").
S3: Feeding the baby?
T: Excellent! What made you think of that? (Teacher continues the discussion).
    I'm going to write that label in the box so I don't forget. This label can help me
    think of more ideas that have to do with feeding the baby, and later, this label
    can help me write my paper.

In the example above, the teacher explains why it is necessary to organize students' brainstormed ideas. In doing so, she helps students distinguish between the knowledge-telling strategy in which poor writers associatively retrieve ideas (i.e., brainstorming), and the important strategy of
pausing to reflect upon the ideas and organize ideas into related groups.
She also provides them with clear labels for the various writing actions that
take place in planning, and increases the likelihood that students will employ similar strategies in their own writing. She has students explain their
thinking to provide them with more opportunities to rehearse the cognitive
strategies and language for talking about writing.

As teachers identify groups of related ideas, they can circle related ideas
or draw a line through them to show which ideas have already been

grouped. Before students are asked to look for groups of related ideas in their own brainstormed ideas, they can be asked to predict or anticipate the types of categories or groups that might be expected for different topics. For example, taking care of animals might be expected to include the categories "health care," "food," "grooming," "selecting a pet"; whereas the topic "mowing the lawn" might include the categories "materials," "setting," and "steps." When student are asked to identify the categories in their own papers, teachers should have them discuss their decisions by asking them "What groups of related ideas did you find?" "What did you call those ideas?" and "Why did you group those ideas together?"

Throughout the demonstration of planning strategies, teachers need to encourage students to participate by asking children to help them construct a class story, and by intermixing modeling with student implementation of strategies. For example, teachers who have just modeled brainstorming topics might immediately have students brainstorm topics and share both their topics and reasons for selecting particular topics with the rest of the class. Similarly, teachers who have demonstrated how to identify writing audiences (who) and purposes (why) might follow the demonstration with guided practice in which students identify their audiences and purposes and share their decisions with their peers. In this way, teachers publicize and make visible students' own plans, strategies, and decisions, resulting in greater acquisition of writing strategies, as well as the vocabulary and self-talk related to writing.

To foster students' generalization of strategies to other settings, teachers also must talk about the *what*, *how*, *when*, and *why* for each of the planning strategies. That is, teachers need to make explicit *what* good writers do when they plan, *how* to plan, *when* writers use particular planning strategies, and *why* they are important. For example, students might be asked to consider what planning strategies they might use when they respond to a test question or when asked to write a science report, why they would use those strategies, and how they could perform those strategies (with or without think-sheets). This makes students' own strategies visible, encourages the flexible use of strategies, and promotes generalization and the independent application of strategies to new situations.

To make strategy adapatations visible to students, teachers should actually use students' think-sheets on overheads as a basis for leading classroom discussions about strategies. For example, one teacher had a fifth grade student named Carrie who spontaneously began to brainstorm in categories related to "materials," "setting," "steps," "care," and "kinds of fish." Carrie had actually scratched through the brainstorming section and skipped ahead to brainstorm in categories (see Figure 7.5). Her teacher took her plan sheet, put it on an overhead, and talked about the ways that writers can brainstorm ideas in categories, or go back and forth between brainstorming in categories and free association to recall ideas. By making Carrie's strategy visible to all her students, she was encouraging

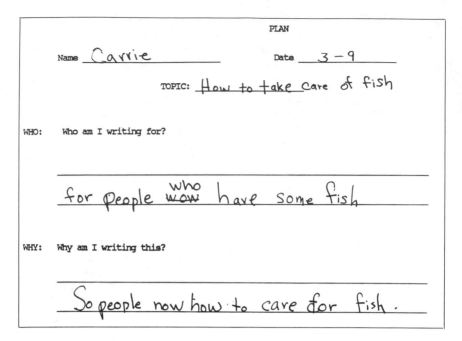

FIGURE 7.5. Carrie's adaptations to plan-think.

generalization, fostering the flexible and thoughtful use of strategies, and making writing strategies accessible to all students.

Organize

In the Organize step, students actually organize their ideas according to the text structure categories. Thus, they consider the text structure questions and key words using a text structure map. The text structure map for an explanation is shown in Figure 7.6. However, the text structure map varies according to the text structure being taught, since each text structure answers a different set of questions. The text structure map for comparison/contrast papers is shown in Figure 7.7.

Text structure maps provide a visual representation of the significant information for each text structure and help students order their ideas as they would appear in their papers. In the Organize step, teachers model decisions related to: considering whether the planned information answers the text structure questions, ordering ideas, and focusing attention on the key words. As with the planning sheet, teachers model how to write notes and questions in the margins of the Organize think-sheet. To discourage copying from the planning to organizing think-sheets, teachers model decisions related to employing phrases or single words to represent an idea,

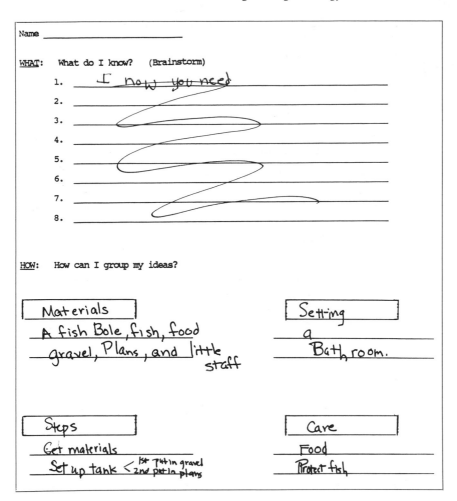

Name _____

WHAT: What do I know?   (Brainstorm)

1. _I now you need_____
2. _____
3. _____
4. _____
5. _____
6. _____
7. _____
8. _____

HOW: How can I group my ideas?

| Materials |
A fish Bole, fish, food
gravel, Plans, and little staff

| Setting |
a
Bathroom.

| Steps |
Get materials
Set up tank < 1st 7utin gravel / 2nd put in plans

| Care |
Food
Protect fish

FIGURE 7.5. *continued*

and using the cues on the Organize think-sheet to generate more ideas or eliminate unnecessary ideas.

Furthermore, teachers need to model the thoughtful use of text structure maps to facilitate the writing process. For example, when Carrie, the student who was writing about fish began to organize her plans, her paper became a jumble of confusing steps related to several different ideas. Her teacher, however, was very sensitive to the problem, and showed her how to use one Organize think-sheet to explain the steps related to "how to care for a fish," and a second Organize think-sheet to explain the steps related to "how to set up the fish tank" (see Figure 7.8). Thoughtful use of think-sheets in response to individual students' needs and problems can not only teach problem-solving strategies, but furthers students' maintenance and adaptation of the strategies.

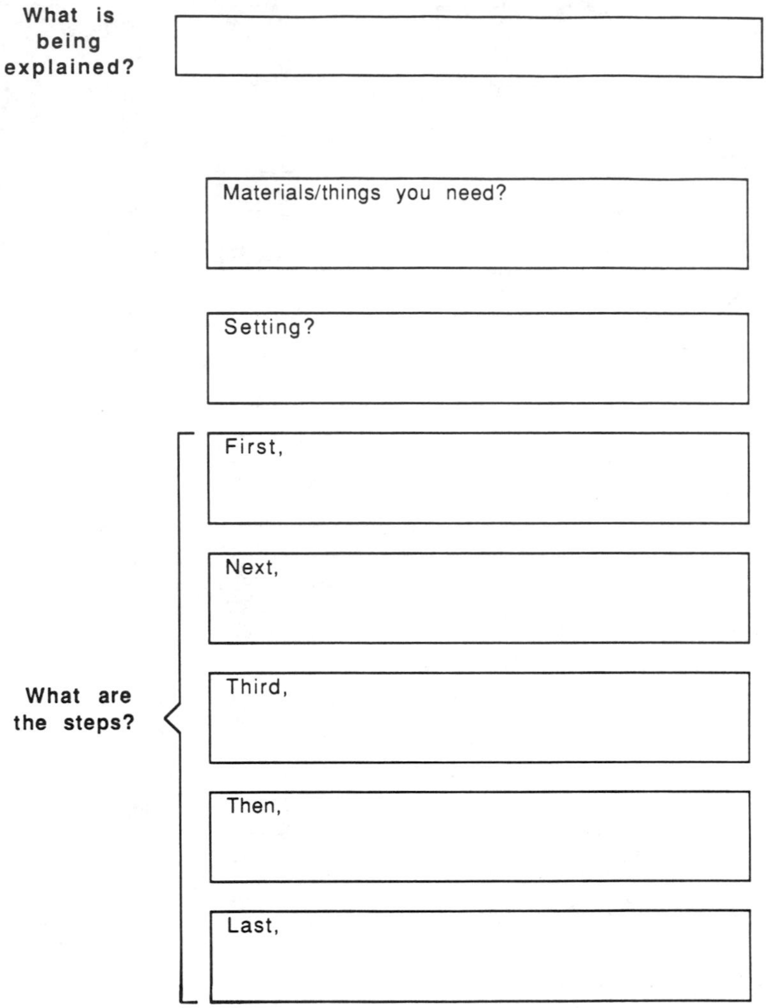

What is
being
explained?

Materials/things you need?

Setting?

First,

Next,

Third,

Then,

Last,

What are
the steps?

FIGURE 7.6. Explanation organize think-sheet. From C.S. Englert, T.E. Raphael, & L.M. Anderson (in press). Cognitive Strategy Instruction in Writing Project. East Lansing, MI: Institute for Research on Teaching. Reprinted with permission.

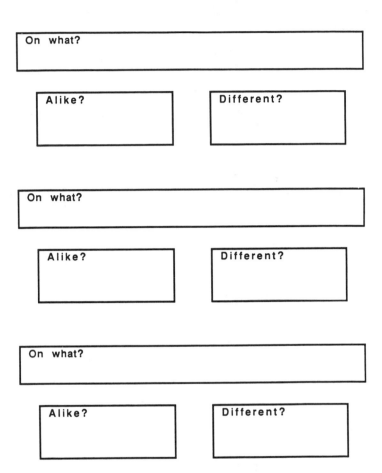

FIGURE 7.7. Compare/contrast organize think-sheet. From Englert & Raphael, 1989. © Jai Press. Reprinted with permission.

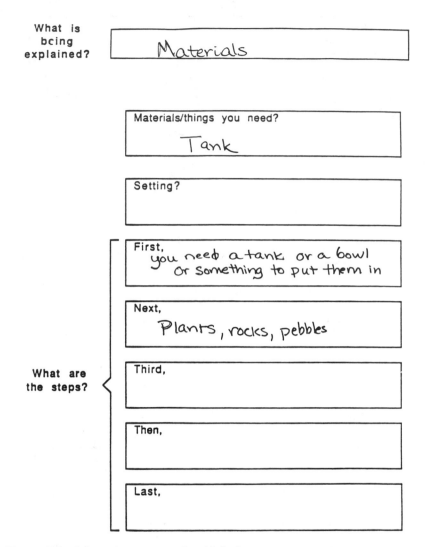

FIGURE 7.8. Adaptations to organize think-sheet.

Write

After planning and organizing their papers, students begin to translate their plans into first drafts using the *Write First Draft* think-sheet. This think-sheet is essentially a lined piece of colored paper. Any color other than white is appropriate to convey to students that this is an initial rather than final draft.

In modeling the drafting process, teachers model how to convey a purpose for writing and how to create an interest in the topic by using dia-

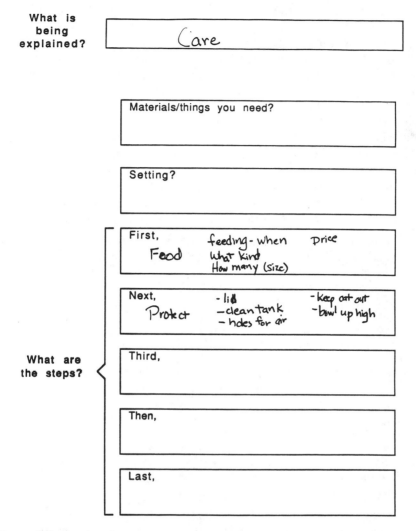

What is being explained?

Care

Materials/things you need?

Setting?

What are the steps?

First, Food   feeding - when   price
what kind
How many (size)

Next, Protect   - lid   - keep cat out
- clean tank   - bowl up high
- holes for air

Third,

Then,

Last,

FIGURE 7.8. *continued*

logue, questions, or problems to enhance readers' interest. Furthermore, in composing the initial part of the first draft, teachers model how to transform the information about purpose from their Organize think-sheets into prose that explicitly conveys a purpose for the paper to the audience. For example, one teacher who was modeling this strategy began her paper by asking a question of her readers, and concluded her paragraph by explicitly stating her purpose (e.g., Have you ever owned a fish? Fish can be very interesting and exciting pets to own. In this paper, I am going to give you step-by-step instructions that will make taking care of a fish simple.).

Another important strategy in drafting is making the text "reader friendly" by communicating the text structure to readers. To do this, teachers model how to transform categories of ideas into text using advance organizers and key words (e.g., "There are many steps to follow when you set up your fish tank. First, you need to buy the materials for your fish tank. You will need a fish tank or bowl, plants, small rocks or pebbles, and objects that the fish can hide in.) Teachers also model how to flesh out tentative ideas with additional details or eliminate unnecessary ideas. For many students, the elimination of unnecessary ideas is particularly difficult (Hillocks, 1986). Throughout the demonstration, teachers also model attention to their audience and monitor their performance by employing self-talk such as "I better tell more about this subject, because my readers probably will not know enough about it," "Will this be clear to my readers?," and "I wonder how I can make this more interesting?" Mary Jones, for example, modeled composing using a think aloud such as the following.

T: I'm thinking that it is important to include how much to feed him. What he should eat. I'd better write, "AJ eats three times a day, morning, noon and night. He eats about one-half a jar of baby food each time. We try to give him some vegetables, meat and fruit at each meal."

T: I'm remembering, too, that I need to tell AJ's grandmother about nap time. I'm thinking of the questions "How long? and When?" I'm going to write those questions in the margins to help me remember those ideas. This is still my first draft, so I can make as many notes to myself as I want.

S1: Bedtime.

T: Oh, you're reminding me that I not only have to talk about nap time, I need to talk about bedtime. I know that I had planned some of these ideas on my Plan and Organize think-sheets, and I'm going to check those ideas right now. But notice how we came up with still other new ideas? This is the exciting thing we can do when we write our first drafts. We can still think of new ideas to put in our drafts and flesh out our plans with additional examples to answer my readers' questions. How can I introduce the idea about putting AJ to bed since I've been talking about naps?

As shown in the example, students can be invited to help teachers introduce ideas or categories, and their answers to the teachers' questions can guide the composing process. Teachers also should model the interruptions to the writing process that occur when writers run out of ideas or words, and how writers restart the composing process when they are stuck. The aim of modeling the drafting process is to model the decisions and changes that writers make as they begin to brush their words. Writers backtrack, hesitate, modify, pause and think, and reread during drafting. These processes are modeled for students by teachers, along with the inner thinking and self-talk that guides writers past these problem-solving points. Obviously, students need to come to realize that the final product at the conclusion of the first draft stage is not a perfect paper, and teachers' talk should provide this insight.

Self-edit Think-sheet For Explanations

EDIT

Name _____   Date _____

Read to Check Your Information. Reread my paper.

What do I like best? (Put a * by the parts I like best)

What parts are not clear? (Put a   ? by unclear parts)

Question Yourself to Check Organization. Did I

Tell what was being explained?	YES	sort of	NO
Tell what things you need?	YES	sort of	NO
Make the steps clear?	YES	sort of	NO
Use keywords (first, second)?	YES	sort of	NO
Make it interesting?	YES	sort of	NO

Plan Revision. (look back)

What parts do I want to change?

1. _____

2. _____

Write two or more questions for my editor.

1. _____

2. _____

FIGURE 7.9. Explanation edit think-sheet. From C.S. Englert, T.E. Raphael, & L.M. Anderson. Cognitive Strategy Instruction in Writing Project. East Lansing, MI: Institute for Research on Teaching. Reprinted with permission.

Edit

During editing, three activities occur: writers reread their drafts and self-edit, peer editors read and edit the authors' drafts, and authors and editors meet to discuss their respective evaluations and plan changes. The *Edit* and *Editor* think-sheets guide students during self-editing and peer editing. The Edit think-sheet for explanations is shown in Figure 7.9.

The Edit and Editor think-sheets are designed to overcome LD writers' inabilities to stand apart from their texts as critics. The first part of the Edit think-sheet has authors reread the first draft from the readers' perspective, asking questions such as "What do I like best?" and "What parts are not clear?" To foster students' interactions with the actual draft, students are asked to put a star or question mark by the parts of the text they like best or the parts that are unclear. The purpose of these questions is to help students monitor for comprehension failure, roleplay and imagine readers' confusions, ask questions about the ideas in the text, and evaluate whether the overall text makes sense. Self-reinforcement ("The part I like best is . . .") and self-monitoring ("The part that is unclear is . . .") also are activated at this point in the writing process. Metacognitive processes related to self-talk and self-regulation are cued by the use of self-questions (e.g., "What do I know?") and self-instructions that require an overt response and interaction directly with students' written drafts (e.g., Put a star by the parts I like best).

In modeling editing, teachers actually reread the text and pause to ask questions about parts that are unclear. Teachers think aloud about the source of the confusion and hypothesize about possible solutions to the problem ("I'm wondering if this is clear. I think I need to tell my readers about how much food they can feed their fish. If they feed their fish too much or too often, they can hurt their fish. I better make a note of that in the margins.") The questions and problems noted by the teacher are actually recorded in the margins of the draft, and students should be invited to ask questions which are then recorded in the margins

The portion of the think-sheet that requires the author to check the text structure also must be modeled by teachers. Rather than simply require students to reread drafts with the text structure questions in mind, the Edit think-sheet is designed to simplify this cognitive routine by asking students to systematically consider each of the text structure questions and rate their success in incorporating that text structure feature in their papers. This reduces the memory load of students by providing them with a finite set of effective strategies to employ. In essence, think-sheets perform some of the cognitive work for students until the time they internalize the strategies and can perform them independently.

To model self-evaluation, teachers read each text structure question and then model how to reread the draft with the question in mind. If the draft contains information germane to the question, the teacher or a student reads the section of the text that contains the information, and then consider how well the text answers the question. If the text absolutely answers the question the teacher or a student circles the "YES"; if the text sort of answers the question but is unclear, the teacher or student circle "sort of"; and if the text absolutely omits the information, the teacher or student circle "NO."

Mary Jones reviewed the strategies associated with editing in the following manner.

T: Okay, we are going to reread our papers and think "How can I make my paper better?" The Edit think-sheet can help us use strategies to make our papers better. First, it cues me to read to check my information. I'm going to reread my paper and think to myself, "What parts do I like best? What parts are not clear?" (She begins to read her paper about *horses* aloud: Today my topic is buying horses. I'm going to tell you about buying horses. First, I'll tell you about the cost. A good price for a horse is between 100 and 200 dollars. Some horses cost into the millions. If you buy from a farmer, it will probably cost less than if you buy a registered horse. There are many breeds of horses you can buy. You can buy race horses, show horses, or ponies. A good horse for a child is a pony. Horses come in many different kinds of colors. You can get one in brown, white, grey, or black. They can be spotted or solid. They don't come in blue, purple, or green. They also don't come in stripes.) The first thing I do after reading my paper is ask myself "What do I like best?"

S1: I like the part about costing millions.

T: Why do you like that part?

S1: Because it is interesting.

T: Oh! That's a good reason for picking the part you like best. I'm going to write that down on my think-sheet. Things that are interesting, funny, or strange (records those words above the part that asks students to star the parts they like). I like the part in my paper about the colors of horses. I'm going to star this part, "They don't come in blue, purple, or green. They also don't come in stripes." I like that part because it is funny. Okay, now I think to myself, "What parts are not clear?" If I forget to do this, I can look at the think-sheet to help me remember the strategies for editing my paper.

T: Okay, I'm going to reread my paper and I'm asking myself, "What parts are not clear?" (She begins to read her paper, "Today my topic is buying horses. I'm going to tell you about buying horses"). I like that part, so far no questions. ("First, I'll tell you about the cost. A good price for a horse is between 100 and 200 dollars. Some horses cost into the millions"). I have a question, Why do they cost a million? What horses cost more? I'd better record these questions in my paper in the margins and put a question mark in the text so I know where to write the answers to these questions. ("If you buy a registered horse, it will cost more"). I have a question, Why will it cost more? What is a registered horse? I'll write those questions in the margin. I don't explain these things very well, so I'll put question marks next to these parts because my readers may not understand these parts very well. ("A good horse for a child is a pony.")

S3: Why?

T: Good question!!!

T: I'll record that question in this part. See how I can get ideas from other people? ("Horses come in many different kinds of colors. You can get one in brown, white, grey, or black. They can be spotted or solid. They don't come in blue, purple, or green. They also don't come in stripes") I have a question here, 'Why can't you get horses in these colors?' . . . One strategy I used as I read my paper is I try to put myself in the place of my reader. I try to imagine that I'm a reader who doesn't know very much about the topic. I think about the questions my reader has, and I mark the places in my paper with question marks where it is unclear. Have I looked for capital letters? Sloppy letters? Periods? (Students say "No.") That's right. I'm looking at my ideas and thinking "What parts do I like best? and "What parts are not clear?" I try to think like my reader.

T: Now I read to check my organization. Did I tell what was being explained?

S: Yes!

T: What tells you what the paper is about?

S: The first part of the paper.

T: Can you read it to us? (Student reads the first two sentences, then Mary asks the students whether they think that she definitely explained what the paper was about, sort of explained, or did not explain what the paper was about. Teacher has students justify their thinking and then repeats that interaction pattern for the remaining text structure questions).

As students are involved in analyzing text, Mary is helping them learn to self-analyze and monitor their writing performance. Furthermore, when students complete the Edit think-sheet, they are already on their way to editing and revising their text since every question mark they have recorded on their draft, as well as every "sort of" and "no" response, can be turned into a question for the editor or made part of the revision plan. In this way, the Edit think-sheet can provide a clear direction to guide students' revision efforts.

Research suggests that the implementation of writing scales and criteria, such as that included in CSIW, has a powerful effect on students' writing performance. Over time, students internalize criteria and bring them to bear in writing and editing new material (Hillocks, 1986). Our own experience suggests that students typically do not show the growth in terms of the changes and revisions they make from first to final draft; however, there is substantial growth from the first draft of one paper to the first draft of another paper. Thus, students appear to internalize the facets of editing and writing related to their audience and text structure that fuels their next drafting efforts.

Editor

The next think-sheet, *Editor*, parallels the *Edit* think-sheet. It guides peer editors to reflect on the paper they were editing, focusing on both content and organization and helping writers plan revisions based on constructive suggestions from their editors. Editors place stars next to their favorite parts, put question marks where they were confused, evaluate the organization of the feature according to the text structure questions, and brainstorm with the author on ways to improve the paper. There are three important benefits of peer editing on the performance of students with learning disabilities.

First, collaboration with peers is useful in making the needs and concept of audience visible and real to authors. When students share their writing, they are confronted with real readers who make them aware of the importance of communicating with an audience, their concerns and needs. Peers serve as monitors for what "works" and what does not, providing important feedback that helps young writers identify problems and communication breakdowns until that time when such criteria and the perspective of the audience is internalized.

Second, as readers themselves of others students' drafts, students begin to roleplay the perspective of readers, and learn to distance themselves from the written text. In essence, they practice the essential reading and monitoring skills they will need to regulate and monitor their own texts, but they do it in the context of monitoring others' texts, a task considerably easier than reading their own.

Third, participation in peer editing activities contributes to the overall success of strategy instruction through two additional means. First, as students talk to others about their writing, they practice the inner dialogue of the writer, with opportunities for peers to monitor, as well as provide feedback and assistance. This offers individual opportunities for students to rehearse the language and writing dialogue modeled by the teacher. Second, peer collaboration provides opportunities for authors and peers to work together in meaningful problem-solving activities. Collaboration requires that students go beyond themselves to resolve problems that a single student might not have been able to solve alone. In the process, students benefit from hearing writing alternatives and strategies proposed by peers and can evaluate whether or not the alternatives would improve their paper. Thus, peer collaboration and the creation of a community of writers and readers furthers writers' cognitive development as they are furnished with opportunities to internalize their audience's perspective, to rehearse the inner dialogue, and to problem-solve alternative responses to writing problems.

Revise

Finally, students consider how to revise their text with the *Revision* think-sheet (see Figure 7.10). The revision think-sheet simply prompts authors to (a) put a checkmark next to the suggestions on the Edit and Editor think-sheets that they will use, (b) consider how to make their paper more interesting, and (c) make their revisions directly on the first draft. At the completion of this stage, students advance to write their final draft. Many teachers, however, elect to serve as copy editor before students write their final drafts to help students monitor their texts for mechanical errors (i.e., spelling, punctuation, etc.). After students produce their final draft, the papers are published in a class book to make writing a public occasion and to create a literacy community of writers and readers.

Teaching Strategies and Goals

Although the think-sheets are the most visible component of the CSIW curriculum, they are merely one small facet of an integrated curriculum that emphasizes teaching and learning strategies for writing. An even more important part of the curriculum that determines its effectiveness involves the instructional and teaching features (for further description of these in-

```
                              REVISE

  Name  _____        Date  _____


  1.   What revision do you plan to make? (Put a  ✓  next to the suggestions
       on the Edit and Editor sheet that you will use.)


  2.   How will you make your paper more interesting?

       _____

       _____

       _____


  3.   Go back to your first paper and make your revisions directly on the paper.


  Revision Symbols

    Type                Symbol              Example
                                                little
    Add Words              ∧            The ∧ girl is my sister.

    Take words out         —            The woman has tried to give

    Change Order           ∿            He had (go to) home
                                                                    Tell
    Add Ideas here         ⌐            The ˅ dog is friendly.      which
                                                                    dog
```

FIGURE 7.10. Revision think-sheet. From C.S. Englert, T.E. Raphael, & L.M. Anderson. Cognitive Strategy Instruction in Writing Project. East Lansing, MI: Institute for Research on Teaching. Reprinted with permission.

structional strategies and teaching methods, see Englert & Raphael, 1989; Englert et al., 1990; Englert et al., 1989; Raphael & Englert, 1990). Briefly, these instructional features pertain to three essential elements: an emphasis on dialogue related to writing, the provision of scaffolded instruction, and a focus on generalization.

Emphasizing the Role of Dialogue in Writing Development

As already stated, effective strategy instruction involves the development of language tools and an inner dialogue for talking to oneself about one's writing and talking to others (Daiute, 1985). Mature writers conduct an inner dialogue about the text and its content, the writing process, and the structure of text as they mutter to themselves when they encounter a complex problem, instruct themselves in how to solve the problem, and self-monitor to determine the outcome (Daiute, 1985; Dyson, 1987). This language is acquired through interactions with a more knowledgeable language user who thinks aloud while initially doing much of the cognitive work (see Vygotsky, 1978).

This literature suggests that good strategy instruction in writing requires that teachers and students engage in social speech and conversation in the context of composing text. As demonstrated in the lessons of Mary Jones, teachers have an important responsibility to model writing strategies as they "think aloud" to make visible the normally invisible cognitive processes related to planning, drafting, and revising text. Thus, teachers actually plan, draft, edit, and revise text in front of students as they think aloud about their own cognitive processes. This ensures that students not only see the writing products produced by adults, but observe the actions and hear the inner dialogue that skilled writers use to direct and monitor writing behavior.

Equally important, students need to participate in this collaborative and public dialogue as they take increasing responsibility for the inner speech and writing actions. Although the sample lesson dialogues presented in this chapter are largely teacher-directed because they illustrate how teachers can introduce writing strategies, this teacher control is faded as students take increasing control of the dialogue and strategies. Students, for example, need to have opportunities to think aloud themselves as they perform the writing subprocesses, with feedback from teachers and other students on their success in using the writing strategies and self-talk, and with on-the-spot assistance and feedback whenever they falter in the use of the strategies or self-talk. Teachers also should foster this transfer of control by asking individual students to direct the rest of the class through an aspect of writing or self-evaluation using the think-sheets as a guide (see Palincsar & Brown, 1984).

Providing Scaffolded Instruction

Second, effective strategy instruction includes a temporary and adjustable support to scaffold the learners' development of new skills and abilities (Tharp & Gallimore, 1988). Good strategy instruction consists of assisted teaching that bridges the gap between the child's actual developmental level and the level required for independent problem solving, a gap that Vygotsky (1978) refers to as the zone of proximal development.

Teachers can scaffold learning in various ways. One way that teachers scaffold performance in writing is by providing graduated prompts or questions that add increasing support until students can perform in the expected manner. For example, teachers can scaffold the performance of students who have difficulty activating background knowledge by asking a series of graduated questions until students successfully retrieve relevant information. Teachers might scaffold performance during editing by coaching and leading the dialogue for a student who fails to monitor his paper for distortions of meaning. While the teacher leads the spoken dialogue and thinks aloud about text confusions, the student might be asked to perform the actions related to editing and detecting violations to text meaning. However, this support is temporary in nature, and the student gradually assumes increasing responsibility for the dialogue related to editing and monitoring text over time. In this manner, teachers act as "cognitive coaches" who provide tips, strategies, dialogue, and cues that "rouse to life" the strategies, self-talk, and processes necessary for independent problem solving (Tharp & Gallimore, 1988).

A second way teachers scaffold learning is through procedural facilitation, a more formal way to help students carry out sophisticated composing strategies (Scardamalia & Bereiter, 1986). In procedural facilitation, students are provided with a series of oral or written prompts that cue them to use or consider specific strategies. However, all students are given the same set of prompts and strategies, and there is less emphasis on the on-line diagnosis of response to writing difficulties. Scardamalia and Bereiter (1983), for example, used procedural facilitation by providing students with a series of written prompts on cuecards to guide them through the editing and revising process. These prompts supplied a structure for thinking and acting that helped students organize and sequence their actions until the cognitive processes were internalized. Similarly, we designed "think-sheets" as a form of procedural facilitation with a set of written prompts to activate writing strategies for planning, organizing, drafting, editing, and revising. Procedural facilitation through the use of think-sheets is intended to help students execute strategies even though they had not entirely mastered the strategies. They serve as a crutch until the time that students can activate and monitor the strategies independently.

Teaching for Generalization

Finally, strategy instruction is based on the assumption that the role of teachers is to put themselves out a job. In other words, good teachers help students become independent and strategic so that the teacher and support materials are no longer needed. There are three ways that teachers using CSIW foster generalization.

First, teachers need to have students continually consider *what* strategies they are learning, *how* to perform those strategies, and *when* the strategies are to be used and *why* they are important. That is, teachers review the strategies that students are learning, and have them consider the multitude of situations in which those strategies may or may not be used (with and without the think-sheets). In addition, teachers continually encourage and model the flexible adaptation of strategies for different subject areas (i.e., reading) or activities (i.e., using organize think-sheet for note-taking). By

Expert Organization Form

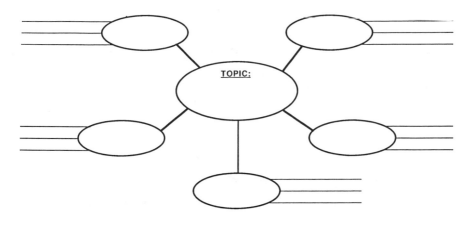

TOPIC:

1 How can I group my ideas into categories?

2. How can I order my ideas?

FIGURE 7.11. Expert organize think-sheet. From Englert & Raphael, 1989. © Jai Press. Reprinted with permission.

modeling and making public the adaptations of strategies for different audiences, purposes, and contexts, teachers encourage generalization and independent strategy use.

Second, teachers need to promote the independent use of strategies by presenting different types of text structures. Although we focused on explanations in this chapter because it is a text structure that makes the informancy role of students apparent, teachers can introduce other text structures to students. For example, the expert text structure is a more functional text structure for students to learn because it contains categories of superordinate and subordinate ideas. The expert Organization think-sheet, shown in Figure 7.11, is similar to other semantic maps and easily can be adapted for reading comprehension tasks. However, other text structures can be taught and introduced to students. One teacher, for example, introduced autobiographical writing by having her LD students brainstorm features of well-written autobiographies. These features then became the basis of the organize and edit/editor think-sheets. Such activities empower students by showing them how they can independently adapt the plan, organize and edit strategies to accommodate different writing purposes and text structure goals.

Third, teachers need to fade out the think-sheets as students become proficient in the writing strategies. Teachers can guide students to do this

---

Grill Cheese

To start to make grill cheese. First you get all of the

materials like cheese and pan and butter and bread. And you

go and get some people like Mom, dad, sister, and brother,

teacher names are Mrs. Gordon and Mr. Gordon. You get some

bread and butter, and cheese.

First, you get the bread and then you put the cheese on the

bread and then you butter one side and then you stick the

buttered side in the pan and then you put the other butter on

the other side that you did not put it on. Flip it and you

may take it out of the pan and then you may get a glass of

milk and you go watch TV and you eat the grill cheese and

drink the milk and you got the best grill cheese.

THE END

FIGURE 7.12. Heather's explanation on the posttest.

by asking them to perform strategies mastered mentally rather than make overt responses on the think-sheets. Teachers also must encourage students to use specific think-sheets on an optional basis to promote the further internalization of strategies.

The Effectiveness of CSIW

The most important consideration in implementing a program is determining its effectiveness. Our research suggests that the LD students of teachers who used CSIW in a year-long intervention showed significant improvements in the organization of their expository texts over control students (Englert, Raphael, Anderson, Anthony et al., 1989), and significant qualitative changes in the cognitive and metacognitive processes in their knowledge about writing (Englert, Raphael, & Anderson, 1989).

To demonstrate the changes in students' writing, Heather's posttest ex-

```
                         Cats and Dogs
    Cats are different in two ways.  Dogs say Bark when they talk

or her a mice.  Cats are the same.  Cats say meow.  And they

both have four legs and they both are good pets.  But some

people hate cats and some people like both.

    Cats have litter box and dogs go outdoors.  But some cats

and dogs are not good to have.  Some dogs are wildcats and

some cats are good to have.  Some dogs are wild.  But they

are good pets to have and good animals.

    The cats eat cat food and milk.  Dogs eat dog food and water.

                            THE

                            END!
```

FIGURE 7.13. Heather's comparison/contrast posttest.

planation and comparison/contrast papers are shown in Figures 7.12 and 7.13. In contrast to her pretest shown at the beginning of the chapter, Heather clearly knows the purposes of the two types of expository text structures. Her explanation answers the questions "What is being explained? What are the materials? and What are the steps?," her comparison/contrast paper answers the questions "What is being compared and contrasted? On what attributes (e.g., sounds they make, how people like them, kinds of pets they make)? and How are they alike and different?" Her papers' organization has greatly improved over the pretests, and with this organization comes the addition of details and increasing length. Her papers have become more informative and purposeful. Interestingly, examination of her pretest and posttest papers revealed that Heather has made many more changes on her posttest papers than pretests. Although there were erasures on both sets, Heather's erasures on her posttest are more substantial and she has even inserted words above the line and in the margins. Clearly, Heather has increasingly gained tools related to monitoring and regulating her performance.

Nevertheless, Heather's papers still suggest that she needs teacher modeling that focuses on organizational strategies and self-talk related to how to project her own author's voice in the paper and increase its interestingness to her audience. Like many other LD children, Heather's writing shows that writing instruction is an ongoing process, requiring continual assessment and attention to the cognitive and metacognitive goals. Furthermore, although Heather's progress is substantial, these results suggest that instruction in cognitive strategies is a lifelong endeavor that cannot be accomplished in a single year, or even confined to a single unit on expository writing taught between September and December, as many teachers do.

Heather also was interviewed about the writing process. In contrast to the preintervention student, Emily, discussed at the beginning of the chapter who lacked awareness of writing strategies for writing; Heather has gained knowledge of the strategies and subprocesses in writing, as indicated by her responses to the interviewers' questions shown below.

I: Now, before she starts writing, can Sally do anything to help her organize her ideas?

H: Like if she is brainstorming and she is all done grouping her ideas and stuff . . .

I: Can you explain more about what she can do to organize her ideas?

H: Well . . . her ideas like they can be mixed up in order . . . and she has to put them in the right order . . . . Okay. If she is writing pancakes, she goes who like your mom and your dad, and your materials like flour, batter, and a bowl and spoon . . . and then with this you do how does she cook it . . .

I: Can you tell Sally the steps she should follow in writing her report?

H: Well, think who you are writing for . . . your mom and your dad and teachers and stuff; and why are you writing this and then she can go so people can get a grade on it; and then on the back it says brainstorming, she can mix up something like say she writes down alligator, she can go an alligator has a long tail . . .

I: So, what are you telling her to do in brainstorming?

H: She writes down the stuff that she really needs. Then she organizes her paper. (How do you do that?) Well, you write down the stuff that you wrote and you group the ideas.

I: Can you tell Sally what kinds of information she can include in her animal report?

H: Alligator has a long tail, big mouth, small feet, big tongue, big teeth . . . And when she groups her ideas she can go like, she can put in how does it look like? (Child spontaneously groups her ideas that have been written on cards and puts them in piles).

I: I see you have put the ideas in groups already for Sally. Are there any other groups you would tell Sally to include?

H: What they eat—they eat fish. Where do they live—they live in the water and sometimes walk on the sand. And when it is really hot, they go swimming in the water.

I: Now, what should I tell Sally to do with these cards with your ideas when I see her?

H: Say, that they were all mixed up, and they she goes "Which one should go first?" And I say, Well, put the ideas in groups—Group A, B, and C. Then she can number the ideas in each group in order. Well, actually, it goes 1, 2, 3, and 4.

I: How will Sally know when her paper is finished?

H: After she is done revising it.

I: After she is done revising it? Is there any other way that she knows she is finished?

H: Well, after people edit it . . .

I: (Later in the interview) Is there anything else when she is finished writing like maybe the first time she writers her paper, is there anything else she should do?

H: Yeah, like she was writing about hot stuff, like pancakes or sausage or something and she can't think of anything and then she can ask somebody, "Well, do you know how to make pancakes?"

The interview suggested that Heather is well on her way to acquiring a language for talking about writing and strategies. In contrast to Emily, she has labels for the subprocesses in writing and shows awareness of the strategies for performing the process. Heather's talk is not teacher-dependent, and reflects a consistent belief that she has the tools and knowledge to make writing decisions. She seems to have acquired the vocabulary and writing labels that would prompt her to engage in specific cognitive activities, and she shows an awareness that writers write for meaningful purposes and audiences. Unlike Emily, she does not generate text associatively, but spontaneously demonstrates how to brainstorm, reflect upon, and organize her ideas. Most interestingly, she also talks about turning to her peers for help, suggesting that she now sees other students as informants, collaborators, and problem-solvers in the writing process.

In summary, these data suggest that CSIW can provide teachers and students with a framework for building a mutual understanding about writing. Through modeling, classroom dialogues, and procedural facilitation, students can become more proficient writers and gain insight into their own cognitive and metacognitive processes. This knowledge can empower LD students to become successful writers. However, the actual curriculum itself is only a small aspect of the instructional program. It is the teacher's insightful modeling and demonstration that activates students to become more proficient informants and strategic problem solvers in the expository writing process.

Acknowledgments. Preparation of this chapter was supported in part by U.S. Department of Education Grant G008530201. The opinions expressed here do not necessarily reflect the position, policy, or endorsement of the U.S. Department of Education.

Thanks are due to Taffy E. Raphael for her comments on an earlier draft, and without whom this research would not have been possible. The help of administrators, teachers and students in East Lansing and Lansing School Districts is most gratefully acknowledged, along with three very special education teachers who taught me a tremendous amount about good writing instruction and special needs students: Louise Gordon, Mary Jenks, and Phyllis Pietka.

References

Bruce, B., Collins, A., Rubin, A.D., & Gentner, D. (1982). Three perspective on writing. *Educational Psychologist, 17*, 131–145.

Daiute, C. (I985). Do writers talk to themselves? In S. Freedman (Ed.), *The acquisition of written language* (pp. 133–159). Norwood NJ: Ablex.

Dyson, A.H. (1987). The value of "Time off task": Young children's spontaneous talk and deliberate text. *Harvard Educational Review, 57*, 396–419.

Englert, C.S., & Raphael, T.E. (1989). Developing successful writers through cognitive strategy instruction. In J.E. Brophy (Ed.), *Advances in research on teaching* (vol. 1, pp. 105–151). CT: JAI Press.

Englert, C.S., Raphael, T.E., & Anderson, L.M. (1989) *Socially-mediated instruction: Improving students' knowledge and talk about writing.* Unpublished manuscript, Michigan State University: Institute for Research on Teaching, East Lansing.

Englert, C.S., Raphael, T.E., Anderson, L.M., Anthony, H.M., Stevens, D.D., & Fear, K.L. (1989). *Making writing strategies and self-talk visible: Cognitive strategy instruction in writing in regular and special education classrooms.* Unpublished manuscript, Michigan State University: Institute for Research on Teaching, East Lansing.

Englert, C.S., Raphael, T.E., Anderson, L.M., Gregg, S.L., & Anthony, H.M. (1989). Exposition: Reading, writing and the metacognitive knowledge of learning disabled students. *Learning Disabilities Research, 5*, 5–24.

Englert, C.S., Raphael, T.E., Fear, K.L., & Anderson, L.M. (1988). Students' metacognitive knowledge about how to write informational texts. *Learning Disability Quarterly, 11*, 18–46.

Englert, C.S., & Thomas, C.C. (1987). Sensitivity to text structure in reading and writing: A comparison of learning disabled and nonhandicapped students. *Learning Disability Quarterly, 10*, 93–105.

Flower, L., & Hayes, J.R. (1981). A cognitive process theory of writing. *College Composition and Communication, 35*, 365–387.

Hayes, J.R., & Flower, L.S. (1987). On the structure of the writing process. *Topics in Language disorders, 7*, 19–30.

Hillocks, G. (1986). *Research on written composition.* Urbana, IL: National Conference on Research in English.

Isaacson, S. (1987). Effective instruction in written language. *Focus on Exceptional Children, 19*(6), 1–12.

Langer, J.A. (1981). From theory to practice: A prereading plan. *Journal of Reading, 25*, 152–156.

Lemke, J.L. (1982). Talking physics. *Physics Education. 17*, 263–267.

Meyer, B.J.F. (1975). *The organization of prose and its effects on memory.* Amersterdam: North-Holland.

Meyer, B.J.F., Brandt, D.H., & Bluth, G.J. (1980). Use of author's textual schema. Key for ninth-graders' comprehension. *Reading Research Quarterly, 16*, 72–103.

Myklebust, H.R. (1973). *Development and disorders of written language. Vol. 2. Studies of normal and exceptional children.* New York: Grune and Stratton.

Palincsar, A.S., & Brown, A.L. (1984). Reciprocal teaching of comprehension-fostering and comprehension-monitoring activities. *Cognition and Instruction*, *1*, 117–175.

Poplin, M.S., Gray, R., Larsen, S., Banikowski, A., & Mehring, T (1980). A comparison of written expression abilities in learning disabled and non-learning disabled students at three grade levels. *Learning Disability Quarterly*, *3*, 46–53.

Poteet, J.A. (1978). *Characteristics of written expression of learning disabled and non-learning disabled elementary school students.* (ERIC Document ED 1590830). Muncie, IN: Ball State University.

Raphael, T.E., Englert, C.S., & Kirschner, B.W. (1986). *The impact of text structure instruction within a process writing orientation on fifth and sixth grade students' comprehension and production of expository text.* Paper presented at the American Educational Research Association, San Francisco.

Raphael, T.E., & Englert, C.S. (1990). Reading and writing: Partners in constructing meaning. *The Reading Teacher*, *43*, 388–400.

Scardamalia, M., & Bereiter, C. (1983). The development of evaluative, diagnostic and remedial capabilities in children's composing. In M. Martlew (Ed.), *The psychology of written language: Developmental and educational perspectives* (pp. 67–95). London: Wiley.

Scardamalia, M., & Bereiter, C. (1986). Written composition. In M. Wittrock (Ed.,), *Handbook of research on teaching* (3rd ed., pp. 778–803). New York: Macmillan.

Scardamalia, M., & Bereiter, C. (1987). Knowledge telling and knowledge transforming in written composition. In S. Rosenberg (Ed.), *Advances in applied psvcholinguistics: Vol. 2. Reading, writing, and language learning* (pp. 142–175). Cambridge: Cambridge University Press.

Tharp, R.G., & Gallimore, R. (1988). *Rousing minds to life: Teaching, learning, and schooling in social context.* New York: Cambridge University Press.

Vygotsky, L. (1978). *Mind in society: The development of higher psychological processes.* M. Cole, V. John-Steiner, S. Scribner, & E. Souberman, Eds. & Trans. Cambridge, MA: Harvard University Press.

Wong, B.Y.L., Wong, R., & Blenkisop, J. (1989). Cognitive and metacognitive aspects of learning-disabled adolescents' composing problems. *Learning Disability Quarterly*, *12*, 300–323.

Commentary
Signposts to Future Directions in Learning Disabilities Intervention Research

Bernice Y.L. Wong

A salient commonality among the five chapters in this section on academic interventions is the use of models. In various forms and ways, each involves a particular model. However, these chapters deal with formulations of models at two different levels/planes. The chapters by Mastropieri and Fulk, Lenz, Bulgren, and Hudson, Bos and Anders, and Englert are concerned with specific models from which they generate their respective programmatic research. Hence, they appear to occupy the same level/plane. In contrast, Groteluschen, Borkowski, and Hales's chapter contains a broader, more general metacognitive model. Relative to the other chapters, it appears to occupy a different, superordinate plane. I shall begin my commentary with Groteluschen et al.'s chapter and use it to lead into my summaries and comments of the other chapters.

On Groteluschen et al.'s Chapter

The model of metacognition proposed by Borkowski and his associates has been described elsewhere (LDQ, etc.). Its raison d'être stems from the problems in strategic transfer in students with learning disabilities. The literature on intervention research with students with LD typically indicates that although they had sufficiently acquired experimenter-designed strategies, they did not consistently transfer learned strategies. For transfer to occur, Borkowski and his associates maintain that students with LD must develop requisite executive control and appropriate attributions of their performance outcomes. The logic of their argument resides in their metacognitive model.

As shown in their diagram, Borkowski et al.'s model of metacognition contains five major components. However, in their present chapter, they chose to focus on three: Specific Strategy Knowledge, Executive Processes, and General Strategy Knowledge (with an emphasis on beliefs about self-control). The component of Specific Strategy Knowledge is readily understandable. Without it, students with LD would be stymied in problem solving, successful learning, and performance. Executive processes are control processes that are deployed in the individual's planful consideration, selection, execution, regulation, and evaluation of strategies. General Strategy Knowledge concerns the individual's awareness that effort is involved in learning strategies, that task-appropriate strategies enhance learning and performance. General Strategy Knowledge has an affective correlate, namely, attributions about the causes of performance success and failure.

Borkowski and his colleagues emphasize the reciprocal influences that General Strategy Knowledge and attributional beliefs have on each other. Specifically, when an individual achieves successful learning through using a particular strategy, his or her sense of self-efficacy becomes enhanced as well as the person's self-esteem and self-confidence in using that strategy. In turn, this enhanced self-efficacy and self-esteem drive the individual to deploy that particular strategy in future occasions. In short, the affective gains increase the likelihood of the individual's future decisions (executive process/control) to use that particular strategy. In these ways, the executive processes and attributional beliefs feed on each other and promote mutual growth.

Borkowski et al.'s metacognitive model is highly relevant to learning disabilities. First and foremost, conceptually and empirically, it provides the best account for the failure to transfer in students with LD. Second, the model underscores the need to instruct students with LD to realize that they must expend effort at learning strategies, and to recognize the value of learning strategies (Paris, Lipson, & Wixson, 1983). Third, the model acknowledges and takes into consideration the research findings on maladaptive attributions in learning disabled students (Pearl, Donahue, & Bryan, 1986). Fourth, the model acknowledges and provides for the lack of self-regulation in students with LD.

In my view, Borkowski et al.'s model of metacognition is conceptually rich and soundly based on research. More important, it is a gold mine for generating basic and instructional research with normally achieving and learning-disabled individuals. It differs from models proposed in the other chapters because essentially it focuses on higher-order mechanisms such as executive processes, various forms of organized knowledge (general and specific), and affective belief systems. It is therefore a broader, more encompassing model. For learners and teachers who are the targeted trainees or subjects in the other models, to achieve consistent transfer, they would most likely need to acquire the kinds of knowledge, executive control, and belief system proposed in Borkowski et al.'s metacognitive model. It is in this sense that I perceive their metacognitive model, relative to the models in the other chapters, to be on a superordinate level.

On Mastropieri and Fulk's Chapter

If one examines the work of Mastropieri and her associates, one would discern two broad stages of development. The first stage of their research focuses on vocabulary and multiple attributes studies in adolescents with learning disabilities. The second stage of their research examines extending mnemonic instruction into content areas of social studies and science.

In their vocabulary studies, Mastropieri and her associates were basically testing the efficacy of mnemonic strategy instruction on enhancing learning and retention of unfamiliar vocabulary in students with LD. These studies unequivocally indicated the superiority of mnemonic strategy instruction over alternate instructional modes. In the attribute studies, Mastropieri and her associates investigated the efficacy of a combined keyword-pegword mnemonic strategy on teaching students with LD information that contained multiple attributes (e.g., hardness levels of minerals). They also tackled interesting questions such as whether students with LD would become confused by cumulative mnemonic images as they receive progressively more information and whether embedding mnemonic instructions in prose passages would enhance learning. The results from the attributes studies replicated those in the vocabulary studies. The impressive consistency of data in both sets of studies in vocabulary and attribute intervention highlight the effectiveness of mnemonic instruction for students with LD in those two areas. From these vocabulary and attribute studies came the evolvement of the researchers' reconstructive elaborations model.

In the second stage of their research, Mastropieri, Scruggs, and their associates dealt with questions of ecological and social validity in extending the use of the keyword mnemonic strategy. Such considerations are inevitable as they continue to research the parameters of its instructional efficacy. Likewise they need to consider the role of the teacher as a partner in the research. Teachers' effective use, attitudes, and evaluations of the mnemonic strategy are important because they provide yardsticks, concomitant to students' enhanced learning, in measuring the efficacy of strategic interventions. In extending mnemonic instruction to content materials, Mastropieri and her associates concerned themselves with necessary modifications of the keyword mnemonic strategy for use with school materials; with producing instructional curricula in which the mnemonic strategy would be embedded; and with training teachers to implement the mnemonic strategy and the modified materials. These efforts resulted in their clear formulations of separate mnemonic strategy instructions: acoustic reconstructions, symbolic reconstructions, and mimetic reconstructions. Acoustic reconstructions are used for content that is completely unfamiliar to the students, symbolic reconstruction for meaningful but abstract materials, and mimetic reconstruction is reserved for information both meaningful and concrete to the students. Mastropieri and their associates found that the acoustic reconstruction condition yielded the best instructional results. Subsequent extensions included a study in which a teacher was trained to produce materials from a science chapter (concepts), and she herself produced the necessary acoustic reconstructions. The results replicated those by Scruggs and Mastropieri in that students given the mnemonic instruction surpassed those in control comparison conditions. Another study included comparing student-generated and experimenter-generated strategies, and studying the effects of longer periods of strategy instruction. The results again replicated those in previous research. An equally important by-product of these studies in content application of mnemonic instruction was the positive reactions to it among both teachers and students with LD.

In sum, the kernel of the research of Mastropieri, Scruggs, and their colleagues is testing systematically and rigorously the efficacy of mnemonic instruction and the parameters of its efficacy. Of import are their results on where it is efficacious and where modifications are necessary to continue its effectiveness (e.g., acoustic reconstructions). The prominence of their work lies in the strength of empirical consistency across their various studies.

On Lenz et al.'s Chapter

At first blush, readers may be a trifle perplexed by the discovery that Lenz et al.'s chapter contains two models instead of one, as indicated in the title. In the absence of sufficient bridging between them, the presentation of two models in one chapter may cause some confusion in readers. Nevertheless, as one understands the assumptions, components, and implementation of the proposed Content Enhancement Model, one realizes the necessity of the parallel model of Good Teacher Thinker.

Essentially, Lenz et al. take a refreshing perspective regarding the information-processing framework that is the prevalent research framework in mainstream psychology by boldly asking how it can be used to generate an effective pedagogy for learning-disabled students. Equally refreshing is their conceptual emphasis on the teacher as the information organizer and instructional agent for the student. In instructional research with learning-disabled students, the focus tends to be exclusively on how to increase strategic repertoires in these students. The teacher's role in inculcating strategies in the most optimal ways is neglected. By focusing on the teacher's role in LD strategic interventions, Lenz et al. restored a badly needed balance.

A pedagogy that is sensitive to the particular information-processing characteristics of learning-disabled students would be one way of translating the information-processing framework into practice. But what should be the meat of this pedagogy? Lenz et al. point to "content." The need to teach content has long been recognized (Wong, 1985), hence their focus on content is justified. Combining an information-processing sensitive pedagogy and content learning results in the Content Enhancement Model.

The core concept of the Content Enhancement Model is the use of particular teaching routines and devices to increase, facilitate, or enrich students' content learning. The teaching routines encompass three major areas: orientation, understanding, and activation. Orientation involves teaching routines that steer students to information to be learned. Understanding involves teaching routines that enable student assimilation of concepts. Activation involves teaching routines that enable students to actively discover, manipulate, recall, and express information. Teaching devices are special devices embedded in the teaching routines. They are designed to further increase/facilitate students' content learning.

The Content Enhancement Model shows that the more teachers engage in using both planned and spontaneous teaching devices within their teaching routines, the more they promote and establish content learning among students. Planned teaching devices are self-explanatory. Spontaneous devices are teaching devices that teachers use in resolving unexpected student learning or behavioral crises. They involve quick, flexible, and appropriate problem-solving skills that presuppose accurate, in-situ diagnosis of a student's learning problem with the content materials. Clearly, spontaneous teaching devices constitute a necessary complement to planned teaching devices in the repertoire of any effective teacher of content.

The Content Enhancement Model places enormous responsibilities on the teacher. The teacher must orchestrate the necessary blend of planned and spontaneous teaching devices in his or her teaching routines so as to maximize effective content instruction. For teachers to be effective selectors and organizers of appropriate content, for them to be effective instructional agents who are aware of and sensitive to the information-processing characteristics of learning-disabled students, and for them to deploy planned and spontaneous teaching devices in a flexible fashion, they must possess certain requisite qualities and training. Central to these is their thinking skills. What kind of a teacher can effectively implement the Content Enhancement Model? The answer lies in what is envisioned by Lenz et al. in their Good Teacher Thinker Model.

The Good Teacher Thinker Model shows the interplay among several factors: teacher's knowledge of subject to be taught, teacher's repertoires of routines in content teaching, behavior management, planning, and strategies. What integrates all these factors is the teacher's thinking processes. Essentially this Good Teacher Thinker Model provides a good balance to Pressley's Good Strategy User Model.

From the above, it can be seen that the Good Teacher Thinker Model is a necessary parallel model to the Content Enhancement Model.

Lenz et al. have outlined interesting avenues for research on the Content Enhancement Model. Other considerations for research may include comparative studies on expert and novice teachers' repertoires of planned devices in teaching; on the responses of expert and novice teachers to simulated learning crises in students; and videotapings of expert teachers' use of spontaneous teaching devices to resolve students' learning and behavioral crises for instructional purposes in inservice training.

Although Lenz et al. aptly suggest that teachers have to hypothesize about the nature of students' information processing in order to tailor instruction, they have not considered how to ascertain the validity of teachers' hypotheses. Checking on whether students are generating appropriate cognitive processes during teacher instruction is an important methodological issue. Unless students generate the kinds of cognitive processes that are targetted by the teacher, appropriate learning cannot be assumed to have occurred. Yet there are difficult problems for teachers and instructional researchers in tracking students' cognitive processing during learning (Winne, 1987).

The Good Teacher Thinker model has important implications for teacher training programs at universities and colleges. For teachers to attend to the information-processing characteristics of students, they must learn about information-processing theories in cognitive psychology. Additionally, they must realize that at the secondary level, content knowledge must be complemented with the need to teach students how to learn (Alley & Deshler, 1979). This means they must learn about the construct of and research in metacognition. Together, these two points imply important additions to teacher training programs, namely, student teachers must acquire a broader knowledge base in cognitive and instructional psychology. It is time for those of us involved in teacher training programs to provide the leadership for making such and other additions in those programs, in order to properly equip student teachers with necessary knowledge and skills for their future roles in schools.

On Bos and Anders' Chapter

Bos and Anders present an interactive model of teaching and learning content, text comprehension, and content-learning strategies. The model has three commendable features: its conceptualization is grounded in related theories of reading and learning; the instructional implementations of the model are guided by relevant theories and empirical data; and the model itself covers both the teachers' and learners' perspectives in that it provides differential operational guidelines for teaching and learning strategies. Clearly, this instructional model has been conceptually well considered.

The authors emphasize the interactive aspect of their model. It highlights students' active constructive processes in text comprehension, and the enhancement in student learning through interactive dialogues with teachers during learning.

Concerning implementations of the model, the authors have carefully detailed instructional principles/implications that shape such implementations. They are drawn from four different theoretical sources: schema theory and the knowledge hypothesis, the psycholinguistic model, concept learning and developmental theory, and the sociocultural theory of learning. Readers may be somewhat overwhelmed by the various sources that generate the instructional principles/implications, and question specifically how they are embodied in the implementations of interactive teaching and learning.

Although the instructional relevance of those four theoretical sources to the interactive model is understandable, Bos and Anders could have used a unifying rationale to explicate why they have been chosen. Moreover, the authors need to highlight and elaborate how the respective instructional principles/implications are embodied in the teaching and learning strategies. The given examples of interactive teaching and learning strategies provide only glimpses of the functional embodiments of those instructional principles/implications. The most clear-cut embodiments of instructional principles ensuing from schema theory and concept development theory are found in the authors' descriptions of their research in validating their model. However, as the interactive model evolves, such functional embodiments of the various instructional principles should become clearer.

In validating the interactive model, Bos and Anders had a three-staged research plan. First, they used researchers to implement interactive teaching strategies, then actual teachers, and finally they concentrated on interactive learning strategies to bridge teaching and learning strategies and promote student use of the strategies. Bos and Anders tested their model with two populations of students and in two school subjects: bilingual (Spanish and English speaking) students with reading/learning disabilities in upper elementary grades studying social studies content, and students with reading/learning disabilities in middle school studying science content. The results of six studies indicated clear support for the interactive model of teaching and learning strategies.

Despite the promising data, Bos and Anders state certain caveats about the use of their model. Of these, the most pertinent ones concern the changes necessary in teaching styles in teachers who want to experiment with the interactive teaching strategies, and the question of how to make such strategic teaching and learning of content merge with the general curricula in school. These are important points, especially the second one which echoes the concern of those who want education in schools to be more dynamic and more focused on thinking (Nickerson, 1988–89).

On Englert's Chapter

In the interesting and detailed account of the instructional program called Cognitive Strategy Instruction in Writing (CSIW), Englert explained its origin, goals, and content (the strategies). Conceptually, it is solidly grounded in current theories of the writing process (Flower & Hayes, 1980;

Scardamalia & Bereiter, 1987), and its components reflect the influence of current thinking on teaching effectiveness (Palincsar & Brown, 1984), cognitive coaching, and student motivation in learning.

There are several important features in the CSIW. The first concerns the pedagogic emphasis on teachers externalizing cognitive and metacognitive processes in the writing process for the benefit of student learning. Specifically, teachers think aloud their thoughts as they proceed to plan, organize their ideas, write, self-check for clarity and writing purposes, and formulate self-questions for subsequent revisions. Teachers also model ways of activating relevant knowledge for writing purposes, grouping and labeling ideas to facilitate writing, and attending to the needs of the audience such as ensuring clarity and being interesting in one's writing.

Second, the CSIW instructional program involves much interactive dialogues between teachers and students, either en masse (whole class or group in resource room) or individually. As shown in the illustrations in Englert's chapter, such interactive dialogues play a pivotal role in student learning. Through skilful dialogues, the teacher elicits from students cognitive and metacognitive processes appropriate and needed for planning, writing and revising. She uses such dialogues to explicate and reinforce the writing strategies in the CSIW program.

Moreover, the CSIW program involves cognitive coaching. Verbally, this is given by the teacher. But it also comes in a nonverbal form, namely, the various think-sheets. These think-sheets fulfill important functions in teaching writings of various genres: they provide structure and serve as prompts.

Conceptually, the CSIW program is well formulated and its nascent data base highly promising. It holds a bright future as a heuristic framework for writing intervention research with learning-disabled students. For it to reach its promising potential however, in future research Englert and her associates may profit from more focus on the following issues: What kinds of effective inservice training can be designed to help teachers of learning disabled students learn to externalize appropriate cognitive and metacognitive processes in writing, and to engage in skilful instructional dialogues with students? What are the conditions that promote student internalization of the writing strategies in CSIW to the point of independent use?

Concluding Comments

The most strikingly consistent aspect of the chapters by Mastropieri and Fulk, Lenz et al., Bos and Anders, and Englert is the emphasis on theory-based intervention. While Mastropieri and Fulk's reconstructive elaborations model has evolved from their initial research data, the others develop their models conceptually. Moreover, there is increasing attention to use theory and prior research to guide the intervention phase of research (see chapters by Lenz et al., Bos & Anders, Englert). The empirical bases in support of the models presented vary because of their different developmental stages. All of them, however, relate comfortably to Borkowski et al.'s model of metacognition.

Altogether what do these five chapters indicate for the learning disabilities field? I think they signal the passing of the era when this field was primarily service oriented. They represent the current aspirations and concerted efforts among us toward making learning disabilities into a scientific discipline. In short, they have clearly marked the future directions of intervention research in learning disabilities: theory-based, rigorous research, and focusing on generalizations of learned skills and strategies!

Acknowledgements. I thank Rod Wong for reading the first draft of this chapter, and Eileen Mallory for word-processing the various drafts.

References

Alley, J., & Deshler, D. (1979). *Teaching the Learning-Drsables Aoolescent: Strategies and Methods.* Denver: Love Publishing Company.

Borkowski, J.G., Estrada, M.T., Milstead, M., & Hale, C.A. (1989). General problem-solving skills: Relations between metacognition and strategic processing. *Learning Disability Quarterly, 12*(1), 57–70.

Flower, L.S., & Hayes, J.R. (1980). The dynamics of composing: Making plans and juggling constraints. In L.W. Gregg & E.R. Steinberg (Eds.), *Cognitive processes in writing* (pp. 31–50). Hillsdale, NJ: Erlbaum.

Nickerson, R.S. (1988-89). On improving thinking through instruction. In R.Z. Rothkopf (Ed.), *Review of Research in Education,* Vol. 15 (pp. 3–57). Washington, D.C.: AERA.

Palincsar, A.S., & Brown, A.L. (1984). Reciprocal teaching of comprehension-fostering and comprehension-monitoring activities. *Cognition and Instruction, 1*(2), 117–175.

Paris, S.G., Lipson, M.Y., & Wixson, K.K. (1983). Becoming a strategic reader. *Contemporary Educational Psychology, 8,* 293–316.

Pearl, R., Donahue, M., & Bryan, T. (1986). Social relationship of learning-disabled children. In J.K. Torgesen & B.Y.L. Wong (Eds.), *Psychological and educational perspectives on learning disabilities* (pp. 193–224). New York: Academic.

Scardamalia, M., & Bereiter, C. (1987). Knowledge telling and knowledge transforming in written composition. In S. Rosenberg (Ed.), *Advances in applied psycholinguistics: Vol. 2. Reading, writing, and language learning* (pp. 142–175). Cambridge: Cambridge University Press.

Winne, P.H. (1987). Students' cognitive processing. In M.J. Dunkin (Ed.), *The international encyclopedia of teaching and teacher education* (pp. 496–509). New York: Pergamon Press.

Wong, B.Y.L. (1985). Skill acquisition in content areas: A topic for consideration regarding learning-disabled adolescents. *Focus in Exceptional Education, 17,* 1–8.

Part III Social and Behavioral Interventions

8
Self-Recording of Attending to Task: Treatment Components and Generalization of Effects

John Wills Lloyd and Timothy J. Landrum

According to special education teachers (Kauffman, Lloyd, & McGee, 1989; Walker & Rankin, 1983) and special educators in the academic community (e.g., Hallahan, Kneedler, & Lloyd, 1983; Kneedler, 1980; Polsgrove, 1979; Rueda, 1981; Rueda, Rutherford, & Howell, 1980), demonstration of self-control is a highly desirable characteristic and teaching atypical learners self-control an important goal of education. Self-control interventions are appealing for many reasons, including the possibility that teaching self-control will (a) increase an interventions's effectiveness (e.g., Kazdin, 1984); (b) save teacher time by decreasing the need for direct teacher intervention (e.g., Rooney & Hallahan, 1988); (c) enhance the maintenance of treatment effects (McLaughlin, 1976); and (d) increase the probability of generalization or transfer of treatment effects (e.g., Neilans & Israel, 1981).

Most models of self-control include several components. The models proposed by Bandura and Perloff (1967), Glynn, Thomas, and Shee (1973), and Kanfer (1970) include (a) self-assessment (observation of one's own behavior), (b) self-evaluation (comparison of one's observations with a standard for behavior), (c) self-recording (noting the results of the observation and evaluation), and (d) self-reinforcement (including both self-determination and self-administration of reinforcement).

Self-recording, which requires self-assessment and self-evaluation, was originally employed as an assessment technique. Clinicians used self-recording to obtain data about their clients' behavior at times the clients were not in the presence of the clinician or about clients' behaviors that were not directly observable (e.g., thoughts or feelings). They taught the clients to observe their own behavior. But it soon became apparent that requiring clients to observe their own behavior had reactive effects—it caused changes in behavior. Since then, the self-recording[1] component in most models has been applied as a treatment procedure because of its reactivity.

Teachers and clinicians concerned with helping people change have taken advantage of the reactive effects of self-recording. There are applications of self-recording in smoking cessation (Abueg, Colletti, & Kopel, 1985; McConnell, Biglan, & Severson, 1984; Singh & Leung, 1988), weight reduction (e.g., Horton, 1981; Israel, Silverman, & Solotar, 1987), depression (e.g., Singer, Irvin, & Hawkins, 1988; Stark, Reynolds, & Kaslow, 1987), diabetes management (Wing, Epstein, Nowalk, & Scott, 1988), and myriad other areas.

In education there are many different applications of self-recording. One of the most extensive literatures about the application of self-recording in education centers on improving attention to task. In this chapter we focus on studies that are of particular concern for educators concerned with the performance of pupils who have difficulties attending to assigned tasks. We have limited our review to studies in which pupils were taught to assess and record their attending behavior. Self-recording has been applied to many other areas of concern as well; see Gardner and Cole (1988), Mace and Kratochwill (1988), Lloyd, Landrum, and Hallahan (in press), and Shapiro (1989) for discussions of some other applications.

In the following section we describe the general characteristics of self-recording interventions designed to improve attention-to-task behavior. In the two subsequent sections we discuss what is known about the components of effective self-recording procedures and the prospects for generalization of the effects of self-recording of attending.

Effectiveness of Self-Recording

Self-recording interventions for attention to task require that participating pupils learn to act as an observer of their own attending behavior. In one of the earliest applications of self-recording, Broden, Hall, and Mitts (1971) taught Liza, an eighth grader in a regular education classroom, to record her own study behavior (looking at the teacher, looking at a pupil who was answering a question, taking notes). A school counselor gave Liza a slip of paper with 30 squares on it and told her

to record her study behavior "when she thought about it" during her history class. . . . Liza was instructed to take the slip to class each day and to record a "+" in the square if she was studying or had been doing so for the last few minutes, and a "−" if she was not studying at the time she thought to record. (p. 193)

---

[1] Some authorities consider the term *self-monitoring* to be more encompassing than *self-recording*; they might argue that the term *self-recording* should be reserved for situations in which, for example, a teacher decides whether a behavior was occurring and signals a learner to record that decision. In contrast, *self-monitoring* would include both assessment and recording of the behavior by the pupil him- or her-self. However, we use the term self-recording rather than self-monitoring in order to discriminate self-recording from the very extensive literature on self-monitoring as that construct is used in personality psychology (e.g., Snyder, 1987).

TABLE 8.1. Basic description of studies.

Authors	Year	Ss	Setting	Question	Dependent variables	Results
Blick & Test	1987	LD BD MR	3 cross categorical resource rooms	Whether self-recording would improve attention to task and whether the cues could be faded successfully	Attention to task	Self-recording resulted in increased on-task behavior; gains were maintained after cues were faded
Broden, Hall, & Mitts	1971	NH	Regular class (history)	Whether self-recording of study behavior would influence attention to task and whether it could be withdrawn effectively	Attention to task (study behavior); teacher attention to S	Clear increases in attention with S-Rec.; addition of self-praise in C phase raised and stabilized effects; self-praise only maintained high levels; maintenance shown over several weeks
Christie, Hiss, & Lozanoff	1984	HA	Regular classroom	Whether self-recording with teacher-controlled signaling would increase attention to task and decrease inappropriate behavior	Attention to task; inattentive behaviors; inappropriate behaviors	Attending increased and disruption declined for 2 of 3 Ss
Glynn & Thomas	1974	NH	Language lessons in classroom	Whether self-recording of attention with more frequent cuing and with directions about variations in the meaning of appropriate behavior would produce effects on attention to task	Attention to task	First s-r had inconsistent effects; s-r with more frequent cues had clearer effects

TABLE 8.1 *Continued*

Authors	Year	Ss	Setting	Question	Dependent variables	Results
Glynn, Thomas, & Shee	1973	NH	Regular classroom	Whether introducing self-recording of attending after periods of teacher-managed behavior control would result in sustained levels of attention to task	Attention to task	Earlier reinf. phases increased attending; self-control maintained these
Hallahan, Lloyd, Kneedler, & Marshall	1982	LD	Self-contained special education class	Whether teacher-assessed or self-assessed self-recording results in greater effects on attention to task and academic performance	Attention to task; productivity (number of problems completed correctly per session)	Self-monitoring with either teacher assessment or self-assessment resulted in immediate increases in on-task behavior; self-assessment better for on task; conditions not different for productivity
Hallahan, Lloyd, Kosiewicz, Kauffman, & Graves	1979	LD	Special education class	Whether self-recording of attending will affect attention to task and academic performance	Attention to task; academic rate (correct words written per minute, correct math problems per minute)	Self-recording increased both percent on task and academic rate; both increases were maintained after fading treatment components
Hallahan, Marshall, & Lloyd	1981	LD	Self-contained special education classroom	Whether self-recording of attention implemented in a group instruction situation would increase attention to task	Attention to task	Attention increased gradually during treatment, reversed, returned to treatment levels, and was maintained during fading

Author	Year		Setting	Question	Dependent measures	Results
Harris	1986	LD	Self-contained class	Whether self-recording of attention or self-recording and self-charting of academic performance will have greater effects on attention to task and academic productivity	Attention to task; productivity (number of spelling words written correctly)	Self-monitoring of both attention and productivity resulted in gains in the two dependent measures
Heins, Lloyd, & Hallahan	1986	LD	Self-contained special class	Whether cued or noncued self-recording of attending will have greater effects on attention to task and academic productivity	Attention to task; rate of arithmetic production	Both cued and noncued self-recording resulted in gains in attention to task and arithmetic productivity; cued S-R superior for attention to task, somewhat better for arithmetic productivity
Kosiewicz	1981	LD	Self-contained special education classroom	Whether teaching self-recording to one pupil in a group would have effects on other pupils' behavior	Attention to task; productivity	Self-recording had negligible and temporary effects on attention and productivity; effects did not transfer across pupils
Lloyd, Bateman, Landrum, & Hallahan	1989	BD, LD	Resource classroom	Whether monitoring attention or productivity had greater effects	Attention to task; rate of answering; achievement test scores	Attention and productivity increased when s-r introduced; neither markedly superior to other
Lloyd, Hallahan, Kosiewicz, & Kneedler (exp. 1)	1982	LD	Self-contained LD class	Whether self-recording or self-recording without the requirement of making a record (self-assessment) would have greater effects on attention to task and academic productivity	Attention to task; academic productivity (movements per minute)	Self-assessment and self-recording resulted in increased on-task behavior and productivity; neither treatment was superior to the other

TABLE 8.1 *Continued*

Authors	Year	Ss	Setting	Question	Dependent variables	Results
Lloyd, Hallahan, Kosiewicz, & Kneedler (exp. 2)	1982	LD	Self-contained LD class	Whether self-recording or self-recording without the requirement of making a record (self-assessment) would have greater effects on attention to task and academic productivity	Attention to task, academic productivity	Self-assessment alone not particularly effective; addition of S-R resulted in gains in attention to task, though not in academic productivity
Lloyd, Wissick, & Kneedler	1988	BD, LD	Regular classroom	Whether self-recording training completed by the special education teacher in the resource room would affect pupil attention in their regular classroom	Attention to task	Clear effects for first subject, equivocal for second
Marshall	1983	LD	Self-contained special education class	Whether teaching pupils to assess behavior accurately would increase students' accuracy in self-recording and the effectiveness of self-recording	Attention to task	Accuracy retraining increased attention to task
McLaughlin	1983	BD	Self-contained room	Whether self-recording without additional components would affect attention to task and academic accuracy and whether changes would be maintained	Attention to task; percent correct on handwriting, spelling, and math assignments	Attention to task and accuracy on tasks increased; effects were maintained for attention and, less clearly, for accuracy

	Year		Setting	Question	Dependent measure	Results
McLaughlin	1984	BD	Self-contained special education class	Whether self-recording and self-recording plus reinforcement would produce higher levels of attention and assignment completion than a control condition (token system) and would differ from each other	Attention to task; assignments completed; accuracy of self-recording	Both self-recording groups had higher attention to task and assignment completion than the control group; no difference between the two self-recording groups
McLaughlin & Truchlicka	1983	BD	Self-contained special class	Whether self-recording of attending with and without matching and reinforcement will increase the percentage of correct answers on workbook pages	Percent correct	Self-recording + matching + reinforcement higher than self-recording, which was higher than control
McLaughlin, Burgess, & Sackville-West	1981	BD	Self-contained special education class	Whether self-recording or self-recording with reinforcers based on matching with teacher would result in greater effects on percent of correct responding in reading workbooks	Percent correct on reading workbooks	Self-recording with matching (and back-up rfrs) had greater effects than self-recording alone
McLaughlin, Krappman, & Welsh	1985	BD	Special education classroom (math)	Whether self-recording of attending would cause changes in attention that would be maintained	Attention to task	On-task behavior increased clearly for 2 of 4 Ss and seemed to increase for the other 2
Morrow, Burke, & Buell	1985	MR	Classroom periods for mathematics	Whether self-recording of attending influences academic performance as well as attention to task	Attention to task and academic productivity	Attention (and productivity) increased while self-recording was in effect

TABLE 8.1 *Continued*

Authors	Year	Ss	Setting	Question	Dependent variables	Results
Osborne, Kosiewicz, Crumley, & Lee (exp. 1)	1987	BD	Special education classroom	Whether self-recording of attending to task would influence the attention and productivity of pupils with behavior disorders	Attention to task; academic productivity	Attention to task was affected by the introduction and withdrawal of self-recording; marginal effects on productivity
Osborne, Kosiewicz, Crumley, & Lee (exp. 2)	1987	MR	Special education classroom	Whether self-recording of attention to task would influence the attention and productivity of pupils identified as mentally retarded	Attention to task; academic productivity	Attention to task was affected by the introduction of self-recording; there were marginal effects on productivity
Roberts & Nelson	1981	NH	Regular classroom	Whether self-recording of academic accuracy or of attention to task would result in greater effects on academic response rate, academic accuracy, and attention to task	Attention to task; rate of academic performance (arithmetic problems); accuracy of arithmetic problem completion	Attention increased for both conditions; rate increased for 2 of 3 S's; accuracy increased slightly for 1 S, decreased for 1 S, and remained unchanged for 1 S; no differences between conditions
Rooney & Hallahan	1988	LD	Self-contained classroom	Whether changes in attention to task caused by self-recording result in changes in teacher-pupil interactions	Attention to task (students); frequency of adult initiations	As self-recording increased attention, levels of adult interaction declined

Author	Year	Disability	Setting	Question	Behavior	Results
Rooney, Hallahan, & Lloyd	1984	LD, NH	Regular second grade classroom	Whether self-recording could be implemented in regular classroom and whether addition of reinforcement for complying with self-recording would improve performance	Attention to task	Attention increased under s-r compared with base; addition of recording contingency increased effects of s-r
Rooney, Polloway, & Hallahan	1985	LD	Self-contained special education classroom	Whether self-recording of attention or self-recording of answer accuracy has greater effects on attention to task and accuracy and whether the two combined have effects on both measures	Attention to task; percentage correct	Neither treatment was superior to the other; both were effective for 2 pupils but not for 2 others; combined treatments produced clear effects in comparison to later baselines
Sabatos	1986	LD	Self-contained special education class	Whether pupils can record when cues are presented privately and they are required to chart the results of their self-recording	Attention to task; words read (silently)	Attention to task and reading (wpm) both increased when self-recording began; adding self-charting did not enhance effects
Sagotsky, Patterson, & Lepper	1978	NH	Regular elementary math class	Whether self-recording and goal-setting (separately and in combination) would increase pupils' attention to task and academic productivity	Attention to task; task accomplishment	On attention, self-recording > others; on task accomplishment, self-recording > others; pupils' self-recorded data was significantly correlated with observers' data for on task
Seymour & Stokes	1976	—	Vocational skills classroom	Whether self-recording (with reinforcement) increases work behavior and whether behavior can be maintained by self-recording alone	Working	Self-recording with cues and tokens increased work behavior and behavior was maintained after the dropping of tokens (self-recording alone)

TABLE 8.1 *Continued*

Authors	Year	Ss	Setting	Question	Dependent variables	Results
Shapiro & Klein	1980	MR, ED	Hospital special classroom	Whether self-recording introduced systematically after a period of teacher-controlled token reinforcement would maintain improved levels of behavior	Attention to task; disruptive behavior; academic productivity and accuracy	Average attention, productivity, and accuracy increased with token rf and were maintained with self-assessment (with successive increases in pupil responsibility for assessment)
Shapiro, McGonigle, & Ollendick	1980	MR, BD	Hospital school classroom	Whether self-recording and self-reinforcement had different effects on attention to task and disruptive behavior	Attention to task; disruptive behavior	Token economy increased attention, decreased disruption; self-recording didn't maintain levels, initially; after explicit training in self-recording, it maintained effects (with reinforcers)
Thomas	1976	NH	Regular classroom mathematics period	Whether self-recording would increase attention when it had not been preceded by a period of teacher monitoring and to what degree pupils' records would agree with observers' records of attention to task	Attention to task	Attention increased and variability in attention decreased when self-recording was implemented; pupil's accuracy ranged from 56% to 95%
Workman, Helton, & Watson	1982	NH	Classroom	Whether self-recording would increase the attention of a young pupil whom a school psychologist taught to use self-recording of attending and whether effects would also obtain on other variables	Sustained Schoolwork (SS); Compliance (C); Adult Social Attention, Non-Aversive (SA+); Adult Social Attention, Aversive (SA−)	SS improved; C increased slightly; SA+ and − were unchanged. Lots of overlap on some variables

Young, Birnbrauer, & Sanson-Fisher (exp. 1)	1977	JD	Special classroom	Whether self-recording would increase attention to task and whether pupils would record accurately	Attention to task; disruptive behavior	Attention to task increased when self-recording was introduced and stayed high; subject's accuracy varied but was generally high
Young, Birnbrauer, & Sanson-Fisher (exp. 2)	1977	JD	Special classroom	Whether combinations of self-recording, token reinforcement, and matching with teacher's (observer's) would increase attention to task	Attention to task	Self-recording in combination with tokens for completing self-recording and both + matching resulted in improved attention

[a] LD = learning disabled; BD = behavior disorders; HA = hyperactive; NH = nonhandicapped; MR = mentally retarded; JD = juvenile delinquent.

Independent observations revealed that Liza's attention to task increased dramatically when she recorded her own study behavior and dropped precipitously when she did not record.

Since the Broden et al. (1971) study, there have been many additional studies of self-recording of attention to task. Table 8.1 provides a summary of many of these studies.

As can be seen in the table, self-recording of attending behavior has been implemented with diverse populations of pupils; the participants have included pupils not identified as handicapped (e.g., Roberts & Nelson, 1981) and those with special education labels such as LD (e.g., Reiter, Mabee, & McLaughlin, 1985), BD (e.g., McLaughlin, 1984), and MR (Morrow, Burke, & Buell, 1985). Furthermore, participants have included pupils ranging in age from 4 years (Workman, Helton, & Watson, 1982) to adolescence (e.g. Young, Birnbrauer, & Sanson-Fisher, 1977).

Also, self-recording has been implemented in a variety of situations. Pupils have implemented self-recording in hospital classrooms (e.g., Shapiro & Klein, 1980), special education classrooms (e.g, Blick & Test, 1987), and regular classrooms (e.g., Broden et al., 1971). Furthermore, as discussed in a later section, in some studies self-recording has been implemented in one setting and its effects have been assessed in a different setting.

In addition, the effects of self-recording of attending-to-task behavior have been assessed on a variety of dependent measures. Although we focus on this topic in greater detail later, we note that when pupils have recorded their own attending behavior, researchers have also observed beneficial effects on other measures such as academic productivity, accuracy on academic tasks, and misbehavior.

Clearly, self-recording of attending has useful applications. The effectiveness of self-recording is not limited by characteristics of the pupils with whom it is used or the settings in which it is implemented. But are all self-recording of attention interventions created equal? Do some have better effects than others? Should some procedures be preferred over others? What are the features of more successful interventions?

In the next section we discuss the preliminary question of whether attending is an appropriate target for intervention. Following that, we examine the features of successful self-recording interventions.

Attending as a Target Behavior

Although teachers consider attention to task an important classroom skill (e.g., Walker & Rankin, 1983), several authors have raised questions about whether attending is an appropriate target behavior for intervention. For example, Klein (1979) and Snider (1987) have argued that, because improvements in academic performance are a more appropriate goal, direct treatment of academic performance is preferable to treatment of attention to task. There are at least two forms of improvement in academic performance that deserve consideration: productivity (the sheer amount of work produced) and accuracy (the proportion of correct work produced).

Four studies have directly compared the treatment of attention and academic performance with self-recording:

1. Roberts and Nelson (1981) compared self-recording of attending with a self-recording-of-accuracy procedure in which pupils stopped when they heard a cue and scored the correctness of each arithmetic problem completed since the previous cue to assess accuracy. They assessed the effects of these treatments on attention, productivity, and accuracy.
2. Rooney, Polloway, and Hallahan (1985) compared self-recording of attending with self-recording of arithmetic accuracy. In their self-recording-of-accuracy condition, Rooney et al. had pupils stop working at designated problems and compare the accuracy of their answer to the answer on a prepared answer sheet. They also included a condition in which students self-recorded both attention and accuracy and they evaluated the effects of these treatments on attention to task, productivity, and accuracy.
3. Harris (1986) compared a self-recording-of-attention condition with a self-recording-of-productivity condition in which, at the end of a class period, pupils counted and graphed the number of words spelled. She measured attention and productivity.
4. Lloyd, Bateman, Landrum, and Hallahan (1989) compared self-recording of attention to self-recording of productivity in which pupils stopped when they heard a cue and counted the number of problems they had completed since the previous cue to record their behavior. They measured attention, productivity, and accuracy.

To varying degrees, all four studies found that when pupils recorded their own attending, their attention to task increased, their academic productivity increased, and their accuracy increased. Similarly, when pupils recorded their own productivity or accuracy, their attention to task increased, their academic productivity increased, and their accuracy increased.

Thus, as a practical matter, there does not appear to be empirical support for choosing to use one procedure over the other. However, there may be other reasons for making such a choice. For example, some practitioners may consider it more important to obtain attention effects as a by-product of improved academic performance than vice versa and will choose to focus self-recording on productivity or accuracy. Others may consider improvements in attention to task to be sufficiently important (perhaps because inattention is a primary referring problem for an individual pupil) to merit direct intervention. At present, we suggest that the decision about whether attending is an appropriate target for intervention is one that should be made by teachers, students, parents, and administrators on the basis of each individual case. If the decision is to teach self-recording of attending, studies of the components of self-recording training procedures should provide useful direction about how to implement a program.

Components of Self-Recording Training

Although all the studies discussed in this chapter share a focus on self-recording of attending behavior, the procedures for teaching self-recording have varied. Some features of the training procedures that have been used in teaching pupils to record their attending behavior are shown in Table 8.2. In the following paragraphs we briefly discuss several of these features, particularly, who conducts the training, whether pupils are given cues to initiate the self-recording strategy, whether combining self-recording with other procedures such as reinforcement makes self-recording more effective, how matching contributes to the effects of self-recording, and to what extent accuracy in self-recording is important.

Trainers

As can be seen in Table 8.2, many different people have provided self-recording training to pupils. Although researchers, school counselors, and consultants have taught pupils to use self-recording, most frequently, teachers have conducted the training. Given that teachers have often conducted self-recording training and that it often has been studied in actual classroom settings (refer to Table 8.1), there is clear ecological validity in the research on self-recording: The procedures can be applied by teachers in their classrooms.

Cuing

In the Broden et al. (1971) study described earlier, Liza was taught to record her own behavior "when she thought about it" (p. 193); while she was using self-recording, she was not cued or prompted to assess her behavior. It is possible to implement a successful self-recording strategy without the use of cues (e.g., McLaughlin, 1983), but many other studies have used some form of cuing to prompt pupils to perform the self-recording strategy.

Although the signal used to prompt self-recording can be quite novel—Shapiro, McGonigle, and Ollendick (1980) used tape-recorded segments of music as cues—many researchers (e.g., Hallahan, Marshall, & Lloyd, 1981) have used tape-recorded tones as cues. The frequency of cues has varied: Hallahan, Lloyd, Kosiewicz, Kauffman, and Graves (1979) used a tape that played short "beeps" at irregular intervals ranging from 15 to 90

TABLE 8.2. Features of training.

Authors	Year	Trainer	Cuing	Matching	Accuracy assessed
Blick & Test	1987	Teacher	Yes	No	Yes
Broden, Hall, & Mitts	1971	Counselor	No	No	No
Christie, Hiss, & Lozanoff	1984	Consultant	Yes	Yes	Yes
Glynn & Thomas	1974	Teacher	Yes	No	No
Glynn, Thomas, & Shee	1973	Teacher	Yes	No	No
Hallahan, Lloyd, Kneedler, & Marshall	1982	Teacher	Yes	No	No
Hallahan, Lloyd, Kosiewicz, Kauffman, & Graves	1979	Teacher	Yes	No	Yes
Hallahan, Marshall, & Lloyd	1981	Tchr, aide	Yes	No	No
Harris	1986	Teacher	Yes	No	No
Heins, Lloyd, & Hallahan	1986	Teacher	Yes	No	No
Kosiewicz	1981	Teacher	Yes	No	No
Lloyd, Bateman, Landrum, & Hallahan	1989	Teacher	Yes	No	No
Lloyd, Hallahan, Kosiewicz, & Kneedler (exp. 1)	1982	Teacher	Yes	No	No
Lloyd, Hallahan, Kosiewicz, & Kneedler (exp. 2)	1982	Teacher	Yes	No	No
Lloyd, Wissick, & Kneedler	1988	Sp Ed Tchr	Yes	No	No
Marshall	1983	Teacher	Yes	Yes	Yes
McLaughlin	1983		No	No	No
McLaughlin	1984	Not given	No	No	No
McLaughlin & Truhlicka	1983	Teacher	No	Yes	Yes

TABLE 8.2. *Continued*

Authors	Year	Trainer	Cuing	Matching	Accuracy assessed
McLaughlin, Burgess, & Sackville-West	1981	Not given	No	Yes	No
McLaughlin, Krappman, & Welsh	1985	Teacher	No	No	No
Morrow, Burke, & Buell	1985	Teacher	Yes	No	Yes
Osborne, Kosiewicz, Crumley, & Lee (exp. 1)	1987	Teacher	Yes	No	No
Osborne, Kosiewicz, Crumley, & Lee (exp. 2)	1987	Teacher	Yes	No	No
Roberts & Nelson	1981	Researcher	Yes	No	No
Rooney & Hallahan	1988	Teacher	Yes	No	No
Rooney, Hallahan, & Lloyd	1984	Teacher	Yes	No	No
Rooney, Polloway, & Hallahan	1985	Teacher	Yes	No	No
Sabatos	1986		Yes	No	Yes
Sagotsky, Patterson, & Lepper	1978	Researcher	No	No	Yes
Seymour & Stokes	1976	Therapist	Yes	Yes	
Shapiro & Klein	1980	Teacher	Yes	Yes	No
Shapiro, McGonigle, & Ollendick	1980	Teacher	Yes		Yes
Thomas	1976	Teacher	Yes	No	Yes
Workman, Helton, & Watson	1982	Consultant	Yes	No	Yes
Young, Birnbrauer, & Sanson-Fisher (exp. 1)	1977	Teacher	Yes	No	Yes
Young, Birnbrauer, & Sanson-Fisher (exp. 2)	1977	Teacher	Yes	Yes	No

sec and an average inter-tone interval of approximately 45 sec, but Workman et al. (1982) simply set a kitchen timer to ring every 5 minutes. Glynn and Thomas (1974) initially had cues occur at 1, 2, 3, 4, and 5 min. intervals but later switched to using only 1, 2, and 3 min. intervals between cues.

Heins, Lloyd, and Hallahan (1986) directly compared cued and noncued self-recording with a multielement analysis involving four LD boys. They found that although pupil performance was initially high under both cued and noncued conditions, it remained higher under the cued condition; after the first 8 to 12 sessions of self-recording, the boys' attention to task began to drop under the noncued condition.

Cuing does not have to be continued, however. Several studies (e.g., Hallahan et al., 1979; Hallahan, Lloyd, Kneedler, & Marshall, 1982) have shown that the prompts to record can be removed without declines in pupils' performance. For example, Lloyd et al. (1989) withdrew the tape-recorded cues in their study and, for one phase, only required the pupils to record whenever they thought about it; the pupils' attention to task and academic productivity continued at high levels. (See our later discussion of fading and its influence on maintenance of effects.)

Combined Treatments

Some self-recording procedures (e.g., Glynn & Thomas, 1974; Glynn et al., 1973) incorporated self-recording into larger self-control programs. Often, the larger programs included some forms of reinforcement for higher levels of attention to task. For example, the pupils in the studies by Shapiro (Shapiro & Klein, 1980; Shapiro et al., 1980) and his colleagues included self-administration of token reinforcers; pupils not only decided whether they were working on assigned tasks, but also gave themselves tokens if they had been attending. However, other studies (e.g., Hallahan et al., 1979) have revealed that self-recording can have effects even in the absence of additional components such as self-reinforcement.

We hasten to distinguish between providing reinforcers contingent on displaying the behavior pupils are required to assess and record and the use of reinforcement in training pupils to use a recording strategy. Teachers should be sure to praise or, if needed, provide more concrete reinforcers when teaching pupils how to record. In fact, Rooney, Hallahan, and Lloyd (1984) examined the benefits of providing reinforcement for correctly implementing a self-recording program. After observing that some pupils using a self-recording procedure were not correctly executing it (they did not assess and record their behavior each time a tape-recorded cue sounded), Rooney et al. had the teachers institute a reinforcement program in which each pupil who recorded the same number of times as the tones sounded was rewarded with a small candy. Pupils' performance increased dramatically when they received reinforcement for correctly implementing the self-recording procedures.

Matching

In some studies, trainers and pupils have periodically compared their judgments. Comparing or matching may enhance the effectiveness of self-recording. For example, in a study of self-evaluation of several behaviors, Rhode, Morgan, and Young (1983) required that participating pupils assess their own behavior after a given time period had elapsed. At the same time, the teacher also rated their behavior. After completing these ratings, the teacher and each pupil compared their judgments. If the teacher and pupil agreed, the pupil earned additional tokens.

In a more direct evaluation of the contribution of matching, Marshall (1983) identified students for whom self-recording of attending was initially effective but gradually lost its power to change behavior. The teacher in Marshall's study provided additional training to these pupils and the additional training included periods in which (a) the pupil and teacher both recorded the teacher's behavior and then systematically compared their records and (b) the pupil and teacher both recorded the pupil's behavior and systematically compared records. During the later periods, the teacher also introduced distractions so that the pupil would have experience in working and recording under adverse conditions. Marshall observed substantial increments in pupils' attention as well as increased accuracy in their self-recording.

Accuracy of Self-Recording

One of the questions that most frequently arises in discussions of self-recording concerns whether pupils must record accurately. Teachers and others are interested in whether the procedure will be effective when pupils inaccurately judge their behavior. This concern is sometimes expressed as a question: What if the student cheats?

Most of the studies that have assessed pupils' accuracy in self-recording (see Table 8.2) have found that students overestimate their behavior. That is, their self-recording records show that they were attending to task more often than do the records of independent observers. For example, Lloyd et al. (1989) found that in 98% of the observation sessions pupils rated themselves as attending to task 100% of the time. In contrast, observers' records showed that the pupils were virtually never on task for 100% of a session.

Given that observation records of independent observers show clear and consistent effects for self-recording, the question of pupil accuracy seems unimportant. Who cares if the pupils overestimate their attending when the procedure produces independently observed behavior at such high levels as have been repeatedly found with self-recording?

In addition, there are sensible reasons for pupils' overestimating their attention. For example, pupils have access to their own thoughts. Thus, while they are engaging in a behavior that to an observer appears to be inattentive (e.g., "staring into space"), they may actually be thinking about an assigned task. Although to the study's observer they appear off task, to themselves they are working appropriately and could record that they were paying attention at that time. But, of course, this would result in a disagreement between pupil and observer records.

Thus, for the practice of self-recording, we conclude that it is not extremely important to protect against pupils' overestimation of their attending behavior. Self-recording is likely to have beneficial effects even when they do record inaccurately. However, when pupils record extremely inaccurately, as those Marshall (1983) studied, it may be appropriate to incorporate some training that encourages more accurate recording. Such additional training may help to ensure that self-recording will be reactive.

The preceding review of components of self-recording interventions reveals several general guidelines for practitioners seeking effective treatments for off-task behavior. The relative usefulness of self-recording interventions, however, is dependent not only on the effectiveness of the program in bringing about behavior changes, but also on the generalizability of treatment effects. In the next section, we discuss several issues related to the generalization of self-recording treatment effects.

Generalization

In assessing self-recording as an intervention strategy, perhaps the most important aspects of generalization involve response maintenance and transfer of treatment effects (cf. Kazdin, 1984). Maintenance refers to the persistence of treatment effects over time and is generally assessed following the withdrawal of active treatment components. Researchers have most often assessed whether transfer of training has occurred by determining whether self-recording procedures affect other behaviors (i.e., transfer across responses), or whether training students to use self-recording procedures in one setting produces beneficial changes in the students' behavior in other settings (i.e., transfer across settings). Table 8.3 presents information for the selected studies included in this review regarding the degree to which researchers have either programmed for generalization or assessed the generalizability of treatment effects. In the subsequent three sections, we describe in greater detail several examples of the generalization of self-recording intervention effects related to maintenance, transfer across responses, and transfer across settings.

Maintenance

As we suggested earlier, one of the more important features of self-recording as a practical intervention technique involves the degree to which the effects are maintained over time. Broden et al. (1971), for example,

TABLE 8.3. Transfer of effects feature

Authors	Year	Fading	Maintenance	Settings	Responses
Blick & Test	1987	Yes	Yes	No	No
Broden, Hall, & Mitts	1971	Yes	Yes	No	No
Christie, Hiss, & Lozanoff	1984	No	No	No	Yes
Glynn & Thomas	1974		No	No	No
Glynn, Thomas, & Shee	1973	No	No	No	No
Hallahan, Lloyd, Kneedler, & Marshall	1982	Yes	Yes	No	Yes
Hallahan, Lloyd, Kosiewicz, Kauffman, Graves	1979	Yes	Yes	No	Yes
Hallahan, Marshall, & Lloyd	1981	Yes	Yes	No	No
Harris	1986	No	No	No	No
Heins, Lloyd, & Hallahan	1986	No	Yes	No	Yes
Kosiewicz	1981	No	No	No	Yes
Lloyd, Bateman, Landrum, & Hallahan	1989	Yes	Yes	No	No
Lloyd, Hallahan, Kosiewicz, & Kneedler (exp. 1)	1982	No	No	No	Yes
Lloyd, Hallahan, Kosiewicz, & Kneedler (exp. 2)	1982	No	No	No	Yes
Lloyd, Wissick, & Kneedler	1988	No	No	No	No
Marshall	1983	No	No	No	No
McLaughlin	1983	No	Yes	No	No
McLaughlin	1984	No	Yes	No	Yes
McLaughlin & Truhlicka	1983	No	Yes	No	Yes
McLaughlin, Burgess, & Sackville-West	1981	No	Yes	No	Yes
McLauglin, Krappman, & Welsh	1985		No	No	No
Morrow, Burke, & Buell	1985	No	No	No	Yes

Authors	Year	Fading	Maintenance	Settings	Responses
Osborne, Kosiewicz, Crumley, & Lee (exp. 1)	1987	No	No	No	Yes
Osborne, Kosiewicz, Crumley, & Lee (exp. 2)	1987	No	No	No	Yes
Roberts & Nelson	1981		No	No	No
Rooney & Hallahan	1988	No	No	No	No
Rooney, Hallahan, & Lloyd	1984	No	No	No	No
Rooney, Polloway, & Hallahan	1985	No	No	No	No
Sabatos	1986	No	No	No	Yes
Sagotsky, Patterson, & Lepper	1978	No	No	No	Yes
Seymour & Stokes	1976	No	No	Yes	No
Shapiro & Klein	1980	No	Yes	No	Yes
Shapiro, McGonigle, & Ollendick	1980	No	No	No	Yes
Thomas	1976	No	Yes	No	No
Workman, Helton, & Watson	1982	No	No	No	Yes
Young, Birnbrauer, & Sanson-Fisher (exp. 1)	1977	No	No	Yes	No
Young, Birnbrauer, & Sanson-Fisher (exp. 2)	1977	No	No	Yes	No

conducted observations following the removal of treatment procedures (i.e., a return to baseline) and found that Liza's study behavior continued at a high level over a three-week period in the absence of any systematic intervention components. Similar assessments of durability suggest that rates of attending can be maintained above baseline levels from 60 to 330 days following the termination of treatment (Heins et al., 1986; McLaughlin, 1983, 1984).

Holman and Baer (1979) assessed maintenance up to five months following treatment cessation, and further investigated the effects of introducing and withdrawing a treatment component (a leather bracelet with movable beads, which served as the self-recording device during treatment) during these follow-up sessions. In this investigation, the bracelet retained experimental control over 2 of the 3 participants' on-task behavior.

Often researchers promote maintenance by gradually fading the overt aspects of the self-recording procedures (see Table 8.3). Blick and Test (1987), for example, faded the audiotaped verbal cues initially provided to students over successive phases of their active treatment by providing the cues at increasingly infrequent intervals. During the final phase, students were self-recording with only the visual cues provided by the times written under successive blocks on their self-recording sheets. Others (e.g., Hallahan et al., 1979, 1982) often have faded the overt aspects of self-recording by removing components of the active treatments in a sequential withdrawal design. Lloyd et al. (1989) first removed the audiotaped cues ("beeps") and told students to record whether they were paying attention "whenever they thought about it" (p. 319). Following several days of this procedure, the teacher told students that they would no longer need to record their answers on self-recording sheets; they were to ask themselves whether they were paying attention whenever they thought about it, answer the question to themselves, and continue working on their assignments. All of the participants in the Lloyd et al. study maintained high levels of attention to task during the fading phase. Attending behavior also remained high at follow up, assessed on eight days over a five week period.

Transfer Across Responses

Researchers concerned with transfer of treatment effects across responses generally assess whether self-recording of one behavior (e.g., attention) produces therapeutic change in other behaviors (e.g., academic productivity) in addition to the target behavior. In several studies of the effects of self-recording of attention on students' rates of on-task behavior, investigators have also assessed the effects on academic responding (e.g., Sagotsky, Patterson, & Lepper, 1978). Although not all studies have revealed transfer to academic productivity (e.g., Hallahan et al., 1982; Lloyd et al., 1982), some studies have found such transfer. Hallahan et al. (1979), for instance, found that self-recording of attention resulted in increases in the number of handwriting words written and arithmetic problems completed correctly.

The effects of self-recording of attention on accuracy have also been assessed, however. Lloyd et al. (1989) found similar increases in productivity assessed as the number of correct movements (numerals written) per minute when the self-recording treatment was instituted, but additionally found increases in the percentage of correct movements. Thus the students were both completing more work and responding with greater accuracy following intervention. Similar results were obtained by Morrow et al. (1985). McLaughlin (1984) also found that self-recording of attention produced gains in the percentage of assignments completed. These results suggest that the effects of self-recording of attention may transfer to both rate of responding and accuracy of responding.

Transfer Across Settings

Although it has been suggested that one potential benefit of self-recording procedures is that such interventions allow students to display improved behavior initially which might then be maintained by social and environmental reinforcers, the results of investigations examining the transfer of training effects across settings have been inconclusive. Young et al. (1977), for example, found that when students were taught to self-record their study behavior in two of their four class periods per day, the effects of self-recording were apparent for those periods only; no changes in study behavior occurred during the two class periods in which self-recording was not required.

Specific programming for generalization of the effects of self-recording interventions to nontraining settings has produced more promising results. Holman and Baer (1979) taught students to use a bracelet with movable beads to self-record their assignment completion by moving one bead for each workbook page they completed. While training in self-recording took place in a laboratory setting, transfer across settings was facilitated by having the students wear the bracelet in their regular classrooms. The provision of this prompt resulted in increased work completion for each of the participants; these effects were maintained up to one year following treatment. As mentioned earlier, however, the bracelet appears to have retained experimental control over the subjects' behavior. Without this prompt, work completion was not maintained at the improved levels first observed. Thus it appears that the students' initial improvements in work behavior had not come under the control of teacher or environmental reinforcers, nor does it seem that increased work completion had become intrinsically rewarding for these participants to the extent that behavioral gains were maintained in the absence of treatment components.

Summary

Based on this review of studies evaluating the effects of self-recording of attending-to-task behavior, we can make several summary statements:

1. Self-recording of attending is a very robust procedure. It has been applied in a wide variety of settings by a wide variety of trainers with a wide variety of students.
2. Many variations of self-recording of attending have been studied. Although it can be implemented with or without overt cues to record, it appears that self-recording is more effective when cues are incorporated in training (Heins et al., 1986). The requirement to record (as opposed simply to assess) one's behavior is important (Lloyd et al., 1982).

Although it is not necessary (Hallahan et al., 1979), reinforcement may be profitably added to self-recording (McLaughlin, 1984). Overt features of self-recording programs can be systematically removed (e.g., Hallahan et al., 1982) without marked decrements in performance.

3. Enhanced training for accuracy of self-recording (Marshall, 1983) or compliance with the self-recording procedure (Rooney et al. 1984) can be beneficial, but pupils do not have to record accurately for self-recording to have effects.

4. The effects of self-recording-of-attention procedures can persist for extended periods of time even in the absence of the overt aspects of the treatment (McLaughlin, 1983) and can influence performance on other measures of performance (e.g., Lloyd et al., 1989).

As is usually the case, what we know about self-recording of attending raises additional questions. The studies reviewed here do not clearly answer some important questions. For example, we do not know much about the transfer of treatment effects across settings; special educators may legitimately hope for treatment programs that can be implemented in one setting (e.g., the resource room) but which will have beneficial effects in another setting (e.g., the regular classroom). We also do not have a clear understanding about whether academic productivity or academic accuracy might be more appropriate targets for self-recording than attending to task. Thus, despite the extensive literature reviewed here, we are still legitimately able to make the virtually inevitable call for further research on self-recording of attending.

Acknowledgments. We appreciate the contributions of many of our colleagues with whom we have collaborated on research in self-recording, particularly Daniel P. Hallahan and Rebecca D. Kneedler. We also appreciate the support of the Division for Learning Disabilities of the Council for Execeptional Children for the presentation of a paper based on this chaper.

Address correspondence to John Wills Lloyd, Curry School of Education, University of Virginia, Charlottesville, Virginia 22903-2495 or, via BITNET: JOHNL@VIRGINIA.

References

Abueg, F.R., Colletti, G., & Kopel, S.A. (1985). A study of reactivity: The effects of increased relevance and saliency of self-monitored smoking through enhanced carbon monoxide feedback. *Cognitive Therapy and Research, 9*, 321–333.

Bandura, A., & Perloff, B. (1967). Relative efficacy of self-monitored and externally imposed reinforcement systems. *Journal of Personality and Social Psychology, 7*, 111–116.

Blick, D.W., & Test, D.W. (1987). Effects of self-recording on high-school students' on-task behavior. *Learning Disability Quarterly*, *10*, 203–213.

Broden, M., Hall, R.V., & Mitts, B. (1971). The effects of self-recording on the classroom behavior of two eighth-grade students. *Journal of Applied Behavior Analysis*, *4*, 191–199.

Christie, D.J., Hiss, M., & Lozanoff, B. (1984). Modification of inattentive classroom behavior: Hyperactive children's use of self-recording with teacher guidance. *Behavior Modification*, *8*, 391–406.

Gardner, W.I., & Cole, C.L. (1988). Self-monitoring procedures. In E. S. Shapiro & T. R. Kratochwill (Eds.), *Behavioral assessment in schools: Conceptual foundations and practical applications* (pp. 206–246). New York: Guilford.

Glynn, E.L., & Thomas, J.D. (1974). Effect of cueing on self-control of classroom behavior. *Journal of Applied Behavior Analysis*, *7*, 299–306.

Glynn, E.L., Thomas, J.D., & Shee, S.M. (1973). Behavioral self-control of on-task behavior in an elementary classroom. *Journal of Applied Behavior Analysis*, *6*, 105–113.

Hallahan, D.P., Kneedler, R.D., & Lloyd, J.W. (1983). Cognitive behavior modification techniques for learning disabled children: Self-instruction and self-monitoring. In J.D. McKinney & L. Feagans (Eds.), *Current topics in learning disabilities* (Vol . 1, pp. 201–244). New York: Ablex.

Hallahan, D.P., Lloyd, J.W., Kneedler, R.D., & Marshall, K.J. (1982). A comparison of the effects of self- versus teacher-assessment of on-task behavior. *Behavior Therapy*, *13*, 715–723.

Hallahan, D.P., Lloyd, J.W., Kosiewicz, M.M., Kauffman, J.M., & Graves, A.W. (1979). Self monitoring of attention as a treatment for a learning-disabled boy's off-task behavior. *Learning Disability Quarterly*, *2*(2), 24–32.

Hallahan, D.P., Marshall, K.J., & Lloyd, J.W. (1981). Self-recording during group instruction: Effects on attention to task. *Learning Disability Quarterly*, *4*, 407–413.

Harris, K.R. (1986). Self-monitoring of attentional behavior versus self-monitoring of productivity: Effects on on-task behavior and academic response rate among learning disabled children. *Journal of Applied Behavior Analysis*, *19*, 417–423.

Heins, E.D., Lloyd, J.W., & Hallahan, D.P. (1986). Cued and noncued self-recording of attention to task. *Behavior Modification*, *10*, 235–254.

Holman, J., & Baer, D.M. (1979). Facilitating generalization of on-task behavior through self-monitoring of academic tasks. *Journal of Autism and Developmental Disabilities*, *9*, 429–446.

Horton, A.M. (1981). Self-recording in the treatment of obesity: A six-year follow-up. *Journal of Obesity and Weight Regulation*, *1*(2), 93–95.

Howell, K.W., Rueda, R., & Rutherford, R.B., Jr. (1983). A procedure for teaching self-recording to moderately retarded students. *Psychology in the Schools*, *20*, 202–209.

Israel, A.C., Silverman, W.K., & Solotar, L.C. (1987). Baseline adherence as a predictor of dropout in a children's weight-reduction program. *Journal of Consulting and Clinical Psychology*, *55*, 791–793.

Kanfer, F.F. (1970). Self-monitoring: Methodological issues and clinical applications. *Journal of Consulting and Clinical Psychology*, *35*, 143–152.

Kauffman, J.M., Lloyd, J.W., & McGee, K.A. (1989). Adaptive and maladaptive behavior: Teachers' attitudes and their technical assistance needs. *Journal of Special Education*, 23, 185–200.

Kazdin, A.E. (1984). *Behavior modification in applied settings* (3rd ed.). Homewood, IL: Dorsey.

Klein, R.D. (1979). Modifying academic performance in the grade school classroom. In M. Hersen, R.M. Eisler, & P.M. Miller (Eds.), *Progress in behavior modification* (Vol. 8, pp. 293–321). New York: Plenum Press.

Kneedler, R.D. (1980). The use of cognitive training to change social behaviors. *Exceptional Education Quarterly*, 1(1), 65–73.

Kneedler, R.D., & Hallahan, D.P. (1981). Self-monitoring of on-task behavior with learning-disabled children: Current studies and directions. *Exceptional Education Quarterly*, 2(3), 73–82.

Kosiewicz, M.M. (1981). *Self-monitoring of attention in an LD classroom: Across subiect generalization.* Unpublished doctoral dissertation, University of Virginia, Charlottesville.

Lloyd, J.W., Hallahan, D.P., Kosiewicz, M.M., & Kneedler, R.D. (1982). Reactive effects of self-assessment and self-recording on attention to task and academic productivity. *Learning Disability Quarterly*, 5, 216–227.

Lloyd, J.W., Landrum, T.J., & Hallahan, D.P. (in press). Self-monitoring applications for classroom interventions. In G. Stoner, M.R. Shinn, & H.M. Walker (Eds.), *Interventions for achievement and behavior problems.* Harrisonburg, VA: National Association for School Psychologists.

Lloyd, J.W., Bateman, D.F., Landrum, T.J., & Hallahan, D.P. (1989). Selfrecording of attention versus productivity. *Journal of Applied Behavior Analysis*, 22, 315–323.

Lloyd, J.W., Wissick, C.A., & Kneedler, R.D. (1988). *Extending special education's reach: Self-recording implemented in the regular classroom.* Unpublished manuscript, University of Virginia, Curry School of Education, Charlottesville.

Mace, F.C., & Kratochwill, T.R. (1988). Self-monitoring. In J.C. Witt, S.N. Eliott, & F.M. Gresham (Eds.), *Handbook of behavior therapy in education* (pp. 489–522). New York: Plenum.

Marshall, K.J. (1983). *The effects of training to increase self-monitoring accuracy on the attention-to-task of learning disabled children.* Unpublished doctoral dissertation, University of Virginia, Charlottesville.

McConnell, S., Biglan, A., & Severson, H.H. (1984). Adolescents' compliance with self-monitoring and physiological assessment of smoking in natural environments. *Journal of Behavioral Medicine*, 7, 115–122.

McLaughlin, T.F. (1976). Self-control in the classroom. *Review of Educational Research*, 46, 631–663.

McLaughlin, T.F. (1983). Effects of self-recording for on-task and academic responding: A long term analysis. *Journal of Special Education Technology*, 6, 5–12 .

McLaughlin, T.F. (1984). A comparison of self-recording and self-recording plus consequences for on-task and assignment completion. *Contemporary Educational Psychology*, 9, 185–192.

McLaughlin, T.F., Burgess, N., & Sackville-West, L. (1981). Effects of selfrecording and self-recording + matching on academic performance. *Child Behavior Therapy*, 3(2–3), 17–27.

McLaughlin, T.F., Krappman, U.F., & Welsh, J.M. (1985). The effects of self-recording for on-task behavior of behaviorally disordered special education students. *Remedial and Special Education, 6*(4), 42–45.

McLaughlin, T.F., & Truhlicka, M. (1983). Effects on academic performance of self-recording and self-recording and matching with behaviorally disordered students: A replication. *Behavioral Engineering, 8*(2), 69–74.

Morrow, L.W., Burke, J.G., & Buell, B.J. (1985). Effects of a self-recording procedure on the attending to task behavior and academic productivity of adolescents with multiple handicaps. *Mental Retardation, 23*, 137–141.

Neilans, T.H., & Israel, A.C. (1981). Towards maintenance and generalization of behavior change: Teaching children self-regulation and self-instructional skills. *Cognitive Therapy and Research, 5*, 189–195.

Nelson, R.O, & Hayes, S.C. (1981). Theoretical explanations for reactivity in self-monitoring. *Behavior Modification, 5*, 3–14.

Osborne, S.S., Kosiewicz, M.M., Crumley, E.B., & Lee, C. (1987). Distractible students use self-monitoring. *Teaching Exceptional Children, 19*(2), 66–69.

Polsgrove, L. (1979). Self-control: Methods for child training. *Behavioral Disorders, 4*(2), 116–130.

Reiter, S.M., Mabee, W.S., & McLaughlin, T.F. (1985). Self-monitoring: Effects for on-task and time to complete assignments. *Remedial and Special Education, 6*, 50–51.

Rhode, G, Morgan, D.P., & Young, K.R. (1983). Generalization and maintenance of treatment gains of behaviorally handicapped students from resource rooms to regular classrooms using self-evaluation procedures. *Journal of Applied Behavior Analysis, 16*, 171–188.

Roberts, R.N., & Nelson, R.O. (1981). The effects of self-monitoring on children's classroom behavior. *Child Behavior Therapy, 3*, 105–120.

Rooney, K.J., & Hallahan, D.P. (1988). The effects of self-monitoring on adult behavior and student performance. *Learning Disabilities Research, 3*, 88–93.

Rooney, K.J., Hallahan, D.P., & Lloyd, J.W. (1984). Self-recording of attention by learning-disabled students in the regular classroom. *Journal of Learning Disabilities, 17*, 360–364.

Rooney, K.J., Polloway, E., & Hallahan, D.P. (1985). The use of self-monitoring procedures with low IQ learning disabled students. *Journal of Learning Disabilities, 18*, 384–389.

Rueda, R. (1981). Future directions in self-control research. In R.B. Rutherford, A.G. Prieto, & J.E. McGlothlin (Eds.), *Severe behavior disorders of children and youth* (Vol. 4, pp. 16–21). Reston, VA: Council for Children with Behavior Disorders.

Rueda, R., Rutherford, R.B., & Howell, K.W. (1980). Review of self-control research with behaviorally disordered and mentally retarded children. In R.B. Rutherford, A.G., Prieto, & J.E. McGlothlin (Eds.), *Severe behavior disorders of children and youth* (Vol. 3, pp. 188–197). Reston, VA: Council for Children with Behavior Disorders.

Sabatos, M.A. (1986). *Private cues in self-monitoring: Effects on learning-disabled students' on-task performance and reading productivity during sustained silent reading*. Unpublished doctoral dissertation, University of Pittsburgh, Pittsburgh.

Sagotsky, G., Patterson, C.J., & Lepper, M.R. (1978). Training children's self-control: A field experiment in self-monitoring and goal setting in the classroom. *Journal of Experimental Child Psychology, 25*, 242–253.

Seymour, F.W., & Stokes, T.F. (1976). Self-recording in training girls to increase work and evoke staff praise in an institution for offenders. *Journal of Applied Behavior Analysis*, *9*, 41–54.

Shapiro, E.S. (1989). *Academic skills problems: Direct assessment and intervention*. New York: Guilford.

Shapiro, E.S., & Klein, R.D. (1980). Self-management of classroom behavior with retarded/disturbed children. *Behavior Modification*, *4*, 83–97.

Shapiro, E.S., McGonigle, J.J., & Ollendick, T. (1980). An analysis of self-assessment and self-reinforcement in a self-managed token economy with mentally retarded children. *Applied Research in Mental Retardation*, *1*, 227–240.

Singer, G.H., Irvin, L.K., & Hawkins, N. (1988) . Stress management training for parents of children with severe handicaps. *Mental Retardation*, *26*, 269–277.

Singh, N.N., & Leung, J. (1988). Smoking cessation through cigarette-fading, self-recording, and contracting: Treatment, maintenance and long-term followup. *Addictive Behaviors*, *13*, 101–105 .

Snider, V.E. (1987). Use of self-monitoring of attention with LD students. *Learning Disability Quarterly*, *10*, 139–151.

Snyder, M. (1987). *Public appearances/private realities: The psychology of self-monitoring*. New York: Freeman.

Stark, K.D., Reynolds, W.M., & Kaslow, N.J. (1987). A comparison of the relative efficacy of self-control therapy and a behavioral problem-solving therapy for depression in children. *Journal of Abnormal Child Psychology*, *15*, 91–113.

Thomas, J.D. (1976). Accuracy of self-assessment of on-task behavior by elementary school children. *Journal of Applied Behavior Analysis*, *9*, 209–210. [abstract]

Walker, H.M., & Rankin, R. (1983). Assessing the behavioral expectations and demands of less restrictive settings. *School Psychology Review*, *12*, 274–284.

Wing, R.R., Epstein, L.H., Nowalk, M.P., & Scott, N. (1988). Self-regulation in the treatment of Type II diabetes. *Behavior Therapy*, *19*, 11–23.

Workman, E.A., Helton, G.B., & Watson, P.J. (1982). Self-monitoring effects in a four-year-old child: An ecological behavior analysis. *Journal of School Psychology*, *20*, 57–64.

Young, P., Birnbrauer, J.S., & Sanson-Fisher, R.W. (1977). The effects of self-recording on the study behavior of female juvenile delinquents. In B.C. Etzel, J.M. LeBlanc, & D.M. Baer (Eds.), *New developments in behavioral research: Theory, method, and application* (pp. 559–577). Hillsdale, NJ: Erlbaum.

9
Social Skills Training with Learning Disabled Children and Adolescents: The State of the Art

TANIS BRYAN AND JOHN LEE

Studies showing a correlation between problems in childhood peer relationships and adult maladjustment have been accumulating since the 1930s. The results of this research have found that peer interaction plays a vital role in facilitating the development of children's reasoning in personal, societal, and moral domains of knowledge (Piaget, 1970; Turiel & Davidson, 1986). Failure to gain peer acceptance has been shown to be related to later school dropouts, and low acceptance related to aggressiveness has been predictive of later criminality (Parker & Asher, 1987). Kohlberg, LaCross and Rick (1972) argue: "Delinquency, character disorders, neuroses, and learning failures can readily be interpreted as due to retardation in cognitive and social development or to social learning of maladaptive values and behaviors" (p. 1262). It is clear that "Experiences with peers are not superficial luxuries to be enjoyed by some students and not by others. Student-student relationships are an absolute necessity for healthy cognitive and social development and socialization" (Johnson, 1980, p. 125).

Questions about the social skills of children and adolescents with learning disabilities have become a major issue in the field. Indeed, the most recently proposed definitions have called for the inclusion of social problems as characteristics of learning disabilities (Association for Children with Learning Disabilities, 1985; Interagency Committee on Learning Disabilities, 1987). The concern for social problems has been generated by the many studies which have found that students with learning disabilities are more likely than their achieving peers to receive low scores on sociometric scales (Bryan & Bryan, 1990), leading to the conclusion that a significant number of children with learning disabilities may experience difficulty in establishing friendship with their classmates. Studies seeking to identify correlates of peer acceptance have found that the learning disabled differ from their achieving classmates on a variety of cognitive and behavioral dimensions. These studies have discovered that numerous measures of social cognition (Wong & Wong, 1980; Saloner & Gettinger, 1985) and communicative competence (i.e., expressive language skills; Donahue, Pearl, & Bryan, 1983) distinguish students with learning disabilities from their achieving classmates.

Although there is now a data base that attests to the likelihood that children with learning disabilities may be at risk for social skills deficits, the link between their sociometric status and such deficits has not been made. Failure to establish the link between sociometric status and behavior is a serious gap in this research base. Studies of sociometric status signal that a child has not established friendships in the classroom, but these measures do not tell us why. Studies of social cognition and communicative competence may signal that a child is not as developmentally advanced in thinking or speaking as classmates. However, these studies have not examined whether poor sociometric status is necessarily related to deficiencies in social cognition and communicative competence. Until we establish the specific causes for the peer rejection, we will be hard pressed to develop effective social skills interventions. In spite of this gap in our knowledge, the data finding LD youngsters at risk for less acceptance from their peers has led to concern for the provision of social skills training.

The purpose of this chapter is to review research in which LD students were provided with social skills training. To date, however, most social skills training studies have been conducted with children who were not labeled learning disabled. In spite of the many voices calling for social skills training for learning disabled children (cf. de Bettencourt, 1987, Gresham, 1981; 1982; 1983; 1984; Larson, 1987; Schumaker & Ellis, 1982; Spekman & Roth, 1984), very few research studies have actually been conducted. It seems ironic that there are almost as many papers on the implications of social skills training for mainstreaming (cf. Gresham, 1983), and the effects of social skills training on academic performances (cf. Larson, 1987; Mills, 1987; Tolefson, Tracy, Johnsen, & Chatman, 1986) as there are studies assessing the effects of social skills training on students.

The work reviewed here includes social skills intervention studies that used learning disabled children. It should be noted that there were no empirical studies reported prior to 1981.

Components of Social Skills Training

Before reviewing the studies of social skills training, a definition of social skills and a description of the basic components found in social skills training may be helpful. Here we rely on the work conducted by Ladd and Mize (1983) as an exemplar. Although there are any number of definitions, Ladd and Mize's serves well: "[social skills] . . . children's ability to organize conditions and behaviors into an integrated course of action directed toward culturally acceptable social or interpersonal goal" (1983, p. 127). Again, although there are many variants on social skills training, a major conceptual contributor has been the work of Bandura on cognitive-social learning (cf., 1972, 1977, 1981, 1982). Based on Bandura's work, Ladd and Mize translated social skills training into three basic goals: (1) enhancing social concepts, (2) promoting skillful performance, and (3) fostering skill maintenance and generalization.

The first goal focuses on teaching children deficient in social skills appropriate social concepts. The goal is accomplished by: (1) providing children with a rationale for learning the skill to be taught, (2) defining the skill concept in terms of its attributes by identifying relevant and irrelevant features, (3) providing exemplars, both positive and negative, (4) promoting verbal and conceptual rehearsal and recall of the skill concept, and (5) providing feedback to the learner and encouraging the learner to generalize his her understanding of the newly learned concept and its application to other situations.

The second goal seeks to promote skillful performance. This stage of training involves: (1) providing the learner with opportunities for guided rehearsal by requesting overt skill rehearsal in a sheltered context, (2) evaluating the performance of the learner by providing feedback about the match between standards and performance and engendering feelings of self-efficacy in the learner, and (3) fostering skill refinement and elaboration through recommending concept reformulation and skill modification.

The third goal seeks to foster maintenance and generalization, to assist the learner to become independent in his or her use of the newly acquired skills. This goal is accomplished by: (1) providing the learner with opportunities for self-directed rehearsal, (2) encouraging self-initiation of performance while phasing out assistance and withdrawing performance cues or aids, and (3) fostering self-evaluation by promoting self-monitoring.

The training program derived from this model was designed for use with elementary school children low in peer acceptance, and studies using the model with such children have found positive social outcomes. Coached children have been found to increase their skills performance over time and to receive more positive peer responses (Oden & Asher, 1977; Ladd, 1981; Bierman, 1986).

Social Skills Training with LD Children

Empirical social skills training studies that employed students with learning disabilities were conducted by LaGreca and Mesibov (1981); Hazel, Schumaker, Sherman, and Sheldon (1982); Schumaker and Ellis (1982); Berler, Gross, and Drabman (1982); McCloskey and Quay (1987); and Larson and Gerber (1987).

The pioneering study in this area was conducted by LaGreca and Mesibov (1981). In this study the training group consisted of four boys, ages 12.7 to 16.3 years, who were referred by teachers and a program director for "inappropriate social behavior, limited contact with peers, and poor social interaction skills" (p. 197). Four students from the same summer school program who were designated by teachers to have no social interaction difficulties were administered the same assessments.

The training program was conducted by a male and female group leader for 60-minutes weekly for six weeks. The behaviors selected for training were communication-conversation skills and taking the initiative in social situations. Training consisted of modeling, coaching (e.g., discussions of how and when to use the skills), and behavioral rehearsal with feedback (e.g., videotaped practice of skills with group members, assignments to practice the skills with peers). For each skill, the group leaders modeled the skill in appropriate and inappropriate ways, and students observed and discussed the modeled skills in terms of how and when they could use these skills. Then, students role-played the skills with one another. The role-plays were videotaped and played back for students to critique. Students practiced until they could demonstrate the skills. They were given an assignment to practice the skills with other peers during the week, which was then discussed at the next session.

The impact of the program was assessed by having students participate in two role-plays before and after training. These role-plays required students to "talk to a new student in school" as an assessment of conversational skills and to "greet and join two unfamiliar girls who were talking together in the halls" as an assessment of taking the initiative in social situations. The role-plays were scored for specific features (e.g., total number of comments made, questions asked), and for global skillfulness. In addition, students completed a rating form on the frequency of their interactions with peers in a variety of social situations.

The results found that students who participated in the training improved their interpersonal skills and the frequency of their interactions with peers. For example, students increased in the number of conversational statements, generated more topics of conversation and asked more questions. At posttreatment the conversational skills of the students in training approximated the normal comparison group. On the global ratings, students were similar to, though slightly lower than, the comparison group. With regard to self-report data, the trained group reported increase in the frequency of peer interactions.

Although this study suffers from a small N, lack of a true comparison group, no statistical tests on the data, and no test of generalization, it nonetheless paved the way for a new area of research. It is important to note that the behaviors selected for training were ones research had found to be correlates of peer acceptance and also used to differentiate learning disabled from achieving children.

Hazel et al. (1982) also conducted social skills training with adolescents. But the focus in their work was on preparing adolescents with learning disabilities for the job market. The development of this program was based on earlier work assessing occupational social skills. Matthews, Whang, and

Fawcett (1980) had compared learning disabled and normally achieving adolescents' social interactions in occupational situations using a role-playing format. They found that learning disabled adolescents performed significantly worse than achieving adolescents in four of ten situations: participating in a job interview, accepting criticism from an employer, giving criticism to a co-worker, and explaining a problem to an employer. Schumaker, Hazel, Sherman, and Sheldon (1982) then compared the social skills performance of achieving adolescents, learning disabled students, and juvenile delinquents. The learning disabled performed more poorly than the achieving adolescents on seven of eight skills tested. Based on these findings, Hazel, Schumaker, Sherman, and Sheldon (1982) developed and tested a social skills training program.

The sample included learning disabled adolescents attending an alternative high school (6 males, 1 female), nonlearning disabled adolescents attending the same school (7 females), and court-adjudicated youths on probation with a juvenile court (5 males, 2 females). Since the alternative high school enrolled students following a period of "dysfunctional" behavior in a traditional educational setting (e.g., chronic truancy, noncompliance with teacher and parents), all three groups of participants had evidenced problems in the social domain.

The skills selected for training were six of the seven on which Schumaker et al. (1982) had found LD students deficient: giving positive feedback, giving negative feedback, accepting negative feedback, resisting peer pressure, negotiation, and problem solving in social situations (i.e., verbally describing a social problem, generating three solutions, and evaluating the consequences).

The training took place for two hours once a week for ten weeks. Training sessions began with a review of previously learned skills, followed by a discussion of rationales for using the skills. The third step in training involved a discussion of situations in which the skill could be used, followed by the group leader modeling the skills in a role-play situation. The participants then had an opportunity to rehearse the new skills. The youths then gave feedback to the performing student on his or her performance. Behavioral checklists were used to assess performance of each skill. Both the verbal and nonverbal components for each skill had been identified and an observer rated each performance using a three-point rating scale. The subjects were pretested individually on each skill, and then tested weekly during the treatment and at the end of the program using novel situations that had never been practiced in the group meetings. The youths were trained until they were able to perform at 100 % accuracy without prompts from their peers or the group leaders. Performance of the skills was assessed through behavioral role plays in novel situations.

To evaluate the program a multiple-baseline-across-skills design was used. Results indicated that the three groups maintained or increased their skills level, with the exception of problem-solving skills. The learning disabled students performed at a lower level on problem solving than the other two groups (59% compared to 77%, respectively). It was also reported that there were no significant group differences on the number of trials to criterion performance.

In sum, three groups of students who were clearly having problems in the social domain, at least with respect to getting along with adults, were found to test quite similarly on a number of social skills believed important for occupational performance. In addition, the three groups responded quite similarly to social skills training. The singular exception was social problem solving, an area of greater difficulty for the learning disabled than the other groups.

It is difficult to evaluate the effectiveness of this training program. As Hazel et al. (1982) point out, the sample size was small and there were sex differences in the groups. In addition, there was no control group and there were no statistical analyses of the student's progress in the program. Given the initial focus on occupational skills, it may not be quite fair to criticize the study for failing to include some type of sociometric measure; nonetheless, there is no way of knowing if these students were experiencing problems getting along with their peers, or whether the treatment had any impact on their relationships with peers, teachers, or parents.

The LaGreca and Mesibov (1981) and Hazel et al. (1982) studies evaluated the impact of training through the use of role-plays. Serious questions have been raised about the validity of role-plays as they are not direct measures of the impact of social skills training on social behavior (i.e., "a training-related change in social behavior in settings where subjects normally interact" (Foxx, McMorrow, Bittle, & Ness, 1986, p. 299). When the generalizability of training to the natural environment was tested, it was found that students used a small percentage of the components of the skills, or, used the skill infrequently (Gorney-Krupsaw, Atwater, Powell, & Morris, 1981). One interpretation of this finding is that the students did not have opportunities to use their newly acquired skills. In order to test whether failure to demonstrate generalization of skills was the result of few opportunities to use them, Schumaker and Ellis (1982) injected contrived, unobtrusive events into the classroom to provide opportunities and test for generalization. In this study, subjects were three learning disabled high school students, one male and two females. These three students had achieved the lowest scores on the Social Skills Assessment Instrument (Hazel, Schumaker, Sherman, & Sheldon-Wildgen, 1981a) and another device developed by Hazel, Schumaker, Sherman, & Sheldon-Wildgen 1981b) which had been administered to all the LD students in a high-school resource room program.

Based on the assessment, three or four skills were targeted for each student (the student performed less than 45% of the steps for that skill). The skills for Student 1 were: asking questions, accepting negative feedback, and giving negative feedback; for Student 2, skills included giving negative feedback, following instructions, asking questions, and resisting peer pressure; for Student 3, skills were negotiation, personal problem solving, and giving negative feedback. Students were also assessed in the classroom. Two resource room teachers and three students served as confederates who were trained to create specific problematic situations and to respond to the target students' interactions. These were situations that required the use of the targeted skills that had been developed based on reports of typical problem situations in the resource room setting.

Each student then received individual instruction on each targeted skill. Training was provided by a LD teacher in sessions ranging from 20 minutes to one hour on alternating days. Each skill was taught to 100% performance of the skills components without teacher prompts until all the skills targeted for that student had been trained. Skills were tested using role plays and contrived situations. With a multiple-baseline design, the performance of each student on each targeted skill was charted. On the category Negotiation, Student 1 progressed from 69% correct (role-play) and 26% correct (contrived) to 94% after training in the contrived situations. For problem solving, she went from 28% and 30% correct to 66% correct in the contrived situation. On giving negative feedback, she went from 32% and 26% correct to 22% correct in the contrived situation. On two of three skills, Student 1 showed progress in generalizing the classroom.

Student 2 showed no generalization to the classroom contrived situations on giving negative feedback, following instructions, or resisting peer pressure, although some improvement occurred after training on how to ask questions. Student 3 showed a similar pattern wherein role playing performance improved on the 3 skills, but performance in the classroom contrived situations improved on 2 skills but deteriorated on the third. Unfortunately, as pointed out by Schumaker and Ellis (1982), the "students' gains were not large and, at best, their performances only approximated a performance level which can be considered adequate (at least 80% of skill components performed correctly") (p. 413).

The preceding studies represent trips into hitherto uncharted areas. The results can be viewed as a testimonial to the difficulty of training social skills such that they will generalize outside the confines of the training room. The results suggest that some behaviors may be more amenable to training than others, that we do not know the amount and length necessary for successful training, or whether other factors such as trainer characteristics, or prior histories in the natural setting might not have significant impact on the likelihood of successful generalization. Again, there was no measure of the impact of training on social status. Most important, in the Schumaker and Ellis study there were no measures taken of the confederates or other classmates' responses to the students' performance. Given long-standing patterns of social interactions—that is, subjects' interpersonal histories—it may be very difficult to break such patterns. Perhaps generalization training needs to prepare significant others in the natural environment to respond differently to subjects' attempts to change traditional patterns of behavior. It would seem to be necessary to include time for practice and error in the generalization of new skills.

Similar difficulties in generalization were reported by Berler, Gross, and Drabman (1982). In this study, six learning disabled boys, 8.2 to 10.10 years, who received the lowest ratings on a roster and rating sociometric questionnaire and whose teachers identified them as having poor peer relationships were selected. Three of the boys were randomly assigned to an experimental group and three to a control group. The experimental group received skills training for about 30 minutes, two to three times per week for five weeks.

The behaviors selected for training were based on the children's performance during baseline. The behaviors found to be deficient for most of the six children were: eye contact, appropriate verbal content in responding to unfair criticism, initiating social interactions, giving compliments, and requesting new behavior. Duration of speech was an untrained corollary measure. The control subjects received the same pre- and posttreatment measures.

The training was conducted in a group with three boys and two adult group leaders. First, the group leader described the target behavior, and provided a rationale for its use. Group leaders then presented one of 12 training scenes. Children took turns role-playing the scenes with one child prompting and the other responding. The adults coached the children, modeled correct responses, and gave feedback and praise. The role-playing was videotaped to provide children with feedback on their performance. Training procedures to facilitate generalization included using two trainers (the use of a teacher was thought to serve as a discriminative stimulus), group training (so that peers might serve as discriminative stimuli), devoting 5 to 10 minutes of each session to rehearse responses to scenes developed by the children, and verbal and written instructions to classroom teachers to provide feedback to the subjects concerning their interactions with peers.

The six boys were tested for generalization using: role-play tests, social interactions in a free play situation, and sociometric ratings. The role-play tests were done on the second and fourth day following the termination of treatment. Twelve trained and eight untrained role-play scenes were administered by novel experimenters. The free play interactions were observed in an outdoor area where it was difficult to obtain reliable recordings of behaviors taught in the training sessions. Observers thus recorded frequencies of verbalizations and play behavior (e.g., participation in a cooperative activity). To assess maintenance, the six boys were reassessed one month following the termination of treatment, again using role-plays, observations in the free play session, and sociometric ratings.

Results of the multiple baseline analysis averaged for the 12 role-play training scenes found an increase of eye contact (.03 to .75), an increase in appropriate verbalizations (.18 to .63), and a slight increase in speech duration. No such changes were found for the control subjects. On the untrained role-play scenes there were trends toward improved eye contact and appropriate verbal content and speech duration. Using novel experimenters yielded essentially the same results for the six children. The free play observational data found increases in play behavior and verbalization directed toward peers for experimental and control subjects but no changes in verbal behavior directed and received from individual peers. There were no changes in sociometric status from baseline to post-treatment tests. The one-month followup found about the same performance on the role-plays, inconsistent changes in the free play setting, and sociometric ratings either remained unchanged or declined. In sum, the results found that in structured situations, targeted social skills can be taught and maintained. But the training did not have an influence on their interactions with individual classmates, nor any impact on their sociometric status.

Insofar as this study attempted to build in various ways of ensuring generalization, the results were disappointing. Berler et al. (1982) suggested that the lack of treatment impact on peer status and interactions might have resulted from the teachers' failure to follow through in the classrooms, the use of different categories of behavior to assess generalization in the free-play situation and, most important, the failure to select target behaviors that have an empirically demonstrated relationship with a criterion measure of social competence. In addition they suggest that perhaps students with learning disabilities represent a different population; that there is some unique reason why the results of training had such limited impact.

McCloskey and Quay (1987) also used a coaching model to train social skills in mainstreamed handicapped children. What differed in this study was the use of student teachers as trainers. In this study, subjects were 26 first through fourth grade children (20 boys and 6 girls) in classrooms that had student teachers. The children were selected on the basis of low peer acceptance as measured by a nomination or picture rating scale and teacher recommendations. Sixteen of the children were diagnosed as behavior disordered, four were learning disabled, and six were extremely withdrawn. Children were randomly assigned to one of three treatments: cognitive coaching, individual instruction, no training. In the cognitive coaching condition, student teachers were given 6 hours of training and scripts to conduct eight coaching play sessions over a 4-week period. The coaching sessions included: (a) participation (getting started, paying attention), (b) cooperation (taking turns, sharing), (c) communication (talking with and listening to others), and (d) validation support (looking at others, smiles, help or encouragement). In individual instruction, student teachers were taught to individualize instruction for a target child. In the No Training condition, children participated only in the assessments.

The effects of the training were assessed by: (a) sociometric measures administered before selection, immediately after the intervention, and about 4 to 6 weeks later; (b) observations made after selection, immediately following the intervention, and 4 to 6 weeks later; and (c) student teachers and classroom teachers' evaluations of changes in academic and social behavior. The results found no changes in sociometric status or observations as a function of treatment. Student teachers and classroom teachers' ratings found social improvement cited for children in the coaching condition, and no changes for the no-training control group. Since teachers knew which children were in which condition this last measure is confounded.

Although the results of this study did not find significant impact of coaching on sociometric status and observational measures, closer analysis demonstrates a critical problem in social skills training. Some of the children did profit from the training; these children tended to be socially withdrawn. The children for whom there was little or no change were those whose problems were related to acting-out behavior. Children with problems in paying attention, following rules, and arguing were not helped or only partially helped by the coaching. The significant point here is that coaching has to be individualized, matched to the social deficits of the child. It is not sufficient to train children in social skills found correlated with peer acceptance if at the same time these children engage in behaviors that are highly aversive to their peers. Furthermore, behaviors may not even be "social" in the sense of being interactive. Children who pick their noses or have temper tantrums, who hold up the class by virtue of being off-task may not have social interactions that are inappropriate, yet may be highly rejected. The important factor is to determine the source of the child's rejection when selecting targeted behaviors for training.

Finding adolescents with learning disabilities to differ from juvenile delinquents and other adolescents with social problems on measures of social problem solving, even after training, led Hazel et al. (1982) to suggest that the social skills deficits of learning disabled students may be related to cognitive processing rather than to general social skills deficits. Larson and Gerber (1987) indirectly tested this hypothesis in a social skills training program. In this study the effects of metacognitive training on negative behavior were tested using 34 learning disabled and 34 low-achieving incarcerated 16- to 19-year-old delinquents. Subjects were randomly assigned to metacognitive training or an attention or a test-only control group.

In the metacognitive training subjects were coached in verbal self-instructions on how to think before responding (3 sessions), social metacognitive awareness on what to think about when facing a social problem (9 lessons), and social metacognitive control skills (how to work out step-by-step procedures when looking for solutions to problems (10 lessons). The subjects in the attention control condition received lessons on daily living skills. Role-playing and group discussions were similar to the metacognitive group, but no interpersonal skills were discussed or taught. Students in the metacognitive and attention conditions received 22 1 $\frac{1}{2}$ hours of training over a 7-week period.

Following training, subjects were tested on metacognitive awareness of self and others. The results found that LD and NLD subjects in the metacognitive training condition were significantly better than LD and NLD subjects in the two control conditions in identifying meta-other and meta-self variables. On meta-control knowledge, the LD subjects identified more metacognitive control steps than LD subjects in the two control groups. Changes in behavior were reported by the staff at the institutions. The LD and NLD treatment groups were rated higher on reducing negative behavior than subjects in the control groups. Unfortunately, it is not known whether the staff were blind as to the subject's condition of training, nor are specifics provided on the ratings. Since this is the only measure of generalization, it is an oversight. Nonetheless, the results do provide support for the authors' claim that "parallel improvement in metacognitive skills and significant correlations between social metacognitive scores and indicators of effective behavior support the notion that social metacognition mediates overt social behavior in novel contexts without specific cueing from the environment" (1987, p. 201).

Summary

The purpose of this chapter was to review the use of social skills training with students who have learning disabilities. The results of these studies demonstrated that children and adolescents with learning disabilities can be trained to increase the frequency of the targeted skills they use in structured settings. The verdicts on the generalizability of targeted skills to natural settings and the impact of training on sociometric status and peer interactions in natural settings, however, are not yet in. Although the research found that children and adolescents with learning disabilities could be trained to use specific social skills, tested primarily using role-plays, carryover of such training to classrooms and increases in peer popularity were not demonstrated.

Clearly, the issue of generalization is a major one. Unless generalization of social skills training can be demonstrated in the natural environment it will be hard to defend the investment of resources in such endeavors. The lack of generalization, it might be noted, is not limited to studies of students with learning disabilities. The lack of generalization in other studies has led to skepticism concerning the social validity of training, a call for a moratorium on training, and conceptual reformulations of social skills (Foxx, McMorrow, Bittle, & Ness, 1986). In response, Foxx et al. (1986) tested whether a number of situational constraints might not influence generalization using a sample of elderly, mentally retarded female residents in a community facility. Although their sample was radically different from that of interest in this chapter, their study identified a number of situational variables that appear likely to influence generalization of social skills training irrespective of characteristics of the trainees.

The first important finding was that generalization of training may be delayed. Subjects in their study who failed to show generalization during training were found to show it in a followup 15-weeks later. Second, the subjects were found to be more likely to use the trained skills in some situations than in others. The situation in which generalization is tested may be very critical. They reported that subjects were more likely to use the trained behaviors when they interacted with others who exhibited similar behaviors. The trained behaviors were less likely to be reinforced by peers who themselves did not use such behaviors. The skills of significant others and the norms of the group must be taken into account when testing generalization.

Other factors are related to the subjects. As mentioned earlier, it is unlikely that social skills training will be effective unless the behaviors targeted are those causing the child's social problems. Social niceties are not likely to outweigh socially aversive behaviors; hence the results of the studies underscore the importance of individualized training. However, in the absence of socially repugnant behaviors it makes good sense to teach learning disabled students social behaviors correlated with peer acceptance. Assuming that LD disabled youngsters are not likely to be engaging in aggressive acting-out behavior (or they would be diagnosed behavior disordered), why did the social skills training fail to result in sociometric status improvements (cf. McCloskey & Quay, 1987; Berler, Cross, & Drabman, 1982)? We suggest that a possible clue can be found in the Hazel et al. (1982) study. Recall that in this study learning disabled, juvenile delinquents, and achieving students acquired a variety of social skills at about the same rates, with the exception of one category: problem solving. The LD adolescents were less skilled at problem solving and showed greater difficulty in acquiring the skills associated with social problem solving. Although the coaching studies all start training by providing some type of rationale and examples of the uses of the behavior being trained, it may be that there is inadequate emphasis on the cognitive learning of social skills. It is probably not sufficient to teach children specific social skills; they need a great deal of information regarding the situations in which such skills can be appropriately deployed. When, with whom, how, where: basic principles governing how to read social situations may be sorely undertaught in these training programs.

Also ignored in social skills training studies are such factors as developmental and sex differences, and affect. There is an accumulating body of data outlining the ages/stages of developmental differences in peer interaction and friendships. The coaching studies (e.g., LaGreca & Mesibov, 1981; McCloskey & Quay, 1987) are geared toward elementary aged children; the training studies that focus on occupational skills (Hazel et al.,

1982) are aimed at adolescents. If learning disabled youngsters are developmentally delayed in their acquisition of social cognitive skills, the targeted behaviors may be much more difficult for them to learn. The training programs may require more time, more trials, more varied types of training and testing.

None of the training studies analyzed learning and performance differences, or appropriateness of the training given male and female differences in friendship styles. Since LD females may be at greater risk for problems in social status (Bryan, 1974; Scranton & Ryckmon, 1979), future studies should pay closer attention to sex differences.

In a related vein, subjects selected for training are likely to have established patterns of interaction. Although this issue is covered in the discussion of generalization, it is also important to consider when grouping selected children for training. Children come to the intervention setting having known their classmates, often since kindergarten. It may be difficult to change the social relationships of children who have had histories of mutual antagonism and dislike. Children who have no prior established antipathy may be more likely to respond to intervention efforts since their histories will be less likely to interfere. In addition, the characteristics of the group are likely to influence whether targeted skills are accepted. Wright, Giammarino, and Parad (1986) showed how aggressive children tend to be better accepted in groups that endorse aggression than in groups that are more laid back; conversely, quiet children are more likely to be better accepted in more passive groups than in aggressive groups. Social skills training is not likely to be effective if it tries to teach behaviors that are not endorsed, valued, or reinforced by the child's peer group.

Finally, missing from social skills training, indeed, from much of the social cognitive research, is concern for affective variables. Feelings, emotions, moods, are generally ignored in assessments, training, and evaluation of program impact. Does the training elicit anxiety? Does meeting criterion generate joy or positive feelings of accomplishments/efficacy? Wouldn't affective responses mediate the likelihood the child will use the trained behaviors outside the training sessions?

The social skills training studies have opened up a new vista for understanding and helping children with learning disabilities. It is clear that we have a great deal of work to do.

References

Asher, S.R., Oden, S.L., & Gottman, J.M. (1976). Children's friendship in school settings. In L.M. Katz (Ed.), *Quarterly review of early childhood education. 1*(1).

Asher, S.R., & Renshaw, R.P. (1981). Children without friends: Social knowledge and social-skill training. In S.R. Asher and J. Gottman (Eds), *The development of children's friendship* (pp. 273–296). NewYork: Cambridge University Press.

Bandura, A. (1972). Modeling theory: Some traditions, trends, and disputes. In R. Parke (Ed.), *Recent trends in social learning theory*. New York: Academic Press.

Bandura, A. (1977). Self-efficacy: Toward a unifying theory of behavior change. *Psychological Review, 84*, 191–215.

Bandura, A. (1981). Self-referent thought: A developmental analysis of self-efficacy. In J.H. Flavell & L. Ross (Eds.), *Social cognitiy development: Frontiers and possible futures*. New York: Cambridge University Press.

Bandura, A. (1982). Self-efficacy mechanism in human agency. *American Psychologist, 37*, 122–147.

Berler, E.S., Gross, A.M., & Drabman, R.S. (1982). Social skills training with children: Proceed with caution. *Journal of Applied Behavior Analysis, 15*, 41–53.

Bierman, K.L. (1986). Process of change during social skills training with preadolescents and its relation to treatment outcome. *Child Development, 57*, 230–240.

Bryan, T. (1974). Peer popularity of learning disabled children. *Journal of Learning Disabilities, 1*, 621–625.

Bryan, T., & Bryan, J. (1990). Social factors in learning disabilities: attitudes and interactions. In G. Pavlidis (Ed.), *Dyslexia: Neuropsychological and learning perspective*. New York: Wiley, 245–280.

Donahue, M., Bryan, T., & Pearl, R. (1980). Communicative competence in learning disabled children. In I. Bialer & K.O. Gadow (Eds) *Advances in learning and Behavioral* Disabilitics (Vol II). Greenwich, CT. JAI Press.

de Bettencourt, L.U. (1987). Strategy training: A need for clarification. *Exceptional Children, 54*(1), 24–30.

Foxx, R.M., McMorrow, M.J., Bittle, R.G., & Ness, J. (1986). An analysis of social skills generalization in two natural settings. *Journal of Applied Behavior Analysis, 19*, 299–305.

Gorney-Krupsaw, B., Atwater, J., Powell, L., & Morris, E.K. (1981). *Improving social interactions between learning disabled adolescents and teachers: A child effects approach* (Research Report No. 45). Lawrence: The University of Kansas Institute for Research in Learning Disabilities.

Gresham, F.M. (1981). Social skills training with handicapped. A review. *Review of Educational Research, 51*(1), 139–176.

Gresham, F.M. (1982). Misguided mainstreaming: The case for social skills training with handicapped children. *Exceptional Children, 48*, 420–433.

Gresham, F.M. (1983). Social skills assessment as a component of mainstreaming placement decisions. *Exceptional Children, 49*, 331–336.

Gresham, F.M. (1984). Social skills and self-efficacy for exceptional children. *Exceptional Children, 51*, 253–261.

Hazel, J.S., Schumaker, J.B., Sherman, J.A., & Sheldon-Wildgen, J. (1981a). *ASSET: A social skills program for adoelscents*. Champaign, IL: Research Press.

Hazel, J.S., Schumaker, J.B., Sherman, J.A., & Sheldon-Wildgen, J. (1981b). The development and evaluation of a group skills training program for court-adjudicated youths. In D. Upper & S.M. Ross (Eds.), *Behavioral group therapy*, Champaign, IL: Research Press.

Hazel, J.S., Schumaker, J.B., Sherman, J.A., & Sheldon-Wildgen, J. (1982). Application of a group training program in social skills and problem solving skills to learning disabled and non-learning disabled youth. *Learning Disability Quarterly, 5*, 398–408.

Johnson, D.W. (1980). Group processes: Influences of student-student interaction on school outcomes. In J.H. McMillan (Ed.), *Social psychology of school learning* (pp. 123–168). New York: Academic Press.

Kohlberg, L., LaCross, I., & Ricks, D. (1972). *The predictability of adult mental health from childhood behavior. In B.B. Wolman (Ed.), Manual of child psychopathology* (pp. 1217–1284). New York: McGraw-Hill.

Ladd, G.W. (1981). Social skills and peer acceptance: Effects of a social learning method for training verbal social skills. *Child Development, 52*, 171–178.

Ladd, G.W., & Mize, J. (1983). A cognitive-social learning model of social-skill training. *Psychological Review, 90*(2), 127–157.

LaGreca, A.M., & Mesibov, G.B. (1979). Social skills intervention with learning disabled children: Selecting skills and implementing training. *Journal of Clinical Child Psychology, 8*, 234–241.

LaGreca, A.M., & Mesibov, G.B. (1981). Facilitating interpersonal functioning with peers in learning-disabled children. *Journal of Learning Disabilities, 14*, 197–199.

Larson, K.A. (1987). *Project main street: The efficacy of social problem solving training for high-risk adolescent students.* Paper presented at the annual meeting of the American Educational Research Association, April, Washington, DC.

Larson, K., & Gerber, M.M. (1987). Effects of social metacognitive training for enhancing overt behavior in learning disabled and low achieving delinquents. *Exceptional Chidren, 54*(3), 201–211.

Matthews, R.M., Whang, P.L., & Fawcett, S.B. (1980). *Behavioral assessment of occupational skills of learning disabled adolescents* (Research Report No. 5). Lawrence: The University of Kansas Institute for Research in Learning Disabilities.

McCloskey, M.L., & Quay, L.C. (1987). Effects of handicapped children's social behavior and teachers' attitudes in mainstreamed classrooms. *Elementary School Journal, 87*, 425–435.

Mills, M.C. (1987). An intervention program for adolescents with behavioral problems. *Adolescence, 22*(85), 91–96.

Oden, S., & Asher, S.R. (1977). Coaching children in social skills for friendship making. *Child Development, 48*, 495–506.

Parker, J.G., & Asher, S.R. (1987). Peer relations and later personal adjustment: Are low-accepted children at risk? Psychological Bulletin, *102*, 357–389.

Piaget, J. (1970). *Structuralism.* Trans. and edited by Chaninah Maschler. New York: Basic Books.

Saloner, M.R. & Gettinger, M. (1985). Social inference skills in learning disabled and nondisabled children. *Psychology in the Schools, 22*, 201–207.

Schumaker, J.B., & Ellis, E.S. (1982). Social skills training of LD adolescents: A generalization study. *Learning Disability Quarterly, 5*, 409–414.

Scranton, T.R., & Ryckman, D.A. (1979). Disabled children in an integrative, program: Sociometric status. *Journal of Learning Disabilities, 2*, 402–407.

Spekman, N.J., & Roth, F.P. (1984). Intervention strategies for learning disabled children with oral communication disorders. *Learning Disability Quarterly, 7*, 7–18.

Tollefson, N., Tracy, D.B., Johnsen, E.P., & Chatman, J. (1986). Teaching learning disabled students goal-implementation skills. *Psychology in the Schools, 23*(2), 194–204.

Turiel, E., & Davidson, P. (1986). Heterogeneity, inconsistency and asynchrony in the development of cognitive structures. In I. Levin (Ed.), *Stage and structure*. Norwood, NJ: Ablex.

Wong, B.Y.L., & Wong, R. (1980). Role-Taking in normal achieving and learning disabled children. *Learning Disability Quarterly*, *3*, 11–18.

Wright, J.C., Giammarino, M., & Parad, H. (1986), Social status in small groups: Individual-group similarity and the social "misfit" *Journal of Personality and Social Psychology*, *50*, 523–536.

10
Why Social Skills Training Doesn't Work: An Alternative Model

Sharon Vaughn, Ruth McIntosh, and Anne Hogan

"Man is biologically predetermined to construct and to inhabit a world with others" (Berger & Luckmann, 1966, p. 168).

In the past ten years the interest in social skills training has increased dramatically. Social skills training programs have been developed and evaluated with a range of populations—delinquents, alcoholics, managers, criminals, the elderly (see, for review, Hollin & Trower, 1986), and for a range of purposes, for example, peer acceptance (Bierman & Furman, 1984), intercultural skills training (Bochner, 1986), interpersonal problem solving (Shure, 1985), and self-control (Meichenbaum & Goodman, 1971). Not surprisingly, social skills training programs have been developed that represent a number of models and theories including behavioral (Beck & Forehand, 1984), cognitive-social (Ladd & Mize, 1983), cognitive-behavioral (Vaughn, Ridley, & Bullock, 1984), and cognitive (Shure & Spivack, 1982).

Why all the interest in social skills training? The most likely explanation is that early failure to make and maintain appropriate peer relationships has significant influence on children for many years to come, even into adulthood (Parker & Asher, 1987; Alexander & Entwisle, 1988). Early peer difficulties, particularly peer rejection, bodes unfavorably for later adjustment problems, dropping out of school, and difficulties at school, on the job, and at home.

The link between social skills training and low peer acceptance receives intuitive and some empirical support. The rationale is that children are not well accepted by their peers because they lack the critical social skills to secure peer and teacher acceptance. Thus, social skills interventions provide an opportunity for low accepted children to acquire the appropriate skills. It is thought that the acquisition of these needed skills will result in increased popularity by peers and adults for the target children.

The purpose of this chapter is to review the literature relating social skills training to peer acceptance specifically for children with learning disabilities. This chapter will present a social competence/contextualist model for increasing the peer acceptance of low accepted children. How social skills training has been developed and conducted with learning disabled children will be discussed and an intervention program that has received initial success in increasing the peer acceptance of children with learning disabilities will be presented.

Social Skills Training and Peer Acceptance

While we view social skills as only a piece of the social competence model, considerable research has focused on increasing the peer acceptance or likability of children through social skills training. Such training has been used with a wide range of populations including isolated and withdrawn children, children with behavior disorders, autistic children, and children with learning disabilities (Gunter, Fox, Brady, Shores, & Cavanaugh, 1988; LaGreca & Mesibov, 1981; Schneider & Byrne, 1987; Tiffen & Spence, 1986). The primary assumption underlying social skills interventions is that children are not liked by their peers because they have a social skill deficit that interferes with appropriate peer interactions. Once children are taught appropriate social skills they will be more likable and the result will be increased positive peer acceptance. A review of the efficacy of social skills interventions (McIntosh, Vaughn & Zaragoza, in review) indicates that many studies demonstrate significant changes in social behavior and few studies demonstrate significant changes in peer acceptance.

The problem with the skills deficit assumption is that a number of other factors contribute to low peer acceptance including low academic achievement, physical ability, and appearance. Thus, it is not surprising that changes in social status following social skills training have yielded mixed results, with positive gains in peer acceptance reported in some studies (Ladd, 1981; Oden & Asher, 1977; Vaughn, Lancelotta, & Minnis, 1988), no changes in peer acceptance in other studies (Bierman, Miller, & Stabb, 1987; LaGreca & Santogrossi, 1980), and partial improvements in peer acceptance in other studies (Bierman & Furman, 1984; Coie & Krehbiel, 1984; Vaughn & Lancelotta, in press).

Most studies designed to increase the peer acceptance of rejected students have focused on skills training alone. Bierman et al. (1987) provided an intervention for rejected boys that included one group who received both skills training and prohibitions/response cost. The results of this study indicated that only the combination of social skills training and prohibitions led to increased peer acceptance ratings from nontarget partners. This study suggests that we need to both increase desirable social skills and decrease undesirable behaviors to alter the rejection status of target children.

An examination of the relations between skill acquisition and treatment outcome (Bierman, 1986) found that regardless of the target child's pretreatment skills, rejected children who acquired the most in conversational skills and peer support during treatment were the students most likely to show significant increases in positive peer interactions in a naturalistic setting.

Csapa (1982) increased the peer acceptance of six subjects by teaching children to ask questions, give directions, praise, and control socially negative behaviors. Gresham and Nagle (1980) found that coaching, modeling, and a combination of coaching and modeling were effective for increasing the "play with" sociometric ratings of target isolated children, but there were no significant changes in how much their peers would like to work with them. This finding is not surprising, as classmates who are selected as desirable work partners may have different skills and attributes, for example, academic abilities, task persistence, neat work, than classmates chosen as desirable play partners.

In addition to social intervention programs that have focused primarily on increasing the peer acceptance of target students, social intervention programs have also focused on other outcomes, particularly increasing the social problem-solving skills of target youngsters. Shure and Spivack (1980, 1982) have conducted the seminal work in this area. Their findings demonstrate a relationship between increased problem-solving skills in young children and increased adjustment. Of most significance was the finding that children who were either the most impulsive or most inhibited showed the greatest improvement. Following the work of Shure and Spivack, a number of studies have investigated relations between interpersonal problem solving and adjustment as well as the efficacy of social problem-solving interventions with behavior disordered children. A thorough review of interpersonal problem-solving intervention studies is beyond the scope of this chapter (see Hughes, 1988), yet social problem solving is an important skill for children to acquire and is related to such positive outcomes as increases in positive teacher ratings, alternative thinking, positive interactions with peers, and reductions in impulsivity (Gesten et al. 1982; McClure, Chinsky, & Larcen, 1978; Vaughn et al. 1984; Vaughn et al. 1983).

A major component of interpersonal problem solving is the ability to generate a wide range of alternative solutions to problems. Asarnow and Callan (1985) found the number of alternatives generated to hypothetical problem situations was related to the extent the student was identified as popular. A similar study found different results. White and Blackham (1985) found no significant differences between subgroups of social status (popular, rejected, neglected, and controversial) and their scores on an interpersonal problem-solving test.

With few exceptions (Vaughn & Lancelotta, in press), social problem-solving interventions have not yielded changes in children's social status with peers (Gesten et al. 1982). A recent study with severely emotionally disturbed youngsters found that students involved in a social problem-solving training program made significant gains in the number of alternatives generated to problem situations (Amish, Gesten, Smith, Clark, & Stark, 1988), however, they made no significant gains on the sociometric measure. The overall pattern is that training on problem-solving skills often leads to increases in problem-solving behaviors but does not generalize to peer relations.

Social skills intervention training programs typically teach the same social skills to all target individuals. The assumption is that if target children need social skills interventions, they all need to acquire the same skills. While a more individualized approach to social skills training would seem more effective, there is little data that document the advantages of individualization in social skills training. Since individualized social skills training programs require extensive time for the interventionist, data that support the efficacy of individualized social skills training programs are necessary. Schneider and Byrne (1987) evaluated the efficacy of individualized social skills training by providing social skills training to two groups of behavior disordered children. One group received social skills intervention based on unmet social skills criteria (IT group), and the other group received social skills training on all the components (NIT). Following training there were no significant differences between the IT and NIT groups; however, when compared with a wait-list control group, both groups demonstrated significantly greater mastery of the social skills objectives. The IT group demonstrated significantly more cooperative behavior than the other two groups, and there were no differences in aggression scores. This study provides limited support for the individualization of social skills training.

Social Skills Training and Learning Disabled Students

Research findings are far from convincing regarding the efficacy of social skills interventions with students who are learning disabled. Of particular concern is the lack of empirical evidence that documents increases in peer acceptance as a result of such interventions. In fact, few measures involving self, peer, teacher, or parent scales, checklists, or ratings show promising change for LD students involved with these interventions. When positive behavioral changes are documented by trained observers (Northcutt, 1987; Williams, 1983), teachers and peers do not perceive the positive change. Even when increases in appropriate social behaviors are observed in controlled settings, they are not generalized to more natural settings (Berler, Gross, & Drabner, 1982). Though changes in social behavior are observed, these changes do not yield significant changes in peers' and adults' perceptions.

Table 10.1 provides a summary of findings from studies evaluating the efficacy of social skills interventions for children with learning disabilities. These studies were examined to determine if particular factors such as age, group size, intervention duration, and type of intervention were related to

TABLE 10.1. Summary of studies of social skills intervention for children with learning disabilities.

Author(s)	Subjects	Procedure	Measures	Results
Amerikaner & Summerlin, 1982	46 resource LD 1st & 2nd graders were divided into 3 groups: social skills, relaxation, and control groups.	Two interventions included small group counseling for social skills and relaxation. Interventions carried out over 12 biweekly sessions.	Self-concept ratings measured personal, social, and intellectual self. Teacher ratings measured acting out and distractibility.	Social skills group was significantly higher on social self subscale scores. Relaxation group was lower on acting out and control group was higher on distractibility.
Berler, Gross, & Drabner, 1982	Six male 8- to 10-year-old students were selected from classes in a school for LD children. Selection was based on low peer sociometric ratings. Subjects were divided equally into treatment and control groups.	Group training for treatment group was two to three, 30-minute sessions per week for five weeks. Intervention included coaching, modeling, rehearsal, role play, & feedback.	Multiple baselines measured target behaviors of eye contact and appropriate verbal responding. Sociometric ratings and free play observations of target behaviors in natural settings were assessed.	Marked increases of target behaviors in structured & role-play settings, but no increases in sociometric ratings were observed. One month followup showed little generalization.
Blackbourn, 1989	Four, elementary aged resource LD students (3 M/1 F), selected through teacher and parent referral for poor social development.	Target behaviors were selected for each child that interfaced with successful peer interaction. Intervention for 12 weeks in Spring semester. Follow up for 9 weeks in Fall semester. Training in LD resource room by LD teacher included discussion, explanation, prompting, corrective feedback, & verbal rehearsal combined with systematic positive attention.	Multiple baselines measured frequency counts of target behaviors by teachers and parents during initial 12 weeks of training in LD resource room, regular classroom, and home, & during 9 weeks of followup after summer vacation in new regular classroom.	Subjects acquired specific desired behavior across each of the trained environments and demonstrated generalization of the target behavior to environments other than those trained. Subjects exhibited a high level of proficiency in the skill of interest over the course of the final observation.

TABLE 10.1. *Continued*

Author(s)	Subjects	Procedure	Measures	Results
Byham, 1984	Fourteen, 7th grade, LD students were selected from two classes. One class acted as treatment group, the second as control.	Structured learning approach used modeling, role play, feedback, & transfer training during fourteen weeks of biweekly sessions.	Teacher checklists of targeted structured learning skills & self ratings scale of self-concept were used.	No significant differences were found between treatment & control groups for any of the measures.
Grayson, Gadow, & Sprafkin, 1987	Ninety-two, 5 to 13-year-old students from a school for LD children were trained. Treatment group (27 M/18 F) and control group (34 M/13 F) were matched on age and IQ.	Treatment group received television-based social problem-solving curriculum, with group discussions and assignments. Intervention was conducted during a five-week period with two 30-minute sessions per week.	Social problem analysis checklists were assessed.	Increases in attention and class participation during training were observed, however, no significant differences were found between groups in problem solving, behavior adjustment, or peer relationships.
Hazel, Schumaker, Sherman, & Sheldon, 1982	Seven LD students (6 M/1 F, mean age 14–9), with adjustment problems were selected. Other groups included subjects from the same alternative school and subjects on probation from a nearby detention center.	Small group training on behaviors known to be performed poorly by LD students. Intervention during 20 one-hour sessions over a 10-week period by trained group leaders unaware of group classification.	Measures included behavior checklists, multiple baselines of pre and post target behaviors, and role-play observations.	Intervention increased levels of target behaviors for all groups, however, the LD group performed poorest on all measures when compared with other groups.

LaGreca & Mesibov, 1981	Eight male LD students, mean age 14–2, from a summer program for LD children were placed into treatment and control groups. Treatment group selected through referral for poor social skills. Control group determined to have average social skills and used for normative data assessment data comparison measures only.	Intervention during 6 weeks with one-hour sessions each week. Training on initiating social interaction & communication skills through modeling, coaching, and behavioral rehearsal strategies. Role play after group instruction with videotape replay for self-monitoring.	Pre/post assessments of videotaped role plays measured conversation skills, greeting and interaction skills, plus self reports of social interactions.	Increases observed, in all measures, however, post-ratings remained consistently lower than average functioning LD control group.
Larson & Gerber, 1987	34 high school LD students (entire school resource LD population), age 16–19 matched with 34 NLD low achieving students. Paired students were randomly assigned to full treatment group, attention control group, and test only control group.	Social metacognitive training on impulse control, metacognitive awareness & control for enhancing overt social adjustment was trained. Intervention over 7 weeks consisted of 22 (1 1/2 hour) sessions.	Observations and school level promotion for appropriate school behaviors.	Significant behavior improvement for full treatment group when compared with other groups. Stronger gains for LD subjects than for NLD students.
Merz, 1985	40 LD students, ages 8–10, placed equally into treatment & control groups.	Intervention over 8 weeks with one session each week included skills training targeting social interaction, greeting, complimenting, & appearance.	Pre and post teacher behavior checklists, peer ratings, and self report.	No significant treatment effects observed on any of the measures.

TABLE 10.1. *Continued*

Author(s)	Subjects	Procedure	Measures	Results
Northcutt, 1987	30 male LD students from a resource room in grades 3–5 were selected.	Intervention was during a nine-week period. Training focused on parent-child and teacher-child relations with emphasis on attention, task orientation, and compliance.	Meausres included pre, post, and 4-week follow up using teacher and parent rating checklists.	No significant effects found in checklist measures, however, improvements were reported by parents and teachers in anecdotal reports.
Schumaker & Ellis, 1982	Three high school LD student (1 M/2 F) were selected who scored lowest on 10 specific social skills assessed.	Each student received individual instruction assessed to be deficit for that student. Skills were taught, ranging from 20 minutes to one hour on alternating days until the student performed 100% of the skill components correctly in training without prompts.	Multiple baselines were used across social skills design based on skill performance on randomly selected role play and natural environment situations before and after training.	Results were mixed. Students were found to be more likely to show improved skill performance in novel role play situations than in contrived situations in the natural environment. LD students did not necessarily generalize their use of newly learned social skills in natural settings.
Smilon, 1985	39 high school students, ages 11–18, from resource LD rooms were placed into treatment and control groups. A third treatment group of 23 NLD low achievers was included.	Intervention consisted of 12 45-minute sessions for 12 weeks with training to improve self esteem.	Student and teacher checklists measuring self-esteem were assessed.	No significant changes in self-esteem found. Significant differences found between treatment groups on teacher ratings of self-esteem.

Stark, 1984	21 male LD students, ages 9–12, were placed equally into 3 groups: social skills training only, social skills training plus cognitive training, and control.	Intervention was during 4 weeks, with 8 sessions emphasizing social skills training and cognitive self-instruction.	Teacher observations and checklists were measured at pre, post, and six month followup.	No significant differences found between groups; however gains were found for all three groups, including the test only control group, at about the same rate of improvement.
Straub & Roberts, 1983	Thirty-three (26 M/7 F) 2–6 grade self-contained LD students from two schools were randomly assigned to experimental and test-only control groups.	Group training in small groups for 4 weeks of daily 20-minute sessions of training in social awareness with emphasis on nonverbal communications followed by 4 weeks of maintenance with a 20-minute review of the program per week. Control received equal small group instruction on academic related topics.	Pre and post measures of friendship, peer ratings of acceptance and peer social affect ratings concerning interpersonal affect impressions were assessed.	Significant results for both measure across intervention period. Peers rated subjects who received the training higher on both peer acceptance & social affect than those subjects in the control group.
Trapani, 1987	29 male elementary school LD students were placed equally into experimental and control groups.	Social skills training in conjunction with training to tutor spelling to NLD 2nd graders.	Pre/post spelling achievement scores, teacher behavior checklists, and behavioral observations were assessed.	Significant differences between groups on greeting and answering questions, but other measures did not show significant effects.

TABLE 10.1. *Continued*

Author(s)	Subjects	Procedure	Measures	Results
Vaughn, Lancelotta, & Minnis, 1988	One female LD 4th grader who received the lowest peer acceptance socre in her grade, paired with an NLD same sex classmate who ranked highest in peer acceptance in the class.	Intervention was over 10 weeks, 3 days each week for 25 minutes each session. Social skills training, peer pairing, and regular classroom involvement using cognitive-behavioral approach and mnemonic strategy training was used.	Pre/post social status ratings and nominations of regular class were assessed.	Ratings from below average to above average on posttest, nominations from rejected to popular status were observed.
Vaughn, McIntosh, & Spencer-Rowe, 1983	10 resource LD students (7 M/3 F) in grades 3–6 having low peer acceptance ratings and rejected status, paired with 10 high status NLD classmates.	Intervention was for 20 weeks at 2 to 3 30-minute sessions each week. Training done in groups with 2 to 4 students using a contextualist model.	Pre, post, & six-month followup measures on teacher behavior checklists, peer ratings and nominations, subject interviews and self reports.	Change and lasting effects found for peer nomination classifications, and increases for positive peer nominations.
Wanat, 1983	30 high school students from LD resource rooms, in grades 10–12, mean age 17.2, placed into treatment and control groups (12 M/3 F each group).	Intervention over 16 weeks consisted of 80 one-hour sessions with group training using films and filmstrips, interpersonal problem-solving strategies, and cognitive behavioral approaches.	Self-rating checklists of self-concept, plus teacher behavior checklists were assessed.	Significant differences found between groups on posttest measures.

Whang, Fawcett, & Mathews, 1984	2 high school students (1M/1F) in a resource room for learning disabled students who also held part-time jobs outside of school were trained.	Training procedures and materials were designed to teach 6 job-related social skills. Each subject trained to mastery on each skill, then was observed in job setting.	Multiple baselines accross skill categories for baseline condition, during and after skills training, and at a follow-up observation one month after training.	Bopth subjects increased target skills after training, and maintained target skills above baseline measures at the follow up observation in a real job environment.
Williams, 1983	40 LD students in grades 4–6 who scored in the bottom quartile in LD class for peer acceptance were placed into treatment and control groups.	Intervention in 6 one-hour sessions over six days. Training emphasized physically and psychologically attending, greeting, making requests and complying with requests, modeling, self-monitoring, and feedback.	Peer ratings, self report of locus of control, teacher expectation ratings and social skill observations of peer and teacher interactions were assessed.	Significant results found between groups on social skill observations; however, no differences found between groups on peer ratings, measures of locus of control, or teacher expectations.

outcomes. Studies that reported intervention effects were compared with studies that reported few or no intervention effects.

Age of Subjects

Studies were about equally divided by age with seven studies selecting elementary students, five studies selecting middle school students, and seven selecting high school students. One study (Grayson, Gadow, & Sprafkin, 1987) selected students with a larger age range, from five to thirteen years.

An examination of the efficacy of treatment by·age range indicates that those studies selecting elementary or high school subjects reported a greater degree of significant intervention effects than studies selecting middle school children. Five of the seven studies selecting elementary students reported positive intervention effects (Amerikaner & Summerlin, 1982; Blackbourn, 1989; Straub & Roberts, 1983; Vaughn et al., 1988; Vaughn, McIntosh & Spencer-Rowe, in press). Six of the seven studies selecting high school students reported positive intervention effects (Hazel, Schumaker, Sherman, & Sheldon, 1982; LaGreca & Mesibov, 1981; Larson & Gerber, 1987; Schumaker & Ellis, 1982; Wanat, 1983; Whang, Fawcett, & Mathews, 1984), and only one of the five studies (Berler et al., 1982) with middle school students reported significant results.

These results suggest several explanations. One is that there may be developmental stages during which children may be more sensitive to social skills interventions. From an analysis of these studies, elementary and secondary students are more susceptible to social skills intervention than are middle grade students. A second explanation may be that middle school children require a different social skills intervention program than previously used. It could be that the social needs of middle school children need to be more carefully identified with social skills interventions developed specifically to meet those needs.

Gender of Subjects

In the studies reported here, a total of 481 students who were learning disabled participated in social interventions and the gender of 268 of the subjects was discernible (215 males, 53 females). While students who are female and learning disabled appear to be unusually troubled by low peer acceptance and poor social skills (Bruck, 1985; Bryan, 1974), there have been disproportionately few LD females who have been included in social skills interventions.

Of the five studies that selected only males for intervention, two reported intervention effects (Berler et al., 1982; LaGreca & Mesibov, 1981). Only one study (Vaughn et al., 1988) selected a female for intervention. The remaining studies selected subjects of both genders. The available research provides little support for greater responsiveness of either males or females to social skills intervention.

LD classification

Students who are learning disabled are frequently provided educational programming in either a full-time or a part-time placement. As full-time students in LD programs, LD students interact primarily with other students who are learning disabled. In part-time LD placements, students interact with children in their regular classroom as well as other LD peers in the resource room. These settings would obviously influence the peer comparison group of target children with learning disabilities. Seven studies selected subjects who were full-time LD students in classes or schools serving only children who are learning disabled. Of these seven studies, only three (Berler et al., 1982; Hazel et al., 1982; Straub & Roberts, 1983) reported intervention effects. Eleven studies selected subjects who received LD services part-time. Of these eleven studies, nine reported intervention effects (Amerikaner & Summerlin, 1982; Blackbourn, 1989; Hazel et al., 1982; Larson & Gerber, 1987; Schumaker & Ellis, 1982; Vaughn et al., 1988; Vaughn et al., in press; Wanat, 1983; Whang et al., 1984).

It appears that studies using students placed in LD programs full-time have been less successful in affecting social change as a result of intervention than have studies using subjects who are receiving LD services part-time. It is likely that LD students attending LD programs full-time have more significant difficulties in academic and social areas than do LD students attending LD programs part-time, thus their social difficulties are less amenable to change. A further possibility is that LD students who primarily interact with their LD peers are provided inadequate opportunities to interact with nonhandicapped children.

Subject Selection Based on Need for Social Intervention

Two methods of subject selection were used to identify students for intervention. Either subjects were chosen for intervention solely because they were in programs for the learning disabled, or because they were both LD and demonstrated a need for social intervention. Twelve of the studies selected subjects who were LD with no other selection criteria. Of these twelve, four reported intervention effects (Amerikaner & Summerlin, 1982; Hazel et al., 1982; Larson & Gerber, 1987; Straub & Roberts, 1983). Eight studies selected LD students who demonstrated deficits in social skills, peer interaction, or social acceptance. Of these eight, seven studies reported intervention effects (Berler et al., 1982; Blackbourn, 1989; LaGreca & Mesibov, 1981; Schumaker & Ellis, 1982; Vaughn et al., 1988; Vaughn et al., in press, Whang et al., 1984).

The success of social skills intervention programs that select students who are both learning disabled and have social skills deficits may be due to the extensive needs of this target group that increases the likelihood for change as a result of intervention. When students are selected who have significant social difficulties the likelihood of producing significant gains is far greater than when students are selected simply because they are in a program for the learning disabled. Students who are selected solely on the basis of being in a program for the learning disabled may or may not have social difficulties. In fact, many students in programs for the learning disabled have strengths in the social area and are considered highly popular by their peers and teachers. It is unlikely that these popular students would benefit significantly from social skills interventions and, furthermore, "ceiling" effects on both skill acquisition and acceptance measures would make training effects undetectable.

Intervention Group Size

The size of the intervention group is related to intervention effectiveness. Of the four studies that used single subject intervention designs, all four reported intervention effects (Blackbourn, 1989; Schumaker & Ellis, 1982; Vaughn et al., 1988; Whang et al., 1984). Eight studies incorporated small group training, from two to ten subjects per group. Of these studies, six of the eight reported intervention effects (Amerikaner & Summerlin, 1982; Berler et al., 1982; Hazel et al., 1982; LaGreca & Mesibov, 1981; Straub & Roberts, 1983; Vaughn et al., in press). Seven studies used large group instruction and training. Of these only one study (Wanat, 1983) reported significant intervention effects.

Time of Intervention

The average intervention period was 9.2 weeks for the ten studies that reported both intervention effectiveness and length of intervention. For the seven studies that reported few or no intervention effects intervention duration averaged 7.6 weeks.

Nine studies with intervention effects reported the amount of time students were engaged in the intervention ($M = 23.3$ hours), and five studies with few or no intervention effects reported intervention time averaging 6.4 hours. The overall conclusion is that the amount of time students are involved in the social skills intervention is related to significant changes in outcome measures.

Individualized Skills Training

Only two (Blackbourn, 1989; Schumaker & Ellis, 1982) of the twenty studies specified that skills training was designed to meet the individual child's deficits or skills level. Both studies reported significant intervention effects.

Regular Classroom Involvement

Seven of the studies designed interventions to include nonlearning disabled (NLD) students. Of the seven studies, six reported intervention effects (Blackbourn, 1989; Hazel et al., 1982; Larson & Gerber, 1987; Schumaker & Ellis, 1982; Vaughn et al., 1988; Vaughn et al., in press). of the remaining thirteen studies that trained LD subjects within environments exclusively for LD students, six reported intervention effects (Amerikaner & Summerlin, 1982; Berler et al ., 1982; LaGreca & Mesibov, 1981; Straub & Roberts, 1983; Wanat, 1983; Whang et al., 1984). There is some indication that involving NLD peers in the intervention is related to positive outcome.

Components of Cognitive Behavior Modification

Thirteen of the studies incorporated components of cognitive-behavioral models and/or metacognition. These components include coaching, modeling, role play, verbal rehearsal, corrective feedback, and strategy training. Of these fourteen studies, eleven reported intervention effects (Berler et al., 1982; Blackbourn, 1989; Hazel et al ., 1982; LaGreca & Mesibov, 1981; Larson & Gerber, 1987; Schumaker & Ellis, 1982; Vaughn et al., 1988; Vaughn et al., 1989; Wanat, 1983; Whang et al., 1984). Of the six studies that did not indicate cognitive or metacognitive components, only one (Amerikener & Summerlin, 1982) reported intervention effects. Thus, instructional procedures that incorporate principles of learning from cognitive-behavioral models and/or metacognition are associated with positive outcomes.

Intervention Follow Up

Six of the twenty studies indicated intervention followup measures. Berler et al. (1982), Northcutt (1987), and Whang et al. (1984) reported one-month follow up measures. Blackbourn (1989) reported a four-month followup and Stark (1984) and Vaughn et al. (1989) reported six-month followup measures. Of the six studies that included followup, four reported intervention effects lasting across intervention and followup periods (Berler et al., 1982; Blackbourn, 1989; Vaughn et al., in press; Whang et al., 1984).

Generalization to Other Settings

Twelve of the studies indicated generalization to other settings. Of the twelve studies, ten reported intervention effects (Berler et al., 1982; Blackbourn, 1989; Hazel et al., 1982; LaGreca & Mesibov, 1981; Larson & Gerber, 1987; Schumaker & Ellis, 1982; Straub & Roberts, 1983; Vaughn et al., 1988; Vaughn et al., in press; Whang et al., 1984). Of the eight studies that did not indicate components of generalization, only two reported intervention effects (Amerikaner & Summerlin, 1982; Wanat, 1983).

In summary, it appears that certain factors of social interventions with learning disabled students do affect intervention results. A summary of factors found in the examination of studies in Table 10.1 that were related to positive outcomes included: selecting subjects who were both learning disabled and were either poorly accepted by their peers and/or demonstrated social skills deficits, use of a model that incorporated components of cognitive-behavior modification, regular classroom involvement, individual or small group instruction, and long term intervention and training programs.

Social Competence Model

The position we have taken (Vaughn & Hogan, 1990) is that social skills are only a piece of the social competence puzzle. We view social competence as an elusive higher-order construct somewhat analogous to intelligence.

There are many behaviors that combine for effective social competence. First, *positive relations with others*, includes peer status, friendship patterns, and relations with significant others in the family and neighborhood. Positive relations with others begins with the newborn and continue through adulthood, with peer interactions for many children beginning as early as infancy. Second, *accurate/age-appropriate social cognition* includes interpersonal problem solving, self perceptions and attributions, and judgments about others' feelings, motivation, and behavior. Most of our work has focused on accurate/age-appropriate social acceptance and academic competence. Third, *absence of maladaptive behaviors*, includes the absence of serious behavior problems and noxious social behavior. This includes such behavior problems as aggressiveness, attention disorder, anxiety, disruptive conduct, and also the development of self-control. Fourth, *effective social behaviors*, includes the range of specific social skills often targeted for behavioral observation. With young children, our focus on social behaviors has been on two factors: outgoing/initiating and cooperating/responding.

A number of factors that while not part of the molar notion of social competence, significantly influence aspects of social competence. Achievement is perhaps the most notable example. Academic achievement, particularly in the early grades, is highly associated with components of social competence, particularly peer acceptance. Thus, children with atypical profiles on the behavior problem component of social competence may have the negative effects of their behavior problems attenuated by their high academic achievement. In a recent study (Vaughn, Hogan, Lancelotta, Shapiro, & Walker, in review.), we found that high achieving children with behavior problems did not receive significantly lower peer ratings of acceptance than did their high achieving peers without behavior problems. The group most at risk for peer problems was low, achieving children with behavior problems.

A Contextualist Model for Increasing Peer Acceptance with Learning Disabled Children

Background

Wertsch and Sammarco (1985) argue that one of the assumptions seldom made explicit in cognitive developmental psychology is that the individual provides the boundaries upon which psychological processes are analyzed. Much of the criticism of this traditional approach to studying social behavior is offered within the social constructionist movement in modern psychology (see, for review, Gergen, 1985). The social constructionist perspective challenges the positivist-empiricist conception of knowledge and focuses on the active and changing interrelationships that occur within society more generally.

Within the broader movement of the social constructionist, a contextualist model for guiding understanding of social relationships has developed. A contextualist model assumes that social relationships are a function of interactions between individuals, the social setting, and values. Social status and peer relationships are viewed as a dynamic, interactive process in which the child is both influenced by and influences the social processes of others. Drawing from the work of Sullivan, Piaget, and Vygotsky (Doise & Mugny, 1984; Vygotsky, 1981; Wertsch, 1985; Youniss, 1980), a contextualist perspective views the child as a member of interpersonal relationships in which reciprocity and interaction are simultaneous processes. For both Sullivan and Piaget, understanding of self and others occurs by understanding and forming a joint view of social reality. The interpersonal relationship forms the unit of understanding and the process for viewing social order. One of the fundamental assumptions that guided Vygotsky is that understanding the social behavior of the individual requires first understanding the social relations and interactions in which the individual exists (Wertsch, 1985). "Formerly, psychologists tried to derive social behavior from individual behavior. . . . The first problem is to show how the individual response emerges from the forms of collective life" (p. 59).

From a contextualist perspective, a deficit model of social relations is inadequate because it fails to address important components of social relationships, environmental influences, the interactions between the target child and others, and values of the culture, child, and others. A deficit model assumes that the problem is "within" the child. Thus, the reason for a child's poor acceptance by peers is the child's deficient social skills repertoire. The deficit model is child centered and seeks to solve the problem by making changes within the child. Pepper (1948) describes this model as a mechanistic theory in which by wishing too hard to create a determinate order the reality of a good many things has to be denied. Vygotsky was also critical of mechanistic behaviorism and encouraged a more holistic examination of development. In contrast with a mechanistic theory, a contextualist model assumes that the low peer acceptance of a child is a function of a number of variables including the interaction between the child and others and environmental expectations. A contextualist model assumes that individual relationships can be understood only in light of the social-structural context (Berger & Luckmann, 1966). While teaching social skills and behaviors may be a part of a contextualist model, it would not be viewed as sufficient to alter social status.

Integration of Contextualist and Competence Models for Increasing Peer Acceptance with Learning Disabled Children

This chapter has provided two models to guide social intervention: a social competence model and a contextualist model. In our judgment, these models are viewed as compatible, with each model providing guidance for social development and intervention. The contextualist model provides a framework for establishing procedures for determining who should be involved in the social skills training, what social and environmental variables should be considered, and perhaps even how data should be collected and analyzed. The social competence model presented at the beginning of the chapter provides guidance for assessing and identifying behaviors to be included in social skills training. Since the social competence model identifies several components (positive relations with others, accurate/age-appropriate social cognition, absence of maladaptive behaviors, and effective social behavior), these components can be examined in the target population and social intervention training can be developed that attempts to change these behaviors.

Table 10.2 illustrates how the contextualist and social competence models combine to provide a structure for social intervention training. The contextualist model defines the procedures necessary to increase social competence. It is important to note that the components of the models are artificially separated for further understanding. Social competence is a unified construct and the interaction and interrelationship between behaviors result in social competence.

The initial study applying a contextualist model to social skills intervention was conducted with a case study of a female student with learning disabilities (Debra) who had been rejected by her peers (Vaughn et al., 1988). Debra had been in the LD resource room program at her school since second grade and was now in fourth grade. All children in the fourth

TABLE 10.2. Relationship between contextualist and social competence models for increasing peer acceptance and appropriate social behavior.

Procedures		Desired Outcome
Contextualist Model		Social Competence Model
Skills Training		
Increasing Appropriate Social Skills	←————————→	Effective Social Behavior
Increasing Social Cognition	←————————→	Appropriate Social Cognition
Decreasing Inappropriate, Interfering Behaviors	←————————→	Absence of Maladaptive Behavior
Informant Status		
Social Skills Trainer for class/ school	←————————→	Positive Relations with Others/Elevated Status
Teaching Social Skills to classmates	←————————→	Positive Relations with Others/Elevated Status
Significant Interactions		
Peer Pairing	←————————→	Positive Relations with Others
Recognition from school and parents	←————————→	Elevated Status

grade were administered a peer rating scale and based on this scale, Debra, and a popular same age, same sex, student from Debra's class, were selected as social skills trainers for their class. The announcement of who was to be social skills trainers for the class was done with cooperation from the classroom teacher and the building principal. Children in the class responded to the selection as though it were a privilege.

There were two phases to the intervention. During the first phase, which occurred for approximately six weeks, Debra and her popular classmate were removed from the regular classroom (3 days per week, 25 minutes per session) to participate in friendship-making/problem-solving training. First, Debra and her classmate designed a problem-solving box (a decorated shoe box with a slit for inserting problems) for their classroom. The classroom teacher informed children in the classroom that they could use the problem-solving box to write problems they had with peers either on the playground or in the classroom. The problem solving trainers, Debra and her high peer accepted partner, used these problems in two ways. One, to role play and apply skills learned during friendship-making/problem-solving training, and, two, to read selected problems to the class (omitting names), and discuss what the class might do to solve the problems. Debra and her classmate stood in the front of the room during these once-a-week sessions and provided leadership in terms of how they thought the problem could be solved.

During the second phase of the intervention, the two girls were removed from the classroom for only two days per week and spent the third day in the regular classroom teaching the social skills strategies they had learned and role playing problems from the problem-solving box. At the beginning of this four-week session the two girls were awarded by the school principal and in front of their classmates a certificate indicating they were the "official problem-solving trainers" for the school.

During the intervention phases, the components of the contextualist model included peer involvement, teacher involvement, principal involvement, and even the PTA were informed who were the social skills trainers for the school. The names and pictures of the social skills trainers were included in the school newsletter. Additionally, the informant status component of the model was illustrated by placing the target student in the position of being "knower." Debra was teaching others the social skills strategies she was learning and was viewed by others in the classroom as a source of information for solving problems with classmates.

The results of this intervention for the rejected LD student, Debra, were quite dramatic. Debra's pretest peer rating score was $M = .62$ and her posttest score was $M = .90$. Prior to intervention her social status classification was rejected and following intervention her social status classification was popular. These gains were maintained the next year.

As a followtup to the case study design, we conducted an intervention with 10 LD students who were identified as rejected by their peers (grades 3–6; 3 females, 7 males). In this study, all children in grades 3 through 6 were involved in peer rating and nomination tasks. High accepted students were paired with peer rejected classmates who were learning disabled. The principal and classroom teacher announced that based on the "lottery" these children were selected as the social skills trainers for the school. The social skills intervention occurred in a similar format to the case study design with one exception, target children were even more involved in teaching the social skills strategies to their classmates. One of the social skills strategies taught by the target students to their classmates was the "FAST" mnemonic strategy, a four-step strategy for solving problems.

*F*REEZE! Don't act too quickly. What is the problem?
*A*lternatives! What are all my possible solutions?
*S*elect one! What is the best solution in the long run?
*T*ry it! What do I need to do to implement the solution? And if it doesn't work, what else can I try?

After the social skills trainers learned the strategy and could apply it to problem-solving situations, they taught the strategy to their classmates. Teaching the strategy included large group instruction in which the social skills trainers presented large letters representing F-Λ-S-T and rehearsed with their classmates what each letter represented. Additionally, they provided motivation for their classmates to learn the strategy by giving examples of how they applied it to real-life problems.

The results from this intervention were mixed with boys making significant gains in peer acceptance, while peer acceptance ratings for the entire group of target students approached significance. Further support for the social difficulties of female LD students was identified (Bruck, 1985; Bryan, 1974) with females making nonsignificant gains as a result of the intervention.

The intention of applying a contextualist model to increasing the peer acceptance of rejected children who are learning disabled was to develop a model that involved the target child, peers, and significant others (popular peers, teachers, school principal). The focus was on increasing the peer acceptance of the target children by placing them in the role of the "knower," and by providing systematic opportunities for them to demonstrate their skills to their peers. The program was established within the classroom setting and required the cooperation of the classroom teacher and school principal.

Summary

Heretofore, social skills interventions have largely represented skills deficit models in that they have focused on teaching appropriate social skills as a means to increasing the peer acceptance of target students. This chapter has presented an alternative model that integrates a social competence and a contextualist model for developing and structuring social interventions with children who are not liked by their peers.

A review of social skills interventions with learning disabled students identified several factors that likely influence the success of social skills training including: length of intervention, number of subjects in the training groups, and intervention procedures used. Considering these factors when developing social skills interventions should increase the likelihood for success.

References

Alexander, K.L., & Entwisle, D.R. (1988). Achievement in the first 2 years of school: Patterns and processes. *Monographs of the Society for Research in Child Development, 53*(2), 157.

Amerikaner, M., & Summerlin, M.L. (1982). Group counseling with learning disabled children: Effects of social skills and relaxation training on self-concept and classroom behavior. *Journal of Learning Disabilities, 15*, 340–343.

Amish, P.L., Gesten, E.L., Smith, J.K., Clark, H.B., & Stark, C. (1988). Social problem-solving training for severely emotionally and behaviorally disturbed children. *Behavioral Disorders, 13*(3), 175–186.

Asarnow, J.R., & Callan, J.W. (1985). Boys with peer adjustment problems: Social cognitive processes. *Journal of Consulting and Clinical Psychology, 53*, 80–87.

Beck, S., & Forehand, R. (1984). Social skills training for children: A methodological and clinical review of behavior modification studies. *Behavior Psychotherapy, 12*, 17–45.

Berger, P.L., & Luckmann, T. (1966). *The social construction of reality.* Garden City, NY: Doubleday.

Berler, E.G., Gross, A.M., & Drabner, R.S. (1982). Social skills training with children: Proceed with caution. *Journal of Applied Behavior Analysis, 15*, 41–53.

Bierman, K.L. (1986). Process of change during social skills training with preadolescents and its relation to treatment outcome. *Child Development, 57*, 230–240.

Bierman, K.L., & Furman, W. (1984). The effects of social skills training and peer involvement on the socialfadjustment of preadolescents. *Child Development, 55*, 151–162.

Bierman, K.L., Miller, C.L., & Stabb, S.D. (1987). Improving the social behavior and peer acceptance of rejected boys: Effects of social skill training with instructions and prohibitions. *Journal of Consulting and Clinical Psychology, 55*(2), 194–200.

Blackbourn, J.M. (1989). Acquisition and generalization of social skills in elementary-aged children with learning disabilities. *Journal of Learning Disabilities, 22*, 28–34.

Bochner, S. (1986). Training inter-cultural skills. In C.R. Hollin & P. Trower (Eds.), *Handbook of social skills training* (pp. 155–184). Oxford, England: Pergamon.

Bruck, M. (1985). The adult functioning of children with specific learning disabilities. In L. Siegel (Ed.), *Advances in applied developmental psychology* (pp. 91–129). Norwood, NJ: Ablex.

Bryan, T. (1974). Peer popularity of learning disabled children. *Journal of Learning Disabilities, 7*, 261–268.

Byham, L.W. (1984). Social skills training to improve the social skills and self-concept of learning disabled adolescents. *Dissertation Abstracts International, 45*, 412–413A.

Coie, J.D., & Krehbiel, G. (1984). Effects of academic tutoring on the social-status of low-achieving, socially rejected children. *Child Development, 55*, 1465–1478.

Csapa, M. (1982). Effects of social learning training with socially rejected children. *Behavior Disorders, 8*(3), 199–208.

Doise, W., & Mugny, G. (1984). *The social development of the intellect.* Oxford, England: Pergamon.

Gergen, K.J. (1985). The social constructionist movement in modern psychology. *American Psychologist, 40*(3), 266–275.

Gesten, E.L., Rains, M. H., Rapkin, B.D., Weissberg, R.P., deApodaca, R.F., Cowen, E.L., & Bowen, R. (1982). Training children in social problem-solving competencies: A first and second look. *American Journal of Community Psychology, 10*, 149–153.

Grayson, P., Gadow, K.D., & Sprafkin, J. (1987). *Evaluation of a television-based social problem solving curriculum for learning disabled children.* Presented at the Society for Research in Child Development, April, Baltimore, Maryland.

Gresham, F.M., & Nagle, R.J. (1980). Social skills training with children: Responsiveness to modeling and coaching as a function of peer orientation. *Journal of Consulting and Clinical Psychology, 48*(6), 718–729.

Gunter, P., Fox, J.J., Brady, M.P., Shores, R.E., & Cavanaugh, K. (1988). Nonhandicapped peers as multiple exemplars: A generalization tactic for promoting autistic students' social skills. *Behavioral Disorders, 13*(2), 116–126.

Hazel, J.S., Schumaker, J.B., Sherman, J.A., & Sheldon, J. (1982). Applications of a group training program in social skills and problem solving to learning disabled and non- learning disabled youth. *Learning Disabilities Quarterly, 5*, 398–408.

Hollin, C.R., & Trower, P. (1986). *Handbook of social skills training.* Oxford, England: Pergamon.

Hughes, J.N. (1988). *Cognitive behavior therapy with children in schools.* New York: Pergamon.

Ladd, G. (1981). Effectiveness of a social learning method for enhancing children's social interaction and peer acceptance. *Child Development, 52*, 171–178.

Ladd, G.W., & Mize, J. (1983). A cognitive-social learning model of social skill training. *Psychological Review, 90*, 127–157.

LaGreca, A.M., & Mesibov, G.B. (1981). Facilitating interpersonal functioning with peers in learning-disabled children. *Journal of Learning Disabilities, 14*(4), 197–199.

LaGreca, A.M., & Santogrossi, D.A. (1980). Social skills training with elementary school students: A behavioral group approach. *Journal of Consulting and Clinical Psychology, 48*, 220–227.

Larson, K.A., & Gerber, M.M. (1987). Effects of social metacognitive training for enhancing overt behavior in learning disabled and low achieving delinquents. *Exceptional Children, 54*, 201–211.

McClure, L.F., Chinsky, J.M., & Larsen, S.W. (1978). Enhancing social problem-solving performance in an elementary school setting. *Journal of Educational Psychology, 70*, 504–513.

McIntosh, R., Vaughn, S., & Zaragoza, N. (in review). Social interventions for students with learning disabilities: An examination of the research.

Meichenbaum, D., & Goodman, J. (1971). Training impulsive children to talk to themselves: A means of developing self-control. *Journal of Abnormal Psychology, 77*, 115–126.

Merz, M.A. (1985). Social skills training with learning disabled children. *Dissertation Abstracts International, 46*, 1231A.

Northcutt, T.E. (1987). The impact of a social skills training program on the teacher-student relationship. *Dissertation Abstracts International, 47*, 3712A.

Oden, S., & Asher, S.R. (1977). Coaching children in social skills for friendship making. *Child Development, 48*, 495–506.

Parker, J.G., & Asher, S.R. (1987). Peer acceptance and later personal adjustment: Are low-acpeted children "at risk"? *Psychological Bulletin, 102*, 357–389.

Pepper, S.C. (1948). *World hypotheses: A study in evidence.* Berkeley: University of California Press.

Ridley, C.A., & Vaughn, S.R. (1982). Interpersonal problem solving: An intervention program for preschool children. *Journal of Applied Developmental Psychology, 3,* 177–190.

Schneider, B.H., & Byrne, B.M. (1987). Individualizing social skills training for behavior-disordered children. *Journal of Consulting and Clinical Psychology,* 55(3), 444–445

Schumaker, J.B., & Ellis, E.S. (1982). Social skills training of LD adolescents: A generalization study. *Learning Disabilities Quarterly, 5,* 409–414.

Shure, M.B. (1985). Interpersonal problem-solving: A cognitive approach to behavior. In R.A. Hinde, A. Perret-Clermont, and J. Stevenson-Hinde (Eds.), *Social relationships and cognitive development.* Oxford: Clarendon Press.

Shure, M.B., & Spivack, G. (1980). Interpersonal problem-solving as a mediator of behavioral adjustment in preschool and kindergarten children. *Journal of Applied Developmental Psychology, 1,* 29–43.

Shure, M.B., & Spivack, G. (1982). Interpersonal problem-solving in young children: A cognitive approach to prevention. *American Journal of Community Psychology, 10,* 341–356.

Smilon, R. (1985). The effect of social skills training of self-esteem and teacher ratings of adolescents. *Dissertation Abstracts International, 45,* 3924–3925B.

Stark, P.A. (1984). Evaluation of a social skills training program for middle elementary aged boys with learning disabilites. *Dissertation Abstracts International, 44,* 2570B.

Straub, R.B., & Roberts, D.M. (1983). Effects of nonverbal-oriented social awareness training program on social interaction ability of learning disabled children. *Journal of Nonverbal Behavior, 7,* 195–201.

Tiffen, K., & Spence, S.H. (1986). Responsiveness of isolated versus rejected children tosocial skills training. *Journal of Child Psychology and Psychiatry,* 27(3), 343–355.

Trapani, C. (1987). The effect of social skills training on the use of social skills by LD boys. *Dissertation Abstracts International, 47,* 3398A.

Vaughn, S., & Hogan, A. (1990). Social competence and learning disabilities: A prospective study. In H.L. Swanson & B.K. Keogh (Eds.), *Learning disabilities: Theoretical and research issues.* Hillsdale, NJ- Erlbaum.

Vaughn, S., Hogan, A., Lancelotta, G.X., Shapiro, S., & Walker, J. (in review). Subgroups of children with severe and mild behavior problems: social competence and reading achievement.

Vaughn, S., & Lancelotta, G.X. (in press). Teaching interpersonal social skills to low accepted students: Peer-pairing versus no peer-pairing. *Journal of School Psychology.*

Vaughn, S.R., Lancelotta, G.X., & Minnis, S. (1988). Social strategy training and peer involvement: Increasing peer acceptance of a female LD student. *Learning Disabilities Focus,* 4(1), 32–37.

Vaughn, S., & McIntosh, R.M. (1989). Interpersonal problem solving: A piece of the social competence puzzle with LD students. *Journal of Reading, Writing and Learning Disabilities International,* 4(4), 321–334.

Vaughn, S.R., McIntosh, R.M., & Spencer-Rowe, J. (in press). Peer rejection is a stubborn thing. Increasing peer acceptance of rejected students with learning disabilities. *Learning Disabilities Research*.

Vaughn, S.R., & Ridley, C.A. (1983). A preschool interpersonal problem solving program: Does it affect behavior in the classroom? *Child Study Journal, 13*(1), 1–12.

Vaughn, S.R., Ridley, C.A., & Bullock, D.D. (1984). Interpersonal problem solving skills training with aggressive young children. *Journal of Applied Developmental Psychology, 5*, 212–223.

Vygotsky, L.S. (1981). The genesis of higher mental functions. In J.V. Wertsch, *The concept of activity in Soviet psychology*. Armonk, NY: ME Sharpe.

Wanat, P.E. (1983). Social skills: An awareness program with learning disabled adolescents. *Journal of Learning Disabilities, 16*, 35–38.

Wertsch, J.V. (1985). *Vygotsky and the social formation of mind*. Cambridge, MA: Harvard Universlty Press.

Wertsch, J.V., & Sammarco, J.G. (1985). Social precursors to individual Cognitive functioning: The problem of units of analysis. In R.A. Hinde, A. Perret-Clermont, and J. Stevenson-Hinde (Eds.), *Social relationships and cognitive development*. Oxford: Clarendon Press.

Whang, P., Fawcett, S., & Mathews, R.M. (1984). Teaching job-related social skills to learning disabled adolescents. *Analysis and Intervention in Developmental Disabilities, 4*, 29–38.

White, P.E., & Blackham, G.J. (1985). Interpersonal problem-solving ability and sociometric status in elementary school children. *Journal of School Psychology, 23*(3), 255–260.

Williams, V.R. (1983). The effects of a classroom social skills training program on socially maladaptive learning disabled elementary students. *Dissertation Abstracts International, 44*, 1424A.

Youniss, J. (1980). *Parents and peers in social development: A Sullivan-Piaget Perspective*. Chicago: University of Chicago Press.

11
The Use of Schema in Research on the Problem Solving of Learning Disabled Adolescents

Joanna P. Williams

The purpose of this chapter is to explore the value of the notion of *schema* in the development of a program of research and intervention concerned with learning disabled adolescents' "real-life" *problem solving*. We have addressed our attention to two schemata. One represents the structure of a series of problems presented as short texts. We present a theoretical analysis of the *problem-representation* schema underlying such problems and demonstrate its psychological reality. We are using this schema in a series of studies that investigate differences between the ways in which learning disabled and nondisabled adolescents formulate problems and also how difficulties in problem formulation lead to difficulties in *problem solving*.

The second schema, which we employed in our intervention research, consisted of a series of steps that led to a successful solving of a problem. The theoretical work undergirding this schema, as well as some previous examples of the use of such a *problem-solving* schema in the literature, are presented, followed by a description of an initial study designed to evaluate the effectiveness of this approach in teaching learning disabled adolescents to think critically about real-life problems and to make good decisions.

According to the National Assessment of Educational Progress (1985), many of today's adolescents do not comprehend what they read; they have basic reading skill and can carry out simple reading tasks, but have not developed proficiency in advanced reading comprehension. Many are also deficient in critical thinking; they have very poorly developed problem-solving strategies. But literacy demands (Venezky, 1987) as well as demands for a more highly skilled work force (Etzioni, 1989) are growing, and there have been many calls for educational reform (Kearns, 1987; National Commission on Excellence in Education, 1983; Ravitch & Finn, 1987).

In recent years there has also been an increase in social and personal problems manifested by adolescents, as reflected, for example, in suicide and crime rates (Statistical Abstracts of the U.S., 1987, pp. 79 and 170). The urgency of instituting educational reforms in both school organization and curriculum that will counter these trends has been noted (Hornbeck, 1989).

Learning disabled (LD) students are at particular risk in these areas. By far the largest proportion of those who are identified as learning disabled are thus labeled because of failure in learning to read (Stanovich, 1986), and the difficulties these students exhibit persist well beyond the acquisition phase. They often do not spontaneously use reading strategies (Torgeson, 1977, 1980; Wong, 1980); they do not recognize and use text structure cues (Englert & Thomaa, 1987); they are less able to monitor their comprehension than their nondisabled (ND) peers (Bos & Filip, 1984; Wong, 1986); they detect inconsistencies in text less often (Chan, Cole, & Barfett, 1987). Taylor and Williams (1983) found that even when matched on IQ and reading vocabulary, LDs were less able than NDs to detect deviant structures when they appeared late in paragraphs, indicating that LDs were less adept at getting the point of a text.

While there are fewer studies that address the problem-solving area, the research that exists suggests that LDs have difficulties in this domain: they are less able than NDs to apply strategies in solving arithmetic problems (Fleischner & Garnett, 1987), do less well in a 20-questions game (Barton, 1988), and perform more poorly in a class decision-making task (Bryan, Donahue, Pearl, & Sturm, 1981). Moreover, these difficulties spill over into the real of social competence, including peer acceptance, social skills, self-perception, and behavioral adjustment (Vaughn & Hogan, in press).

Instruction that is focused on comprehension and problem-solving strategies can be very productive. However, there is little assurance that these strategies will be generalized to problems in content domains other than the one addressed in training (Alley, Deshler, Clark, Schumaker, & Warner, 1983; Bransford, Arbitman-Smith, Stein, & Vye, 1985). Instructional programs that take a schema approach and that include many concrete and real-world instances of application are more likely to be successful in producing transfer (Adams, 1989); such an approach has been used effectively in a few projects involving learning disabled students, e.g., Vaughn (1987); Schumaker, Deshler, and Ellis, 1986; and Larsen and Gerber (1987), and it is this approach that we have taken here.

While recommendations to include more critical thinking and problem solving in the classroom abound, one cannot simply decide to introduce new content into the curriculum; there are limits to the school day. It is the ultimate goal of the research program described here to develop an instructional program that can be incorporated into the standard curriculum—that is, into instruction in reading and writing. The aim is to present LD adolescents with content that is interesting and relevant because it is similar to problems they will face and decisions that they will have to make in their own lives, and to present a structured way or dealing with this content.

This chapter reports beginning steps toward this goal. Our model is in line with recent recommendations for what has been called infusion instruction (National Council of Teachers of English, 1982; National Dissemination Study Group, 1989).

The Problem-Formulation Schema

One distinction often made in research on problem solving is between well-structured and ill-structured problems (Slmon, 1978). In a well-structured problem, the goal is clear, the way to get to it is often well specified, and much of the information needed for solutlon is included in the presentation of the problem. In contrast, the ill-structured problem typically has no explicit goal, there is no algorithm for reaching the goal, and the criteria for determining whether in fact the goal has been achieved are indefinite. Most work in the area of problem solving has been done with well-structured problems (Mayer, 1983), and, not surprisingly, arithmetic and science (along with puzzles and other material unrelated to school curricula) have been studied.

"Real-world," or soclal/personal, problems are generally considered to be ill structured (Wilensky, 1983), and they are contrasted with problems in mathematics or science on this dimension. But another dimension may in fact be worth noting: School arithmetic problems as we are used to thinking about them have already been formulated so that there is a specified goal, etc. When we think of "real-life" problems, we conceive of them as they appear *before* formulation. In fact, much psychotherapy and counseling provides help in formulating, or structuring, personal problems in a way that positive action can be taken and results evaluated.

Personal/social problems have often been presented in a well-structured format, within narratives, for example, and as case histories. The same general schema that appears in arithmetic word problems (Kintsch & Greeno, 1985) can be used to structure personal/social problems. In our work, we have written such problems according to a simple and well-formulated schema, because we felt that our questions would be more profitably attacked initially in the context of well-structured materials for which the scoring and interpretation were relatively clear.

Our first question, to be discussed below, was whether LD adolescents are sensitive to this type of text structure. Is there a psychological reality to the "problem" schema in this regard? Subsequent concerns in our research will relate to how LD adolescents, compared to their ND peers, solved such problems, and how variations in presentation within such a well-structured schema affected problem formulation and problem solving.

The Analysis of the Schema

Following is an analysis of a problem-representation schema in terms of its basic information structure. The analysis is based on the work of Kintsch and Greeno (1985) and the earlier model of Kintsch and van Dijk (1978) and van Dijk and Kintsch (1983).

A complete problem-solving schema is multilevel. It can be described as a compilation of three subachemata, two for text representation (problem formulation) and one for problem solution. First, the *textbase schema* is a semantic representation of the information in the input discourse in episodic memory; it reflects the literal information presented by the author in the text. According to Kintsch and Greeno (1985), "textbases are constructed by arranging the propositions of a text into a coherent network on the basis of appropriate knowledge schema" (p. 116). Here, the textbase schema is the fundamental appropriate knowledge schema.

Second, the *situation schema*, also constructed in episodic memory, represents not only the information from the textbase but also information concerning associated events, actions, and persons. This elaborated situation schema incorporates the textbase and the experiences the reader retrieves from his or her long-term (episodic and semantic) memory in order to understand events in the text or to make these events coherent. Thus, following van Dijk and Kintsch (1983), the textbase schema is, so to speak, the semantic "content" of the problem-solving act, and the situation schema extends this content by incorporating the referential basis. In comprehending the problem text and representing it in memory, the reader relates the discourse to some (appropriate) existing knowledge structures in his or her episodic and more general semantic memory to instantiate a situation schema for the text.

Third, the *problem solver's schema* represents the processes that the problem solver uses to solve the problem. In describing the comprehension processes involved in solving arithmetic word problems, Kintsch and Greeno (1985) write, "The task of comprehending a problem text is to construct from the verbal form of the problem a conceptual representation upon which problem solving processes can operate" (p. 116). In this model, the conceptual representation is constructed on-line, and problem-solving operations are triggered by "certain constellations of propositions. Whenever a proposition is completed that triggers one of the set-building strategies, the appropriate set is formed and the propositions currently being processed are assigned their places in the various slots of the set schema" (1985, p. 120). Successful understanding of strategies and the organizing of the problem solver's schema depend more on the knowledge structures existing in the problem solver than in the text. As van Dijk and Kintsch (1983) explain, "The basis for problem solving is not the textbase directly, but the model derived from it" (p. 341).

Within this multilevel schema, categories of information can be grouped into *setting slots* and *problem slots*. The setting slots include those categories of information that "set the stage" or provide context for the actual problem. These setting slots are:

1. ANTECEDENTS: descriptive information relevant to the problem representation. This information can be presented in a variety of ways, for example, with more or less detail, in a narrative mode or not, etc.
2. INITIATING EVENT: the action that marks the initial state of the problem.

The essential problem slots include:

1. GOAL: what the person with the problem wants to accomplish. There may or may not be CONSTRAINTS—that is, information that refines or limits the goal.
2. OBSTACLE(s): What prevent(s) the person from achieving the goal as stated.

Further problem slots (which are not essential to the basic problem representation) include:

3. CHOICES: What options are available for action. Sometimes these choices are delineated explicitly in the textbase, but they are not necessarily so delineated. In the latter case, the reader must formulate choices; he or she does so via the operations in the third subschema, the problem solver's schema.
4. PRIORITIES: How the person with the problem weights the available choices.

As the reader constructs a problem representation, the propositions in it provide cues that (1) trigger the placement of those propositions into the schema; and (2) trigger problem-solving operations.

What happens as a reader constructs (from a text or otherwise) a problem representation containing a goal and an obstacle, as described above? One problem-solving operation that is triggered is *formulating choices* (options) of alternative actions that will lead to the goal and take the obstacles into account. These options as formulated appear as an unordered array. This array, when it consists of more than one option, triggers another problem-solving operation: the ordering or weighting of options. The outcome of this operation is, in fact, the solution to the problem, in the sense that the top-weighted choice will be selected for action.

The information provided can, of course, go beyond the statement of the goal and the obstacle(s). If the set of possible options is provided explicitly, the trigger is directly of the *ordering* operation; formulating options is not required. Another type of information may also be provided in the text: the character's priorities. This information is the basis for the operation of ordering, or weighting, the options, and when the operation is completed, the problem is solved, in the sense that the action that the character will take has been decided.

Relationship to Main Idea

This analysis can be related to main idea, an important concept in reading comprehension. One way of conceptualizing main idea is as that portion of the text—that proposition or propositions—highest in the informational hierarchy; that is, that portion which represents an adequate summary statement of the information contained in the text. It also can be described as that portion of the text most useful to retain in memory during the reading of subsequent text. The information at the highest point in the informational hierarchy within a single paragraph will fit into the overall informational hierarchy of the larger text in which that single paragraph is embedded at a higher level than any other information appearing in the paragraph.

In the problem schema addressed here, certain slots in the schema must be filled in, namely, the goal and obstacle, for the schema to be triggered. Beyond these mandatory instantiations, additional slots may or may not be filled in. The important and special attribute of this schema is that the information that appears at the highest level of the informational hierarchy *changes* as a function of how much of the schema—how many slots—are instantiated. In other words, the main idea changes.

Description of Our Problems

The problems we used were based on interviews with LD specialists (teachers and clinicians), who identified several issues as being of special importance to LD adolescents. These issues had to do with dealing with authority figures and peers; how to allocate one's money and one's time, and so forth. Each problem text consisted of a short paragraph containing a brief description of the character and his or her situation. Two variations in the presentation of these problems were prepared. In the first variation, which we call a No Priority problem, the character's *goal* is presented, as well as the *obstacles* that make it difficult to achieve the goal, and two *choices*, or alternative courses of action. With no further information provided, the reader cannot determine from the text what the character will do. The second variation, called a Priority problem, also presents the *goal*, *obstacles*, and *choices* for action. In addition, there is a statement of the character's *priority*, from which can be inferred which of the two choices or action he/she will make. In some sense, this latter problem is not a problem (for the reader) at all, in that the priority determines the (probable) solution.

An example of each type of problem follows:

No Priority Problem.   Josh is 19 years old. He is putting himself through a two-year program at a community college by earning money as a night watchman at a local factory. He is often able to study while he works. He wants to continue his education after he graduates and, in order to do so, he needs to save more money than he can with his current salary. He knows that there are going to be some construction jobs available in his neighborhood soon because a new building has been planned. Working on a construction job will be far more tiring than working as a night watchman and will leave him with little time for studying. He isn't certain what he wants to do.

Priority Problem.   Daniel is 16 years old and his mother has asked him to start thinking about his future. She'd like him to look for work this summer in an area that he's interested in, so that he can decide if he'd like to do that kind of work after he graduates from high school. He thinks that he'd like to be a car mechanic, so he asked his sister's friend to teach him how to repair cars. He agreed to teach Daniel, but he can't afford to pay him a salary. Learning how to repair cars would prepare Daniel for a good job in the future, though. He has also been offered a job working at McDonald's and he'll earn money if he does that. He cares less about earning money this summer than he does about earning a good salary in the future.

In the No Priority mode, the array of choices presented to the reader is the most important information. In the Priority mode, the main priority of the character is the most important information presented to the reader. In these two modes, the structure is nearly the same—only one piece of information is added to the Prority mode that is not in the No Priority mode. This piece of information—the character's priority—is in a hierarchically higher position, however, and is therefore a more important piece of information than the array of choices. "Important" here implies that the information is what is most useful to retain and carry over to the next portion of the text. The structure of the two paragraphs is basically the same, but the main idea is different.

The main idea of a problem cannot be defined in the same way that the main idea of a paragraph of expository prose can be defined, because it is not an umbrella term or a more inclusive or more general term. What is important or "main" depends on the structure of the problem as a whole and on which slots in the schema have been filled with information already. The slot that contains the highest level of information that has been filled becomes the main idea. Starting with the top of the hierarchy and working down, these slots in a problem are: (1) the solution (which can be inferred, as explained above, from the priorities that the character used to determine the solution); (2) the array of choices or options for action available; and (3) the goal and obstacle(s)—which, as the problem solver becomes aware of them, invoke the problem schema.

The schema guides us as we read—we fill the slots of the schema with information, and then most of that information is deleted when we construct, or formulate, the problem. If we know the priorities, for example, then we can delete information regarding the alternative choices, because what becomes important (and what is to be retained in memory during the reading of the subsequent text) is the choice dictated by the character's priorities. The problem schema dictates that the solution to a problem or the keys to problem solution are the most important pieces of information. If no priorities are given, however, then the information regarding the number of choices that are available and the key information regarding each choice become the most important pieces of information, and this is what is likely to be retained in memory during the reading of the subsequent text.

TABLE 11.1. Characteristics of the students.

		Group	
		LD	ND
Age	Mean	14.7	14.5
	S.D.	.8	.9
Grade-equivalent reading scores (Range)		2.6–6.1[a]	4.8–9.9[b]

[a] 8 scores available.
[b] 9 scores available.

Sensitivity to the Problem Structure

Twelve students, 9 male and 3 female, classified as LD by school placement, were drawn randomly from their ungraded classrooms, in which they
had been placed along with students falling into other special education
categories. A group of 12 ND students (9 male and 3 female) was then
selected with a mean age comparable to that of the LD group; they were
drawn from seventh, eighth, and ninth grade classrooms.* Table 11.1 presents information concerning the ages of these groups as well as reading
scores. Students read a text, retold the problem, and answered a series of
questions. Each student read three texts, all presented in the same mode,
either Priority or No Priority.

Each student was given a score on overall effectiveness in recalling the
problem-schema of each problem. One point was given for each component reported correctly: goal, obstacles, choices, and (depending on presentation mode) priority or a statement of the character's uncertainty.
Thus the score for each individual problem ranged from 0 to 4. Table 11.2
presents the mean number of problem-schema components accurately reported as a function of type of student and type of problem presentation.

The data from both LD and ND subjects were combined, and it was
found that there were significantly more obstacles, $X^2 (1) = 10.19$, $p < .01$,
and choices, $X^2 (1) = 6.24$, $p < .05$, reported in the No Priority mode than
in the Priority mode, but no significant difference in number of goals reported, $X^2 (1) = .96$. The priority in the Priority problems was less often
reported than the uncertainty in the No Priority problems, $X^2 (1) = 7.73$,
$p < .01$; this was true only for LD subjects.

---

*This is part of a larger study, a complete description of which can be found in
Williams (1988).

TABLE 11.2. Frequency of correct responses on components of the problem schema.

	Priority				No Priority		
	LD	ND	Total		LD	ND	Total
Goal	10	15	25	Goal	9	12	21
Obstacles	1	1	2	Obstacles	4	9	13
Choices	2	2	4	Choices	4	9	13
Priorities	6	13	19	Uncertainty	15	15	30

Maximum per cell = 18.

This difference in pattern of recall appears to reflect a fundamental difference in the main idea of the two kinds of problems. Consider the Priority problem; in some sense, it is not really a problem, because the final statement indicates what the character will do. If a reader were to come across such a paragraph within the context of a story, what would be important to remember would be the goal, and what the character decided— or would decide—to do. On the other hand, if the priority is not given, as in the No Priority problem, it is important to remember the obstacles and choices. Thus, the priority statement changes the informational hierarchy of the paragraph content and therefore the main idea. The data reflect this.

These findings demonstrated the sensitivity of both learning-disabled and nondisabled students to the text structure and the psychological reality of the problem schema, and they have encouraged us to use such well-structured problem texts in our further work on how variations in presentation will affect problem formulation and problem solving.

The Problem-Solving Schema

In addressing this topic, the third subschema in the Kintsch and Greeno (1985) analysis cited above, we found it valuable to go directly to the clinical and educational literature, where a wide variety of applications based on a schema approach can be found. The programs that we looked at essentially took the approach recommended by Adams (1989); they taught a general strategy, or schema, for solving a problem, and ways to utilize this general schema in solving specific problems.

We were strongly influenced by the work of Janis (1982), who used a schema approach in individual counseling to help clients make effective life decisions. According to Janis, uncertainty about an important decision can cause stress that leads to poor decision making; people can be taught to cope with their stress and improve their decisions by learning a general schema for decision making. This is schema involves five steps: (1) appraise the challenge; (2) survey alternatives; (3) weigh alternatives; (4) deliberate about commitment; (5) plan ways to encourage adherence despite initial negative feedback.

D'Zurilla and Goldfried (1971) identified five sets of cognitive operations that play a part in successful social problem solving: (1) general orientation; (2) problem definition; (3) generation of alternatives; (4) decision making; (5) verification. Subsequent studies (D'Zurilla & Nezu, 1980; D'Zurilla & Nezu, 1981) demonstrated that college students who were given training that was focused specifically on one or another of these cognitive operations, or aspects of a problem schema, improved in their problem solving. Spivak and Shure (1974, 1985) have used a similar schema as a basis for training interpersonal problem solving in kindergarteners and elementary school children.

This approach has also been utilized by investigators working in the field of learning disabilities. Larson and Gerber (1987) developed a social meta-cognitive training program for use with delinquent youth. One important component of this curriculum consisted of a series of lessons that presented a seven-step general problem-solving strategy, to use when attempting to make good decisions about social risk situations that might occur in the course of daily living. After 22 training seasons, both LD and ND adolescent boys received fewer negative behavior reports and higher ratings on potential for rehabilitation; the LD delinquents' improvement was greater than that of the other boys.

Vaughn and her colleagues have developed interventions for teaching interpersonal problem solving to elementary and secondary students with learning disabilities (Vaughn, 1987; Vaughn & McIntosh, 1988). In these training programs, the schema for successful problem resolution includes problem formulation, generation of alternatives, solution selection, and solution implementation. Vaughn's training, which involves a problem schema incorporated into a complex set of classroom manipulations, has led to improvement in interpersonal skills shown in role-play situations and to increased acceptance by normally achieving peers.

An extensive research and demonstration project at the University of Kansas has focused on helping learning-disabled students improve their thinking and problem-solving skills (Ellis, Deshler, & Schumaker, 1989; Schumaker, Deshler, & Ellis, 1986). This instruction includes curriculum packets, which also incorporate the use of a problem schema within the learning strategies that are taught. Results have demonstrated genuine gains in the ability to generate problem-solving strategies for learning disabled adolescents who received this instruction.

In the work to be reported here, a problem-solving schema was developed in the tradition of the studies described above, primarily that of Janis (1982). Nancy Ellsworth and I designed an instructional program specifically organized around teaching learning disabled adolescents to (1) identify a general problem-solving schema, and (2) apply the schema to problems presented in short narratives to reach appropriate decisions (Williams & Ellsworth, in press).

The problems were somewhat longer than those used in our earlier studies. In general, the same issues were presented—getting along with family and friends, finding and holding a job, and so forth. Many problems used later in the instruction were suggested by the students themselves. All the problems were presented in the No Priority mode.

Here is one of the problems (Edward) used in the study:

Edward is a good athlete. He's on a winning football team, and he is sometimes the only lineman who can stop the other team. He gets along with all the other athletes, and he was voted most valuable player last year. He loves basketball also.

Edward is not good with numbers, and he has a hard time remembering the plays. He often has to ask another player what the quarterback's call means. The other players don't seem to mind; in fact, they kind of make a joke of it. His coach gets really upset and yells at him, which makes Edward mad. The coach has threatened to kick him off the team if he doesn't learn all the plays within two weeks. Edward is so embarrassed that he feels like quitting the team.

Edward isn't sure what to do.

The schema that we adopted consisted of a sequence of questions that would be applicable to problems in general—certainly to all the problems used in our instruction.

The general schema included eight questions:*

1. What is the main problem?
2. What alternative solutions are there?
3. What additional information is needed to make the best decision? How could it be obtained?
4. What are the advantages and disadvantages of each alternative?
5. What is the best decision? Why? Is it appropriate?
6. What would be a good back-up decision?
7. What could the person do in implementing this decision to improve the chances of success?
8. What could the person do to improve the chances of adhering to this decision despite some initial negative feedback? What problems might the individual encounter?

---

*It should be noted that students derived these questions inductively during the early instructional sessions. The actual wording of the schema as it was generated by each instructed group was somewhat different, although the main point of each question in the schema was the same. For instance, for Question 2, one group's wording was "What are all the possible decisions?" rather than "What alternative solutions are there?"

The instructional model used was based on both an inductive teaching approach and Vygotsky (1962). The instructor led the students, through discussion, to generate the problem schema. The actual wording of the schema as it was generated by each instructed group was somewhat different; for example, for Question 2, one group's wording was "What are all the possible decisions?" rather than "What alternative solutions are there?"

Each problem was presented for discussion as well, during which students generated alternative solutions and critiqued them. Along with this emphasis on inductive teaching went considerable support and guidance. For example, after the students had generated the components of the schema, the instructor explained how the problem schema was of value in helping to develop effective problem-solving strategies. (This was reiterated frequently.) The instructor also modeled the critical thinking processes that she herself used in making decisions concerning the specific problem narratives.

As the instructional sessions proceeded, the teacher's support became gradually less needed, and so she gradually withdrew it, leaving the students to rely on their own critical thinking processes and to gain confidence by doing so. This approach has been described as "modeling plus explanation and instruction marked by a gradual press for student independence in the context of supportive coaching" (Corno, 1987, p. 256)

The instructional activities for each session included:

1. *Motivation.* During the first session, the instructor gave examples of people who faced an important decision. The examples were supported by newspaper clippings. During the second session, the instructor told the students about a recent crisis that she herself had had with her teenage daughter, and she asked their suggestions for ways in which she could have better solved the problem. Thereafter, many of the students volunteered their own or their friends' problems on which a decision was needed, which provided excellent motivation.
2. *Prereading preparation.* The instructor reviewed the general purpose of the program, and introduced the day's lesson.
3. *Reading the narrative.* The instructor read the day's narrative aloud as students read silently from their own copies of the text.
4. *Inductive generation of the schema.* The instructor asked, "What questions should you ask yourself when you need to make a tough decision? She recorded an abbreviated version of the students' schema on the chalkboard as they contributed. This procedure was followed during each session.
5. *Application of the schema.* The instructor guided the group through the application of the schema to the problem presented in the story. She began by saying, "What's the real problem here?" (question 1 of the schema). Again, the chalkboard was used. The discussion continued until a decision had been reached and implementation and contingency

planning had been accomplished. (The instructor's own contribution in terms of modeling, explanation, and support decreased gradually over the course of the instructional sessions.)

6. *Conclusion.* Each instructional session closed with an activity that recognized the progress made that day in learning to reach better decisions on personal problems. For example, the instructor might ask the students what they had accomplished during the session. Following their responses, she would suggest that they try to apply this decision-making strategy in their own lives.

Evaluation of the Program

The students who participated in the study were 70 mainstreamed learning-disabled students in two large heterogeneous New York City public high schools. All four grades from 9 to 12 were represented in the sample. The mean age of the 70 subjects was 16.5 years (SD = .9), and the mean grade-equivalent reading level, based on the Wide Range Achievement Test (WRAT), was 7.6 (SD = 1.1).

A pretest, consisting of an audiotaped individual interview, was administered. In this interview, students were asked to recall two problem narratives, to describe the steps to be taken in solving a problem (to identify a general problem-solving schema), and to answer the eight questions in the problem schema with respect to each of the two problem narratives (to apply the general schema).

At the end of instruction, a posttest was administered to all 70 students. The posttest was the same as the pretest except that different stories (written in a similar format) were used.

There were 10 intact special education resource room classes, all together including 35 students, that were given instruction. The size of the classes ranged from 2 to 4 students. There were also 10 comparison groups (total $N = 35$), matched on size, grade level, and reading level. Seven 40-minute instructional sessions were given on a twice-a-week basis. (The comparison groups received their regular language arts program, which included comprehension and critical thinking but did not take a schema approach.)

Five measures were used to evaluate students' ability to identify and apply the problem schema, scored on the basis of questions about each narrative. Separate analyses of covariance were conducted on the posttest scores on each of the measures, using pretest score as the covariate. On all five measures, there was a significant difference in favor of the instructed groups at the .01 level or better.

Table 11.3 presents the main findings. The first measure, Identifying the Schema, was a count of the number of parts of the problem schema that the subject could report (0–8).The other four measures focused on schema application. The score for Solution Generation was the number of accept-

TABLE 11.3. Instructional study: Means and standard deviations on all posttest measures.

	Instructed groups		Comparison groups	
	Mean	*S.D.*	*Mean*	*S.D.*
Schema Identification[a]				
Mean No. of Components Reported	6.25	1.44	.35	.39
Solution Generation[a]				
Mean No. of Solutions Generated	5.15	.80	2.95	.39
Fact Finding[a]				
Mean No. of Additional Facts Identified	2.77	.70	.77	.32
Implementation Planning				
Proportion of Students with Satisfactory Plan	.73	.32	.36	.20
Contingency Planning				
Proportion of Students with Satisfactory Plan	.63	.27	.31	.15

[a] Adjusted scores.

able solutions that each subject generated. For Fact Finding, the score was the number of additional pieces of information that the subject identified as being needed to reach the best decision. Implementation Planning was a measure of whether or not a subject devised a satisfactory plan to increase the probability of successfully implementing his or her decision, and Contingency Planning was a measure of whether or not a subject stated a plan that could improve the likelihood of adhering to a given decision. In both cases, each subject's response was judged either acceptable or not acceptable, and the score for each group was the proportion of students in that group who succeeded.

Questions 4, 5, and 6 of the schema were not scored. The diversity of the students who participated in the study was great, and it was not reasonable to evaluate the personal appropriateness of the decisions that they offered.

In summary, our instructional program was effective in improving students' ability to identify a problem schema and to apply it to novel problem narratives similar to those used in training. These findings support the view that application of a general schema to problems presented in narratives can be an effective instructional method to improve decision making and critical thinking. Teenage students' needs in this domain are widely acknowledged, and those of LD adolescents are even greater; we suggest that the education of these students will be enhanced by the addition of instruction in critical thinking based on the use of a schema. Of course, this is just an initial step in developing such instruction. Transfer of the training to solving problems and making decisions in one's own life has not yet been demonstrated, and further research is needed to explore potentially effective ways of developing the transfer capability of this type of cognitive instruction.

Conclusion

We initially conceived of this program as an addition to remedial instruction in reading comprehension and writing skills. This goal is more modest than the goal of helping adolescents actually to improve their real-life decision-making skills and demonstrating that they have been so helped. It certainly appears from the students' enthusiasm generated in the present study that the discussion of urgent personal problems provides compelling motivation for attentive participation. Remedial instruction is often seen as boring, and to capture atudents' interest with a set of compelling materials is not always easy.

Instructionally, writing is a logical extension of the critical thinking process (Bereiter & Scardamalia, 1985). Writing narratives that describe problems can be introduced as a group writing experience and can progress to individual writing. Students can also record alternative solutions and additional facts needed before coming together for discussion, and they can compose their own decisions and the rationale underlying them. Providing sufficient stimulation is often the heart of getting students such as these to write, and the immediacy of the issues under consideration is likely to be successful in providing that incentive. Ellsworth and I are currently working on such ways to incorporate reading and writing instruction into the program.

We feel that this decision-making program is especially usable because of its simplicity and economy. It can be effectively implemented by classroom teachers without purchased materials or teacher aides. While it was designed and evaluated on the basis of small group instruction, it would also lend itself to use with a larger group broken into smaller cooperative learning groups.

Summary

The notion of schema has proved very useful in our work with learning disabled adolescents, and we plan to continue using this approach as we do further work to develop our intervention.

Acknowledgment. The theoretical and empirical work on the problem schema was done with the assistance of Laura Gussoff, Linn Marks, and Kenneth Smith. The intervention research was conducted jointly with Nancy J. Ellsworth.

References

Adams, M.J. (1989). Thinking skills curricula: Their promise and progress. *Educational Psychologist, 24*, 25–77.

Alley, G.R., Deshler, D.D., Clark, F.L., Schumaker, J.B., & Warner, M.M. (1983). Learning disabilities in adolescent and adult populations: Research implications (Part II). *Focus on Exceptional Children, 15*, 1–14.

Barton, J.A. (1988). Problem-solving strategies in learning disabled and normal boys: Developmental and instruction effects. *Journal of Educational Psychology, 80*(2), 184–191.

Bereiter, C., & Scardamalia, M. (1987). *The psychology of written composition.* Hillsdale, NJ: Erlbaum.

Bos, C.S., & Filip, D. (1984). Comprehension monitoring in learning disabled and average students. *Journal of Learning Disabilities, 17*, 229–233.

Bransford, J.D., Arbitman-Smith, R., Stein, B.S., & Vye, N.J. (1985). Improving thinking and learning skills. An analysis of three approaches. In S.F. Chipman, J.W. Segal, and R. Glaser (Eds.), *Thinking and learning skills* (Vol. 1, pp. 133–208). Hillsdale, NJ: Erlbaum.

Brown, A.L., Bransford, J.D., Ferrara, R.A., & Campione, J.S. (1983). Learning, remembering and understanding. In P. Mussen (Ed.), *Child psychology*, Volume III, J. Flavell & E. Markman, Eds. New York: Wiley.

Brown, A.L., & Smiley, S.S. (1978). The development of strategies for studying texts. *Child Development, 49*, 1076–1088.

Bryan, T., Donahue, M., Pearl, R., & Sturm, C. (1981). Learning disabled children's conversational skills: The "TV Talk Show." *Learning Disabilities Quarterly, 4*, 260–270.

Campagna, A.F., & Harter, S. (1973). Moral judgment in sociopathic and normal children. *Journal of Personality and Social Psychology, 31*, 199–205.

Chan, L.K.S., Cole, P.G., & Barfett, S. (1987). Comprehension monitoring: Detection and identification of text inconsistencies by LD and normal students. *Learning Disability Quarterly, 10*, 114–124.

Corno, L. (1987). Teaching and self-regulated learning. In D. Berliner & B. Rosenshlne (Eds.), *Talks to teachers.* New York: Random House.

D'Zurilla, T.J., & Goldfried, M.R. (1971). Problem solving and behavior modification. *Journal of Abnormal Psychology, 78*, 107–126.

D'Zurilla, T.J., & Nezu, A. (1980) . A study of the generation-of-alternative process in social problem solving. *Cognitive Therapy and Research, 4*, 67–72.

D'Zurilla, T.J., & Nezu, A. (1981) . Effects of problem definition and formulation on decision making in the social problem solving process. *Behavior Therapy, 12*, 100–106.

Ellis, E.S., Deshler, D.D., & Schumaker, J.B. (1989) . Teaching adolescents with learning disabilities to generate and use task-specific strategies. *Journal of Learning Disabilities, 22*, 108–119.

Englert, C.S., & Thomas, C.C. (1987). Sensitivity to text structure in reading and writing: A comparison between learning disabled and non-learning disabled students. *Learning Disability Quarterly, 10*, 93–105.

Etzioni, A. (1989). School reform: A serious challenge for business. *Challenge, 32* (3), 51–54.

Fleischner, J.E., & Garnett, R. (1987). Arithmetic difficulties. In K. Ravale, S. Forness, & M. Bender (Eds.), *Handbook of learning disabilities*. Boston: Little, Brown.

Hornbeck, D.W. (1989). *Turning Points: Preparing American youth for the 21st century*. Report of the Task Force on Education of Young Adolescents, Carnegie Corporation of New York.

Janis, I. (1982). *Counseling on personal decisions*. New Haven: Yale University Press.

Kearns, D.T. (1987). Foreword. In A.N. Appleby, I.A. Langer, and I.V.S. Mullis, *Learning to be literate in America: Reading, writing, and reasoning*. Paper commissioned by "The Nation's Report Card."

Kintsch, W., & Greeno, J.G. (1985). Understanding and solving arithmetic word problems. *Psychological Review, 92*(1), 109–129.

Kintsch, W., & van Dijk, T.A. (1978). Toward a model of text comprehension and production. *Psychological Review, 85*(5), 363–394.

Larson, K.A., & Gerber, M.M. (1987). Effects of social metacognitive training for enhancing overt behavior in learning disabled and low achieving delinquents. *Exceptional Children, 54*(3), 201–211.

Mayer, R.E. (1983). *Thinking, problem solving, cognition*. New York: Freeman.

National Assessment of Educational Progress. (1985). *The reading report card: Trends in four national assessments*. Princeton, NJ: Educational Testing Service.

National Commission on Excellence in Education. (1983). *A nation at risk*. Washington, DC: U.S. Department of Education.

National Council of Teachers of English. (1982). *Essentials of English*. Urbana, IL: NCTE.

National Dissemination Study Group. (1989). *Educational programs that work, Edition 15*. Longmont, CO: Sopris West, Inc.

Ravitch, D., & Finn, C.E., Jr. (1987). *What do our 17-year-olds know?* New York: Harper & Row.

Schumaker, J.B., Deshler, D.D., & Ellis, E.S. (1986). Intervention issues related to the education of LD adolescents. In J.K. Torgesen & B.Y.L. Wong (Eds.), *Psychological and educational perspectives on learning disabilities*. New York: Academic Press.

Simon, H.A. (1978). Information-processing theory of human problem solving. In W.K. Estes (Ed.), *Handbook of learning and cognitive processes, Vol. 5, Human information processing*. Hillsdale, NJ: Erlbaum.

Spiro, R.J. (1979). *Etiology of reading comprehension style*. (Tech. Rep. No. 124). Urbana: University of Illinois, Center for the Study of Reading.

Spivak, G., & Shure, M.S. (1974). *Social adjustment of young children: A cognitive approach to solving real-life problems*. San Francisco: Jossey-Bass.

Spivak, G., & Shure, M.B. (1985). ICPS and beyond: Centripetal and centrifugal forces. *American Journal of Community Psychology, 13*, 226–243.

Stanovich, K.E. (1986). Cognitive processes and the reading problems of learning-disabled children: Evaluating the assumption of specificity. In J.K. Torgesen and B.Y.L. Wong (Eds.), *Psychological and educational perspectives on learning disabilities*. Orlando, FL: Academic Press.

Statistical Abstracts of the U.S.A., 108th Edition. (1987). Washington, DC: U.S. National Center of Health Statistics.

Taylor, M.B., & Williams, J.P. (1983). Comprehension of learning-disabled readers: Task and text variations. *Journal of Educational Psychology*, *75*(4), 743–751.

Torgesen, J.K. (1977). The role of nonspecific factors in the task performance of learning disabled children: A theoretical assessment. *Journal of Learning Disabilities*, *10*, 27–34.

Torgesen, J.K. (1980). Conceptual and educational implications of the use of efficient task strategies by learning disabled children. *Journal of Learning Disabilities*, *13*, 364–371.

van Dijk, T.A., & Kintsch, W. (1983). *Strategies of discourse comprehension*. New York: Academic Press.

Vaughn, S.R. (1987). TLC—Teaching, learning, and caring: Teaching interpersonal problem-solving skills to emotionally-disabled adolescents. *Pointer*, *31*, 25–30.

Vaughn, S., & Hogan, A. (in press). Social competence and learning disabilities: A prospective study. In H.L. Swanson and B.K. Keough (Eds.), *Learning disabilities: Theoretical and research issues*. Hillsdale, NJ: Erlbaum.

Vaughn, S., & McIntosh, R. (in press). Interpersonal problem solving: A piece of the social competence puzzle for LD students. *Journal of Reading, Writing, and Learning Disabilities*.

Venezky, R. (1987). *The subtle danger: Reflections on the literacy abilities of America's young adults*. Princeton, NJ: Educational Testing Service.

Vygotsky, L.S. (1962). *Thought and language*. Cambridge, MA: MIT Press.

Wilensky, R. (1983). *Planning and understanding*. Reading, MA: Addison-Wesley.

Williams, J.P. (1986). Teaching children to identify the main idea in expository texts. *Exceptional Children*, *53*, 163–168.

Williams, J.P. (1988). Teaching problem-solving skills to learning-disabled adolescents. Final Report: Grant No. G008530043, U.S. Department of Education.

Williams, J.P., & Ellsworth, N.J. (1990) Teaching learning-disabled adolescents to think critically using a problem-solving schema. *Exceptionality*, *1*, 135–146.

Wong, B.Y.L. (1980). Activating the inactive learner: Use of questions/prompts to enhance comprehension and retention of implied information in learning disabled children. *Learning Disability Quarterly*, *3*, 29–37.

Wong, B.Y.L. (1986). Problems and issues in the definition of learning disabilities. In J.K. Torgesen and B.Y.L. Wong (Eds.), *Psychological and educational perspectives on learning disabilities*. Orlando, FL: Academic Press.

Commentary
The Effectiveness of Social and Behavioral Interventions

Barbara K. Keogh

Authors of chapters in this section have focused on a range of interventions and on somewhat different targets of intervention. Bryan and Lee review social skills intervention studies that address particular component skills. Vaughn and her associates approach social skills training from a contextualist perspective. Lloyd discusses self recording of attention to task. Each chapter draws on evidence from research with learning disabled pupils, yet the content is clearly of relevance to a broader range of problem conditions. Despite differences in emphases, a number of problems and limitations have emerged in common. These include obvious questions of generalizability, maintenance, relevance, and importance. These issues are fundamental to all intervention programs and deserve our consideration. They provide a backdrop against which we may examine specific questions of program content and effects.

Considering social skills training programs first, the chapters by Vaughn, McIntosh, and Hogan and by Bryan and Lee provide comprehensive overviews of interventions aimed at improving learning disabled pupils' social skills. The topic is important, as the social problems of learning disabled pupils are well documented (see reviews by Bryan & Bryan, 1981; and Gresham, 1981, 1989). As evidenced in the content of the chapters, interventions differ in the particular social skills targeted, in the specific content of instruction, in the length and intensity of intervention, in who does the training, and in the structure or format for implementing the training. All these are likely contributors to program effectiveness as defined as maintenance and generalization. Given the variations among programs described, we should not be surprised that the outcomes also differ, and that it is difficult, if not impossible, to draw solid inferences about the effectiveness of "social skills training." Like psychotherapy, social skills training takes many forms. Like psychotherapy, sometimes it works and sometimes it doesn't. And, like psychotherapy, when it works we are often not quite sure why, although it is tempting to attribute success to the program and failure to the individual.

In addition to underscoring the variability among programs, the reviews by Bryan and Lee and by Vaughn et al. raise important questions about outcome indices. Asked directly, what should we measure to test program impact? There are a number of possible answers to the question: The application of trained behaviors in role-taking scenarios, problem solving in "real-life" situations, change in peer status as defined sociometrically, spontaneous increase in targeted behaviors in the classroom, or improved ability to articulate socially positive responses to stressful situations. All have been used in various social skills training programs, yet they clearly differ in level, sensitivity, importance, and possibly relevance. Because of the differences in program content and techniques and in the variations in outcome measures, it should not surprise us that findings about the effectiveness of training programs are inconsistent and inconclusive, a point well documented in the two chapters.

Assessing program impact is obviously confounded further by sampling variability, including the well-known heterogeneity captured within the Learning Disabilities rubric. Some, but certainly not all, learning disabled individuals have social problems and limited social competence. Among those with social problems some may have deficits in social perception, some may lack particular social skills, others may be poor social problem solvers, and some may have deficits in all. Recognizing these differences, both sets of authors have called for more individualized training programs, and for consideration of context. These are logical inferences or extensions of earlier training efforts. Yet I am somewhat pessimistic that short-term training models, even individualized and "contextualized" ones, will work effectively.

My reasons for pessimism are several. First, as the authors of these chapters have documented, social competence is not a unitary "trait," but rather has many facets that interact with a range of setting and situational demands. It is probably naive to assume that training specific, molecular skills will improve social performance in general, as the demands for social performance are complex and vary by setting and time.

Second, while the behaviors and interactional styles of children referred for social skills training may not be viewed as positive by others (especially adults), the behaviors may effectively serve the needs of the individuals themselves. Fighting and acting out behaviors, as example, may be viewed as target behaviors for training programs, yet may be relatively unamenable to change as they provide children with powerful reinforcement and social position. Why change if the behaviors pay off?

Third, and closely related, most children in social training interventions are referred by others, usually adults. One of the accepted tenets of psychotherapy is that problems must be acknowledged and "owned" by the individual receiving services. It may well be that many of the children in training programs do not see themselves as having social problems. Thus, the content of the training programs may not be important nor relevant as viewed by the children themselves. This may be particularly true for children viewed as shy, withdrawing, or reticent. In recent work at UCLA my associates and I (Keogh, Juvonen, Bernheimer, & Ratekin, 1990) used peer sociometric techniques to identify fifth and sixth grade children as socially rejected, neglected, or popular. As a group the rejected children's self-views of their own social competencies were more negative than the self-views of children in the other groups, but the neglected children were similar or more positive in self-views than the popular children. Further, examination of the friendship patterns of the sociometrically defined neglected children revealed that all but a few had mutually selected friends. That is, although they were not chosen by many children, their friendship choices were reciprocal, suggesting that they were not really neglected or without friends. These findings suggest that identification as neglected by peer sociometrics does not necessarily infer social skills deficits or social problems. Yet, sociometrics are often the basis of selection for social skills training programs.

Finally, despite recognition of the importance of "context," many training programs are narrow in scope. I refer not just to the specificity of the social skills taught, but to the limited setting or situational influences considered. Compared to home and family experiences, children are in school or are in intervention programs for limited time periods. Training programs focused on school specific skills may not be powerful enough to overcome the influences of family and home. The point is well illustrated in ongoing work by Evans (1989) in Canada. In Evan's study "very quiet" or reticent children identified by their kindergarten and first grade teachers were compared to highly verbal children of comparable age and gender. The reticent children were viewed as less talkative and less expressive by both teachers and parents. The mothers of the reticent children were also less expressive, and there was not much pressure for language development in the homes (e.g. fewer parent-child reading sessions, fewer social/educational outings, and less encouragement for social visits with friends). Given the scope and power of home/family influences, it is possible that training programs focused on school specific skills may not be powerful enough to overcome the effects of family socialization.

Similarly, training programs focused on individual target children may overlook peer attitudes and behaviors that contribute to the context of the classroom. Pupils with social problems may learn particular skills or strategies, but interactional histories with peers may preclude their application. Said directly, peers may reinforce maladaptive rather than socially adaptive social behaviors. Failure to demonstrate transfer from the training program to the classroom or playground may be due to the power of the context rather than to the weakness of the training. Perhaps we have selected the wrong targets of intervention.

The social skills training picture is not all bleak, however, as both sets of authors have pointed out. It is probably accurate to say that this is an aspect of intervention work that is just beginning to receive the systematic attention it deserves. The directions for future work recommended in these chapters are promising. Bryan and Lee call for consideration of a range of individual differences that affect social skills and social interactions. Vaughn and her colleagues underscore the importance of the context in which social interactions occur. Both sets of authors recognize individual and developmental differences that influence social competence and social skills problems. Both also emphasize the fundamental issues of generalization and maintenance, and their analyses provide insight into the limited effectiveness of many training programs. Taken together, the two chapters allow a realistic and cautiously optimistic view of the future of social skills interventions.

The chapter by Lloyd addresses a different, but related aspect of learning disabilities: self-control and attending to task, with a primary emphasis on self-recording procedures. The chapter contains a selective but comprehensive review of self-recording interventions as implemented with a range of problem and nonproblem pupils. Drawing on his own research as well as the work of others, Lloyd has provided a useful overview of some components of self-recording training. These include questions of who does the training, the use of cueing, matching, reinforcement, and whether accuracy in self-recording is essential. The chapter as a whole provides good introductory reading for those considering implementing self-control programs with problem learners.

Like the social skills literature, the particular interventions reviewed by Lloyd differ in targeted behaviors, in specifics of techniques or procedures, and in outcome indices. In general, the results of self-recording studies are positive, suggesting that these procedures are useful for problem learners. A comparison of four interventions based on somewhat different self-recording procedures indicated that all lead to improved attention and greater productivity. In my view a particularly important section of the chapter is focused on issues of generalization. Despite evidence that self-recording is a "robust" procedure, that self-recording increases productivity, and that there is maintenance over time, transfer across settings is less well demonstrated, indeed, results of empirical studies are generally inconclusive and disappointing.

The last point is particularly interesting when considered against the findings of social skills training programs. Bryan and Lee and Vaughn et al. have provided evidence demonstrating that specific skills can be taught, and Lloyd's review of self-recording is consistent with their findings. The content of both reviews also suggests that there is limited generalization or transfer of skills to other situations. Thus, whether the content of training is specific educational tasks (e.g. arithmetic, spelling, reading) or social skills, the question of transfer is critical, and the reasons for limited transfer effects remain uncertain. It may well be that this is the fundamental issue in understanding learning disabilities. A range of studies demonstrate that learning disabled children can learn a variety of specific skills. Those who work with learning disabled pupils will attest to the "real-world" validity of that finding. Yet laboratory research as well as real world evidence indicates consistently that the skills are not spontaneously or appropriately applied in different situations. Hypotheses proposed to explain the lack of transfer include but are not limited to: learning disabled children do not read setting and context accurately, they do not see the relationship of specific skills to new situations, they are inactive problem solvers. These and other hypotheses deserve consideration and test, as they get to the heart of the puzzle of learning disabilities, that is, the lack of spontaneous generalization. From a practical perspective, the generalization issue should direct our research on intervention.

References

Bryan, T.H., & Bryan, J.H. (1981). Some personal and social experiences of learning disabled children. In B.K. Keogh (Ed.), *Advances in special education, socialization influences on exceptionality* (Vol. 2, pp. 147–186). Greenwich T: JAI.

Evans, M.A. (1989). Cognitive personality, social and background characteristics of reticent young children and their more talkative peers. Presented at the ISSBD Meeting, Jyvaskyla, Finland, July 1–6, 1989.

Gresham, F. (1981). Social skills training with handicapped children: A review. *Review of Educational Research, 51* (1), 139–176.

Gresham, F. (1989). Social competence and motivational characteristics of learning disabled students. In M. Wang, M. Reynolds, and H. Walberg (Eds.), *The handbook of special education: Research and practice* (Vol. 2, pp. 283–302). Oxford, England: Pergamon Press.

Keogh, B.K., Juvonen, J., Bernheimer, L.P., & Ratekin, C. (1990). Childrens' self-views of competence, sociometric status, and teachers' ratings. Manuscript in review.

Part IV   Postsecondary Interventions

12
Intervention Effectiveness at the Postsecondary Level for the Learning Disabled

Susan A. Vogel and Pamela B. Adelman

This research reflects the increased awareness of the chronicity of learning disabilities, the question of long-term prognosis, and the need to determine intervention effectiveness at the postsecondary level. The study is part of a larger descriptive, eight-year followup study on educational and employment attainments of a group of self-referred college students with diagnosed learning disabilities who received LD support services for at least one semester between 1980–88 at Barat College, a small, moderately selective private college that offered comprehensive, highly coordinated support service.

This specific program is based on a four-pronged approach to assist students:

1. To use course support as needed (subject-matter tutoring).
2. To improve basic skills deficits through remediation.
3. To access and use appropriate accommodations (e.g., modified examination procedures).
4. To develop and use compensatory strategies based on self knowledge, that is, understanding the results of diagnostic testing and how these relate to their strengths and deficits and learning styles.

Several factors combined that fueled our interest in this study. First, LD children identified in the 1970s have grown up. Many (and in increasing numbers) are attending colleges and universities as a result of Section 504 and the increase in available services and accommodations for the handicapped in postsecondary settings. Recent national reports indicate that 1% (approximately 160,000) of all first-time, full-time college freshmen self-identified as LD (Astin, Green, Korn, Schalit, & Berg, 1988), and this is probably a minimal estimate because many LD university students are not included in these statistics since they transfer from one PSI to another or take a part-time load.

Section 504 of the Rehabilitation Act of 1973 mandates equal access for handicapped students, including the learning disabled, to institutions of higher education. This law prohibits discrimination in admissions and in

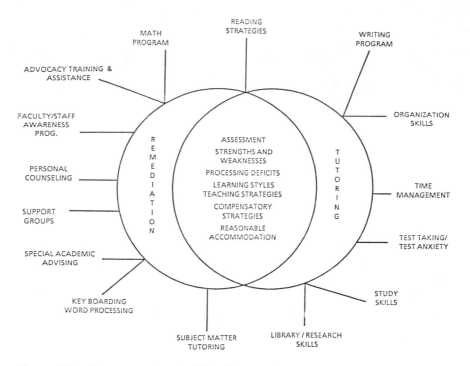

FIGURE 12.1. Support services for LD college students.

program accessibility to qualified handicapped students, and mandates that accommodations be made to ensure access. Mandated accommodations require modifications of the ways teachers present information, ways students acquire knowledge, and the means by which faculty assess student learning. Commonly available accommodations include allowing a student to tape-record lectures and providing extended time on examinations (Abrams & Abrams, 1981; Ballard, Ramirez, & Zantal-Wiener, 1987). The specific services are not mandated, but commonly provided are tutoring, priority registration, personal counseling, and notetakers (Vogel, 1982; Vogel, 1985a). Additional services offered on this campus included comprehensive assessment, one-on-one remediation with a certified LD specialist for one to three hours per week, special academic advising, advocacy, developmental courses and workshops in reading, written language, and study skills, and career counseling (see Adelman, 1985; Adelman, 1988; Adelman, & Olufs, 1986; Konrad, 1984; Vogel, 1982; Vogel, 1987; Vogel & Adelman, 1981, for elaboration).

Section 504, increased pressure from advocates, lack of clarity on the definition of "qualified," perhaps fear of legal battles, dwindling applicant pools, and the search for new student markets have all resulted in this increase. Moreover, along with this significant growth in the last 10 years in the number of students with learning disabilities attending colleges and universities, there is also an equal if not greater concern for the academic failure rate of these students (the "revolving" door syndrome).

Even with such large numbers of students with learning disabilities enrolling in postsecondary institutions, very little is known about effectiveness of the accommodations, services, and modifications that are presently in widespread use. One way to assess their effectiveness is to examine the graduation and failure rate of LD college students in various postsecondary settings. This study was, therefore, designed to assess intervention effectiveness at the postsecondary level by addressing: How do LD college students compare to a random sample of peers on high school preparation and performance, college admissions testing (in this specific college setting, the American College Testing (ACT) program is used), college performance, graduation rate, and academic failure rate.

Only one study thus far has addressed this question (Bursuck, Rose, Cowen, Yahaya, 1989). Bursuck et al. (1989) sent a survey to the 336 members of the LD Special Interest Group of the Association on Handicapped Student Service Programs in Postsecondary Education (AHSSPPE) (Bursuck, Rose, & Cowen, 1987). Members of this organization are directors or coordinators of services for handicapped students in two-year and four-year colleges or universities. Out of the total number of 197 respondents, only 20 (or 10%) responded to the question regarding the percentage of students who graduated or completed a course of study. The average graduation or completion rate for those who responded was 30%. However, the authors neglected to describe the respondents' institutions or separate out those that reported graduation rate versus completion of a course of study. Moreover, it is unknown if the reporting institutions were two-year degree or four-year degree granting institutions, making interpretation of this information unclear.

Neither do we have any substantial information about LD students' high school performance or college entrance examination scores. Cordoni and Harman (1985) studied the relation of ACT scores and first semester college freshman grade point average (gpa) for a group of 107 LD college students. Vogel (1985b) compared the mean subtest and composite scores for this group to a second LD college sample and a national LD sample and noted that though the hierarchies were different in each sample, the means were similar.

In a critique of Cordoni and Harman's research design, Vogel (1985b) questioned the use of first semester gpa as the criterion measure since LD college freshmen entering with low ACT scores frequently are advised to take a part-time or minimum full-time load (12 credit hours) consisting of developmental courses, a beginning writing course, and perhaps one heavy reading course, resulting in an inflated gpa. On the other hand, LD freshmen entering with higher ACT scores and performing better on placement tests may be encouraged to take typical college freshmen courses and a full course load (15 credit hours), resulting in poorer grades for the stronger LD students. Vogel, therefore, recommended using student exit gpa as the criteria measure rather than first semester freshmen gpa.

The Method

Subjects

A group of 110 LD students were compared to a random stratified sample (RSS) of 153 peers attending the same college for at least one semester between 1980 and 1988. None of the RSS students had been referred for LD support services. All had English as their primary language and were accepted as degree candidates. Students in the LD group were matched with the RSS students on (1) gender, (2) college experience (first-time freshmen or transfer students), and (3) semester and year of entry to the college. Females outnumbered males 2:1 because this school had been a women's college until 1982. Excluded from the LD sample were students with uncorrected visual or auditory impairments, known brain damage, or history of primary emotional disorders.

The mean age of the RSS students at entrance to the college was 23 years and they were significantly older ($p < .001$) than the LD students ($\bar{x} = 21$). This college was perhaps typical of urban and suburban, moderately selective, private women's colleges in that the student body was very heterogeneous and consisted of many transfer students and women returning to school after raising a family. However, the LD sample was both younger and more homogeneous, perhaps because the LD students were attracted to the college specifically because of its comprehensive LD support services.

Based on examination of college transcripts, each group was divided into two subgroups: the college graduates (G) and the nongraduates (NG). Nongraduates were those students dismissed due to academic failure (defined as a gpa of < 2.0 on a 4.0 scale). The following group comparisons were made:

LD X RSS
LD G X RSS G
LD NG X RSS NG
LD G X LD NG

Diagnosis of LD was verified for students previously identified by examination of past psycho-educational evaluations, current WAIS and academic achievement testing, LD specialists' reports, and/or recent IEP (available for 97% of the subjects). Because early intervention and exten-

TABLE 12.1. Age in months and years.

Group	$\bar{X}$ (years)	SD	Range in months
LD total	257 (21)	73.88	194–768
RSS total	298 (23)[a]	96.87	206–609
LD males	240 (20)	23.68	209–322
RSS males	279 (23)[b]	79.40	206–563
LD females	266 (22)	88.96	194–768
RSS females	306 (26)[b]	103.37	212–609

[a] $p < .001$.
[b] $p < .01$.

TABLE 12.2. Significance levels for group comparisons on age.

	RSS—total	LD—males	RSS—males	RSS—females
LD-total	.000			
LD-males			.004	
RSS-males				.114
LD-females		.076		.009

sive remediation may diminish aptitude-achievement discrepancies in same LD adults, early history of learning problems was weighted more heavily than the presence of a specific degree of aptitude-achievement discrepancy or underachievement. Therefore, applicants and their families (if appropriate) provided extensive history information regarding birth, developmental, medical, and educational history, and family background. In addition, prior to acceptance, students visited the campus, were interviewed by an admissions officer, the director of the LD program, and dean of students, and took three screening tests. The screening tests consisted of a timed reading comprehension test (Stanford Diagnostic Reading Test—Blue Level Subtest 1) (Karlsen, Madden, & Gardner, 1977), a writing sample on an assigned topic, and a measure of knowledge of sentence structure (Sentence Structure Test from the Descriptive Tests of Language Skills of the College Board published by Educational Testing Service, 1977). These screening instruments provided an indication of present functioning levels, type and severity of learning disability, as well as relative standing as compared to their peers.

LD Sample Profile

The mean Verbal, Performance, and Full Scale IQ were at average and quite even (103, 105, and 104, respectively) with Similarities and Comprehension the two highest mean scaled scores ($\overline{X}$ of approximately 12.00) and the "ACID"subtests the four lowest. The pattern of grouped subtests according to the Bannatyne categories was similar to other samples of LD and nonLD college students in the average IQ range with Verbal Conceptualization the highest or next to highest, and 'ACID' the next to the lowest (Cordoni et al. 1981; Vogel, 1986).

Academic achievement abilities ranged from a high of 12.9 on silent reading vocabulary as measured by the Stanford Diagnostic Reading Test (SDRT) Blue Level to a low of mid-seventh grade on Phonetic Analysis (SDRT). Timed reading comprehension on the SDRT was mid-ninth grade level, while untimed reading comprehension as measured by the Passage Comprehension subtest of the Woodcock-Johnson Psychoeducational Battery (Woodcock & Johnson 1977) was mid-tenth grade level. Because many LD adults report that they are hindered by their slow reading rate, we expected the mean score on the Fast Reading Subtest (SDRT) to be lower than all the other reading measures. Much to our surprise, Phonetic Analysis, a measure of phonological segmentation abilities and word attack skills, was the lowest ($\overline{x} = 7.6$ grade equivalent), confirming the chronicity of phonological disabilities and incomplete mastery of word attack skills in learning disabled adults.

Results and Discussion

High School Performance

The high school variables of greatest interest were those found to be most highly correlated with college performance. Though most predictive studies use college freshmen gpa as the criterion variable, exit gpa was used in this study for the following reasons:

1. Exit gpa is typically based on longer than one year of college work and encompasses a more representative course of studies than freshman year courses.
2. Many LD students in the sample were transfers (a common phenomenon among LD students). Transfer credits are commonly accepted as a "package" and, therefore, freshman gpa is unavailable and cannot be calculated.
3. Exit gpa is available for all subjects.
4. Exit gpa correlated very highly with both freshman and senior year gpa for the total group and graduate subgroups.

The high school variables that were most highly correlated with exit gpa were the number of regular (rather than developmental or remedial) English and math high school courses completed with a grade of C or better ($r = .40$ $p < .000$ and $r = .26$ $p < .012$, respectively) and the number of D

TABLE 12.3. Correlation of college exit GPA and high school preparation and performance.

Variable	r	p
Regular English courses	.40	.000
Regular Math courses	.26	.012
D grades (Total)	−.18	.058
E/F grades (Total)	−.40	.000
D grades (Non-core Courses)	−.25	.016
D grades (Core Courses)	−.39	.219
F grades (Non-core Courses)	−.31	.003
F grades (Core Courses)	−.29	.006

TABLE 12.4. Univariate F tests of significance between LD and RSS groups on the high school variables.

Variable	$F(1,78)$	MS	p
English	5.18	24.92	.026
Math	7.59	35.71	.007
D grades	11.46	376.05	.001
E/F grades	6.51	66.63	.013

and failing grades ($r = -.25$ $p < .016$ and $r = -.40$ $p < .000$, respectively). Not surprisingly, these four variables differentiated between the groups at the $p < .008$ level with the total number of D grades contributing the most. Moreover, the number of D grades in non-core curriculum and elective courses was more discriminating than the number of Ds in regular core curriculum courses. Through qualitative analysis of transcripts, it was seen that many more Ds were received in physical education than in any other subject. Since it is customary to give a C or better grade for attendance, following dress code, positive attitude, and good sportsmanship, this finding is thought to reflect noncompliance with school regulations and a poor attitude rather than athletic skills, balance, coordination, endurance, speed, or strength. Possible reasons for the observed poor attitude or non-compliance could also be related to the student's learning disability, that is, memory deficits (causing students to forget to bring appropriate gym shoes, uniform, or towel), or poor social-interpersonal skills.

ACT Performance

The second kind of information used traditionally in predicting college success is performance on college entrance examination. Table 12.5 compares the LD sample to a national LD sample, (Laing & Farmer, 1985) and the RSS group to the total college population and a national sample of 1988

TABLE 12.5. ACT subtests and composite means on the random stratified sample, Barat College freshmen (1980–1988), national norms (1988), LD sample, and national LD sample (1985).

Group	English	Math	Social studies	Science	Composite
RSS	18.48	16.83	19.74	21.39	19.17
College	18.56	15.89	18.22	19.56	18.11
National norms	18.50	17.20	17.40	21.40	18.80
LD sample	13.17	9.90	11.38	16.49	12.73
National LD sample	13.50	10.90	13.40	17.20	13.90

TABLE 12.6. ACT subtest and composite mean scores, SDs, and ranges for RSS and LD groups.

Variable	X (SD)	Range	F	p
English				
RSS (46)	18.48 (5.03)	4–28		
LD (63)	13.17 (5.05)	3–28	29.44	.000
Math				
RSS	16.83 (6.75)	3–25		
LD	9.90 (6.14)	1–27	31.04	.000
Social studies				
RSS	19.74 (6.73)	7–32		
LD	11.38 (5.91)	3–31	47.28	.000
Science				
RSS	21.39 (5.34)	8–33		
LD	16.49 (5.01)	7–28	24.04	.000
Composite				
RSS	19.17 (5.01)	9–31		
LD	12.73 (4.10)	6–22	54.36	.000

high school graduates (ACT, 1988). As can be seen on the ACT composite score, the RSS group performed slightly better than the national sample while the LD group mean composite was 1.2 points lower than a national LD sample. Differences mainly on the Social Studies and Math subtests seemed to be contributing to the discrepancy in the LD samples' composite scores.

The LD group scored significantly poorer than the RSS group on all four subtests and the composite. However, a different pattern emerged in comparing the LD and RSS graduate subgroups. The LD graduates scored significantly poorer only on the English and Social Studies subtests, perhaps because they are the most verbal subtests and the LD graduate

TABLE 12.7. ACT performance for RSS and LD Barat graduates and non graduates.

Variable		X (SD)	Range	F	p
English					
RSS	G	16.00 (3.50)	11–21		
LD	G	12.20 (4.33)	7–21	4.96	.037
RSS	NG	16.31 (5.85)	4–24		
LD	NG	13.30 (6.65)	3–21	.79	ns
Math					
RSS	G	11.00 (3.35)	6–17		
LD	G	11.29 (5.99)	3–24	.01	ns
RSS	NG	16.23 (6.88)	3–26		
LD	NG	6.70 (4.06)	1–15	10.29	.004
Social studies					
RSS	G	15.56 (5.25)	10–24		
LD	G	9.60 (4.73)	3–20	8.22	.009
RSS	NG	17.46 (7.16)	8–30		
LD	NG	11.70 (5.89)	6–23	5.27	.032
Science					
RSS	G	17.33 (3.39)	13–24		
LD	G	14.93 (3.73)	7–21	2.48	ns
RSS	NG	21.85 (6.12)	8–30		
LD	NG	17.00 (5.27)	10–26	3.91	ns
Composite					
RSS	G	15.11 (3.02)	11–20		
LD	G	12.20 (3.63)	6–19	4.08	.056
RSS	NG	17.92 (5.62)	9–26		
LD	NG	12.40 (3.92)	7–19	6.64	.017

were still experiencing the effects of their language learning disability. However, these deficits did not preclude college graduation. The correlation of ACT subtest scores and college exit gpa confirmed this finding. Namely, for the RSS group, there was a significant, albeit low, correlation for the English subtest score and college exit gpa, while for thc LD group, there was a significant correlation only for the math subtest with exit gpa. These findings confirm the importance of examining the ACT subtest profile and discrepancies rather than relying solely on composite scores. Because LD applicants score significantly poorer than nonLD college applicants on the ACT, even when they use modified examination procedures, and performance may partially reflect the disability in addition to college preparation, we posed the question as to the predictive power of the ACT for LD individuals. This question has relevance for college counselors,

TABLE 12.8. Correlation of college exit GPA and ACT composite score for LD and RSS groups.

Variable	r	p
English		
LD	.18	.074
RSS	.29	.023
Math		
LD	.29	.011
RSS	.18	.112
Social studies		
LD	.02	.436
RSS	.14	.178
Natural science		
LD	.03	.417
RSS	−.07	.329
Composite		
LD	.16	.099
RSS	.17	.122

TABLE 12.9. Multiple regression analysis with graduation status as criterion variable and the four subtests of the ACT as predictor variables in LD college students.

Variable	r	Partial r	Beta weight	F	p
English	−.08	−.01	−.01	.00	ns
Math	.28	.52	.66	10.32	.00
Social studies	−.20	−.34	−.47	3.52	ns
Science	−.18	−.18	−.19	.86	ns

Mult $R = .56$ $R^2 = .31$ F(EQN) = 3.08 $p < .033$

TABLE 12.10. Multiple regression analysis with graduation status as criterion variable and the four subtests of the ACT as predictor variables in random stratified sample.

Variable	r	Partial r	Beta weight	F	p
English	−.68	−.17	−.22	.89	ns
Math	.28	.59	.85	14.84	.000
Social studies	−.20	−.25	−.33	1.86	ns
Science	−.18	−.30	−.37	2.73	ns

Mult $R = .62$ $R^2 = .39$ F(EQN) = 4.28 $p < .008$

high school guidance counselors and academic advisors, LD advocates, LD individuals and their parents, and college admissions officers.

For this LD population, the ACT was found to be an accurate predictor of college success, but not as powerful a predictor as in the nonLD population. The ACT accounted for 31% of the variance in graduation status for LD students compared to 39% in the RSS. These findings indicate that the ACT subtest and composite scores do have relevance and predictive power. However, we recommend that this information is supplemented by careful analysis of the high school transcript and other relevant information such as recent results from the WAIS-R, academic achievement levels, previous psychoeducational reports, case history information, letters of recommendation, and interviews.

College Performance

The next question posed was: How did the LD college students perform in college in comparison to their nondisabled peers? Learning disabled students' gpa was significantly lower at the end of each year of study and when they exited from the college (either graduated, transferred, failed, or dropped/stopped out). Their transcripts had significantly more D and P grades. The latter is to be expected in the LD sample because many college developmental courses that advisors highly recommend for the LD students are only offered P/F. Surprisingly, no differences were found on number of withdrawals (W), incomplete, and F grades, perhaps because of the special academic advising available to the LD students, close monitoring of drop/add deadlines, and frequent communication between the LD students and advisors/LD specialists.

On closer examination of the college transcripts of the LD and RSS graduates, it can be seen that the LD graduates had a lower gpa at the end of their sophomore, junior, and senior year and at exit from the college. They had significantly more withdrawals, D grades, and passing grades as well. However, not surprisingly, the LD and RSS academically failing students did not differ, except on the number of P grades, as was expected because of the large number of developmental courses offered only at P/F.

Given that the LD students performed significantly poorer in high school, scored lower on all ACT subtests and composite, and had a lower mean gpa at the end of each year of study in college and at exit, it was expected that fewer LD students would graduate and a larger number would have been dismissed as a result of academic failure.

When the number of LD and RSS graduates and academic failures were compared to the total groups, we found that during the eight year period 23% of the total LD group and 30% of the total RSS group graduated (a nonsignificant difference). However, 43 (37%) of the 110 LD students are still in school as compared to 36 (24%) of the RSS group. Therefore, we calculated the ratio of graduates as compared to the total group minus

TABLE 12.11. College performance for RSS ($N = 153$) and LD ($N = 110$) groups.

Variable (N)	$\bar{X}$ (SD)	Range	F	p
Freshman GPA				
RSS (71)	2.82 (.72)	1.06–4.00		
LD (68)	2.52 (.47)	1.28–3.70	8.23	.005
Sophomore GPA				
RSS (83)	3.07 (.68)	1.57–4.00		
LD (50)	2.55 (.67)	.00–4.00	18.38	.000
Junior GPA				
RSS (62)	3.20 (.53)	1.79–4.00		
LD (34)	2.69 (.48)	1.71–3.76	21.71	.000
Senior GPA				
RSS (44)	3.24 (.46)	2.29–4.00		
LD (28)	2.82 (.39)	2.05–3.71	16.23	.000
Exit GPA				
RSS (153)	2.74 (.96)	0–4.00		
LD (110)	2.43 (.71)	0–4.00	5.77	.017
Exit Hours				
RSS (153)	75.22 (42.88)	0–153		
LD (110)	62.35 (42.71)	0–157	8.49	.004
W Grades				
RSS (153)	.60 (1.43)	0–10		
LD (110)	.76 (1.42)	0–10	.83	.362
Incomplete Grades				
RSS (153)	.08 (.29)	0–2		
LD (110)	.21 (.88)	0–7	2.93	.088
F Grades				
RSS (153)	.88 (1.72)	0–10		
LD (110)	.89 (1.52)	0–9	.00	.967
D Grades				
RSS (153)	.63 (1.18)	0–6		
LD (110)	1.15 (1.41)	0–7	10.44	.001
P Grades				
RSS (153)	.97 (2.03)	0–17		
LD (110)	4.04 (3.18)	0–14	90.56	.000

those still in school and found graduates constituted 37% of the LD group and 39% of the RSS group. Moreover, the academic failure rate was almost identical—18% for the NG and 17% for the RSS NG group. These findings seem to indicate that the support services available to the enrolled LD students were effective in helping LD students overcome the effects of the learning disability and complete their degree at the same rate as their nondisabled peers.

TABLE 12.12. College performance for RSS and LD Barat graduates (G) and non graduates (NG).

Variable	N	$\bar{X}$	SD	Range
Freshman GPA				
RSS G	19	2.86	.66	1.67–4.00
LD G	17	2.59	.42	1.83–3.41
RSS NG	8	1.65	.33	1.06–2.12
LD NG	7	1.85	.38	1.28–2.33
Sophomore GPA				
RSS G	36	3.18	.64	1.65–4.00
LD G	23	2.58[a]	.78	.00–4.00
RSS NG	4	2.10	.61	1.72–3.00
LD NG	5	1.83	.22	1.56–2.03
Junior GPA				
RSS G	45	3.21	.52	2.12–4.00
LD G	25	2.68[b]	.52	1.71–3.76
RSS NG	1	3.05	—	—
LD NG	1	2.00	—	—
Senior GPA				
RSS G	43	3.24	.46	2.29–4.00
LD G	24	2.83[a]	.40	2.05–3.71
RSS NG	0	—	—	—
LD NG	0	—	—	—
Exit GPA				
RSS G	46	3.21	.51	2.03–4.00
LD G	25	2.84[a]	.39	2.05–3.71
RSS NG	26	1.09	.65	.00–1.87
LD NG	20	1.39	.55	.00–2.00
Exit Hours				
RSS G	46	125.13	8.24	120–153
LD G	25	123.64	5.44	120–138
RSS NG	26	28.73	24.70	0–104
LD NG	20	28.30	23.30	0–86
W Grades				
RSS G	46	.30	.84	0–5
LD G	25	.92[c]	1.19	0–4
RSS NG	26	1.57	.51	1–2
LD NG	20	.85	1.46	0–5
Incomplete Grades				
RSS G	46	.02	.15	0–1
LD G	25	.32	1.41	0–7
RSS NG	26	.12	.33	0–1
LD NG	20	—	—	—
D Grades				
RSS G	46	.67	1.33	0–6
LD G	25	1.48*	1.92	0–6
RSS NG	26	2.07	1.54	1–6
LD NG	20	1.40	1.19	0–4

TABLE 12.12. *Continued*

Variable		N	$\bar{X}$	SD	Range
F Grades					
RSS	G	46	.26	.61	0–3
LD	G	25	.64	1.08	1–4
RSS	NG	26	3.64	2.34	1–10
LD	NG	20	2.70	2.39	0–9
P Grades					
RSS	G	46	1.83	2.92	0–17
LD	G	25	6.44[b]	3.77	0–14
RSS	NG	26	.31	.74	0–3
LD	NG	20	3.00[b]	2.53	0–9

[a] $p < .05$.
[b] $p < .001$.
[c] $p < .000$.

TABLE 12.13. Credit hour load and time to complete undergraduate degree for RSS ($N = 46$) and LD ($N = 26$) Barat graduates.

Variable		X (SD)	Range	F	p
Years of study					
RSS	G	6.61 (2.47)	3.5–14.0		
LD	G	6.85 (3.58)	4.0–21.5	.12	ns
$\bar{X}$ credits earned per semester					
RSS	G	10.38 (3.26)	4.3–17.3		
LD	G	9.43 (2.53)	3.2–14.6	1.54	ns
$\bar{X}$ credits attempted per semester					
RSS	G	10.49 (3.26)	4.3–17.3		
LD	G	9.61 (2.71)	3.4–16.6	1.28	ns
Credits attempted minus credits earned					
RSS	G	5.82 (7.58)	1–28		
LD	G	5.56 (4.39)	2–16	.01	ns

As another indirect measure of intervention effectiveness, a time study was conducted to determine if it took the LD graduates longer than their nondisabled peers to complete their degree. Contrary to our expectations, we found it did not take the LD students longer to complete their undergraduate degree. However, this finding has to be interpreted with caution since it may reflect specific characteristics of the RSS sample on this campus who often have to carry a part-time load due to family and financial responsibilities. This finding also seems to relate to one aspect of the support services, namely, the advisement system.

Three of the major tasks of academic advisors are to assist students in determining the right course load, to select a balanced array of courses, to enroll in courses in the correct sequence within a specific department or across the curriculum, and to monitor deadlines for drop/add, pass/fail grading options, and withdrawing from a course. Advisors also have the responsibility of monitoring warning signals during the semester and adjusting the student's schedule, reviewing end-of-semester grades, and re-evaluating the courses selected for the next semester during pre-registration. The finding that LD students did not differ significantly from the RSS group in "credits attempted minus credits earned" is thought to indicate that advisors were effective in their jobs.

Summary

When students with learning disabilities self-refer at admissions, and are screened for intellectual abilities, type and severity of LD, and motivation and attitude toward the teaching-learning process, and when they seek out and use comprehensive, highly coordinated support services designed along the four-pronged approach described above, and use special academic advisors, they graduate at the same rate and within the same time frame as their nondisabled peers. Moreover, their academic failure rate is no higher. These findings are thought to indicate the effectiveness of the comprehensive, highly coordinated four-pronged approach utilized in this setting. In light of these results, replication is needed to determine graduation and failure rate for LD students on campuses that have different admissions requirements, screening procedures, and support services. At present, though encouraging, these findings cannot be generalized to other settings, but can serve as a first step in validating current postsecondary practices.

Acknowledgment. This research was supported in part by grants from the Butz and Thorn River Foundations.

References

Abrams, H., & Abrams, R. (1981). Legal obligations toward the post-secondary learning disabled student. *Wayne Law Review*, *27*, 1475–1499.

Adelman, P.B. (1985). Developing a reading program for dyslexic college students. *AHSSPPE Bulletin*, *3*, 87–92.

Adelman, P.B. (1988). An approach to meeting the needs of the learning disabled student in a four-year college setting. In C. Mangrum and S. Strichart (Eds.), *College and the learning disabled student* (pp. 240–249). Philadelphia: Grune & Stratton.

Adelman, P.B. & Olufs, D. (1986). *Assisting college students with learning disabilities*. Columbus, OH: AHSSPPE

American College Testing. (1988). *1988 ACT High School Report*. Iowa City, IA: Author.

Astin, A., Green, K., Korn, W., Schalit, M., & Berg, E. (1988). *The American freshman: National norms for 1988*. Los Angeles: University of California.

Ballard, J., Ramirez, B., & Zantal-Wiener, K. (1987). *Public Law 94-142, Section 504, and Public Law 99-457: Understanding what they are and are not*. Reston, VA: Council for Exceptional Children.

Bursuck, W., Rose, E., & Cowen, S. (1988). A nationwide survey of services for students with learning disabilities in postsecondary education settings. In D. Knapke & C. Lendman (Eds.), *Capitalizing on the future AHSSPPE '87* (pp. 44–52). Columbus, OH: AHSSPPE.

Bursuck, W., Rose, E., Cowen, S., & Yahaya M.A. (1989). Nationwide survey of postsecondary education services for students with learning disabilities. *Exceptional Children*, *56*(3), 236–245.

Cordoni, B.K., & Harman, D.E. (1985). Are commonly used predictors of college success applicable to the learning disabled? *Thalamus*, *5*(1), 1–61.

Karlsen, B., Madden, R., & Gardner, E. (1977). *Stanford diagnostic reading test (Blue Level)*. Chicago: Harcourt Brace Jovanovich.

Konrad, D.C. (1984). The Barat College writing lab. In W.M. Cruickshank and J.M. Kleibham (Eds.), *Early adolescence to early adulthood: The best of* ACLD, Vol. 5. Syracuse, NY: Syracuse University Press, 177–182.

Laing, J., & Farmer, M. (1985). ACT assessment results for specially-tested examinees with learning disabilities. *ACT Research Bulletin*, *85–1*.

The rehabilitation act of 1973, Section 504, 29 U.S.C. Section 794 (1977).

Vogel, S.A. (1982). On developing LD college programs. *Journal of Learning Disabilities*, *15*, 518–528.

Vogel, S.A. (1985a). Syntactic complexity in written expression of LD college writers. *Annals of Dyslexia*, *XXXV*, Orton Dyslexia Society.

Vogel, S.A. (1985b). *The college student with a learning disability: A handbook for college LD students, university admissions officers, faculty, and administration*. 2nd ed. Pittsburgh, PA: ACLD.

Vogel, S.A. (1985c). Comments on "Are commonly used predictors of college success applicable to the learning disabled?" *Thalamus*, *5*(1), 62–74.

Vogel, S.A. (1986). Levels and patterns of intellectual functioning among LD college students. *Journal of Learning Disabilities*, *19*(2), 71–79.

Vogel, S.A. (1987). Issues and concerns in LD college programming. In D. Johnson and J. Blalock (Eds.), *Adults with learning disabilities: Clinical studies* (pp. 239–275) Orlando, FL: Grune & Stratton, Inc.

Vogel, S.A., & Adelman, P.B. (1981). Personnel development: College and university programs designed for learning disabled adults. *ICEC Quarterly*, *1*, 12–18.

Vogel, S.A., & Moran, M.R. (1982). Written lanauage disorders in learning disabled college students: A preliminary report. In W. Cruickshank and J. Lerner (Eds.), *The Best of ACLD 1981, Volume III, Coming of Age*. Syracuse, NY: Syracuse University Press.

Woodcock, R., & Johnson, M. (1977). *Woodcock-Johnson psychoeducational battery*. Hingham, MA: Teaching Resources Corp.

Index

A

Advance organizers, 137–139
American College Testing Program,
    331, 335–339
  LD students performance, 335–339
Aptitude-treatment interaction, 73–74
Assignments, 144–146
  Homework, 143, 144
  Seatwork, 145
Association on Handicapped Student
    Service Programs in Post-
    Secondary Education (AHSSPE),
    331
Attention, 40, 246–248, 257
  academic performance, 247, 257
  accuracy, 247, 257
  aids to, 40
  orienting, 40
  productivity, 247, 257
  selective, 40
  self-recording of, 247
Attributional processes, 81, 83, 85, 87
  development of, 88–89
  LD students, 89
  retaining, 90–92, 97–98

C

Categorization, 40, 144
Cognitive Strategy Instruction in Writ-
    ing, *see* Writing
College performance of LD students,
    339–343
Concept learning, 140–141, 168–169
Content analysis, 173–175

Content enhancement model, 131–152,
    227–228
  components of, 135–152

D

Definition of LD, 67–68
Direct instruction, 124

E

Effect size, 7, 17–18, 69
Effectiveness, 4, 68–69, 218–221, 236–
    246
Elaboration, 40
Empiricism, 5
Enriched strategy instruction, 84–86
Evaluation, 6
Executive processes, 81, 83, 87, 92,
    224–225
  deficits in, 92–94
  training in, 94–97

G

Generalization, 49, 86, 92, 95, 216–218,
    253–257
Good Teacher Thinker Model, *see*
    Teacher
Grade point averages, 334–335

H

High school performance of LD
    students, 334–335

I

Illinois Test of Psycholinguistic Abilities
    (ITPA), 6, 9, 69
Imagery, 40
Information-processing, 45, 123–124,
    125, 129, 130
Interactive teaching, 167–182, 229–230

L

Learner characteristics, 52
Locus of control, 87

M

Main idea, 308–309, 311–312
Maintenance, 253–254
Memorizing, 41
Meta-analysis, 7–19
    diet modification, 16–17
    efficacy of special education, 13–14
    interventions in learning disabilities,
        17–19, 21
    modality testing and teaching, 11–12
    perceptual-motor training, 10–11, 69
    process training, 12–13
    psycholinguistic training, 6, 8–10, 69
    stimulant medication, 14–16
Metacognition, 69, 81–84, 225
    metacognitive model, 224–225
    metamemory, 41
Mnemonic instruction, 103–121, 147–
    149, 226–227
    acoustic reconstruction, 226–227
    attribute studies, 104
    initial investigations, 103
    mimetic representations, 226
    multiple attribute studies, 226
    symbolic relationships, 226
    theoretical support of, 118
    vocabulary studies 103, 226

N

National Assessment of Educational
    Progress (1985), 304

O

Organization, 46, 149, 202–205

P

Peer acceptance, 274, 279–296
Practice, 143
Prior knowledge, 141, 142, 147, 167
Problem formulation schema, 306
Problem-solving, 41, 281–287, 304–305,
    312–316
Problems in instruction of LD students,
    19–25
Process training, 12, 70
Process-based instruction program, 95–
    97
Production deficiency, 54

R

Reading, 167, 168
Reciprocal teaching, 124, 125
Reconstructive elaboration, 105–118,
    231–232
    acoustic reconstructions, 107
    mimetic reconstructions, 107
    symbolic reconstructions, 107
    validation study of, 108–109
Rehabilitation Act of 1973, 329–331
Rehearsal, 40
Remediation, 69–70
Research, 5–6, 152–157
    basic, 71–72
    classroom practices, 74–76
    ethical issues, 76
    implementation in mnemonics, 109–
        118
    instructional routines, 152–157
    intervention, 66–67, 72
    laboratory practices, 74
    purposes of, 69–70
    qualitative, 23
    synthesis, 7–19

S

Sampling, 68
Scaffolding, 125, 136–137, 171, 215–218
Schema, 167, 306–308
    formating choices, 308
    ordering, 308
    problem slots, 307–308
    problem-solver's schema, 307
    setting slots, 307

situation schema, 307
textbase schema, 307
Science instruction, 113–118
Screening instruments, 333
Sentence Structure Test, 333
Stanford Diagnostic Reading Test,
333–334
Wordcock-Johnson Psychoeducational Battery, 334
Section 504, *see* Rehabilitation Act of
1973
Self-control, 225, 235, 325
Self-esteem, 87, 90
Self-instruction, 41–43
Self-recording, 236–258, 325
accuracy, 252–253, 258
cuing of, 248–249
effectiveness of, 236–246
generalization of, 253–257
maintenance, 253–256
training components, 248–253
transfer, 256–257
Semantic mapping, 141
Social competance, 280, 294–299, 323
Social skills, 264–275, 322–326
developmental differences in, 274–
275
generalization, 273–274, 325–326
individualization of, 282, 292
LD children, 265–273
outcome indices, 323
self-recording, 325
training programs, 264–275, 322,
324–325
variability, 323
Social Studies, 109–119
elementary, 112

U.S. History, 106, 109–110
World History, 106–107
Strategy instruction, 35–58
Support services in post-secondary
education, 329

T
Teacher,
decision-making, 127–129
Good Teacher Thinker Model, 150–
151, 227–229
planning, 126–129, 150–152
routines, 126–129, 136–146
teacher-made materials, 113–114
training, 71
Teaching devices, 146–148
Teaching strategies, 172–179
Theory-based intervention, 231–232
Think aloud, 49, 50
Transfer of effects, 256–257, 324
Transformation, 40, 56–60

V
Variance in intervention, 17–19

W
Writing, 186–221
Cognitive Strategy Instruction in
Writing (CSIW), 194–213, 230–231
editing, 209–213
self-regulation, 189–191
sensitivity to audience, 191–192
teaching strategies, 213–218
text structure, 186–189